EDUCATION AND WORK IN GREAT BRITAIN, GERMANY AND ITALY

In the current economic crisis which has given rise to high and persisting levels of unemployment, the relations between education and training, on the one hand, and work and employment, on the other, have been the object of lively debates and have stimulated a large body of research. *Education and Work in Great Britain, Germany and Italy* analyses the literature in this field and establishes an institutional and intellectual cartography for these three countries.

This volume examines the multiple connections between education, broadly defined, and work, through an analysis of the literature on the transition from school to work, on vocational training and on the labour market. It summarises the major debates in each country and, on the basis of this, contributes to an understanding of different intellectual traditions. It shows that concepts such as skill, unemployment rates, young people and the transition from school to work are socially constructed and are thought about in ways which are nationally specific.

Education and Work in Great Britain, Germany and Italy is essential reading for students of European training systems and for those conducting comparative European research.

Annette Jobert is a CNRS Researcher at the Université Paris X–Nanterre. Her research interests are in the field of industrial relations and training policy at different levels (company, sector and region) on a comparative basis. **Catherine Marry** is a LASMAS Researcher at the Institute of Research on Contemporary Societies (IRESCO), Paris. Her research has been on the comparison of education systems and employment in France and Germany and on women in scientific and technical occupations. **Lucie Tanguy** is a CNRS Research Director at the Université Paris X–Nanterre. She has researched on the historical and sociological dimensions of the institutions, policies and contents of vocational training. She leads the CNRS research programme on education and training in Europe. **Helen Rainbird** is Professor of Industrial Relations at Nene College, Northampton and an Associate Fellow of the Industrial Relations Research Unit at the University of Warwick. She has researched in the field of industrial relations and vocational training.

ROUTLEDGE INTERNATIONAL STUDIES IN THE
PHILOSOPHY OF EDUCATION

EDUCATION AND WORK
IN GREAT BRITAIN,
GERMANY AND ITALY

*Edited by Annette Jobert, Catherine Marry,
Lucie Tanguy and Helen Rainbird*

London and New York

First published 1997
by Routledge
11 New Fetter Lane, London EC4P 4EE

Simultaneously published in the USA and Canada
by Routledge
29 West 35th Street, New York, NY 10001

Typeset in Garamond by Routledge
Printed and bound in Great Britain by Redwood Books,
Trowbridge, Wiltshire

British Library Cataloguing in Publication Data
A catalogue record for this book is available from the British Library

Library of Congress Cataloguing in Publication Data
Education and work in Great Britain, Germany and Italy/edited by
Annette Jobert, Catherine Marry, Lucie Tanguy and Helen Rainbird
Includes bibliographical references and index.
1. Labor market – Great Britain. 2. Labor market – Germany. 3. Labor
market – Italy. 4. Education – Economic aspects – Great Britain. 5.
Education – Economic aspects – Germany. 6. Education – Economic
aspects – Italy. I. Jobert, Annette.
HD5765.A6E37 1996
331.11'423 – dc 21
97 – 1854
CIP

ISBN 0–415–15333–6

CONTENTS

v

CONTENTS

ILLUSTRATIONS

FIGURES

TABLES

CONTRIBUTORS

David Ashton is Professor of Sociology and Director of the Centre for Labour Market Studies at the University of Leicester. His current interests focus on the relationship between education, training and employment from a comparative perspective. His latest book (with Francis Green) is *Education, Training and the Global Economy*, published by Edward Elgar in 1996.

Luciano Benadusi is Professor of Sociology of Education at the University of Rome, La Sapienza. He is the scientific director of the Sociology of Education section of the Italian Sociological Association and editor of the journal *Scuola Democratica*. His research is on sociological theory, socialisation, educational inequality, the relationship between training and jobs, and the organisation of schools and universities.

Paolo Botta is Researcher at the Institute for the Development of Vocational Training of Workers (ISFOL), Rome, and teaches at the University of Rome. His research is on young people, social identity, vocational training, professionalism, training and the labour market.

Paolo Calza Bini is Professor of Social Change at the University of Rome, La Sapienza. He has conducted research on agriculture and the South of Italy, new technologies in public administration, employment policies and youth unemployment.

Vittorio Capecchi is Professor of Sociology of Education at the University of Bologna. He has conducted research on the 'industrial districts' in Italy, on the relationship between training and socio-economic development and between technological and social innovation. He has been engaged in international comparisons of education and training systems and is the president of the regional observatory on labour market and training for Emilia-Romagna.

Lynne Chisholm works at the DGXXII Reflection Group Secretariat at the European Commission. She is a specialist in education, training and youth transitions in comparative European research and policy contexts, with a particular interest in contemporary social change.

Ingrid Drexel is Senior Researcher in Sociology at the Institut für Sozialwissenschaftliche Forschung (ISF), Munich. Her research has been in the fields of Industrial Sociology, the Sociology of Education and vocational training, the development of educational and training systems and their interrelations with companies' workforce strategies. She has conducted international comparative work on Germany, France and Italy.

Margit Frackmann is Professor of Berufspädagogik (educational sciences applied to vocational training) at the University of Hannover. Her work is concerned with initial and continuing vocational training, the training and professions of women and the educational qualifications of those who teach continuing training.

Marinella Giovine is Senior Research Fellow and director of the labour policies section of the Institute for the Development of Vocational Training of Workers (ISFOL), Rome. She specialises in labour law and economics and has conducted research on the evaluation of public policies for training and employment. She supervises the evaluation unit of the European Social Fund in Italy.

Walter Heinz is Professor of Sociology and Social Psychology and the Chair of the Research Centre 'Status passages and risks in the life course' at the University of Bremen. His research interests and publications lie in the fields of socialisation and work, labour markets and careers and the life course.

Annette Jobert is a CNRS Researcher at the Université Paris X – Nanterre. Her research interests are in the areas of industrial relations and training policy at the company, sector and regional level. She has been engaged in a number of international comparative studies.

Beate Krais is Professor of Sociology at the Technical University of Darmstadt. Her main research interests are in sociological theory, the Sociology of Education and Science, class and status and in gender relations.

Catherine Marry is a LASMAS Researcher in Sociology in a team at the Institut de Recherches sur les Sociétés Contemporaines (IRESCO), Paris. Her research has been on the comparison of training systems and employment in France and Germany and on women in scientific and technical occupations.

David Marsden is Reader in Industrial Relations and Associate of the Centre for Economic Performance at the London School of Economics. He is currently vice-president of European Commissioner Edith Cresson's reflection group on education and training in the European Union. His current research is on training and labour market structure and public sector pay reforms in Europe.

Saul Meghnagi is Director of the Istituto Superiore per la Formazione (ISF), Rome. His main research interests concern the relationship between work and education. His publications are on learning processes in different social and occupational contexts.

Ulrike Nagel is Senior Researcher in the Department of Sociology at the University of Jena. Before this she was Senior Research Assistant at the University of Bremen and Visiting Professor at the University of Kassel. Her research interests include microsociology, qualitative research methods, life course studies and studies of the professions.

David Raffe is Professor of Sociology of Education at the University of Edinburgh, where he directs the Centre for Educational Sociology and co-directs the newly formed Institute for the Study of Education and Society. His research interests cover secondary and post-secondary education, training and the labour market, and he has conducted several comparative studies, especially within Europe.

Helen Rainbird is Professor of Industrial Relations at Nene College, Northampton and an Associate Fellow of the Industrial Relations Research Unit at the University of Warwick. Her research interests cover the interface between industrial relations and vocational training and she has worked on a number of comparative international projects on different aspects of continuing vocational training.

Klaus Schömann is Research Fellow at the Wissenschaftzentrum für Sozialforschung (WZB), Berlin. His major fields of research are labour market policy and development, life-long learning policies and the development of statistical methodology for the analysis of longitudinal data.

Lucie Tanguy is a CNRS Directeur de Recherche at the Université Paris X – Nanterre. She leads the CNRS research programme on education and training in Europe and has conducted historical and sociological research on the institutions, policies and contents of training. She is the editor of *L'Introuvable Relation Formation-Emploi. Un État des Recherches en France*, La Documentation Française, 1986.

ACKNOWLEDGEMENTS

This book is the result of research financed by the French Ministère de l'Enseignment Supèrieure et de la Recherche. The papers were originally presented at a conference held in Paris in March 1994 which was financed by the Programme Europe of the CNRS (Centre National de la Recherche Scientifique), the Task Force of the European Union, CEDEFOP (European Centre for the Development of Vocational Training), ESRC (Economic and Social Research Council) and the DFG (Deutsche Forschungsgemeinschaft). The editors are grateful to Charlotte Knight and Michelle Webster at the Nene Centre for Research for their work in preparing the manuscript for publication.

1

COMPARISONS BETWEEN AN AREA OF RESEARCH IN GERMANY, GREAT BRITAIN AND ITALY

Annette Jobert, Catherine Marry, Lucie Tanguy

IMPROVING MUTUAL UNDERSTANDING WITHIN A RESEARCH COMMUNITY AND PROMOTING SCIENTIFIC COMMUNICATION

This research is an extension of work carried out a number of years ago in France by a group of researchers and published as *L'introuvable relation formation-emploi. Un état des recherches en France* (1986).[1] The objective of the project was to conduct a review of the literature on the relationships between education and work, which is a field of research characterised by its multidisciplinarity, its division by themes and disciplines and a bias towards the collection of empirical data. Through a process of critical reflection on this literature, it was intended to break down academic and thematic divisions and to provide a better basis for accumulating knowledge and theoretical development. The reception given to this work revealed the strength of interest in this area. This has intensified with the primacy given to the problems of employment and unemployment in the majority of European countries over the past fifteen or twenty years and, within this context, the greater role assigned to education and training as instruments capable of offering responses. Increasing pressure is also being exerted by European institutions to develop comparative research in this field notwithstanding the various obstacles confronting studies of this nature, such as preconceived ideas embodied in the use of national classification systems age and socio-economic categories which are specific to each country. Moreover, the use of concepts such as qualifications, skills, competence or transition differ in meaning from one country to the next. In short, the difficulties encountered by researchers engaged in comparative analysis derive not only from their lack of understanding of the 'other' reality but also from the fact of belonging to different cultural and intellectual traditions.

Comparative analysis, however, is still a young discipline, though it could be claimed that it has proved to be one of the most fertile avenues of investigation in this area, leading to the gradual constitution of a body of knowledge. In Great Britain, where the policy debate about training and

1

economic efficiency is particularly intense, international comparisons are highly developed. Certain comparative studies have already acquired a land-mark status, notably the societal analysis developed by the Laboratoire d'économie et de sociologie du travail (LEST) in Aix-en-Provençe. This ana-lysis stresses the features and patterns specific to each country, thereby making it possible to obtain an understanding of a system as a whole. However, the limitations of this type of analysis become apparent when attempts are made to compare the intermediate level and more specific real-ities. Internal diversity, eliminated in the model, then emerges as an insurmountable and unavoidable obstacle. This is true for the German or British systems of education; it is also true for comparisons of employment where differentiation by gender, generation and nationality, specific to each country, cannot be ignored if the aim is to take account of situations in a state of flux. The case of Italy, where regional differences are extremely marked, is particularly significant in this respect.

The intention here is not to provide a comparative analysis of research fields as such, but simply to present the conceptual and methodological tools needed for comparisons. This work represents a stage in research that involves describing the contours of the research field in a given country, identifying the principal research questions and fields of research, reflecting on the categories and terminologies used. This is, in our opinion, a vital step for the development of comparative research. The approach requires a mutual understanding on the part of the academic communities as well as an understanding of historical realities and the intellectual traditions of each community.

This volume gathers together the papers presented at a conference organ-ised in Paris, 17–19 March 1994, entitled *Education et travail, état d'un champ de recherche en Allemagne, Grande-Bretagne et Italie* (Education and work: state of a research field in Germany, Great Britain and Italy), representing the culmination of research funded by the French Ministry of Higher Education and Research. Each section begins with an introduction presenting the insti-tutional and political context characterising the field studied in each of the three countries in question; five texts devoted to each country then focus on the main currents of research within this area. These different currents include work devoted to educational systems, research focusing on the labour markets for young people, as well as studies adopting an economic approach. In this introduction, the objectives of the work are outlined, including a consideration of the conceptual tools required for a comparative analysis of this nature. This necessarily involves a consideration of the char-acteristics of the field of education and work in France, where this project was initiated.

AN AREA OF RESEARCH WITH BLURRED AND SHIFTING CONTOURS

We have tried, therefore, to characterise the academic traditions and social and political conditions (strong or weak identity of the disciplines, links with what in France is called 'social demand' emanating from trade union organisations and public administration, types of publication, etc.) which provide a framework and the basis for development of this research area with a view to appreciating the particular forms it takes in each country. Research is organised differently in each country but the characteristic configurations of each remain difficult to understand by outsiders. This is why we have tried, first of all, to establish a kind of 'intellectual map' for each of the three countries, giving a condensed image of research in this area. We then set out to define the principal currents of research (distinguished on the basis of research questions, methods and interpretative frameworks) covering the relation between the world of education and that of work. In this, our aim is not to be exhaustive but rather to highlight the theoretical approaches and topics which best characterise the three countries included in our study. The result is a picture of the principal features and currents of research drawn up by a group of researchers active in this area.

Before identifying these various aspects, we consider it vital to examine the identity of this field and its underlying concepts. We shall not discuss the concept of 'field' as applied to an area of research characterised by blurred and shifting contours. Obviously, this field is not as well defined or as neatly organised around a stable subject with clearly delineated secondary themes as, for example, the Sociology of Education. This, in part, is due to its nature: the analysis of relationships between two spheres of social activity, education and work.

We must also justify the concepts used in the title of this book: 'education and work' rather than 'training and employment' which are more often referred to in public debate. We are thus led to consider the association of the concepts 'education' and 'training', which are sometimes used synonymously but at others to convey a difference. The concept of training, taken in its broad and general meaning, appears alongside that of education, either clearly to differentiate itself (when related to in-company training, for example) or to compete directly with it. Although in France school occupies a central position in society and virtually all young people remain in education until the age of 18, the role of the school in the transmission of knowledge and values is being increasingly challenged. At present, the principle of combining school and work experience is being promoted by the majority of European societies. In this way, a certain shift can be observed away from the concept of education towards that of training, in forms that differ from one country to the next.

Mindful of semantic slides and the consequent shifts in meaning, we

3

would also like to emphasise the need for comprehensive analyses which take into consideration the meaning attributed by different societies to apparently synonymous concepts. This is the case for the concept 'education' which is frequently used in France to refer narrowly to schooling, owing to the central role played by schools in this country; 'education' has a far broader meaning in Great Britain, where the school as an institution does not have the same importance in society for all social groups. The expression used in Great Britain 'participation in education' cannot be translated into French as *scolarisation* (schooling); instead, a broader term – that of *études* (studies) – is more appropriate, to emphasise the fact that they may be pursued in different places and in different forms. In fact, in Great Britain, the realities described by 'education' and 'training' resist attempts to put them into neat institutional categories. The colleges of further education represent an excellent instance of this diversity. They accept both young people and adults, whether in employment or not. Most of the students attend vocational training courses but others study full-time or part-time in general education, attending day- or evening-classes. The diversity of curricula and institutions in Great Britain contrasts with the standardisation of the educational establishment in France and is the consequence of a tradition where education has been the responsibility of local authorities.

The identity of the fields covered by the concepts of 'work' and 'employment' is problematic. This lack of clarity in the meaning of words and their respective status can be seen in their association in the titles of periodicals such as *Travail et Emploi* in France, *Work, Employment and Society* in Great Britain. Researchers seek to convince their audience that a shift in interest from work to employment is necessary, not only because employment has become a problem but because it structures work and thereby contributes to social stratification. Other researchers dispute the primacy given to the concept of employment and, instead, consider that work (in the wider sense of the term, including domestic work and voluntary unpaid work) remains central to an understanding of social relationships. In practice, however, the reference to waged work remains central.

To conclude these comments about the concepts used, we could point out that they are rarely scrutinised by the researchers who use them most frequently as social categories. This is also the case for the concept of training, which covers activities as diverse as the transmission of knowledge and know-how, advice to individuals in an increasingly complex institutional environment or actions directed at social integration.

We should also remind readers that this broad field of research which examines relationships between a series of changes – ranging from technical changes in production processes and work organisation to the definition of qualifications and the transmission of knowledge – necessarily calls for the use of multidisciplinary approaches. Every discipline has its own tools for analysing a particular aspect of reality but cannot cover the totality. We argue therefore for a division of labour between disciplines which construct different objects of study on the basis of similar empirical data. This way of proceeding enables us to approach our subject from many different angles, to identify distinct but related levels of the same reality, and requires a comparison of results. It makes it possible to avoid the often mechanical explanations of the relationship between training and employment and to analyse the complex relationships between the two concepts and the mediations between them.

THOUGHTS ABOUT TOOLS AND CONCEPTS

All analysis, and *a fortiori* all comparative analysis, requires appropriate conceptual tools and the use of indicators developed intentionally, which are not necessarily those referred to in public debate to support partisan viewpoints. The measurement of unemployment among young people provides a good example of the problems encountered in international comparisons. Germany stands apart from the other countries with its relatively low unemployment rate among young people. This situation is generally attributed to the dominant form of organisation of vocational training, the 'dual' system, so-called because it is based on the principle of taught courses in school and workplace supervision. The unemployment rate among young people aged between 15 and 24 stood at 4.5 per cent in Germany in 1990 compared with 19 per cent in France (and for the labour force as a whole at 5 per cent and 9 per cent at the same date). Nevertheless it is extremely difficult to determine what these statistics actually mean. To begin with, the relevance of these age categories is debatable. Although the significance of the age of 15 was justified in an earlier period, this is not the case today when almost all young people of this age in France continue in some kind of full-time education. It would seem more appropriate to measure the unemployment rate of young people at higher ages, when the majority of them enter the labour market. By adopting this approach, we note that substantial differences remain but are reduced somewhat: the 20–29 age-group represents 44 per cent of all unemployed people in France and one third of this population in Germany. Account must also be taken of demographic differences. In Germany, the size of the age cohorts is decreasing. In 1990 there were more than one million young people aged 23 or 24 but only 650,000 aged between 16 and 17. In France in the same year both age cohorts stood at approximately 800,000. Lastly, the major obstacle to a measurement-based comparison derives from the forms of social reality themselves – in this case, the type of vocational training set up in each country which results sometimes in the inclusion of young people in the working population, sometimes in the non-working population.

Most European countries define the working population by the same criteria in surveys of employment. This includes everyone who works, even for one hour, is looking for work or is active during the week of reference. In other words, young people in full-time education or following vocational training courses, including unpaid periods in companies, are not included in the working population. In contrast, those who take courses but are paid a wage – apprentices, for example – are included in this category. Although, in France, the population of young people included in the latter has increased over the past decade, their numbers remain substantially lower than those noted in the dual system. In West Germany in 1990, 1.5 million young people aged 16 to 22 followed dual training leading to a wide range of jobs, ranging from baking and banking to the metalworking industry. In France, there were only 212,000 apprentices, concentrated in the food and car repair sectors for young men, and in shops and personal care for young women.

The activity rates of young French people are consequently much lower than those for young Germans, particularly before the age of 20: 12.2 per cent for young men aged 15–19, 6.8 per cent for young women of the same age in France, compared to 40.1 per cent and 34.8 per cent for young Germans. This weakness in young people's activity rates distinguishes France not only from Germany and the countries in northern Europe, but also from those in southern Europe. It therefore seems more appropriate, in order to appreciate the social position of young people in different societies, to relate the numbers of young unemployed people to the entire population of young people rather than to that of the active population alone. More generally, unemployment cannot be divorced from all the training and employment situations in which young people may find themselves. For example, when youth unemployment levels are calculated on this basis for the 15–24 age-group in France and Germany in 1990, the discrepancy between them shifts. Whereas the German rate declines from 4.5 per cent to 3.5. per cent, the French rate declines from 19 per cent to 7 per cent.

Similar comments may be made about other indicators – the length of periods in unemployment, for instance – which provide an objective measure of the seriousness of this phenomenon. However, in the parts of southern Italy where unemployment is massive, this indicator masks as much as it reveals. Indeed, young people from the poorest families are obliged to accept any temporary work, even if it is underpaid and unrelated to their qualifications. As a result, they are excluded from the statistics on long-term unemployment, while young people supported by their families are included. The differences in the unemployment rates of men and women provide another example of the distortions inherent in a non-contextualised use of statistical indicators. Thus, unlike other European countries, women's unemployment rates in the United Kingdom are lower than those of men and stood at 9.2 per cent and 12 per cent respectively in 1992 (Eurostat 1993). This apparent advantage obscures the way in which married women are often excluded from the unemployment statistics. Moreover, many women work

6

part-time. This form of employment accounted for 43 per cent of female employment in 1990 compared with 5 per cent of male employment. The category of part-time work includes categories of employment of variable duration (sometimes less than 15 hours per week), and includes workers who are exempt from employment protection. All these examples demonstrate inequalities between the sexes with respect to conditions of employment, and the greater exposure of women to labour market deregulation.

NATIONAL RESEARCH ISSUES

The relationship between education and work is also conceptualised differently from one country to the next, reflecting varying social realities and ways in which these are perceived and analysed at a given point in time. Problems, such as economic recession or increasing youth unemployment, which have arisen at the same time have produced different public debates and issues in each country. Indeed, the debates and issues are closely linked to the national context, the history of vocational training institutions and the development of related social representations and practices. As a result, we cannot limit the analysis to the current state of research but must take account of changes over the past twenty years and maybe more. This approach, adopted in most of the contributions to the book, allows continuities, shifts and breaks within research traditions to be emphasised.

One of the characteristics of Great Britain is that, traditionally, the majority of young people have left school at the age of 16, at the end of compulsory schooling, to enter employment or to start an apprenticeship. Until the early 1980s, apprenticeships constituted the most sought-after form of training in this country and early labour market entry was explained by the fairly wide range of jobs available and by the relatively high wages offered to young people aged 16. As a result, young people were disinclined to continue their studies. With the rapid decline in apprenticeships due to the recession in the manufacturing industry and with the growing level of unemployment among young people, the postponement of their entry into the labour market and the provision of training became important. This change has only recently been translated into an extension of the length of schooling. This situation explains why studies have focused on the transition from school to work and on the policies supporting it, particularly for young people in the 16–18 age-group who were the target group for many policies.

In Germany, the main issues raised in this debate are closely related to the very nature of the German system of education and training – notably, the emphasis given to the dual system into which young people move when they leave secondary school, and which continues to be the main form of occupational socialisation for the young in Germany. There is also a distinction within secondary education between academic education, in the *Gymnasium* or grammar school, leading directly to the university, and other forms of secondary education which do not give direct access. Even if the dual system is widespread, and attracts students whose level of general education continues to rise, the most prestigious route remains that of the *Gymnasium* and university which, in practice, leads to the most sought-after and highly paid professions. Increasingly, young people are being attracted into this route and in 1993, for the first time, the number of university students exceeded that of young people enrolled in the dual system.

When these changes in the educational system and in vocational training are taken in conjunction with the problems resulting from reunification (particularly the high level of unemployment in the *Länder* of the former German Democratic Republic and the 'restructuring' of education, training and research institutions), they provide a backcloth for the main issues being debated in German society and in the research community. The majority of the questions focus on the operation of the dual system and its future. This system has long represented a major research subject in Germany but, at present, its relative loss of attraction casts the entire debate in a new light.

Whereas interest in Great Britain and, particularly, in France is focused on the transition from school to work, in Germany emphasis is on a broader concept of transition, applied to the life course of young people and adults (family, professional activities etc.). Using longitudinal studies, research tends to discriminate between the effects related to age (life cycle), period (or economic context) and generation. This specific approach is undoubtedly based on the nature of labour market entry in Germany: the blurring of the frontiers between the status of being at school and belonging to the working population in the dual system, the possibility of moving between these statuses for a great number of years, and the relatively low level of unemployment among young people in Germany.

In Italy, two phenomena raise key questions in the area of education and work. The first, concerning education, is the strong propensity both in the North and in the South of the country for young people to remain in secondary and higher education. This trend deserves emphasising: in a country where compulsory education ends at 14, 90 per cent of students continue their studies beyond, and frequently well beyond, the legal age limit. The second major characteristic is that regional differences in the level and nature of unemployment are much more acute in Italy than in other European countries. This regional disparity corresponds to a deep and long-standing social and economic divide between the Northern and Central regions on the one hand, and the South on the other. This is illustrated by the marked differences in the unemployment levels in each of these regions: 7 per cent in the Central/Northern region and more than 20 per cent in the South, with peaks of almost 60 per cent for women under the age of 30 living in this region. Two categories are affected more severely by unemployment than in the other countries studied: women and young people (a category which extends to the age of 30 in Italy). With the exception of female unemployment, which recently became more visible with the massive entry of women into the labour market, these characteristics are not new, even if the current scale of the phenomenon requires the adoption of new approaches.

The structural nature of these phenomena explains why so much attention has been focused for so long on unemployment, the functioning of the labour markets and on training as a factor of economic development. Although the role of training remains a major subject of research, the contradiction between a constant increase in the level of training and the persistence of high levels of unemployment among young people no longer lies at the heart of current thinking as it did in the 1970s and early 1980s. The focus of research is also tending to shift away from broad themes of interpretation at the macro-social level in favour of more diversified analyses framed, for the most part, within a regional context. Among the more recent tendencies, two have a particular bearing on the debate about the relationship between education and work: the first focuses on the implications of a highly decentralised system of vocational training and on the role of the State; the second focuses on vocational and in-service training provided for employees, especially those who are in employment but are faced with major organisational and technological changes.

A certain number of transversal issues emerge from comparisons made between countries, namely male/female differences, long-term exclusion from the labour market and the importance of vocational training within employment policy. This varies from one national context to another, as does the question of the appraisal of the educational, vocational training and employment policies.

SOME ELEMENTS OF COMPARISON WITH FRANCE[2]

Employment in France is characterised more and more by a substantial shortening of the time spent at work. Employment levels are at their lowest for young people aged 15–24 and adults aged 55–64. This situation is the consequence of various measures taken to combat unemployment as well as the effect of choices made regarding educational and corporate policies. The result is that the population most protected against unemployment is aged 25–55. In contrast, the susceptible categories are young people aged less than 25 (for whom the level of unemployment is 17 per cent for young men and 22.6 per cent for young women), the least qualified (14.1 per cent against 4.5 per cent for the most highly qualified) and manual workers (11.8 per cent against 3.1 per cent for executive staff). Among the western industrialised countries, it is in France that the employment rate of young people has declined most sharply (by 14.2 per cent between 1979 and 1991).

The difficulties encountered by young people in finding employment cannot be divorced from another characteristic feature of France, the rapid development of full-time education. This took place at an exceptional rate in the second half of the 1980s. The increase in the numbers of students sitting the *baccalauréat* is undoubtedly the most eloquent indicator – this rose from 30.2 per cent in 1985 to 50.5 per cent in 1992. Thus virtually all young people aged 17 (91.7 per cent to be precise), four-fifths of 18-year-olds (79.6 per cent) and almost two-thirds of those aged 19 (64.1 per cent) are engaged in full-time education. The result of structural changes, this propensity to remain in education has been encouraged by education and employment policies for young people. It could be said, therefore, that young people no longer join the labour market as employees and at the employer's expense, but through a series of measures set up and regulated by the State.

From the end of the 1970s to the middle of the 1980s, the shortage of skills was deemed to be the major cause of unemployment, and training was seen as the ideal instrument for correcting this situation. Gradually, however, youth employment policy became a central element of public policy distinct from, yet closely linked to, training. It seems more important to emphasise the extent of the measures taken to promote youth employment than the different forms they have taken over time. The annual numbers of young people benefiting from one or another of these actions rose from approximately 433,000 in 1980–1 to 1,113,000 in 1987 and 845,000 in 1992. It emerges from the observations carried out by the *Centre d'Études et de Recherches sur les Qualifications* (CEREQ), in particular, that the use of these structures is absolutely essential for all young people leaving school after middle school (*collège*) as well as for those who have followed vocational training leading to a CAP (*certificat d'aptitude professionnelle*) or BEP (*brevet d'études professionnelles*). The situation facing young people in the labour market cannot fully be understood without taking account of changes in employers' recruitment practices over the same period. Indeed, there is no linear correlation between the decline of employment and the economic inactivity or unemployment of young people. Between 1982 and 1990, young people's employment decreased by more than 19 per cent while the volume of employment increased by almost 4 per cent.

One of the other major changes observed in education and youth employment seems to be the creation of a variety of practices designated by the term 'work experience'. This term describes a common feature of a range of practices gradually introduced over the past fifteen years: the search for co-operation between training institutions (schools or specialist bodies of different statuses, both public and private) and industry. This joint action serves as a principle guiding both the redefinition of the way training is provided at school as well as the organisation of training offered in youth employment schemes. Although the vocational training which the school system has long provided remains dominant, it has been considerably transformed. The relationships established between the educational institutions (vocational and technical high schools, in particular) and industry are producing work experience programmes that differ from the German dual system in at least one major respect. In the latter, the company occupies the central place while this position is held by the school or college in the French system.

Finally, the fact that a training market has been created cannot be overemphasised even if it has not been adequately analysed. 'Training' includes not only actions aimed at the transmission of general or specialised knowledge through initial or continuing education in institutions of various types, but also efforts made to offer counselling (provided through appropriate structures), integration into the social environment, or even work of a psychological nature with unemployed people.

On this basis, a body of research has been developed that we cannot describe in these pages. We shall merely mention that, to date, this research has focused more specifically on certain themes such as young people's experience of the labour market as well as in the family and their leisure activities. The development of continuing training, under the provisions of the French law of 1971 obliging companies to fund training programmes for their employees, has inspired a great deal of research focused specifically on the policies implemented and the people concerned (in 1991, 39 per cent of employees attended continuing training courses). In addition, there is a body of work which has traditionally focused on 'qualification'. This is a concept which in France designates the practices and agreements which define the relationship between individual attributes and job descriptions, which are currently being redefined in terms of competences. This shift in meaning noted in France is similar to that observed in Great Britain, where the concept of 'competence' is replacing that of 'skills', a semantic shift which in both countries expresses a change in the nature of the relationship between training and work. In other words, the same trend can be observed in different national contexts. In both cases it undermines existing sets of relationships. In France, it affects the wage classification grids negotiated at industry level. In Great Britain, skill has been linked to the exercise of job controls by craft unions in the workplace and their ability to restrict the supply of skills in local labour markets. Lastly, it should be emphasised that comparative analyses have also been developed in France and have substantially deepened our understanding of the relationships between education and work. More specifically, this research has been used to examine a certain number of propositions made by LEST's societal analysis, focusing the research on intermediate levels: specific occupations, differentiation within the training systems and differences between men and women, for example.

REFERENCE POINTS AND PROPOSALS

To conclude these introductory remarks, it is important to emphasise that this account of research in different countries, in a field which is not highly institutionalised, cannot be presented in the positivist terms of tables of results and established knowledge. Rather it is an attempt to take account of the principal questions raised by a body of research at a particular point in time. This shows that the relations between education and work, which are currently perceived as being of vital importance, are the result of a long chain of interconnected relationships that need to be examined. This implies that the review of the research presented in this book results from a construction of reality that cannot be considered as a definite and comprehensive expression of that reality. This construction has been controlled through interactions and debate between researchers from all three countries and the French co-ordinators who first initiated the investigation. An informed reader could well object, however, that the overall picture errs through a poor understanding of features which we consider of secondary importance – perhaps wrongly – and/or through a selection of analytical categories common to European countries which are the most visible but perhaps not the most appropriate when trying to take account of current research. Still, one of the concerns guiding this study has been to recognise and to bring to public attention the questions and analytical approaches which are distinctive to particular countries. In other words, if this type of work is to promote communication between researchers in the Social Sciences in Europe it should not encourage a standardisation of these approaches in any way. That would represent a negation of the specific nature of historical realities which are undergoing different processes of transformation, though the research questions raised have some similarities.

NOTES

1 Tanguy, L. (ed.) (1986) *L'introuvable relation formation-emploi. Un état des recherches en France*, Paris: La Documentation Française.
2 This analysis is developed in more depth in Tanguy, L. (1994) 'La Formation, une activité sociale en voie de définition', in M. de Coster and F. Pichault (eds) *Traité de Sociologie du Travail*, Brussels: De Boeck-Wesmale.

2

EDUCATION, VOCATIONAL TRAINING AND EMPLOYMENT IN GERMANY

A close relationship between education and work

Catherine Marry

Since early 1990, the majority of researchers and social science research institutions in the Federal Republic of Germany have been asked to examine and analyse the rapid and often dramatic economic and social transformations resulting from the fall of the Berlin Wall in November 1989 and the subsequent reunification process of the eleven 'old' *Länder* (regions) of the West with the six new Länder of East Germany.[1] The issues of education and work, and the question of employment policies in particular, lie at the heart of these analyses. Reunification has also led to the 'restructuring' of research bodies in former East Germany and to an increase in exchanges and joint comparative projects conducted by researchers in both East and West.[2]

After introducing the institutional framework for research in education and employment, the complexity and exclusiveness of the dual system of vocational training will be examined. This remains the principal method for training young people and the German working population in general, despite the growth in the student population in the past twenty years. A general outline of changes in employment and unemployment will be presented before concluding this chapter with an examination, from the vantage point of a 'French' perspective, of certain ideas and lines of inquiry which seem specific, incomplete or innovative in German sociological thinking and research in this domain. This is characterised by poorly defined and overlapping boundaries of the education/employment relationship: namely, the question of transitions *(Übergänge)*, 'life-courses' *(Lebensverlaüfe)* and profession *(Beruf)*.

AN OVERVIEW OF SOCIAL SCIENCE RESEARCH IN GERMANY

Since the end of the Second World War, social science research in Germany has tended towards the stabilisation and institutionalisation of relations between the three leading actors in this area: the Federal Government *(Bund)*, the Länder and the scientific organisations both within and outside the university. A framework law enacted in 1975 regulated the long-standing conflictual relationship between the Bund and the Länder by redefining their respective spheres of competence and sources of funding. The Länder, whose sovereignty in research matters was guaranteed in the 1949 constitution, accepted the loss of a part of their authority over scientific organisations in exchange for greater financial support from the Federal Government. In the 1970s, Federal Government intervention in these matters was stepped up, notably through the co-financing of the Max Planck Society and of the federal research organisation in Germany (Deutsche Forschungsgemeinschaft, DFG). The DFG was particularly active in the early 1980s in establishing long-term theme-based research projects in universities, carried out jointly by researchers in different disciplines (economists, sociologists, political scientists).

The security resulting from the permanence of federal subsidies and from co-operation agreements enabled the Länder to define their own scientific policies. This was particularly true during the 1980s. For scientific organisations, the 1975 framework agreement eliminated uncertainties over funding by guaranteeing a minimum 50/50 split between the Federal Ministry for Research and Technology and the Regional Education and Research Ministries.

The recession brought about a shift in focus from questions of inequality of opportunity in education towards questions of segregation on the job market (unemployment, lack of job security, social exclusion). At the same time, the multiplicity of networks of relationships among researchers and institutions in different disciplines has favoured a narrowing of traditional divisions between fundamental or theoretical research (usually carried out in the universities) and the more 'applied' or 'empirical' research conducted by the institutes.

It should be noted, however, that this process has been accompanied by an increase in academic specialisation, even if the subjects treated are given a broad interpretation. Specialists in work, employment and industry, whether economists or sociologists, rarely fully integrate the 'education' dimension into their analyses. Similarly, specialists in education are reluctant to include job market analyses or public employment policies in their work. The contributions to this book testify to this continuing divide, this *introuvable relation formation-emploi*' (the elusive relationship between training and employment), which has also been observed in France (Tanguy (ed.) 1986).

The proliferation of institutes examining education and work in the late 1960s

The Max Planck Institute for Research on Education (Max-Planck Institut für Bildungsforschung) was founded in Berlin in 1963 and remained the most influential institution in this field until the end of the 1960s. Its purpose was to provide a scientific foundation for federal education policy. At the beginning, its work was chiefly centred on university teaching but its focus was subsequently widened to embrace the entire education system.

The late 1960s saw the emergence of a great many large institutes, leading to an increase in statistical studies, more research on the dual system and, more recently, to an interest in the difficult domain of the quantitative and qualitative appraisal of continuing education *(Weiterbildung)*. Encouraged by the government coalition between the social democrats of the SPD and the Liberal Party (1969–82), these institutes set out to implement and evaluate the 1969 laws on vocational training *(Berufsbildungsgesetz)* and on the 'promotion' of work *(Arbeitsförderungsgesetz)*. Adopted at a time of economic growth and a shortage of skilled labour, these laws were meant to improve the quality of individuals' initial and continuing vocational training and thereby satisfy the desire for greater mobility expressed by the workers as well as the employers. For workers, this professional mobility meant promotion; for employers, it meant 'adaptability' to technical and geographical change. This consensus of opinion about the goals of initial and continuing vocational training and about the relevance of the measures taken has been questioned, however, by a number of researchers (Baethge 1992; Lampert 1989).

Four institutes seem to play a major role in the promulgation of these two 1969 laws:

- The IAB (Institute for Research on Work and the Professions). Created in 1967 in Nuremberg, it carries out studies on behalf of the Federal Employment Ministry.
- The Bundesinstitut für Berufsbildung (BIBB, Federal Institute of Vocational Training). Established in 1969 in Berlin, it is dependent on the Federal Ministry of Education and Sciences and plays an important role as an expert and mediator in negotiations between workers' representatives, employers, the Länder and the Federal Government over what is to be included in new in-company training schemes.
- The Wissenschaftszentrum Berlin für Sozialforschung (WZB, Berlin Centre for Social Science Research) was founded in 1969; its four departments specialise in the analysis of the labour market and public employment policy.
- The Munich-based Deutsches Jugendinstitut (DJI, German Youth Institute), as its name suggests, focuses on issues concerning young people, but also on subjects related to the family and women. It is chiefly funded by the Federal Ministry of Women and Youth.

The substantial contribution of university institutes specialising in this field should also be mentioned. Among these are the Göttingen-based Soziologisches Forschungsinstitut (SOFI, Institute for Sociological Research), known for its publications on changes in the division of labour in large-scale manufacturing industry and in the service sector, the Wissenschaflisches Zentrum für Berufs- und Hochschulforschung (Centre for Research on Professions and Higher Education) at the University of Kassel and the independent Institute for Social Science Research (ISF) in Munich.

Other institutes, affiliated to workers' or employers' organisations, represent valuable sources of information and analysis in this field.

THE SYSTEM OF EDUCATION AND TRAINING: THE STRENGTH AND SELECTIVITY OF THE DUAL SYSTEM

In Germany, as in most other European countries, general education has expanded in the past thirty years and this is frequently noted in studies on youth, social mobility and the relationship between education and employment. This trend implies longer full-time education and increased friction between the education system and employment structures. The early academic and social selection of young Germans into three hierarchical tracks at the end of four years of primary school *(Grundschule)*, in other words, at the ages of 10 and 11, persists. At this age, children are sent either to upper primary school *(Hauptschule)*, middle school *(Realschule)* or high school *(Gymnasium)*. Only the Gymnasium (see Figure 2.1) allows direct access to university after obtaining the high-school diploma *(Abitur)*, taken after thirteen years' schooling as opposed to ten years' for the Hauptschule and Realschule. Between 1976 and 1989, the distribution according to social origin of 13- and 14-year-olds in these three types of school changed very little. Workers' children remain over-represented in the Hauptschule (60 per cent of the pupils in 1989) and poorly represented in the Gymnasium (14 per cent). In contrast, more than 50 per cent of the children of civil servants *(Beamte)* and self-employed professionals were attending the Gymnasium (Köhler 1992). These three types of general secondary school, the legacy of a distant past, have resisted reform efforts to combine them into one. The *Gesamtschulen*, a type of comprehensive school, have never enjoyed widespread development and, in 1990, accounted for merely 7 per cent of all 13-year-olds.

This apparent stability, however, masks significant underlying changes. Along with the greater standardisation of curricula and the reduction of barriers to the possibility of switching educational tracks, the principal trend noted in all the Länder between 1970 and 1990 was the sharp drop in both absolute and relative enrolments in the Hauptschule in favour of the Realschule and Gymnasium. The proportion of 13- and 14-year-olds in the Hauptschule declined from 55 per cent to 31 per cent and rose from 19 per cent to 26 per cent in the Realschule and from 20 per cent to 31 per cent in the Gymnasium. Some researchers (Köhler 1992) maintain that the privileged track leading from the Gymnasium to university and, from there, to

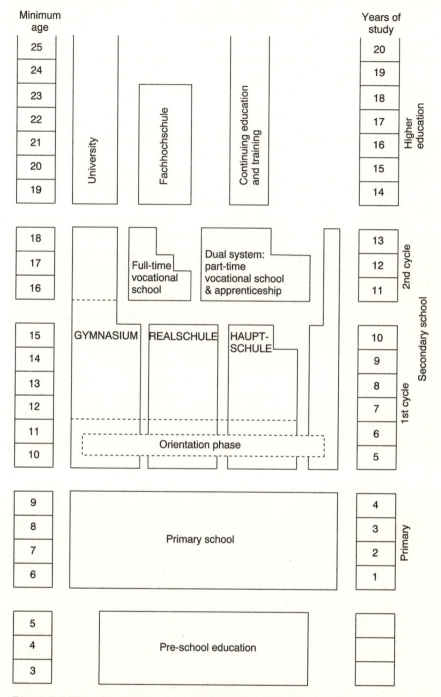

Figure 2.1 The education system in the Federal Republic of Germany, 1987
Source: Max-Planck-Institut für Bildungsforschung, 'Traditions et transformations. Le système éducatif en RFA', *Economica* 1991

the most prestigious and well-paying jobs (Tessaring 1993) has been able to preserve its social status thanks to the expansion of the Realschule and to the possibility offered to its graduates to go on to post-secondary studies in the *Fachhochschulen* (higher technical schools) after attending a *Fachoberschule*. In 1971, the Fachhochschulen replaced the engineering schools which had traditionally been considered secondary schools and which enabled holders of the diploma from the dual system given to manual and white-collar workers to take the title and position of 'graded' engineer. This theory would tend to contradict recurrent fears (Krais 1980, 1992) of the relative depreciation of university graduates *(Akademiker)* following the sharp increase in student numbers and the employment problems they encounter.

The professional importance attributed to the dual system as a means of promoting a workers' élite is a feature largely emphasised in comparative research, especially in studies comparing France and Germany (Maurice *et al.* 1982; Campinos-Dubernet and Grando 1988; Möbus and Verdier 1992; Géhin and Méhaut 1993). Less emphasis is placed on the academic and social gap that persists between those who choose this track and those who go to the Gymnasium and university. However, the 'technical culture' of technicians and non-university engineers continues to be opposed, in an ambivalent relationship based on a mixture of pride and feelings of inferiority, to the 'classical' culture of the Akademiker (Beckenbach 1991). This enduring hierarchy of values is illustrated by the long struggle of the *Technische Hochschulen* (technical universities) to obtain equality with the 'scientific' universities in the nineteenth century. This struggle ended at the turn of the century with the decision to allow the Technische Hochschulen to confer the prestigious title of *Doktor* on their graduates (Stück 1986).

Despite the growth of secondary school enrolments, and above and beyond these controversies, value judgements and worries about its future, the dual system continues to remain the dominant mode of professional socialisation for young Germans (Tessaring 1993). As shown in Table 2.1, 45 per cent of the total population of 18-year-olds in 1990 were following the dual system, 25 per cent general secondary education and 13 per cent vocational training (*Berufsfachschule* or *Fachschule*). Only 12 per cent were active, of which 2 per cent were unemployed. At the age of 21, one-third remained in full-time education and were evenly divided between the dual system and higher education.

The number of students tripled between 1970 and 1990. In 1994, at 1.8 million,[3] this number is marginally greater than the numbers of young people in the dual system (1.6 million). This numerical comparison, however, can be deceptive. Only 27 per cent of any given generation had gone on to higher education in 1990, and university (or equivalent) graduates represented only 15 per cent of the active population in the 30–44 age-range.[4] In contrast, half of the total working population of the Federal Republic of Germany had benefited from vocational training (the vast

Table 2.1 Occupational position of young people aged 16 to 24 in West Germany (1970–1990)

Age	Year	Gen. ed.	Full-time voc. ed.	Dual training	Higher tech. ed. Universities	Active pop. in employment	Unem- ployed	Non- working	Total
16	1970	25.50	8.00	44.80	0.00	18.30	0.40	2.90	100.00
	1990	62.10	13.60	16.90	0.00	2.90	1.00	3.10	100.00
17	1970	16.00	7.90	41.60	0.00	31.30	0.40	2.80	100.00
	1990	35.40	17.50	35.80	0.00	7.50	1.90	1.90	100.00
18	1970	11.00	6.40	22.50	1.30	53.70	0.40	4.70	100.00
	1990	25.50	13.40	44.70	0.20	10.70	1.90	3.60	100.00
19	1970	5.00	5.60	8.90	4.50	69.90	0.40	5.70	100.00
	1990	13.50	10.00	34.60	3.70	30.50	2.80	4.70	100.00
20	1970	1.50	3.60	3.20	7.20	75.00	0.40	9.00	100.00
	1990	3.10	8.00	22.20	9.00	48.40	4.20	5.20	100.00
21	1970	0.50	2.10	1.20	8.70	75.30	0.40	11.70	100.00
	1990	0.50	5.50	12.50	12.70	58.80	4.40	5.50	100.00
22	1970	0.30	1.80	0.60	8.60	74.10	0.40	10.10	100.00
	1990	0.20	3.90	6.10	14.60	64.80	4.50	5.90	100.00
23	1970	0.20	1.60	0.50	7.80	72.20	0.40	17.20	100.00
	1990	0.10	2.90	3.20	15.50	66.80	4.40	7.20	100.00
24	1970	0.10	1.30	0.40	6.50	72.80	0.30	18.60	100.00
	1990	0.00	2.20	2.10	15.30	66.90	4.40	9.10	100.00

Source: IAB. M. Tessaring (1988) (figures updated in 1990)

majority in the dual system) and this proportion reached almost two-thirds (57 per cent) of the working population in the 30–44 age-range. In 1975, as in 1988, more than half of the young people coming out of the Hauptschule or the Realschule turned towards the dual system. A new development in the 1980s was that secondary-school graduates (*Abiturienten*), the over-whelming majority of whom have always gone straight to university, started to opt for the dual system in sizeable proportions (4 per cent in 1975, 10 per cent in 1980, 14 per cent in 1994). Even if it meant taking a roundabout route while waiting for an opening in the university department or Fachhochschule of their choice, this diversification and elevation of the level of general education of those entering the dual system testifies to the vitality of the system itself. These characteristics are based on the involvement and support (even when conflictual) of unions and management, workers' and employers' associations and representatives of the state at federal and regional level (Länder). Known as 'dual' owing to the alternation between the places where the training is given and the people providing it (two days at school, the *Berufschule*, and three days in industry), the organisation of the dual system allows the intervention of a complex combination of different actors: representatives of both employees and employers, experts from the

State at federal (Bund) as well as regional (Land) level. A large number of publications describe how the system functions and its importance (the regulations negotiated within the dual system have force of law) but they also point to its unwieldy nature. For example, the reform of the metallurgical and electricity/electronics professions, initiated by the 1969 law (BBG), took twenty years to materialise in an agreement governing the content and duration of training.

However, the rise in the level of general education and the age at which young people enter different forms of in-company vocational training, along with the decline in the jobs available, has resulted in stiffer competition among these groups of more highly trained young people, notably, between those coming from the Realschule and those, following a negative selection procedure, graduating from the Hauptschule.

It is these selection mechanisms based on education, social class and gender that play a role at the beginning, during and at the end of the dual system that need clarification. The aim is not to denounce the system, as some highly critical sociologists such as Offe (1975) did in the 1970s, but to use the work of German researchers and the official statistics in an attempt to describe the complexity and poor visibility (outside Germany, in particular) of the way in which the dual system functions and its relationship to continuing and higher education.

Although institutionally independent of general secondary schools, the different routes through the dual system recruit young people whose academic backgrounds are correspondingly higher when the routes in question lead to the more socially attractive occupations and offer the greatest potential for professional advancement. High-school graduates (Abiturienten) who opt for dual training are concentrated in the most attractive occupations, namely management and administration in banks, industry and trade. In 1989, for example, two-thirds of the students training to be bank employees (*Bankkaufmann/Bankkauffrau*), whose numbers have risen constantly in recent years, had obtained their high-school diploma. Conversely, activities related to the craft industry (such as the food trade for boys, hairdressing for girls), the building trade and retail distribution (sales assistants), which offer little attraction for young people and whose workforce is declining rapidly, accounted for two-thirds of Hauptschule graduates in 1989. This opposition is somewhat reductionist, however, since the middle school or Realschule now sends the same proportion of students into the dual system as the Hauptschule (almost 40 per cent).[5] It also competes with Gymnasium graduates in the careers mentioned above.

The absolute and relative numbers of young people leaving the Hauptschule without any kind of diploma decreased from 143,000 in 1970 (17 per cent) to 53,000 in 1990 (9 per cent). Young people are finding it more difficult to obtain positions as trainees today, except in certain small craft or agricultural businesses or, in the case of young women, in service jobs (cleaning ladies). Many of them face unemployment or attend a one-year course of vocational training to prepare them for entry into the dual system. It should also be noted that there has been an increase in the percentage of children of non-German nationality (Ausländer in the German statistics) who leave school without a diploma (20.6 per cent in 1985, 30 per cent in 1990).[6] This penalisation of these children is also visible in their under-representation in the Gymnasium (9.7 per cent study at this level compared with 31 per cent of ethnic German children) and their over-representation in the Hauptschule (70 per cent compared with 31 per cent).

Although it has not been possible to find data regarding the socio-professional origin of the young people in the dual system, and even less about those in the different specialities of vocational training, the large number of young people involved and the diversity of their educational background force us to suppose that the same diversity applies to their social origin. Yet this question is rarely examined by researchers. In addition, the socio-professional classifications most frequently used in the statistics mention only five categories embracing extremely heterogeneous groups: the self-employed (Selbständige) and, among wage-earners, workers (Arbeiter), white-collar workers in the private sector (Angestellte), public-sector employees (Beamte) and home helps. In contrast, as mentioned above, this information is available for general and higher education. Thus, among the 18–21 age-group, only 5 per cent of workers' children went to university in 1990, and 6.7 per cent to the Fachhochschulen, compared with 46.9 per cent and 12.8 per cent respectively of children of public-sector employees (Köhler 1992).

Since the early 1980s, a great many studies have endeavoured to show the unequal division between males and females in the different tracks and areas of specialisation in the education system. In order to give greater perspective to the following analysis, it should be remembered that in Germany, as in other European countries, there has been a great increase in 'general' schooling for girls. In 1990, girls represented half of the students graduating from the Realschulen and Gymnasium and half of university entrants but only accounted for one-third of the students entering the Fachhochschulen because most of these schools specialise in engineering science. Their numbers have also increased substantially in advanced studies opening the way to careers other than teaching, such as law, economics, pharmacology and medicine, but their presence still remains weaker in the scientific and technical disciplines than in France (Marry 1992).

Discrimination is much more pronounced in the vocational training system. Young women are under-represented in the dual system (45 per cent) and concentrated in a small number of largely female specialities offering fewer prospects of advancement than those dominated by young men. In contrast, they attend school full-time more often than males (Berufsfachschulen or Fachschulen) (65 per cent of students), mostly in 'personal service' jobs (teaching, health care, work with the elderly, cleaning). These schools, which are often privately run and fee-charging, are responsible to the Länder alone. The training they provide consequently varies considerably both in quality and duration (one to two years, in general). Above all, they do not benefit from the federal control that the 1969 law on vocational training imposed on courses organised within the dual system which gives them a general validity recognised outside the place of training. Krüger (1992) emphasises that it is not the combination of training in vocational schools and in the company that constitutes the major advantage of the dual system over full-time vocational training in an educational establishment. The latter also offer a mixture of practical and theoretical apprenticeship. The handicap of school-based vocational training resides in the business community's failure to recognise this form of training, even when the successful completion of the course is guaranteed by a diploma (which is not always the case). No account is taken of these diplomas in sectoral collective agreements and the rate of pay is always inferior to that offered not only to male graduates from the dual system but also to young women coming from this system in similar professions with comparable qualifications.

THE MAIN CHANGES IN OCCUPATIONS AND EMPLOYMENT OVER THE PAST TWENTY YEARS

The decline of the agricultural workforce, the increase in the number of service-industry jobs and working women are strong trends shared by all the countries in Europe. Yet the scope of these phenomena and their occurrence in time differ from one country to the next. In Germany, urban development and industrialisation created an enormous mass of workers in a short period of time. In a mere twenty-five years, from 1882 to 1907, the working class grew from 4 to 8 million workers, principally due to the movement *en masse* of people from the land and to the transition from artisanal to industrial forms of production (Sellier 1984). This may explain the power enjoyed by a relatively homogeneous working class which succeeded in achieving trade union unity after the Second World War. In 1992, only 3.5 per cent of the population worked in agriculture, compared to 7 per cent in France, 8 per cent in Italy and 2 per cent in Great Britain, while 50 per cent worked in industry and construction, the highest percentage of all the European countries, compared to around 30 per cent in France and Italy and 41 per cent in Great Britain.[7] Recent changes, between 1981 and 1992, in the distribution of the German working population into broad occupational categories indicate a relative decline in the numbers of manual workers (-4 per cent) but their numbers still hovered near the 11 million mark in 1992 out of a total employed population of 26 million. In contrast, the so-called Angestellte, covering non-manual workers in the private sector, grew by 25.4 per cent and the Beamte, or civil servants, by 2.8 per cent (Datenreport 1992).

22

Female employment in industry and agriculture has developed more slowly in Germany than in France. Women represented 37.5 per cent of the active population employed in 1980, 41.6 per cent in 1992. Despite the growth in the numbers of working women, linked to the rapid increase in paid employment for women − notably in the service industries − this rate remains lower than in France, especially in the age range where women marry and have children. In 1991, 48 per cent of mothers aged 20 to 39 worked (20 per cent full-time, 28 per cent part-time) versus 61 per cent in France (44 per cent full-time, 17 per cent part-time).[8] Their pattern of activity is still discontinuous. The majority of women stop working between the ages of 25 and 40, when they have children, and subsequently return to work when their children grow up. The lack of child-minding facilities explains, in part, the reason for this pattern. Kindergarten which are private, do not offer enough places and are, like primary and secondary schools, only open part-time. The portrayal of motherhood (*Mutterlichkeit*) in German society undoubtedly also contributes to this withdrawal from the labour market. However, in Germany, as in all European countries, the growth of the working population in recent years is essentially due to the growth in women's employment, representing 2 million out of the 3 million additional jobs between 1980 and 1992. This tendency has intensified since the middle of the 1980s. Nearly half a million women enter the job market every year. When they are laid off, they register as unemployed more often than before. The considerable progress made in women's academic levels in general, in addition to the development of sectors employing women ('people-oriented' services, in particular) where they are concentrated, frequently in part-time work, also underlie these changes. In 1994, part-time work represented 33 per cent of female employment in Germany compared with 28 per cent in France.

Between 1980 and 1993, the unemployment rate for women remained higher than for men, although the gap narrowed in the last three years owing to the sharp decrease in male employment, particularly in heavy industry. The rates were 3 per cent and 5.2 per cent respectively in 1980, and 8 per cent and 8.4 per cent in 1993. In contrast, in the former GDR, women suffered more than men from economic restructuring and 21 per cent of women were unemployed in 1993 against 11 per cent of men. During this entire thirteen-year period, we note a steady rise in unemployment in the Federal Republic of Germany between 1980 and 1985 (from 3.8 per cent to 9.3 per cent), a drop in the unemployment rate until 1991 (5.8 per cent) followed by the higher rate mentioned above from that year on (Table 2.2).

Analysis of the unemployment rate by gender and level of training reveals some significant differences between men and women. The rates are by far the highest for both sexes when the individual concerned lacks a vocational training diploma (18.6 per cent in West Germany, 39.7 per cent in East

Table 2.2 Changes in unemployment rates among wage-earners according to gender in the former and new Länder between 1980 and 1993 (as a percentage)

	1980	1981	1982	1983	1984	1985	1986	1987	1988	1989	1990	1991	1992	1993
Men - former Länder	3	4.5	6.8	8.4	8.5	8.6	8	7.9	7.8	6.9	6.3	5.8	6.2	8.2
Women - former Länder	5.2	6.9	8.6	10.1	10.2	10.4	10.5	10.2	10	9.4	8.4	7	7.2	8.4
Total - former Länder	3.8	5.5	7.5	9.1	9.1	9.3	9	8.9	8.7	7.9	7.2	6.3	6.6	8.2
Men - new Länder												8.5	10.5	11
Women - new Länder												12.3	19.5	21
Total - new Länder												10.3	14.8	15.8

Germany in 1993) (Buttler and Tessaring 1995). Male graduates from the dual system, and especially those who have received complementary training as technicians or as foremen in a Fachschule, are much better protected from unemployment than women (1.6 per cent of unemployed men compared with 9.3 per cent of unemployed women in 1987) (Tessaring 1988). This disparity is also significant among Fachhochschulen graduates, based on the horizontal segregation of training and employment. The areas related to technology, science and heavy industry are largely traditional male enclaves. Service-sector jobs (health, teaching), particularly in the public sector, are dominated by women. This horizontal segregation also accounts for unemployment rates twice as high for women with university degrees as their male counterparts (8.3 per cent against 4.3 per cent) (ibid.).

One of the characteristics of unemployment in Germany which is frequently emphasised in comparisons with the rest of Europe is its relatively minor impact on young Germans compared with the situation in other countries. This observation is a priori irrefutable. In 1994, the unemployment rate in Germany of young people between the ages of 15 and 24 was 8.7 per cent (8.4 per cent for the 15–64 age-group) compared with 28.8 per cent in France (12.4 per cent for the 15–64 age-group). Comparisons of this nature raise two problems, one of which is related to the definition of the term 'young people'. The extension of full-time education for 15- to 24-

year-olds in both countries means that, for the purpose of comparison, only the unemployment rate for 20- to 24-year-olds is relevant (or even 20- to 29-year-olds).

The second difficulty stems from the definition of 'working population' standardised in European surveys. Young people in full-time education are not deemed to be members of the working population but young people in the dual system are included in the working population in view of the fact that they are paid for their work. The extension of schooling in the dual system in Germany, and in full-time education in France, therefore requires unemployment indicators which make it possible to distinguish between young people under and over the age of 20, and to relate the numbers of unemployed to the total population of each cohort. The difference between the unemployment rates of 15- to 24-year-olds in France and in Germany then diminishes greatly (3.7 per cent in Germany in 1989, 8.6 per cent in France). In an article devoted to changes in the labour market since 1980, Tessaring (1988) has suggested a similar presentation of all the possible situations in which young people could find themselves at a given age. Table 2.1 illustrates this for young people aged between 16 and 24 in 1970 and 1990. It summarises the evolution, mentioned above, of the rise in the age of young people in the dual training system, the growth of higher education and the marginal increase in unemployment among young people under the age of 20 (1 per cent for 16-year-olds, 2.8 per cent for 19-year-olds in 1990) and a substantial increase for those aged 20–24 (0.4 per cent in 1970, 4.4 per cent in 1990).

SPECIFIC CONCEPTS AND LINES OF INQUIRY

The absence of systematic inquiries into young people's entry into the workforce seems specific to Germany, particularly in comparison with France which, at the beginning of the 1970s, set up a national body to study and assess the entry of young people into an active working life. The renewal and extension of the 'measures for young people', combining employment and training policies aimed at reducing the difficulties of the least educated in finding employment, has increased the demand for surveys and appraisals of these mechanisms. In Great Britain and, to a lesser extent in Italy, there has been a shift of academic emphasis towards young people who have difficulty in finding their first jobs, or are simply excluded from stable employment on the labour market on a long-term basis.

Limited surveys do exist in Germany (most frequently carried out by specialised institutes) on the occupational outcomes of young people leaving the dual system and university graduates. The researchers, whether they are sociologists specialising in youth or in education, usually replace the notion of occupational integration focused on the passage from school to work with that of 'transition', which they conjugate in the plural (*die Übergänge*), thereby emphasising their interest in young people's entire life-cycle histories (Mayer and Blossfeld 1990; Blossfeld 1990; Brock *et al*. 1991; Evans and Heinz 1994). Entry into employment is considered by these researchers as an essential step in individual destinies, particularly in terms of occupational careers. Nevertheless they consider it important not to divorce this 'entry' from the economic context in which it takes place (the 'period' effect) and to connect it to the other stages or transitions from one status to another in the entire life cycle. This includes changes in status related to age (childhood–adolescence–adult life) and family status (moving away from home to live alone, living in a couple, becoming a parent, etc.).

The greater overlapping or blurring of the boundaries in Germany between the status of 'student' and 'person engaged in the labour market', which is due to the preponderance of the dual system in the socialisation of young people, explains, in part, this weaker focus on their professional insertion or first job experience. Another explanation is the lower rate of unemployment among young people in Germany compared with the rate for young people in other European countries.

The notion of Beruf – usually translated as 'profession' – seems to play a central role and be much more widely accepted in German society and sociology than in Anglo-Saxon countries where the model is based on the 'liberal professions', or in France where both academic and non-specialist usage refer to a schema of graded socio-professional categories. It applies to all the higher professions, employees in the public sector (teachers, the legal profession) and private sector (engineers) as well as the self-employed (doctors, lawyers) – all professions whose legitimacy derives from professional skills or from expertise sanctioned by a university degree (Krais 1992). It also applies to artisanal professions, commerce and industry, whose access is conditioned (in theory, at least) by the possession of a diploma acquired in the dual system and whose validity is widely recognised.

For Weber (1964), this central importance can be traced back to the Lutheran concept of work as a 'vocation' or duty assigned by God. He supports his thesis with the assertion that Luther uses the same word, Beruf, to translate words in the Bible referring to the secular activities of 'job' or 'work' (*Werk, Arbeit*), and those signifying religious vocation (*Berufung*) or a calling from God (*Ruf*). Because of this association between occupation and vocation, Luther overturned both the negative portrayal of work as 'labour', or punishment even, and the corresponding positive portrayal of poverty and contemplation conveyed by the Catholics, thus enhancing the value of work and 'profession' as the principal means for individual fulfilment. As Nipperdey puts it, with Luther, 'profession replaces good works' (1992).

In Germany professional status is linked to the recognition of an individual's competence and importance is attributed to personal effort in making progress in one's professional life, especially through continuing education. The apparent lack of concern with hierarchical status possibly explains the difficulties of distinguishing hierarchical divisions in socio-professional classifications both in official statistics and in sociological research. It can also explain the classification used for training courses and diplomas, used in particular by the IAB, which makes a clear distinction between the diplomas awarded at the conclusion of 'general' education (at the end of the three pathways in secondary education) and vocational qualifications. This last schema is the most frequently used and would seem more relevant when assessing the highest level reached since it alone includes the degrees awarded in higher education.

The concept of Beruf, however, applies mainly to men working in industry and is considerably less relevant to occupations in commerce and the services. At intermediate and higher levels, loyalty to the firm is as necessary as a diploma, or even more so (cf. Kocka's work (1989) on the Angestellte). At lower levels, where there are more women employees, especially in 'people-oriented' occupations (health, social work, cleaning), one does not often speak of Beruf because these activities are considered an extension of a woman's role in the family, as if they involved 'feminine qualities' (such as 'devotion') and are not assumed to need any form of regulated and recognised training. Krüger (1992) points out an interesting analogy between the arguments advanced today about women's exclusion from technical occupations and the debate at the beginning of the century on the dangers facing women who enter upon the Beruf. At that time, the aim was to prevent women, against their will, from taking part in any professional activity because of the risk that it would destroy their humaneness, their feelings, their warmth.

More generally, the power of the concept of Beruf and the central importance of the dual system and industry in German society have reinforced the neglect (also present in French sociology) of employment not conforming to this 'model', namely, that of women and foreigners. In her contribution to this work, Drexel shows that the preoccupations of German industrial sociology are focused on the professional worker in manufacturing industry, the social standard of the 'good job' or the 'socially desirable job'. The work of feminist researchers in Germany has done a great deal to highlight these differences and hierarchies and to build bridges between the different specialist fields in sociological research (youth, education, family, work).

NOTES

1 In fact, the reunited Germany has only sixteen Länder, since those of East and West Berlin are now consolidated into one.
2 It is not possible to offer a detailed discussion of these phenomena in this paper, which relies primarily on data predating most of these changes; however, some statistics which are now available will be cited.
3 1,676,000 in former West Germany; 180,000 in former East Germany (Source: Grund-und Strukturdaten 1995/96).

4 10 per cent coming from university, 5 per cent from Fachhochschulen (Source: Datenreport 1992).
5 In 1993, 38 per cent of all apprentices came from the Hauptschule, 36 per cent from the Realschule, 14 per cent from the Gymnasium, 12 per cent from another type of training institution (Source: Berufsbildungsbericht 1995, Ministry of Education).
6 Source: Datenreport 1992.
7 Source: Eurostat, Labour Force Survey, 1991.
8 Source: *Bulletin sur les femmes et l'emploi dans l'Union Européenne* 6, April 1996.

BIBLIOGRAPHY

Baethge, M. (1992) 'Die vielfältigen Widersprüche beruflicher Weiterbildung', *WSI Mitteilungen* 6.
Beckenbach, N. (1991) *Industriesoziologie*, Berlin: De Gruyter.
Blossfeld, H.-P. (1990) 'Berufsverläufe und Arbeitsmarktprozesse. Ergebnisse sozialstruktureller längschnituntersuchungen', *Kölner Zeitschrift für Soziologie und Sozialpsychologie* 31: 577–95.
Brock, D., Hantsche, B., Kühnlein, G., Meulemann, H. and Schober, H. (eds) (1991) *Ubergäng in den Beruf. Zwischenbilanz zum Forschungsstand*, Munich: Deutsches Jugendinstitut.
Buttler, R. and Tessaring, M. (1995) 'Le capital humain facteur de l'implantation industrielle en Allemagne: une discussion du point de vue du marché du travail', *Sociologie du Travail* 4, special issue 'Contre le chômage, la formation?'.
Campinos-Dubernet, M. and Grando, J. M. (1988) 'Formation professionnelle ouvrière: trois modèles européens', *Formation-Emploi* 22, April-June, special issue 'Entreprise, État et formation en Europe (Allemagne, France, Grande-Bretagne, Italie)'.
Datenreport (1992) Einführung: Walter Müller, *Zahlen und Fakten über die Bundesrepublik Deutschland. Bundeszentrale für politische Bildung*, Statistisches Bundesamt (ed.), in *Zusammenarbeit mit dem WZB und dem Zentrum für Umfragen, Methoden und Analysen*, Mannheim.
Evans, K. and Heinz, W. R. (1994) *Becoming Adults in England and Germany*, London: Anglo-German Foundation.
Géhin, J. P. and Méhaut, P. (1993) *Apprentissage ou formation continue? Stratégies éducatives des entreprises en Allemagne et en France*, Paris: L'Harmattan.
Kocka, J. (1989) *Les employés en Allemagne, 1850–1980. Histoire d'un groupe social*, Paris: EHESS.
Köhler, H. (1992) 'Bildungsbeteilung und Sozialstruktur in der Bundesrepublik', Max-Planck-Institut für Bildungsforschung, *Studien und Berichte* 1992, 53.
Krais, B. (1980) 'Der deutsche Akademiker und die Bildungsexpansion oder die Auflösung einer Kaste', *Soziale Welt* 1: 68–87.
——(1992) 'Pourquoi n'y a-t-il pas de cadres en Allemagne? Note de recherche', *Sociologie du Travail* 4: 497–507.
Krüger, H. (ed.) (1992) *Frauen und Bildung, Wege der Aneignung und Verwertung von Qualifikationen in weiblichen Erwerbsbiographien*, Kritische Texte, Karin Böllert, Bielefeld: KT-Verlag.
Lampert, H. (1989) '20 Jahre Arbeitsförderungsgesetz', *MittAB* 2.
Marry, C. (1992) 'Les ingénieurs: une profession encore plus masculine en Allemagne qu'en France?' *L'Orientation scolaire et professionnelle* 21, 3: 245–67.

Maurice, M., Silvestre, J. J. and Sellier F. (1982) *Politique d'éducation et organisation industrielle en France et en Allemagne. Essai d'analyse sociétale*, Paris: PUF.

Mayer, K. U. and Blossfeld, H.-P. (1990) 'Die gesellschaftliche Konstruktion sozialer Ungleichheit in Lebenslauf', in P. A. Berger and S. Hradil (eds) Lebenslagen, Lebensläufe, Lebensstile', *Soziale Welt* 7: 297–318.

Möbus, M. and Verdier, E. (1992) (eds) *Le système de formation professionnelle en République fédérale d'Allemagne. Résultats de recherches françaises et allemandes*, CEREQ, collection des études 61.

Nipperdey, T. (1992) 'Luther et le monde moderne', in *Réflexions sur l'histoire allemande*, Paris: Gallimard (German edition 1986).

Offe, C. (1975) *Berufsbildungsreform. Eine Fallstudie über Reformpolitik*, Frankfurt.

Sellier, F. (1984) *La confrontation sociale en France, 1936–1981*, Paris: PUF.

Stück, H. (1986) 'L'émancipation des écoles supérieures techniques la professionalisation des ingénieurs en Allemagne au XIXème siècle', in A. Grelon (ed.) *Les ingénieurs de la crise, Titre et profession entre les deux guerres*, Paris: Editions de l'Ecole des Hautes Etudes en Sciences Sociales.

Tanguy, L. (ed.) (1986) *L'introuvable relation formation-emploi. Un état des recherches en France*, Paris: La Documentation Française.

Tessaring, M. (1988) 'Arbeitslosigkeit, Beschäftigung und Qualifikation: ein Rück- und Ausblick', *MittAB* 2.

——(1993) 'Das duale System der Berufsausbildung in Deutschland: Attraktivität und Beschäftigungsperspektiven', *MittAB* 2: 131–60.

Weber, M. (1964) *Wirtschaft und Gesellschaft*, Berlin: Kiepenhauer und Witsch (11th edition).

Zimmermann, B. (1996) 'La constitution du chômage en Allemagne. Mise en forme d'une catégorie nationale des politiques publiques', doctoral thesis, Institut d'Etudes Politiques de Paris.

3

THIRTY YEARS OF THE SOCIOLOGY OF EDUCATION

Research questions and debates

Beate Krais

INTRODUCTION

For a long time, the scholarly engagement with education and with the educational system in the Federal Republic of Germany was the uncontested domain of the traditional and influential discipline of Academic Pedagogy. The institutionalised educational system must be regarded as a cornerstone of the western project of modern society. Parsons, for instance, places the 'educational revolution', after the industrial and the democratic revolutions, amongst the most structurally significant processes which constitute modern society. Despite this, the classic German works in sociology did not deal with education in a systematic fashion. Only after educational issues rose to the top of the political agenda in the Federal Republic did this branch of sociology develop in this country as well.

By the mid-1960s, leading representatives of German sociology had entered the debate with a series of articles from an educational–sociological perspective. One example is the special volume on the subject 'Soziologie der Schule' (Heintz 1959) in the *Kölner Zeitschrift für Soziologie und Sozialpsychologie*. With this publication, studies and argument, above all from the United States and Britain, found their way into the West German discussion. In Tübingen, where Dahrendorf was head of the Sociology Department, a whole series of Master's theses and dissertations were written that pursued questions in the Sociology of Education (cf. Peisert 1967). The new, critical Marxist-oriented periodical *Das Argument* had devoted two issues to the theme 'school and education'. In the meantime, studies on the German university had also appeared. One should mention, for instance, the ground-breaking empirical investigation on the political consciousness of university students by Habermas *et al.* (1961).

Educational Sociology had also established itself in an institutional sense. In 1958, a special committee for the Sociology of Education was founded within the German Society for Sociology under the direction of Helmuth Plessner. In the same year, a separate Department of Sociology was established at the Hochschule für Internationale Pädagogische Forschung, today the Deutsches Institut für Internationale Pädagogische Forschung, in Frankfurt. Likewise the Max-Planck-Institut für Bildungsforschung in Berlin, founded in 1963, had a heavy sociological emphasis. In terms of the institutional framework of German Educational Sociology, however, it is clear that the Sociology of Education was from the very beginning part of a comprehensive and wide-ranging branch of scholarship organised along interdisciplinary lines. Above all, it was *Bildungsforschung* (research on education) that took hold in the Federal Republic – in other words, a form of interdisciplinary scholarly specialisation for the study of education. A selective demarcation from studies from other disciplines, for example in Pedagogy and the Economics of Education, is therefore possible only with difficulty. This is even more the case since the majority of professorships in Educational Sociology during the 1970s and 1980s were established in departments of Pedagogy, and thus were committed to a discourse of 'pedagogical practice'. Two advisory committees of experts in education played an important role in the development of educational research, namely, the Deutscher Ausschuß für das Erziehungs- und Bildungswesen and its successor, the Deutscher Bildungsrat.[1]

The debate surrounding education in the 1960s provided the point of departure for the themes and research perspectives of Educational Sociology in the Federal Republic. The discussion on the relationship of education and economic development was conducted throughout the world, and the OECD (Organisation for Economic Co-operation and Development) published reports which compared the educational situations in various countries. These reports revealed that education in the Federal Republic fell behind that in other industrialised countries, as measured for instance in the number of university students and high-school graduates qualified for university study. Moreover, major differences existed in the enrolment rates in secondary school tracks leading to university among the individual federal states within the Federal Republic, which gave rise to the question in the wider public debate as to whether the Bavarians were more stupid than the population in Schleswig-Holstein. This data and information provided the point of departure for the thesis of a 'catastrophe in German education'. In a series of articles in *Die Zeit*, Dahrendorf took up this theme and gave it a new twist. He pointed out a pronounced inequality of educational opportunities in the Federal Republic, and a closely related 'backwardness in modernity'.

'A country can become rich without touching the educational system that has been handed down to it. . . . If a country can remain rich, if it can secure the continued prosperity of its society without opening the doors to its schools and universities to broad sections of the population and fundamentally changing these institutions, this is the question that has awakened interest in educational policies in the last years.' With these words begins Dahrendorf's 'Plea for an active politics of education' (1968). In this way, he took up the debate on the 'catastrophe in education' which establishes the relationship between education and economic growth in modern society, above all, in relation to paid employment. The key concept here for Educational Sociology is 'qualification', which goes hand in hand with 'profession', particularly with the German definition and significance of *Beruf* (vocation). In contrast, Dahrendorf argued strongly for 'education as civil right'. Here he developed a perspective that linked education and social inequality with each other, and a perspective that looked at education and the civilising process. The significance of education as a 'step into a modern world of enlightened rationality' (Dahrendorf 1968: 24) was central to his argument. However, in the debate on education in the 1960s and early 1970s, it was never able to attain the position accorded to issues such as the need for a qualified labour force, and, for a time, inequality in educational opportunities. Nonetheless, this point in Dahrendorf's work belongs to the classic inquiries of Educational Sociology. Together with the other two analytical perspectives mentioned above, it is a main focus of Educational Sociology. They therefore provide the structure of this article. Running through these three analytical perspectives is the question of the mechanisms of reproduction and change in social structures which occur through education or in the educational system. Research on the theme of young people's perspectives and interactions in the 'everyday life' of the school will also be presented. Sociologically informed reporting on education has also analysed the situation and the development of the educational system and its sub-areas. While this reporting is part of Educational Sociology, it will not be presented in detail (cf. Arbeitsgruppe Bildungsbericht 1994; Rolff *et al*. 1980).

EDUCATION AND THE CIVILISING PROCESS

When Parsons talks of the significance of the 'educational revolution' for modern society, he is not primarily concerned with the modernisation of human-capital resources. Rather, what interests him is the significance of the educational system. For Parsons the 'cognitive rationality' of modern society is institutionalised and develops, in the first place, in the university. The individuals who are socialised there, the individual personalities in Parsons' terminology, transfer cognitive rationality into other social domains (Parsons and Platt 1990). If, following Norbert Elias, the broader and more general perspective of the civilising process is adopted, the question of the educational system's contribution to the rise of a civil and civilised society belongs to the earliest questions in the Sociology of Education raised in the Federal Republic. The first major empirical investigation concerned with post-secondary students was prompted by the interest in examining students' democratic potential, a social group that had played a highly problematic role in the establishment of the National Socialist régime (Habermas *et al.* 1961). Adorno's work on the social figure of the German teacher (1970b) looked at the educational system in the light of the experience of fascism, as did his article on 'Education after Auschwitz' (1970a). For his part, Dahrendorf saw the primary task of active educational policies in Germany as ensuring that 'the path to modernity is also the path to freedom' (1968: 25).

In this argument, social subjects are seen as the agents of the civilising process. A civil society can emerge only when the development of modern institutions corresponds to that of individuals. This involves, amongst other elements, institutionalised individualism, mutual recognition of individuals as people with equal rights, recognition of individual responsibility, calculable action, cognitive rationality and, finally, the ability to empathise with others in a context of extensive social differentiation, i.e. under social conditions that imply a broad spectrum of life styles and living conditions. Under these conditions, the acquisition of the ability to empathise is not as self-evident as it may appear. It becomes absolutely necessary to be able to relate to 'second-hand' experiences, because 'first-hand' experiences can no longer be apprehended in a highly differentiated society. Modern literature – novels, stories, essays, documentary reports, poems – as well as film, television, newspapers, museums, art exhibitions and concerts deliver a wealth of material for playing out the most diverse social situations, to test out how it is to stand in someone else's shoes, to express feelings, to allow oneself to be swept away by feelings, and so on. However, the ability to decode this material and to use it for one's own purposes in order to transcend the limits of individualised experience must be acquired, not only, but most essentially, in school.

The significance of school for the development of more civilised social conditions was seldom made an explicit subject of research in Educational Sociology in the Federal Republic after 1970. It was most likely to appear in research on socialisation, which tended to address socialisation outside the context of the school. As Baumert remarked with a certain astonishment, 'How little we actually know about the concrete effects of the rise in the level of formal education' (1991: 336). His work numbers among the few attempts to ascertain and measure the longer-term effects of educational expansion. Baumert finds clear evidence for the validity of the thesis that educational expansion has indeed brought about a cognitive mobilisation of the upcoming generation, as its supporters had expected and hoped. On the other hand, the acquired cultural capital of this generation (measured in terms of the level of degree or diploma) seems to cause a stronger differentiating effect in value orientations than that of the older generation.

EDUCATION AND EMPLOYMENT

The study of the relationship of education and employment has to be grasped as a historical question. It requires the generalisation of waged labour on the one hand and the development of an institutionalised and differentiated educational system on the other. In its everyday sense, 'work' has long stood as a synonym for paid employment (the debate about housework, conducted within the women's movement, was the first to call this equation into question). This situation opens up the possibility of conceptualising education in a functional relationship to production and to the use of labour power. The institutionally autonomous educational system can be understood as a place of 'production', i.e. where the education and training of the labour force takes place.

New and unusual viewpoints arose. Labour power is understood as human capital, education is seen as investment in human capital, the need for a skilled and qualified labour force is likewise turned into a problem of adjustment between the education and employment systems. Along with the concept of education emerges the concept of qualification, the key concept in the discussion around the theme of education and employment.

The concept of qualification refers to those abilities, aptitudes and knowledge that allow an individual to perform a given job or to practice a certain vocation (Beruf). A central feature for the concept of qualification is thus the reference to social labour. This brings the concept of qualification into close proximity with concepts such as human capital or labour power in the way Marx used it. At the same time, this concept fits into traditional German thinking in terms of distinct Beruf. In its connection to paid employment, the concept of qualification is distinct in two important aspects from the classic – that is idealistic – German concept of *Bildung*, which is rooted in the philosophical traditions of neo-Humanism. First, the 'qualification' of an individual designates only a part of the entire repertoire of experience and action available to an individual, namely that related to work, and not the total, complex personality. Second, whereas Bildung aims at an idealistic conception of human beings, qualification refers to the ability to solve the real requirements and exacting demands which individuals confront in their work. The concept of qualification has thus been introduced to the discussion around educational theories for good reason – as a realistic corrective to the classical concept of Bildung.

Nevertheless, the concept of qualification has its pitfalls. In both popular and academic debates about qualification, it is common to define qualification as the ability to perform certain tasks in the labour process and to translate qualification requirements in terms of a 'psychology of assets'. To give a classic example, a power to sleep (*vis dormitiva*) must exist in order to explain that people sleep. The ability to accomplish certain tasks, if one regards inner processes of thinking and acting, is determined in a highly complex way. It would be important to understand these 'inner' psychological structures above and beyond their mere tautological designation, as mechanisms for regulating action as is done in the action theory-based labour psychology (cf. Hacker 1986). In this way, one could build a bridge to both the concept and the processes of Bildung.

The discussion surrounding the relationship between education and employment took as its starting-point a problem originally formulated in a narrow economic sense: a model designed to forecast the need for qualified workers in reference to goals for economic growth, the so-called 'manpower requirements approach'. Although originally applied to less developed economies, this approach was quickly applied to the Federal Republic, where an enormous series of manpower forecasts was produced, above all for the highly qualified segments of the labour force, i.e. those trained in polytechnics and universities (together the *Hochschulen*). The debate engendered by this approach, which was very lively around 1970, was, as in other domains of education, conducted with a complete disregard for disciplinary boundaries. Economists, economists of education, representatives of the newly established labour market and occupational research, sociologists of different specialisms, pedagogues and psychologists all contributed to the development of discourse in this field.

The sociological critique of the demand for qualification as presented in the 'manpower requirement approach' focused on the social preconditions and consequences of the existence of labour power as commodity.

Hartung *et al.* (1970) made a strategically important contribution to the critique of the idea of the 'demand for qualifications' in their study of the professional activities of political scientists (the so-called Politologen-Studie). The discipline of Political Science was first established as an independent subject with an academic degree in the 1950s. According to the strict logic of the 'manpower requirement approach', no corresponding demand could have existed before there were graduates in this discipline. Nevertheless, the Politologen-Studie showed that 'the graduates whose qualifications deviate from the articulated demand were absorbed by the labour-market in largely satisfactory conditions of employment' (1970: 157). The authors also examined the conditions for the incorporation of these 'new' qualifications, and in this way criticised the idea implied by the concept of a fixed 'bundle' of qualification requirements. Instead, they point to the complex processes in which professional roles emerge and change.

A whole series of investigations followed the Politologen-Studie. They were often connected to questions in research on education and higher education concerned with the destinations of college and university graduates from a range of disciplines and institutions (cf. on this point Franke *et al.* 1986).

Empirical studies on the theme of Hochschule und Beruf continued to occupy an important place in sociological inquiry (Hartung and Krais 1990;

Krais 1993). The concept of profession has re-emerged strongly in the debate as a means of grasping the relationship of education and Beruf in a theoretical way. This concept has been especially fruitful in research on gender issues for the analysis of social processes of women's exclusion and marginalisation in the area of skilled employment (cf. Wetterer 1992).

The renaissance of Marxism, sparked by the student movement and economically based research on the demand for qualifications, found common ground in assuming the primacy of the economy. The centrality of the employment system thus emerged above all other references of the educational system as a central theme in this discussion. Nevertheless, the debate concerning the concept of demand for qualifications made it clear that the development of the educational system could not be understood as directly dependent on economic development, nor as an autonomous 'pedagogical province' as the idealist model would suggest. Rather, education is best understood as a social field that stands in a position of relative autonomy to other social fields. A whole series of theoretical works aimed to analyse this position of relative autonomy, which draws on Bourdieu's work, in more precise terms (cf. the overview in Baethge and Teichler 1984). These studies are mostly directed towards the relationship of the educational system to the employment system. Offe also developed his analysis from this question but, like others, came to the conclusion that educational planning and educational policies confront 'structural uncertainty' in terms of the scale sizes of demand for qualifications (1975). Offe's attempt to grasp the range of social functions of the educational system gave rise to four functional points of reference: as well as the process of training and qualification there is the social integration of the labour force, the creation of state legitimation in light of an assumed equality of individuals (which is impossible to realise, but which cannot be ignored) and, lastly, the substitution of roles no longer provided by other social sub-systems such as the family. Amongst others, Teichler (1974) analysed the assumption of equality with his thesis of the social demand for social inequality. This thesis accentuates the interplay of training and qualification processes and the distribution of social status. Under conditions of educational expansion, the output of the educational system cannot be adapted to the existing social and occupational structure in the long run and becomes 'surplus', so to speak. In this situation, the educational system's function of distributing status becomes dominant, sacrificing a proper match of qualifications to demand.

The idea of a 'coupling' of social status and Beruf is again taken up in investigations on university graduates (*Akademiker*) and educational processes in the Hochschulen, in the sense of Bourdieu's concept of 'habitus'. Given the significance of the different disciplines in German society for social stratification in the domain of academic employment, empirical investigations have concentrated on the rise of a discipline-specific habitus among students (Engler 1993; Liebau and Huber 1985). The sociological construct of habitus brings together a range of symbolic orders and opens the analytical access to the articulation of social position and qualification. In contrast to the more usual concept of roles, habitus comprehends the physicality of the social agent. This concept therefore allows for a new perspective on learning processes: it directs attention to mimetic processes. (Krais 1996).

EDUCATION AND SOCIAL INEQUALITY

Equal opportunity and the reproduction of social structures

The study of the relationship of education and social inequality is one of the main research issues in Educational Sociology and, in West Germany, it became the basis of its identity. In contrast to what was most commonly assumed, the educational expansion had already started at the beginning of the 1950s (cf. Arbeitsgruppe Bildungsbericht 1994). One can only guess what reasons led many of the population to alter their behaviour on educational matters. The experience of losing possessions, money and property during the Second World War and in the immediate post-war period was perhaps as significant in this change as the idea of education as an ever more important vehicle of social advancement in a society which seemed to have become more mobile. In this way, the issue of how to create equality in educational opportunities took a central place in policy debate.

Dahrendorf (1968) identified four groups in the Federal Republic who were under-represented in upper-level secondary schools and in the universities: girls, children from working-class families, children from rural areas, and Catholics. The debate in Educational Sociology concentrated on two dimensions of structural social inequality: social class and gender. Regional differences in educational opportunities, especially the gap between city and country, and religious differences were repeatedly addressed and analysed though they did not attract the same attention that was devoted to the two other main categories of social inequality. In the 1970s debate on education, the various facets of the educational system's selection and allocation function were inextricably interwoven and the resulting studies in Educational Sociology isolated discrete aspects and questions from this tangled web. They can be roughly divided into three research orientations:

- studies that analysed the structural selection in access, to and within the educational system;
- studies that addressed the relationship of unequal educational opportunities and the acquisition of status;
- studies that looked 'inside the black box' by investigating the mechanisms for the reproduction of social inequality through education, and attempted to reconstruct socialisation processes from the perspective of the subjects.

Sociological research on the reproduction of gender relations through education is also relocated predominantly within these parameters.

Unequal Opportunties in the Educational System

The absence of official data on the social origins of schoolchildren and students which Dahrendorf encountered in his study (1968) continues to be a problem. The collection and analysis of relevant data on inequality in educational opportunities thus became a top priority for the Sociology of Education.

One of the first sociologists in the Federal Republic who was able to produce data on the social background of schoolchildren in upper-level secondary schools was Adam. For his Master's thesis, Adam conducted an investigation in the city of Offenbach and the surrounding county, and later published a short article on his findings in *Das Argument* (1964). He not only looked into the distribution of girls and boys from different social backgrounds in the school population, but also calculated the enrolment rates for children according to their social class.

In the 1970s, a series of monographs on the social selectivity of the school were published with data collected on the basis of diverse regional samples (for a summary see Trommer-Krug 1980). The first nationally representative data are found in the socio-historical work of Kaelble (1975), who documented the social background of students in upper-level secondary schools and universities in the German Reich and the Federal Republic from the period 1910 to 1960. Other nationally representative data are found in studies from the Dortmund Institut für Schulentwicklungsforschung (Rolff *et al.* 1988). In the 1990s, a series of new studies dealing with the question of the effects of educational expansion during the previous three decades gave rise to a renaissance of the debate on educational inequality: Köhler's study on educational enrolment and social structure (1992) has to be mentioned here, as well as the work by Müller and Haun (1994) and Henz and Maas (1995).

The data on inequality in the educational system paint a picture which reveals unequal educational opportunities, even after years of educational expansion and reform. In summary, one can see that all social classes have profited from the expansion in education, even though the structure of inequality did not itself go through any profound change, a development which is often designated as the 'elevator effect'. Above all, the disadvantages faced by children from working-class families in the upper-level educational system have proven to be extraordinarily resilient. The transition from the primary school to the secondary school at the age of 10 still constitutes the decisive threshold for selection in the compulsory school system and has not been changed since the 1920s (cf. Köhler 1992; Müller and Haun 1994; Henz and Maas 1995). Nevertheless, in other aspects, inequality of educational opportunities has been reduced. The differences in enrolment rates according to religion have almost disappeared and in general education the advantage of boys over girls has also vanished. In the areas of vocational education and post-secondary education, however, girls and young women continue to experience highly unequal opportunities (Faulstich-Wieland *et al.* 1984; Köhler and Zymek 1981).

Education and the Acquisition of Status

The burst of educational reform in the years 1965 to 1975 was nourished to a large extent by the hope that the reforms could break the existing class structures. Before empirical investigations provided the answer to this question in the Federal Republic, and even before the success or failure of educational reforms could be examined in this light, sociological debate on the educational system's allocation function had already been influenced by American and French studies. The studies by Bourdieu and Passeron (1971) which appeared as *The Illusion of Equal Opportunity*, in German,[2] was not understood as a polemically formulated challenge to bring up on to the open stage of sociological analysis those processes of class-specific transmission of cultural capital that, so to speak, took place behind the curtains of formal equality. Rather it was taken primarily as proof of the futility of all reform-minded efforts. The conclusions drawn from the widely received book by Jencks *et al.* (1972) followed the same direction. This book collected an abundance of empirical data and examined a range of variables, the relationships between social background, educational success and status acquisition. Jencks came to the conclusion that this relationship was weak, arguing, 'economic success seems to depend on varieties of luck and on-the-job competence that are only moderately related to family background, schooling, or scores in standardized tests' (Jencks *et al.* 1972: 8). In the dominant interpretation, in which representatives of completely different positions on educational policies met, this study was taken as more evidence of the illusory character of the assumption that social inequality could be diminished through reducing unequal educational opportunities. In the meantime, a critique of the equal-opportunity concept had appeared that also contributed to the disappearance of public debate on whether education could open up possibilities for social–structural change, (cf. Büchner 1985; Heid 1988).

As Hopf (1992) points out in his well-founded dispute with this theme, both the study by Jencks *et al.* (1972) and the book by Bourdieu and Passeron (1971) mark the beginning of a whole series of investigations on the selection and allocation function of education, not only in the Federal Republic but in the international context as well. These studies found little resonance in the Federal Republic, and were hardly acknowledged or incorporated into the discussion in Educational Sociology. This is despite the fact that they not only broadened the data available and entered new methodological territory, but also had to modify substantially the way one conceived the reproduction of social inequality through the educational system. Even in the Federal Republic today, there are only a few relevant investigations on this topic. The sociological discussion on social mobility, the acquisition and reproduction of status, conducted in the 1960s and 1970s along such lively and controversial lines, now falls largely outside research in Educational Sociology.

The first study in the Federal Republic to connect social background, education and status acquisition was presented by Müller and Mayer (1976). Rather than giving an answer to the question of the evolution of inequality of educational opportunities and status attainment, this publication developed and tested a programme for quantitative empirical research. Answers to the questions they posed were provided nearly twenty years later. In the context of his project 'Life Course and Social Change', Mayer published the first results concerning the issue (Mayer and Blossfeld 1990; Mayer 1991). Meulemann (1990), who used the data of a follow-up study of tenth-grade Gymnasium students from North-Rhine-Westphalia from 1970, also dealt with this question. The issues of educational opportunities for girls and the significance of education for the social status of women were again raised in this context; along with the authors named above, Handl (1986) pursued this question in a particularly vigorous way.

The methods used in these studies are those developed in sociological research on mobility, involving the compilation and statistical analysis of social mobility. These methods isolate the impact of different factors such as parental occupation in the allocation of status to their children. Complex statistical procedures are used to determine the relative weight of individual factors in the process of status acquisition.

Meulemann (1990) directs attention to the relationship between the prestige of the occupation selected by young men upon graduating from the university, and that of their fathers' occupation. Young men whose fathers have high social status hold a distinct advantage in their professional choices immediately following graduation, even when academic subject, academic success, and similar factors are held constant. Mayer and Blossfeld (1990) and Mayer (1991) have produced results that should lead to a revival of the discussion in Educational Sociology. For these authors it is clear that the 'endogenous connection of the life course' has become narrower. The relationship of social background, educational system and career have not become more open with the expansion in education. Mayer argues that 'overall, the younger the cohort is, the easier it becomes to predict the status upon entry into an occupation on the basis of background and education' (Mayer 1991: 323). According to the author, that also means that the mechanisms of social selection have become somewhat more meritocratic.

In the issue of the periodical *Unterrichtswissenschaft* on the topic 'School and After', Baumert, in discussing Meulemann's and Mayer's results, comes to the conclusion that the school system acts more as a 'wheel' than as a 'steering wheel' in the system of social inequality (Baumert 1991: 333). Other authors, such as Müller and Haun (1994) and Krais (1996b), criticise these conclusions on methodological grounds. The sample of the life course project is too limited to be sensitive to the small changes to be expected in social mobility through educational expansion, and Meulemann's sample is already a highly selected population. Until now, it may be concluded, no empirical study has been published which could answer the question of whether educational expansion and school reforms since the late 1960s have had the effect of changing social reproduction or not.

INSIDE THE BLACK BOX, OR 'WHAT HAPPENS IN SCHOOL?'

There are at least two analytical perspectives concerned with the 'everyday life' of the school: first, a system-oriented perspective that asks how the educational system can master externally produced problem situations and, second, a perspective that addresses the mechanisms and processes in the reproduction of social structures or social barriers to equal opportunity inside the educational system. It is characteristic of both perspectives that the agents, their actions and interactions, also come under scrutiny. Both perspectives will be briefly sketched in the following section, whereby the presentation is limited to research on the school.

The issue of the processes of selection and self-selection in the school runs like a thread throughout the literature. These processes account for the fact that even today, children from working-class families continue to be at a disadvantage in the general education school system. The special issue of the *Kölner Zeitschrift für Soziologie und Sozialpsychologie* on the sociology of the school published in 1959 had already identified the school as a 'middle-class institution' (Lütkens 1959) and the volume *Sozialisation und Auslese durch die Schule* (Socialisation and Selection through the School) (Rolff 1967), a collection of the relevant international research which has evolved into a standard work, has been published again and again in revised and expanded versions. Great attention was paid to the educational expectations and decision-making behaviour of parents and schoolchildren at critical points in the school career (Gerstein 1972; Grimm 1966; Peisert and Dahrendorf 1967; Rolff *et al*. 1988). Research on educational expectations and school preferences of parents and pupils points to a problem that has become more serious over the last two decades, namely, that many pupils attend a *Hauptschule*, a school that neither they, their parents nor the public at large accept. The Hauptschule is the least demanding kind of secondary education and is still in existence because of certain decisions in educational policies. It has even been re-established in the new federal states, although it is rejected by those people who are trained there and should benefit from it. Extensive investigations have been made on the comprehensive school (*Gesamtschule*) on a broad spectrum of pedagogically relevant questions. At the centre of these studies stands the question whether, as supporters of the comprehensive school maintain, the social selectivity of the three-track school system in the Federal Republic should be diminished (Baumert and Raschert 1983; Fend 1982; Leschinsky and Mayer 1990). Since German unification, discussion of the comprehensive school has been revived, sparked by the structural adaptation of the school system in the new federal states to western German conditions. In the current research on these developments and their consequences, questions of selection and differentiation processes take up much space.

It is, however, important to recognise that little is known about the instruction practices and classroom interactions that precede the processes of school selection. While some of the earliest sociological studies on the everyday life of the school include investigations into the role of the teacher (summarised in Grimm 1987), there is still very little information about what really happens between pupils and teachers. This is not just a question of there being bureaucratic obstacles in the way of participant observation but is also due to the absence of a convincing analytical approach to the problem. When looking back at the educational research sparked by the 1960s debate on education, the interest in questions of socialisation is immediately apparent although it is also clear that this research was mainly devoted to socialisation processes in the family. The results of socialisation research on the school were first made available during the 1970s, long after the structural decisions in educational reform had been passed. The imminent development of socialisation research, strongly influenced by Habermas' work on socialisation theory, moved away from questions of class-specific socialisation to fundamental problems in the constitution of the subject. It brought with it a renaissance of symbolic interactionism and a concentration on problems of identity and interaction that have found their way into investigations on stigmatisation processes in the school (Brusten and Hurrelmann 1973) and on peer-group interactions (Oswald 1993). It is the recent emergence of the Sociology of Childhood which may reopen questions of class-specific socialisation, including the everyday life of schools (Zeiher and Zeiher 1993).

In terms of a system perspective, the focal point of interest is occupied by developments in school that go along with social modernisation processes. Amongst these are: the specialisation of instruction and its consequences for the culture of educating; the dualism of education and performance-oriented transmission of knowledge as a structural problem of modern instruction; the erosion of traditional relations of authority in the school and changes in the school climate; and consequences of the superabundance of regulations and bureaucratisation for the internal relationships of the school. All together, these are problem areas in which sociological and pedagogical research continue to be inseparably linked to each other (cf. Arbeitsgruppe Bildungsbericht 1994). In the past, a major role was played by the demands placed on schools by demographic development and migration movements into the Federal Republic.

In this context, a new debate on an unanticipated consequence of educational reform has arisen: the question of co-education for boys and girls in school. It has become clear that direct and indirect discrimination play a role in the transition to employment, producing a pattern of unequal opportunities for women on the labour market, and gender-specific decisions on vocational and academic courses. Co-education has in no way broken the gender-specific segregation of knowledge. On the contrary, results from primarily Anglo-Saxon and Scandinavian investigations show that co-education places girls at a disadvantage in terms of instruction in the Natural Sciences, Technology and Mathematics (Faulstich-Wieland 1991). Although it is not certain in which respects these results are valid for the Federal Republic, they have led to a lively discussion about possible counter-strategies at school.

CONCLUSIONS

This brief survey of the emergence and evolution of Educational Sociology in West Germany has shed light on some characteristic features of this sociological sub-discipline. The Sociology of Education emerged as a discipline when the educational system, and in particular its relation to great social questions such as social inequality and economic welfare, was at the top of the political agenda, and it lost its relevance not only in the general debate but also in Sociology at the moment when other political issues gained priority. It became more differentiated, more specialised, a sub-discipline among others which no longer deals with the 'great' questions of society, even though it still deals with questions such as social inequality and its reproduction via the school system. One of the 'great' questions, namely, education and the civilising process, has been neglected by the Sociology of Education throughout the years. It may be that looking back to the evolution of West Germany from a fascist to a relatively civilised society, an evolution which has scarcely been analysed by sociologists, and the repercussions of the recent unification process will lead to more research in this field. Important sociological issues are dealt with in a mainly interdisciplinary debate on education and school, a debate where the issue − education − occupies the interest and the attention of its participants, whereas disciplinary boundaries seem to have no relevance. It may therefore be stated with little exaggeration that Educational Sociology has achieved most within a comprehensive field of educational research, interwoven with other disciplines such as Pedagogy, the Economics of Education and Educational Psychology. Only later, when the public interest in education vanished, did clearer demarcations of the Sociology of Education appear. However, in part due to its institutionalisation mainly within the confines of Pedagogy faculties, the Sociology of Education still has difficulty in imposing itself as a field of knowledge with a particular, well-defined *sociological* perspective. The dominant normative pedagogical paradigm and, more recently, the equally important economic paradigm, leave just a small place for a genuinely sociological view on education.

NOTES

1 The Deutscher Ausschuß für das Erziehungs- und Bildungswesen existed from 1953 to 1965. It was a board of experts at the national level and fulfilled an advisory function. With the establishment of this committee, a phase of expertise and advice organised across the nation on policy issues in the educational system began. Its influence on the educational system in the Federal Republic can still be felt today. In 1975, the Bildungsrat (advisory council on education), the successor institution of the Deutscher Ausschuß, was dissolved, marking the end of national-level advisory activities in the area of educational policies (cf. Arbeitsgruppe Bildungsbericht 1994).
2 *Die Illusion der Chancengleichheit* was the title of the book which brought together *Les Héritiers* (Éditions de Minuit, 1964) and part of *La Réproduction* (Éditions de Minuit, 1971).

BIBLIOGRAPHY

Adam, H. (1964) 'Bildungsprivileg und Chancengleichheit', *Das Argument* 6: 203–9.
Adorno, T. W. (1970a) 'Erziehung nach Auschwitz', in T. W. Adorno (ed.) *Stichworte. Kritische Modelle* 2: 85–101, Frankfurt: Suhrkamp.
——(1970b) 'Tabus über dem Lehrberuf', in T. W. Adorno (ed.) *Stichworte. Kritische Modelle* 2: 68–84, Frankfurt: Suhrkamp.
Arbeitsgruppe Bildungsbericht am Max-Planck-Institut für Bildungsforschung (1994) *Das Bildungswesen in der Bundesrepublik Deutschland*, Reinbek: Rowohlt.
Baethge, M. and Teichler, U. (1984) 'Bildungssystem und Beschäftigungssystem', in M. Baethge and K. Nevermann (eds) *Organisation, Recht und Ökonomie des Bildungswesens. Enzyklopädie Erziehungswissenschaft*, 5: 206–25, Stuttgart: Klett-Cotta.
Baumert, J. (1991) 'Langfristige Auswirkungen der Bildungsexpansion', *Unterrichtswissenschaft* 19: 333–49.
Baumert, J. and Raschert, J. (1983) 'Gesamtschule', in Skiba, E.-G., Wulf, C., and Wünsche, K. (eds) *Erziehung in Jugendalter, Sedundasshufe I. Enzyklopädie, Erziehungswissenschaft* 8:228–269, Stuttgart: Klett-Cotta.
Bourdieu, P. and Passeron, J.-C. (1971) *Die Illusion der Chancengleichheit*, Stuttgart: Klett.
Brusten, M. and Hurrelmann, K. (1973) *Abweichendes Verhalten in der Schule. Eine Untersuchung zu Prozessen der Stigmatisierung in der Schule*, München: Juventa.
Büchner, P. (1985) *Einführung in die Soziologie der Erziehung und des Bildungswesens*, Darmstadt: Wissenschaftliche Buchgesellschaft.
Dahrendorf, R. (1968) *Bildung ist Bürgerrecht*, Hamburg: Wegner.

Engler, S. (1993) *Fachkultur, Geschlecht und soziale Reproduktion*, Weinheim: Deutscher Studien Verlag.

Faulstich-Wieland, H. (1991) *Koedukation – enttäuschte Hoffnungen?*, Darmstadt: Wissenschaftliche Buchgesellschaft.

Faulstich-Wieland, H., Horstkempter, M., Tillmann, K-J., Weissbach, B. (1984) 'Erfolgreich in der Schule' in Rolff, H-G., Hensel, G., Klemm, K. (eds) *Jahrbuch der Schulentwicklung*, 3:117–143.

Fend, H. (1982) *Gesamtschule im Vergleich*, Weinheim: Beltz.

Franke, H., Kaiser, M., Nuthmann, R. and Stegmann, H. (eds) (1986) *Berufliche Verbleibsforschung in der Diskussion, Hauptband*, Beiträge zur Arbeitsmarkt- und Berufsforschung 90:4.

Gerstein, H. (1972) *Erfolg und Versagen im Gymnasium*, Weinheim: Beltz.

Grimm, S. (1966) *Die Bildungsabstinenz der Arbeiter*, München: Barth.

—— (1987) *Soziologie der Bildung und Erziehung*, München: Ehrenwirt.

Habermas, J., von Friedeburg, L., Oehler, C. and Weltz, F. (1961) *Student und Politik*, Neuwied/Berlin: Luchterhand.

Hacker, W. (1986) *Arbeitspsychologie*, Bern: Huber.

Handl, J. (1986) 'Führt die Angleichung der Bildungschancen zum Abbau geschlechtsspezifischer beruflicher Segregation?', *Zeitschrift für Soziologie* 15: 125–32.

Hartung, D. and Krais, B. (1990) 'Studium und Beruf', in U. Teichler (ed.) *Das Hochschulwesen in der Bundesrepublik Deutschland*, 179-209, Weinheim: Deutscher Studien Verlag.

Hartung, D., Nuthmann, R. and Winterhager, W. D. (1970) *Politologen im Beruf*, Stuttgart: Klett.

Heid, H. (1988) 'Zur Paradoxie der bildungspolitischen Forderung nach Chancengleichheit', *Zeitschrift für Pädagogik* 34: 1–17.

Heintz, P. (ed.) (1959) 'Soziologie der Schule', *Kölner Zeitschrift für Soziologie und Sozialpsychologie* Suppl. 4, Köln/Opladen: Westdeutscher Verlag.

Henz, U. and Maas, I. (1995) 'Chancengleichheit durch die Bildungsexpansion?', Kölner Zeitschriff für Soziologie und Sozialpsychologie, 47:605–633.

Hopf, W. (1992) *Ausbildung und Statuserwerb*, Frankfurt/New York: Campus.

Jencks, C., Smith, M., Acland, H., Bane, M-J., Cohen, D., Grintis, H., Heynes, B., and Michelson, S. (1972) *Inequality, a Reassessment of the Effect of Family and Schooling in America*, New York: Basic Books.

Kaelble, H. (1975) 'Chancenungleichheit und akademische Ausbildung in Deutschland 1910–1960', *Geschichte und Gesellschaft* 1: 121–49.

Köhler, H. (1992) *Bildungsbeteiligung und Sozialstruktur in der Bundesrepublik*, Berlin: Max-Planck-Institut für Bildungsforschung.

Köhler, H. and Zymek, B. (1981) 'Chancengleichheit für Frauen durch Bildungsvoreile?, *Die deutsche Schule*, 73:50–63.

Krais, B. (1993) 'Nachrichten aus der Welt des Geistes', *WSI-Mitteilungen* 46: 240–50.

——(1996a) 'The Academic Disciplines: Social Field and Culture', *Comparative Social Research*, Suppl. 2: 93–111, Greenwich, CT: JAI Press.

Krais, B. (1996b) 'Bildungsexpansion und soziale Ungleichheit in der Bundesrepublik Deutschland', in *JakrbuchBildung und Arbeit*, 1: 118–146.

Krappmann, L. (1993) 'Kinderkultur als institutionalisierte Entwicklungsaufgabe', in 365–376 Markefka M. and Nauck, B. (eds), *Handbuch der Kindheitsforschung*, Neuwied: Luchterhand.

Leschinsky, A. and Mayer, K.-U. (1990) *The Comprehensive School Experiment Revisited: Evidence from Western Europe*, Frankfurt: Lang.

Liebau, E. and Huber, L. (1985) 'Die Kulturen der Fächer', *Neue Sammlung* 25: 314–39.

Lütkens, C. (1959) 'Die Schule als Mittelklassen-Institution', *Kölner Zeitschrift für Soziologie und Sozialpsychologie* Suppl. 4:22–29, Köln/Opladen: Westdeutscher Verlag.

Mayer, K. U. (1991) 'Lebensverlauf und Bildung', *Unterrichtswissenschaft* 19: 313–32.

Mayer, K. U. and Blossfeld, H.-P. (1990) 'Die gesellschaftliche Konstruktion sozialer Ungleichheit im Lebensverlauf', in P. A. Berger and S. Hradil (eds) 'Lebenslagen, Lebensläufe, Lebensstile', *Soziale Welt* Suppl. 7: 297–318, Göttingen: Schwartz.

Meulemann, H. (1988) 'Bildung im Lebensverlauf', *Zeitschrift für Sozialisationsforschung und Erziehungssoziologie* 8: 4–24.

——(1990) 'Schullaufbahnen, Ausbildungskarrieren und die Folgen im Lebensverlauf', *Kölner Zeitschrift für Soziologie und Sozialpsychologie* Suppl. 31, Opladen: Westdeutscher Verlag.

Müller, W. and Haun, D. (1994) 'Bildungsungleichheit im sozialen Wandel', *Kölner Zeitschrift für Soziologie und Sozialpsychologie* 46: 1–42.

Müller, W. and Mayer, K. U. (1976) *Chancengleichheit durch Bildung? Untersuchungen über den Zusammenhang von Ausbildungsabschlüssen und Berufsstatus*, Stuttgart: Klett.

Offe, C. (1975) 'Bildungssystem, Beschäftigungssystem und Bildungspolitik – Ansätze zu einer gesamtgesellschaftlichen Funktionsbestimmung des Bildungssystems', in H. Roth and D. Friedrich (eds.) 'Bildungsforschung', *Deutscher Bildungsrat, Gutachten und Studien der Bildungskommission* 50: 215–52, Stuttgart: Klett.

Oswald, H. (1993) 'Gruppenformationen von Kindern', in Markefke, M., and Nauck, B. (eds), *Handbuch der Kindheitsforschung*, 353–364, Neuwied: Luchterhand.

Parsons, T. and Platt, G. M. (1978) *The American University*, Cambridge (MA): Harvard University Press.

Peisert, H. (1967) *Soziale Lage und Bildungschancen in Deutschland*, München: Piper.

Peisert, H. and Dahrendorf, R. (1967) *Der vorzeitige Abgang vom Gymnasium*, Villingen: Neckar Verlag.

Rolff, H.-G. (1967) *Sozialisation und Auslese durch die Schule*, Heidelberg: Quelle & Meyer.

Rolff, H.-G., Klemm, K. and Tillmann, K.-J. (eds) (1988) *Jahrbuch der Schulentwicklung*, Weinheim: Juventa.

Rolff, H-G. *et al.*, (eds) (1988) *Jahrbuch der Schulentwicklung*, 5, Weinham: Juventa.

Teichler, U. (1974) 'Struktur des Hochschulwesens und "Bedarf" an sozialer Ungleichheit', *Mitteilungen aus der Arbeitsmarkt- und Berufsforschung* 7: 197–209.

Trommer-Krug, L. (1980) 'Soziale Herkunft und Schulbesuch', in Max-Planck Institut für Bildungsforschung, Projektgruppe Bildungsbericht, *Bildung in der Bundesrepublik Deutschland*, 1: 217–81, Reinbek: Rowohlt.

Wetterer, A. (ed.) (1992) *Profession und Geschlecht*, Frankfurt/New York: Campus.

Zeiher, H. and Zeiher, H. (1993) *Organisation von Raum und Zeit im Kinderalltag. Handbuch der Kindheitsforschung*, Neuwied: Luchterhand.

4

RELATIONSHIPS BETWEEN THE EDUCATIONAL AND EMPLOYMENT SYSTEMS

Research in *Berufspädagogik* (Vocational Pedagogy) in the Federal Republic of Germany[1]

Margit Frackmann

INTRODUCTION

Berufspädagogik as an academic discipline is unique within the European university system. This article will therefore present a short discussion of the specific disciplinary character of vocational pedagogy and the history of its development in Germany.

A three-track school system still delineates the German educational landscape. After four years of primary schooling (the *Grundschule*), children must complete at least five or six more years of education. Around the age of 10 they are thus placed either into the basic-skills programme of the *Hauptschule*, the non-classical secondary school (*Realschule*) with ten grades, or the traditional secondary school for university-bound pupils (*Gymnasium*) with thirteen grades. The Hauptschule and the Realschule together form the schools of the secondary level I, and the Gymnasium is the secondary level II school. While the possibilities for transferring among these different schools have become more open in the last decades, the three-track system continues to perpetuate a marked classification of educational opportunities in Germany.

The expansion of education has thus seen a sharp decline in the percentage of children attending the Hauptschule, with more children moving to the Gymnasium. Because the Gymnasium is still widely regarded as the preparatory ground for university study (the *Abitur* or final examination is the university admission requirement), the educational trajectory of the Hauptschule and Realschule usually leads to vocational training in the workplace – the 'dual system'. This designation refers to the pupils' two learning locations, 3–4 days on-site in an enterprise, and 1–2 days in the *Berufsschule* (part-time vocational school). The dual system encompasses vocations ranging from skilled factory work and traditional artisanal trades to administrative positions in both the public and private sectors.

The overall statistics on education for 1988 reveal the different whereabouts of 16- to 19-year-olds: one out of eight was still attending a general education school in the secondary level I; one out of four was in a general education school in the secondary level II; more than one-third participated in dual-system vocational training; and one-seventh could be found in a secondary level II vocational school. After attending a full-time school, two-thirds of all adolescents still pass through the dual system, this despite the higher proportion who pursue a degree from a university or polytechnic college (together, the German *Hochschulen*). The successful completion of a Hochschule course of study results in either a Master's degree or its general equivalent, the *Diplom*; the German system does not grant the Bachelor's degree found in some other countries. These numbers make clear that vocational education continues to play a large role in the German social system. Due to its practice-oriented character, most vocational education and training takes place in an enterprise. This tradition reaches back to medieval artisanal practices, when the guilds created a vocational qualification path from apprenticeship to journeyman to master craftsman. Since the beginning of the twentieth century, industry too has been investing ever more energy in systematic apprentice-training programmes. In fact, schools for general and continuing vocational training date from the nineteenth century, and national legislation has mandated general compulsory vocational schooling since 1938. In the commercial sector, vocational education and training took a different track, with full-time commercially oriented vocational schools set up and running in the eighteenth and nineteenth centuries.

Developmental lines also diverged in the teacher-training programmes for both the craft and technical trades and commercial trades. In the craft and technical trades, teaching preparation and qualification procedures passed through very different phases. Systematic training programmes existed as early as the middle of the nineteenth century, but widespread admissions regulation first came into force during the 1920s with fixed training courses in independent institutes and set courses of study in the universities and polytechnic colleges. After 1933, institute-based training was mandated at the expense of Hochschule study throughout the German Reich; in more and more cases, a certificate of mastercraftsmanship (*Meisterbrief*) or an engineering Diplom served to gain admission to study *Berufspädagogik* (Lempert 1965: 12). Institute-based study remained the rule after 1945, but regulations varied from one federal state to the other. Critics called attention to the resulting differences among the separate training institutes, prompting a broad discussion in the 1960s about how to provide adequate training for teachers. Teachers' organisations pointed out the completely new and increasing burdens placed on the profession and called for a full academic course of study. This was linked to a demand for higher ranking in the public-service salary scales. With a university degree, vocational and trade teachers could achieve both the status (the title 'Studienrat') and the pay of Gymnasium teachers. Last but not least, they also hoped for a better image. Through engagement in interest group politics, they succeeded in securing what is in every respect a better, highly respected position in German society.

In the commercial sector, on the other hand, an 'academic' training has been common since the beginning of this century. The *Handelsschulen* (commercial schools) offered a qualifying course of study in Economics and Pedagogy. The course of study today is very similar to a Diploma in Business Administration and Economics. This diploma also fulfills the first state examination. Teachers in the Handelsschulen have profited from the greater respect accorded to commercial, administrative vocations, and from the firm belief still held in most industrial societies that these vocations demand a higher intellectual level. The establishment of university-based vocational teacher training prompted an expansion in professorial positions for the discipline *Berufs- und Wirtschaftspädagogik* (Pedagogy for Vocational Training and Business Administration). It is my opinion, however, that this discipline lacks both a distinctive theoretical basis and a clear goal-orientation within the larger division of teaching and research tasks. There are a number of different reasons for this.

First, the training to become a vocational teacher consists of mastering the vocational subject itself, the ability to teach an additional subject, and an array of classes in the educational sciences (*Berufs- und Wirtschaftspädagogik*). A specific 'subject didactic' is connected to the vocational and additional subjects. The fact that the sub-disciplines do not need to relate to each other is more problematic in this constellation and an unsatisfactory co-ordination stands in for real co-operative work. Even the Educational Sciences component of the vocational teaching major is, in some federal states and universities, further divided into several subjects (including Pedagogy, Vocational Pedagogy, Sociology, Psychology), and takes up the fewest credit hours. This fragmentation has prevented the creation of a consensus on the curriculum among the university institutions involved in vocational teacher training. A logic of increasing self-determination plagues not only the sub-disciplines generally, but can even affect the disciplines within any particular institution through the opinions and course offerings of the teaching personnel. University-level co-ordinating authorities have come up with few remedial measures, especially since they usually have no recourse to sanctions or other punitive mechanisms.

Second, those students who want to pursue a teaching career at a vocational school are rarely if ever interested in 'academic' study, and neither their professional plans nor their own educational biography and background do much to make that a meaningful goal. Their professional ideas centre more on gaining a practice-oriented qualification for their later teaching activities, although the university has yet to fulfill that goal. Nor for that reason do these students usually strive for a university career. The next generation of those engaged in the university-level study of *Berufs- und Wirtschaftspädagogik* thus has no basic pattern for career planning that culminates in a professorial position. In addition, representatives of the discipline complain that the curriculum lacks sufficient social scientific direction. According to a report from the *Senatskommission für Berufsbildungsforschung* (1990: 102) on research in vocational education and training:

> Even outstanding graduates of *Berufs- und Wirtschaftspädagogik* thus usually still need, in contrast for example to graduates in Psychology or Sociology, several more semesters of study before they are in the position to undertake a promising dissertation in the area of research on vocational education in a broader sense. It would be easier for them to complete an additional academic qualification in technology or economics. Instead, though, they most often turn to the schools and try to pursue a career in teaching.

Thirdly, what results is above all an internal disciplinary dilemma for *Berufs- und Wirtschaftspädagogik*. If one complies with student demands, research and teaching activities will need to be orientated towards the concrete practice of teaching, structured to transmit concrete, professional abilities. These modest disciplinary boundaries do not, however, correspond to what would be expected of university research as it is normally understood in a real academic discipline of *Berufs- und Wirtschaftspädagogik*. Such a discipline would, to cite a related report,

> focus on human developmental processes that not only aim at securing a qualification, acquiring a professional proficiency, but also at the education and development of the individual, a [professional] maturity. . . . In order to research processes of vocational education in a comprehensive way, one must also devote more consideration to processes that influence professional training through changes in larger ecological structures and thus the interrelationships between people and the environment (for example, research on mobility within the system and pupils' whereabouts; [comparative] research on learning sites; research on qualifications; curriculum research; historical research on socialization and qualification processes in industrial society).
> (Senatskommission für Berufsbildungsforschung 1990: 4)

To combine both concerns (broad research and concrete, practical applications), so as also to offer relevant, classroom-related insights for the teaching profession, including applications to university-based teaching practices, has not yet been successful. But neither has this discipline provided many of the comprehensive analyses necessary for understanding the relationships between social developments and processes of professional training. One must also question whether the claimed deficiency in personnel and financial resources can completely explain this research deficit.

Finally, it is important to consider how the recruitment of personnel has influenced the discussion of research topics and orientation. Particularly in the 1970s, when the institutes offering *Berufs- und Wirtschaftspädagogik* underwent significant expansion and quickly absorbed the upcoming junior academics, many graduates who qualified to teach at the Berufsschulen returned to the university after only a short teaching stint. Some of these young academics were then able to climb their own professional ladders to professorships. A profound gap separated the professors of *Berufs- und Wirtschaftspädagogik* from other professors in the Humanities, whose social and cultural capital remained much greater and who occupied a different plane. At the same time, the possession of a university position itself led to the creation of a group or 'clan', which for its part set both the criteria for belonging and the terms of co-optation. Despite apparent differences in the research agenda of *Berufs- und Wirtschaftspädagogik*, we are still dealing with a basically homogeneous group of researchers in terms of their interests.

I will demonstrate the validity of this thesis by examining relevant themes and questions in *Berufspädagogik* over the last twenty years, the results of this research, and its methodological foundations.

THE WEAKNESS OF VOCATIONAL PEDAGOGY AS A DISCIPLINE

In post-war German society public attention has focused on vocational training alongside other major debates on equal opportunities, increasing the priority of education in the social value system, and the widely accepted view that education is an important resource in an industrial society short on raw materials. In this context one can mention the recommendation of the Deutscher Bildungsrat zur Verbesserung der Lehrlingsausbildung (German Education Council for Improving Apprentice Training) in 1969, and especially the empirical analyses of the quality of vocational training carried out in the early 1970s. Four of these studies are relevant for this discussion. Although the investigations were confined to specific regions (five federal states), many of their results can be applied to the overall German situation. These are:

1 The so-called Hamburg study of apprentices by Crusius, Daviter, Eskamp and Laatz. Research was conducted through the Hochschule für Wirtschaft und Politik (School for Economics and Politics), with financial support from the Deutsches Jugendinstitut (German Youth Institute) and the Deutscher Gewerkschaftsbund (DGB, the German Union Federation).

2 A study on the situation of vocational training in the school and workplace,

commissioned by the Federal State Government of Rhineland-Palatinate and by the WEMA Institut für empirische Sozialforschung (WEMA Institute for Empirical Social Research).

3 An investigation of working and training conditions for apprentices in the Saar, commissioned by the Saar Arbeiterkammer (Chamber of Labour) and the Protestant Church.

4 A representative survey of potential apprentices in the federal states of North Rhine-Westphalia and Hesse, commissioned by the Bundes- minister für Arbeit und Sozialordnung (Federal Minister for Labour and Social Order). The goal of this study was to assess the workings of the 1969 Vocational Training Act. The Institut für sozioökonomische Strukturforschung (SAB, Institute for Research on Socio-Economic Structures), Cologne, conducted the survey.

None of these investigations were assigned to an institute for Berufs- und Wirtschaftspädagogik. The Senate report stated:

A large part of the socio-economic research on vocational training during the take-off period [the late 1960s and early 1970s] took place in institutions outside the Hochschulen. . . . Within the universities themselves, on the other hand, an empirical–analytical functioning research on vocational training remained more marginal, an apt description of their role within Berufs- und Wirtschaftspädagogik as well.

(Senatskommission für Berufsbildungsforschung 1990: 17)

Much of this still holds true today. The establishment of a series of larger research institutes outside the traditional universities, whose research agenda also encompasses vocational training and related areas of inquiry, has created strong competition for research on these issues. These institutions include the Bundesinstitut für Berufsbildung (Federal Institute for Vocational Training) created in 1970 under the name Bundesinstitut für Berufsbildungsforschung (Federal Institute for Research on Vocational Training), with national-level financing and over three hundred employees, and the Institut für Arbeitmarkt- und Berufsforschung (Institute for Labour-Market and Vocational Research) founded in 1967, an affiliate of the Bundesanstalt für Arbeit (Federal Employment Agency), from which it also receives its financing. Alongside these institutes, a range of further research institutions can be found in Germany. Part of their financial backing comes from public moneys, with additional resources generated through commis- sioned research projects. The German Jugendinstitut in Munich, the Sozialwissenschaftliche Forschungsinstitut (Institute for Social Scientific Research) in Göttingen, and the Fraunhofer Institut für Arbeit, Wirtschaft und Organisation (Fraunhofer Institute for Labour, Economics and Organisation) in Stuttgart are but some of these partly private research institutions, where larger research projects on vocational training have been carried out in the past.

What remained for university-based research on vocational training was to assume the scholarly work necessary for studies of pilot projects that were either organised by companies (with emphasis on learning sites in the workplace) or as school models (emphasis on the Berufsschule). The universities also took over smaller research projects usually commissioned by the Bundesinstitut für Berufsbildung, whose financial framework did not interest the larger research institutes. Comparable research institutes for those vocational schools under the jurisdiction of the individual federal states were at first lacking. Whereas the university institutes could have been brought in to meet the research needs of this field, the Senate report observed that, 'that did not happen. On the contrary, the federal states founded state-level institutes for School Pedagogy or the like throughout the 1970s and thus tried to compensate for the deficit in school-specific research' (Senatskommission für Berufsbildungsforschung 1990: 17).

These trends explain why university professors in *Berufs- und Wirtschaftspädagogik* did not develop an independent, comprehensive empirical research programme. At the same time, most relevant research results were well-received in university circles and were taken up in individual interpretations. The same applied to the apprentice studies mentioned above, which served as the basis for a series of reforms suggested by those in Berufs- und Wirtschaftspädagogik. Among other points, these studies prompted criticism of a pedagogical disorientation in on-site training (no real training plan in the workplace, and the occupation of apprentices in unqualified activities unrelated to their vocation), an unsatisfactory theoretical foundation for the training, and the lack of training facilities for the systematic practice of complex tasks.

The following years did not bring the enactment of comprehensive reforms. In the mid 1970s, large birth cohorts and an economic recession led to an acute shortage of apprenticeships in the dual system. Those offering on-site apprenticeships were able to use the dual system itself to prevent more sweeping changes in the organisation, financing, and learning sites of the vocational training system (see Frackmann *et al*. 1981; Frackmann 1985).

The research on Vocational Pedagogy from this period contained position statements on the proposed reforms, such as the introduction of a year-long preparatory study of the vocation, a year-long preparation for the vocation, or the labour unions' proposal for financing vocational training through the creation of a fund to which all businesses or factories with vocational trainees would contribute. Most of the statistical material and investigations of the social situation of unemployed adolescents, on the other hand, was collected by the Institut für Arbeitsmarkt- und Berufsforschung and from the Deutsches Jugendinstitut (see for example Schober-Gottwald 1976, 1977).

MARGIT FRACKMANN

THE STUDY OF EXPERIMENTAL TRAINING PROGRAMMES FOR WOMEN

The debate on discrimination against women reached almost every social sphere in Germany during the 1970s and early 1980s, including Vocational Pedagogy. In terms of their educational opportunities, differences between boys and girls no longer existed – on paper, that is. While girls faced the same educational prerequisites for acceptance into a vocational training programme, the statistics reflect a persistent discrimination against girls in the dual system. A disproportionate number of girls were left without an apprenticeship, their share of the total number of apprentices was relatively small (38 per cent in 1980 and 43 per cent in 1988) and the majority of girls entered occupations with lower pay, less job security, and fewer opportunities for professional advancement. The under-representation of women remained particularly marked in the craft and technical vocations. In 1977, for example, there were 186 vocations in which less than 20 per cent of the trainees were women and which could still be called 'men's work'. They included metalworking and electrical occupations, despite the fact that these branches, in the words of one expert, 'would offer employment possibilities and development chances that are relatively favourable in differently structured regions, because many women in this area are employed as unskilled or untrained workers' (Alt 1986: 65).

This situation provided the point of departure for an experimental programme to open up the craft and technical training programmes to girls ('zur Erschließung gewerblich-technischer Ausbildungsberufe für Mädchen'), initiated in early 1978 by the Bundesminister für Bildung und Wissenschaft (Federal Minister for Education and Science) and the Bundesinstitut für Berufsbildung, which also covered the additional costs and co-ordinated the programme. The goal was to reduce the 'unjustified discrimination' against girls and women in the training and occupational system through the creation of new possibilities in skilled manual occupations. From 1978 to 1981, 1,232 women participated in the programme from twenty-one different locations. Of these women, 980 took the examination to be recognised as skilled workers. The focus on the metalworking and electrical occupations is explained in the programme description: 'If it proves possible to open up skilled vocational opportunities in this area to a significant number of girls, then an important step toward abolishing the limited vocational chances for women will have been accomplished.' Furthermore, it was hoped that the experimental projects could help 'to identify the difficulties that arise either from the demands of the training programme or employment in the selected occupations or from the dismissive reactions from the girls' social surroundings, to find the origins of these difficulties, and to develop possible solutions' (BMBW 1978).

Only a very small number of professors in Berufs- und Wirtschaftspädagogik made any contribution to the scholarly analysis of this experimental programme. Perhaps the tiny numbers of women who have been able to gain a professorship in this discipline and the absence of a significant tradition of gender-specific research on vocational training can explain this lack of interest. While a special issue of the *Zeitschrift für Berufs- und Wirtschaftspädagogik* on vocational training for girls identified the possibility for the discipline 'to take a step forward . . . after the conclusion of the experimental programme', this now seems like an appeal to the wrong audience. In the words of one study, 'those in Vocational Pedagogy should advance the analysis of restrictive structural conditions and rigid limitations on personnel in this context, and introduce the results into the different levels of social discussion on this issue' (Pilnei and Geißler 1986: 4).

The most striking results of the experimental programme were above-average attrition rates (17.2 per cent), average test scores and, above all, greater difficulties in entering and remaining in a skilled occupation. The poor state of the labour market of the time was used to explain the fact that women still found few employment opportunities outside the enterprise where they had completed their vocational training. Even within their place of training, women faced several difficulties that still exist today. These are the expectation of employers that women would be less willing to take 'flexible assignments', the assumption that women's length of employment would be short and that their re-entry into the workforce after absence for child-rearing would create problems, the belief that women's double burden results in less individual engagement and accomplishment, and difficulties between women and older colleagues in the workplace (Alt 1986: 84).

The Institut für Arbeitsmarkt und Berufsforschung conducted a longitudinal investigation of vocational trajectories which confirms that younger women in traditional male occupations experience problems in the transition from vocational training to employment. To cite one study, 'the share of unemployed graduates from an enterprise-based training programme in September 1984, among all graduates of this year, was much higher for girls (with 14.4 per cent) than for boys (8.6 per cent) in the twenty most commonly-filled "male vocations"' (Stegmann and Kraft 1986: 443). Women in these occupations do not achieve equality with their male co-workers in terms of compensation and promotion. Overall it appears that 'the career path of women who have learned a "male occupation" compared to that of women in a skilled "female occupation" reveals no clear advantages but also no drastic disadvantages' (Stegmann and Kraft 1986: 445). This is a very dry résumé for a very elaborate programme to improve the vocational chances of young women in a male-dominated occupational branch. Women today may have 'conquered' traditional male vocations, but unfortunately these are those which often lack bright career perspectives, high pay, and good possibilities for advancement, such as gardener, cook, confectioner, skilled restaurant worker (waitress), baker and cabinetmaker.

Related disciplines such as Sociology and Psychology are taking the lead in scholarly work on the problem of persistent discrimination against women in education and professional life. Their research ranges from themes such as gender-specific occupational selection and the situation in typical female occupations (for example, social work and health care), to affirmative action measures in the workplace (see Frackmann (ed.) 1990).

THE DEBATE ON TECHNOLOGICAL DEVELOPMENT AND TRAINING: KEY QUALIFICATIONS

Berufspädagogik contributed actively to the debate on the consequences of technological development for vocational training. In particular, the rapid diffusion of microelectronics to many fields of application prompted discussion on the need for new concepts of teaching and learning. In addition, the comprehensive restructuring of the metalworking and electrical trades, started in the late 1970s, led to the passing of new training requirements for industrial and craft occupations in 1987. This legislation mandated important changes: a common twelve- to eighteen-month basic training to bring together a range of occupations, to be followed by specific subject training, and only then, an eighteen-month training in an actual skilled trade or vocation; a common training lasting three-and-a-half years; detailed descriptions of the contents and time-frame for structuring vocational training, binding on each workplace; and final examinations designed to measure whether a trainee is qualified to plan and check his or her work independently.

The 1987 reforms can also be interpreted as a reaction to two relevant social developments. First, there was a rise in individualism, the result of a shift in the social value system, with the displacement of a clear code of conduct dominated by the family and religion. The possibility for individual design of the non-working environment has prompted the younger generation in particular to assert a voice in workplace design as well. This demand contradicts Fordist work organisation. Second, the limits of the Taylorist division of labour in mass production are now being felt and its regulatory basis does not allow it to improve competitiveness through quality, flexibility and a further increase in productivity (on this point see Frackmann and Lehmkuhl 1993). Both developments, the wish to 'work differently' and a new social organisation of production, necessitate other conceptions of vocational qualification.

At first, the response of Berufspedagogik to these changes was to underscore the danger of attributing too much importance to the needs of the workplace in developing new curricula in vocational training. A well-rounded education of the individual could thus fall by the wayside. The representatives of this discipline were not interested in expanding or defining a different understanding of specialist knowledge. Instead, they wanted to make sure that individuals were equipped with competences above and beyond those tied to the workplace, for example, communication and problem-solving skills. This discussion centred on the concept of 'key qualifications', which needed to be transmitted in new ways. Aside from the definition of a key qualification (itself a subject of endless interpretation), the authors seem caught up in opposing narrowly defined vocational training against comprehensive knowledge as something separate (see for example Reetz 1989; Zabeck 1989). Their work often presumes an impoverished personality reduced to the dictates of Taylorist mass production and which now has to be redeveloped for a post-Fordist age. As mentioned above, this means the transmission of key qualifications. The defenders of key qualifications have yet to come up with a concrete concept for putting them into practice, because it is difficult for them to provide didactic instructions for how abstract abilities can be instilled through concrete human action. A number of critics (Wittwer 1989; Becker 1990; Geißler 1991) have joined this discussion and refute key qualifications as sticking-plaster measures or as means of propping up the status quo. In their view, key qualifications neither offer a basis for handling technical and social change, nor can they better prepare employees for unforeseeable developments. A more fundamental criticism of this theoretical construct has yet to take place.

Independent of the discussion in Vocational Pedagogy, businesses and factories have reacted to the changes brought about by the 1987 regulations and new forms of work organisation. Following the approach of action theory within the psychology of learning, they are forging new paths in training and education. In many industrial training workshops, projects and learning through problem-oriented questioning are found today. These are conceived according to the flow of human action to inform, plan, carry out, check and evaluate the concept of staged learning. It is hoped that these ideas will foster self-reliance in the learning process, to inspire trainees to plan ahead, develop problem-solving abilities, and be aware of quality issues. To date, suggestions for developing the kinds of comprehensive capacity for action over and above that necessary for lean production processes have come more from specialists in the study of work (including Hacker 1978; Skell and König 1990; Volpert (ed.) 1980; on this point see Frackmann 1992) than from the Berufspädagogik.

THE FUTURE OF THE DUAL SYSTEM

A pressing concern in Vocational Pedagogy is the future of the dual system. The quality of argument here often falls well below usual scholarly standards. In several public appearances and press articles, Geißler from the Bundeswehrhochschule (German military academy) in Munich has won wide popular recognition. His argument again reveals how stubbornly vocational pedagogical theory remains wrapped up in internal debates where real social developments barely register, precluding theoretical analyses with any real insight into the acute situation at hand.

After decades of praise and defence from all sides (state, employers and unions), Geißler predicts the end of the German vocational training system (1991). He dismisses reform efforts as 'a system-stabilising enactment of illusions' unable to save the basic conception of the dual system. The main points of his argument are as follows.

To begin with, in the 1990s the number of university students exceeded the number of trainees for the first time, destabilising the established order. Geißler's reliance on absolute numbers unfortunately creates a very superficial and misleading argument. For any one age-group in the educational system, the ratio of first-year university students is still lower, despite a Europe-wide increase in the proportion of high-school students completing the qualifying examination for university study, an increase also present in Germany. The majority of the next generation will still pass through the dual system. A comparison of university graduates and dual-system graduates for 1992 reveals the following data: whereas 154,000 students completed university studies with an academic degree, in the same year 500,000 skilled workers, white-collar workers and artisans graduated from the dual system. The greater number of university students can be explained by both longer lengths of university study and the increase in those selecting a double qualification (apprenticeship and university study).

Second, with recourse to Arendt's classification of social systems (manufacturing, work, commerce), Geißler concluded that ours is a society of work and production, legitimated as 'production machinery, in which human beings belong as a function, not as a person' (Geißler 1993: 57). He presents a societal balance of alienated people in a world of machinery, a world designed for the production of goods with 'fleeting transitory stability'. The dual system can only be dysfunctional, since the pursuit of qualifications is oriented to the manufacturing process. The dual system has its roots in the artisanal training system, which Geißler sees as 'dominated by processes of manufacturing'. He continues:

> Until now this application of the qualification to industrial labour was viewed as productive. Through pre-industrial values and their effect on socialisation, it stabilised the process of industrialisation. The ideology of manufacturing supplied (and continues to supply) the individual's potential for motivation, the horizons of perceptions and emotions for the reality of industrial labour. . . . This means that industrial labour and the qualification to industrial labour allow themselves to be stabilised by a foreign principle, the artisanal model of vocational training.

(Geißler 1993: 58)

To Geißler, the values and character-building elements tied to artisanal manufacturing are completely exhausted at the present state of development of the capitalist system. In a world of constant change and modernisation 'without goal, without purpose, without end, but with an ever faster decomposition and concentration of space and time', there will be no more need for education that helps individuals arrange themselves in this world.

Here the German Berufspädagogiker finally emerge as sharp social and cultural critics, even if their arguments do not engage a concrete social analysis. They generally overlook important insights offered by a range of sociological, business or labour analyses of a social production based on Taylorist principles (including the well-received MIT study 'The machine that changed the world' (Womack *et al.* 1990)). It was precisely the unfolding and diffusion of the Fordist phase of mass production that created a functional vocational training system for this kind of social production. Even before the Second World War, the hold of artisanal traditions over industry had loosened with the introduction of a training system in which all basic proficiencies were conveyed in a systematic and functional manner. The staged training system, as found for example in the 1950s electro-industry, the principle of systematic familiarisation through a series of tasks, and multiple-choice final examinations all testify to the fact that vocational training had adapted to Taylorist forms of labour organisation and had departed from artisanal traditions. Indeed these adjustments of the vocational educational system to the Taylorist approach to work are the source of problems with regard to the expectations of the workforce on the one hand, and those of business on the other. The expectations of individuals are oriented toward a comprehensive organisation of work but business expects forward-looking, problem-solving, responsible, and quality-conscious workers. Another upheaval in our social organisation of work, the kind we see in almost every industrial nation, will also touch our educational and vocational training system. Where narrowly defined proficiencies and knowledge once occupied centre stage, a new organisation of business and labour will demand more comprehensive qualifications for both industry and the service sector.

Despite a series of fundamental problems tied up in the specific organisation of the German vocational training system, it has managed to preserve a certain flexibility. Because a large part of the training takes place in the enterprise, changes in vocational requirements can be quickly registered and incorporated into the vocational training system. Both employers as well as workers – through their organisations, the unions – are involved in this process. All sides, including state institutions, co-operate in the development of new training requirements (stipulating contents, length, goal and examination topics for the different vocations), so that these requirements in their final and binding form always reflect a social consensus. The development of curricula irrespective of changing demands from the world of work (as seems to be the case in German universities) cannot occur in the dual system of vocational training. The sweeping reforms of recent years in the metalworking and electrical professions are a good example of the adaptability of this system.

Interestingly, it is a labour market researcher, Tessaring, not a Berufspädagogiker, who has delivered a penetrating analysis of the problems and perspectives of the dual system (Tessaring 1993). The difficulties of movement between the three tracks of the education system and the limited career advancement for those who opted for the dual system rather than university are now well known. There are proposals to open the university to employees who do not possess the Abitur, for stronger backing for the promotion of skilled workers and clerks within the workplace, and to expand access to vocational qualification below university level. The history of Japan demonstrates that a highly qualified and productive nation can also function without a differentiated vocational training system, and that furnishing all future workers with a high level of general education can be just as successful (Frackmann 1992). At the same time, the German system could be improved in terms of the social requirements of reproduction through appropriate reforms in the general educational and vocational training system, rethinking the allocation of social prestige, and developing a different basis for the remuneration of skilled labour. This would, however, presume several radical breaks with the past: the abolition of the three-track school system; introducing a compulsory general education course of at least ten years, with practical applications to everyday life and better teaching and learning concepts; bringing the level of vocational training among the different sectors up to a common, higher, standard; greater movement between the different tracks of the educational system; and last but not least, reducing the enormous income gap between management and the production workers, a difference much too large to be justified. Here again the Berufspädagogik could and should intervene more forcefully in the discussion process. Such engagement would not side-track its goal of providing the pedagogical support for the development of a well-rounded and educated personality.

Apart from the research areas and themes discussed in this article, a range of related issues has been the subject of other investigations: the historical development of the discipline of Vocational Pedagogy and the dual system; the question of the qualification of unskilled and skilled workers; the qualification of trainees and apprentices; continuing education and adult education; and vocational school didactics. This article was also unable to address the research on Vocational Pedagogy from the former German Democratic Republic and its important contributions, particularly in the field of Psychology.

NOTES

1 For reasons of clarity and precision, this article will leave the distinctively German features of the educational and occupational system in the original with a brief elucidation as necessary.

BIBLIOGRAPHY

Alt, C. (1986) 'Systematischer Überblick über die Modellversuche zur "Erschließung gewerblich-technischer Ausbildungsberufe für Mädchen"', *Zeitschrift für Berufs- und Wirtschaftspädagogik* 6: 64–6.

Becker, W. (1990) 'Schlüsselqualifikationen – ein Schlüsselbegriff für Zielkonflikte in der beruflichen Buildung?', in B. Meifort (ed.) *Schlüsselqualifikationen für gesundheits- und sozialpflegerische Berufe*, Alsbach/Bergstraße.

BMBW (Bundesministerium für Bildung und Wissenschaft) (1978, 1980) *Modellversuchsprogramm zur Erschließung gewerblich/technischer Ausbildungsberufe für Mädchen*, Bonn.

Frackmann, M. (1985) *Mittendrin und voll daneben. Jugend heute*, Hamburg.

——(1992) 'Neue Anforderungen an handlungstheoretisch fundierte Lernkonzepte in der beruflichen Bildung', *Rheinhausener Gespräche zur Theorie und Praxis der Berufsbildung* 1.

——(ed.) (1990) *Ein Schritt vorwärts . . . Frauen in Ausbildung und Beruf*, Hamburg.

Frackmann, M., Kuhls, H., and Lühn, K. D. (1981) *Null Bock oder Mut zur Zukunft. Jugendliche in der Berufsausbildung*, Hamburg.

Frackmann, M. and Lehmkuhl, K. (1993) 'Weiterbildung für Lean Production Anforderungen an einen neuen Arbeitnehmertypus – Qualifizierungskonzept für die Gruppenarbeit', *WSI – Mitteilungen* 2.

Geißler, K. H. (1991) 'Das duale System in der industriellen Berufsausbildung hat keine Zukunft', *Leviathan* 1: 68 ff.

——(1993) 'Hat das duale System der Berufsausbildung noch eine Zukunft?', in *Berufsausbildung im Umbruch. Beiträge zur Berufsbildung* 4, BIGA Schriftenreihe, Bern.

Hacker, W. (1978) *Allgemeine Arbeits- und Ingenieurpsychologie*, Berne.

Lempert, w. (1965) *Gewerbelehrerbildung und Schulreform*, Heidelberg.

Pilnei, M. and Geißler K. H. (1986) 'Vorwort für das Beiheft Berufsbildung für Mädchen', *Zeitschrift für Berufs- und Wirtschaftspädagogik*

Reetz, L. (1989) 'Zum Konzept der Schlüsselqualifikationen in der Berufsausbildung Teil I und Teil II', *Berufsbildung in Wissenschaft und Praxis* 5: 3–10; 6: 24–30.

Schober-Gottwald, K. (1976) 'Jugendliche ohne Berufsausbildung', *Mitteilungen aus Arbeitsmarkt- und Berufsforschung* 2: 174–96.

——(1977) 'Der Weg in die Arbeitslosigkeit – Berufliche und soziale Herkunft von jugendlichen Arbeitslosen', *Mitteilungen aus Arbeitsmarkt- und Berufsforschung* 10: 143–65.

Senatskommission für Berufsbuildungsforschung (1990), *Berufsbildungsforschung an den Hochschulen der Bundesrepublik Deutschland – Hauptaufgaben – Förderungsbedarf*, Denkschrift der Deutschen Forschungsgemeinschaft, Weinheim.

Skell, W. and König, C. (1990) 'Lernen und Arbeiten', in J. Neugebauer (ed.) *Psychologisc Aspekte des Lehrens und Lernens in der Berufsbildung*, Berlin.

Stegman, H. and Kraft, H. (1986) 'Chancen und Risiken von Mädchen mit einer betrieblichen Berufsausbildung für einen "Männerberuf"', *Mitteilungen aus Arbeitsmarkt und Berufsforschung*, No. 3: 439–456.

Tessaring, M. *et al*. (1990) 'Bildung und Beschäftigung im Wandel', Die Bildungsgesamtrechnung des IAB (Institut für Arbeitsmarkt und Berufsforschung der Bundesanstalt für Arbeit), *Beiträge zur Arbeitsmarkt und Berufsforschung* 126, Nürnberg.

Tessaring, M. (1993) 'Das duale System der Berufsausbildung in Deutschland Attraktivität und Beschäftigungs-perspektiven', *Mitteilungen aus Arbeitsmarkt-und Berufsforschung* 2: 131–61.

Volpert, W. (ed.) (1980) *Beiträge zur Psychogischen Handlungstheorie*, Berne/Stuttgart/Vienna.

Wittwer, W. (1989) 'Schlüsselqualifikation. Schlüssel zur beruflichen Zukunft', *Lernfeld Betrieb* 3: 28–9.

Womack, J., Jones, D., and Roos, D. (1990) *The Machine that Changed the World: the Triumph of Lean Production*, New York: Rawson MacMillan.

Zabeck, J. (1989) Schüsselqualifikationen, Zur Kritik einer didaktischen Zielformel, *Wirtschaft und Erziehung* 3: 77–86.

5

SOCIAL CHANGE AND THE MODERNISATION OF SCHOOL-TO-WORK TRANSITIONS

Walter R. Heinz and Ulrike Nagel

INTRODUCTORY REMARKS

In the contemporary sociological discourse, the modernisation process in Germany is addressed from two points of view. On the one hand, research on social structure in the 1980s has shown that the relation between origin (social class), education, occupation and income has not really changed but that the structure of social inequality which is typical for industrial societies has become stabilised. The welfare state with its politics of institutionalisation of the life course, of the so-called 'normal biography', is seen as the mechanism of structural reproduction. The normal biography is characterised by life-long employment and income which provide the individual with access to the benefits of the social security system, and also with chances for social participation. On the other hand, longitudinal analyses as well as analyses of social life worlds, biographies and cultural theory research have contributed to an understanding of recent changes in the social system. These changes are described with reference to processes of differentiation that have resulted in an individualisation of the life course. Thus, social change is discussed as a process of destandardisation of value systems, which is considered to be taking place both despite and, at the same time, along with the process of institutionalisation of the normal biography.

In explaining these contradictory phenomena, attention is drawn to the continuous growth of social problems as a result of economic change, which increasingly forces individuals and entire peer groups to develop new modes of reproducing and constructing their identities. The diversification of life styles and life courses has led researchers to attribute excessive importance to this aspect of the modernisation process and to neglect the objective reality of the social structure, namely, the confirmation of the traditional differences between classes and social strata, between the sexes, age-groups and ethnic groups. The contradictory character of modernisation became apparent when the indicators of social inequality established by cross-sectional research were followed up in longitudinal studies of cohorts in order to study the distribution of these inequalities at different points in the life cycle. This contributes to the explanation of the emergence of social differentiation in its diachronic dimension, while taking into account the sequences of the individual life course and the comparison of different cohorts.

In order to study the relationship between structural reproduction and social change, in the relationship between structure and action in Gidden's terms, the concept of the life course has turned out to be a useful frame of reference for designing empirical studies and for theory formation. The life course is seen as the arena of the modernisation process where determining effects of the socio-economic structure as well as the erosion of traditional life styles and life courses can be observed simultaneously.

In empirical research, (Heinz 1991) special attention is paid to:

1 The sequences in the life courses of members of cohorts, generations, age, and status groups.
2 The bargaining processes between the welfare institutions that structure the life course and individual actors.
3 The investment individuals make in constructing their biography to make coherence of their lives and the management of changes in status which are more or less institutionalised.

In structural and cultural explanations of the modern life course, institutions and their normative power play a central role. As a result, excessive importance is attributed to the socialisation of the life course, neglecting the active role of the individual actor as participant in the bargaining process over his or her personal pathway. The revision of the 'oversocialised' conception of the life course requires a focus on situations and sequences of transitions where the individual has to adjust to changing conditions and to balance individual options with institutional constraints. Transitions within and between social spheres are conceived as status passages. The individual is expected to relate to institutionalised patterns and rhythms and to balance them with the construction of a personal biography.

Modern German society has been described as a 'Risikogesellschaft', a society of risk (Beck 1992). It is a society with a highly differentiated social security system that 'supports' the normal biography. At the same time, to become entitled to the benefits of the welfare system, the individual has to relate life course decisions closely to the normative standards of institutions. This means increasing possibilities for individualisation but also a considerable increase in risk of misinterpreting institutional constraints and thus, of misdirecting the life course. In a situation like this, individual security becomes highly dependent on personal capacities, on the individual's competence to determine the risks and the options resulting from choices, to counteract unwise decisions, to invent corrective strategies and to cope with uncertainties. Individualisation in modern society is said to include opportunities as well as risks. The concept refers to an opening up of opportunities for autonomy, for example, to revise biographical decisions allowing the individual to catch up on lost opportunities. The other side of the coin is that opportunities for individualisation carry with them a great deal of uncertainty as far as their consequences are concerned, i.e. risks of failure. What at first glance appears to be an opportunity, may in the long run prove to be a calamity. The concept of 'Risikogesellschaft' designates a society in which individual life courses could have opportunities for success which are as great as the risks of failure.

TRANSITIONS TO WORK AND THE EXTENSION OF YOUTH

The transition from school to work has always been a major topic of research in German Sociology – and it has gained importance due to the increased individualisation of the life course. The transition to adulthood varies according to socio-economic and cultural contexts that define the opportunities for training and employment with short- and long-term consequences for the individual life course. Comparative research on the transition has substantial significance as industrial societies are transforming into a mix of manufacturing, service and high-technology economies that have to compete in the world market. Germany seems to have an edge in this competition because of its strong tradition of vocational education and training through the dual system. By presenting results of a study of the school-to-work transition in Great Britain and Germany, we attempt to show the potential of comparative research for examining the interaction between institutional structures and individual behaviour in relation to labour market entry. In most advanced industrialised societies the transition from school to employment has increased by years, and a career based on a good education has become important for the construction of identity for both men and women. This development is not only an effect of economic and political processes, but also a matter of human agency. Individuals are constructing their own life course in ways that differ from one or two generations ago. Today, the life course has become a complex sequence of status passages that have to be selected, organised and monitored by the individuals themselves. They have to conceive of themselves as 'planning agencies' concerning life course decisions. The life course is more personalised, consciously chosen, and individuals are accountable for their own behaviour. The new biographical challenge, according to Beck (1992), is to select and revise pathways and life course decisions by using opportunities provided by the market, institutions and social networks in a series of well-calculated life course moves. These observations sensitise transition researchers against falling into the trap of structuralist theories of reproduction by assuming that individuals at career crossroads just have to follow their class habitus, i.e. an internalised apparatus of perceptions, evaluations and rules of action. It is more realistic to assume that individuals adopt 'step by step', 'trial and error' or even 'wait and see' strategies in order to cope with various requirements and contingencies of the transition to work. There is evidence from recent cohort studies comparing high school graduates in the United States that there is not only an extension of transitions but also more disorder in the life course of young people between school and adulthood.

Using data from the national longitudinal survey of the high school class of 1972, Rindfuss *et al.* (1987) demonstrate that young men and women had sequences in their life courses that deviated from the expected pattern. There is sufficient reversibility and diversity of events and statuses in the educational and employment domain to indicate that looking only at the age of first entry into various adult roles and to the sequence of these entries will provide a superficial account of the actual transition processes. This impact of individual action is underscored by Buchmann's (1989) secondary analysis of two US high-school cohorts in the 1960s and 1980s, showing that entry into full adult status has become more complicated and delayed today. Buchmann argues that the increase of skills and knowledge required by a high-technology and service economy has led to more time spent in education which has produced less continuous transition histories of young Americans since the 1970s. Young people who do not enter college have to spend some time in casual jobs in the secondary segment of the labour market before obtaining stable employment. Here they are faced with low income, high risk of job discontinuity and unemployment. Their transition shows no institutionalised pathways either through training or work creation programmes or apprenticeships. Youth research in West Germany has also investigated the causes and consequences of an extension of the youth phase. These studies are treated from either a post-modern perspective or one of a reproduction of social inequality. The former approach is close to Psychology, Education and Social Work, the latter to social class and labour market theory, work and socialisation processes. A favourite metaphor from the post-modern approach is the destructuration and individualisation of the youth phase (Combe and Helsper 1991). The other approach does not rely on speculative rhetoric and proposes an extension and pluralisation of the transition from school to adulthood (Heitmeyer and Olk 1990). In a recent case study on the new timings of the youth phase, Fuchs-Heinritz and Krüger (1991) conclude that the assumption of a destructuration and individualisation of youth was too general to account for the interrelationships between transition patterns and self-concepts of young people. Another recent study has compared the life concepts of young adults and found that most of them entertain a work-centred life concept. They are oriented towards meaningful work that should not interfere with private life; only a small minority subscribe to a leisure-and-fun conception of life (Baethge *et al.* 1988).

This contrasts with youth research in Great Britain, which conceptualises the transition to adulthood either from the reproduction of culture (Willis 1978) or the reproduction of social and gender inequality perspectives

(Banks *et al.* 1992; Allatt and Yeandle 1992). These studies tend to ask why educational and social disadvantage is concentrated in groups defined by class, race or gender in particular British regions.

TRANSPARENCY AND PERMEABILITY OF TRANSITION STRUCTURES

If one wants to compare the status passages from school to work, it is useful to have criteria that show how education and employment are related. In addition to the different opportunity structures with which young people are confronted in their transitions to the labour market, the institutional arrangements that support the progression to adult status differ (for a comparison between the USA and Germany, see Hamilton and Hurrelmann 1993). In contrast to transition processes in the USA and Great Britain, there is a well-organised period for skill development between school and full-time employment in Germany. This institutional arrangement, 'apprenticeship', structures the movement towards adulthood for young women and men who do not go on to higher education (Hamilton 1990). The process of vocational education and training (VET) is formally organised in about 420 occupations which cover most of the blue- and white-collar jobs that do not require college or university training. An apprenticeship lasts three years and combines firm-based training and state-led vocational schools in the 'dual system'. VET is completed with practical and theoretical examinations and confers job titles of skilled blue- or white-collar worker. Despite a declining number of applicants, the majority of Germany's young people still pass through this training and socialisation system which is accepted all over Germany. Vocational education and training was organised in a similar way in East Germany; both training systems have common roots and shared conceptions of how young people should be trained for work. Apprenticeships differ qualitatively in their technical, organisational and social contexts. An apprentice can be trained in a small craft shop with a master craftsman and one apprentice, or in the training workshop of Mercedes-Benz, for example, with many apprentices in different trades. Thus, the scope for skill development, work experience, self-determination, responsibility and social communication is quite variable. Furthermore, the German apprenticeship system is highly segmented along gender lines. Although there are exceptions to the rule, girls normally have access to only a small range of female occupations like hairdresser, sales person, or office clerk with low pay and bad employment prospects. After their apprenticeship some of them are faced with a marginalised labour market position and alternate between unemployment, temporary jobs and domestic commitments.

Currently, about 60 per cent of all German school-leavers between the ages of 16 and 20 enter an apprenticeship. This is because the system provides occupational skills, knowledge, work norms and credentials. In times of high unemployment, even a dead-end apprenticeship can become an entrance ticket to employment at a lower skill level. Finishing an apprenticeship is a stepping stone for entering the employment system, like a ticket which remains valid at each stage of the working life. Furthermore, the apprenticeship system is supported by the employers and their organisations for two main reasons. It supplies inexpensive junior workers for at least three years. This is most relevant for small craft shops, beauty salons and restaurants. More importantly, employers can socialise and select their future employees according to firm or company standards, without being obliged to take on every apprentice completing training. The socialisation dimension of an apprenticeship is also appreciated in a variety of semi-skilled jobs that might eventually lead to entry into the core labour force of a big company.

According to Hamilton and Hurrelmann (1993), Germany's transition system is more transparent than permeable. It does not, however, operate in a mechanical way but is rather a product of negotiations between educators, employers, government and unions in a process of conflict resolution concerning educational values, economic competition in the world market, technological progress and funding. One of the reasons why apprenticeship has not only survived technological change but was internally reformed is this negotiated approach. The arrangements for the transition also contribute to the reproduction of social class, ethnic and gender segmentation. First, it separates the working class from the educated professional class. Second, it creates a hierarchy between white- and blue-collar jobs and male and female occupations. The dual system is more flexible in responding to changes in the qualification structure than contributing to equal opportunities. Permeability between vocational training and higher education, for instance, is possible – but only with extra individual efforts.

In contrast, there is not an organised transition system from school to work in Great Britain. Most young people leaving school at the age of 16 look for employment combined with on-the-job training. In the 1980s, Britain had experimented with one- or two-year Youth Training Schemes (YTS) to provide some sort of school- or firm-based training for young people seeking work. These programmes collapsed because they were accepted neither by the young nor by the business world.

TRANSITIONS WITH UNCERTAIN DESTINATIONS

The German system of transition from school to work, with its differentiated education and vocational training tracks, not only socialises and qualifies, but also serves two other purposes. These are to pre-select young people into different career patterns and to distribute them into male and female segments of the labour market.

For young people who fail to enter an apprenticeship and university, the transition system operates as a mechanism of social exclusion. The German welfare state tends to offer a combination of education, training or work creation programmes for young men and women who have dropped out and who are attempting to re-enter the regular transition system.

The German Youth Institute (Deutsches Jugendinstitut) has interviewed more than two thousand participants in fifty-five programmes which support disadvantaged young people between the ages of 18 and 27 (Lex 1993; Schäfer 1993). The study indicates that this is a heterogeneous group according to its transition patterns: 60 per cent have a school-leaving certificate (*Hauptschule* (upper primary school) or better). They run the risk of becoming excluded from the VET system because they began their transition with spells of unemployment, training schemes, or dropping out of an apprenticeship. Their pathways are characterised by detours that did not take them closer to the regular transition system. It seems that public training programmes define pathways that create the risk of occupational and social marginalisation. The authors found several transition patterns that tend to lead to marginalisation. These patterns range from young people with a low or inadequate level of schooling, who were participants in a scheme and became unemployed afterwards, or who entered a course for vocational preparation, to young people with good school records who opted for a series of short-term jobs or who did not find a job after vocational training.

About a third of all respondents did not manage to get on to a regular pathway, i.e. either an apprenticeship or a contract of employment, after leaving school. Among them, young women are over-represented despite their higher level of educational attainment compared to that of boys. Opportunities to enter a socially acceptable pathway leading to employment decline the more time has elapsed since leaving school and the lower the level of schooling. Early unemployment and participation in training programmes are negative predictors for entering the normal pathways – they become criteria for exclusion.

On the subjective side, the experience of failure feeds into the entire transition phase. In a retrospective study a small sample of thirty-five men were interviewed (average age about 24 years) who participated in a social scheme for work-related preparation in different German regions (Schäfer 1993). Most of these young men had left school without passing their final examination. Their educational experiences were negative and they were fed up with going to school.

Retrospectively, they all had the intention of entering an apprenticeship with a realistic appraisal of their opportunities. They were thinking of craft or manufacturing occupations. After many applications some of them succeeded in locating an apprenticeship, but did not finish it. The main obstacles they reported were the theoretical demands in vocational school.

69

There they experienced failure similar to that earlier in their school careers. The majority of these young men could neither use special education (*Förderunterricht*), vocational preparation, work creation programmes nor training schemes to acquire a school-leaving certificate to improve their situation on the labour market.

The qualitative biographical data show that the majority of these young men were trapped in precarious situations which made access to an occupational career impossible. Work creation schemes, unemployment and short-term jobs structure these transitions with uncertain destinations. Their effect on the individual is an erosion of educational motivation and vocational interests. Therefore young people who experienced educational difficulties and casual work, and who are not able to fulfil the formal requirements and performance standards of apprenticeship training, need not only upgrading courses but also special counselling to help them re-enter the regular system of transition.

TRANSITIONS IN AND OUT OF HIGHER EDUCATION

Employment opportunities for university graduates have declined in the 1990s. Even engineers experience spells of unemployment before finding a stable job. The companies warn new entrants that they may not be employed in their field of specialisation and that they will be placed in other types of work. University graduates in engineering and business are employed on the shop-floor or in customer services. Today, young graduates seeking their first job need patience and a tolerance of frustration. A recent study on the relationship between length of study, examination results and occupational success among economics students has shown that there is no statistically significant relationship between grade point average and job success. Rather, it is practical experience, time spent in a foreign country, personal initiative and enthusiasm for certain tasks that count.

Since the 1980s the method of transition has diversified among students. A longitudinal study of university students who were admitted in 1978 but later dropped out and who were asked about their biography after a period of twelve years shows that almost 30 per cent of them dropped out because of lack of interest, 20 per cent because they anticipated labour market problems and 50 per cent because they felt they could not meet the challenge of their studies. On average they dropped out after four years. The field of study makes a big difference: only 8 per cent of medical students but more than one-third of the students in Humanities, Social Sciences and Economics dropped out. Students who delayed their decision to leave university not only lost time but were also too old to be recruited for an apprenticeship. Personnel managers accept a one-year period of orientation before dropping out, but interpret a longer period as demonstrating a lack of determination. Therefore, if you realise that you are not suited to an academic career it is better to quit as early as possible. Those who did not plan their career carefully and have no realistic alternative run the risk of finding themselves in the lower ranks of employment. Moreover, they not only have a problem with their curriculum vitae, but also with their self-confidence.

Different observations show that the transition from school to higher education becomes more complicated and differentiated. An increasing number of young people attempt to combine vocational training with academic qualifications. There is a growing interest amongst holders of the *Abitur* (high school diploma) to use an apprenticeship as a first step before entering university education. Also, graduates of apprenticeship have an increasing interest in continuing their studies and gaining higher qualifications. In 1990, only a third of the potential university entrance cohort started attending university studies immediately after the Abitur, but more than a third entered the labour market.

There is growing evidence that young people approach and follow their transition to adulthood with less definite plans. This has been criticised by parents, employers and policy-makers as a lack of maturity. However, we may assume that this attitude fits the changing opportunity structures and the weakening of links between school and employment. Transition decisions of young people seem to be less directed by definite occupational goals than by the idea to keep as many educational pathways and job opportunities open for as long as possible. Therefore, for many parents and young people the ideal route has become the Abitur. This certificate permits unrestricted access to all education and training, offers options for attractive jobs and reduces the risk of unemployment. This has created an ever-increasing flow of students into the universities and to a shortage of bright candidates for a 'simple' apprenticeship in industry and commerce. This tendency of increasing educational levels has been accompanied by a corresponding decline in training places and an increase of unemployment among graduates of the apprenticeship system. The level of education has increased in the last decades. The vast majority of apprentices in 1971 were from the Hauptschule and only 1 per cent from the *Gymnasium* (high school); today about 40 per cent have either a Hauptschule or a *Realschule* (middle school) certificate and 15 per cent the Abitur.

Thus, standard biographies from school to employment change not only because of the restructuring of the labour market and the establishment of work creation and training schemes but also because of young people's altered aspirations and criteria in relation to work. In a recent survey young people were asked about their expectations concerning their future work. Here, job security and financial independence were most often mentioned. Enjoyable work, interesting tasks and social environment were rated as very important. There seems to be a slight shift from material and social aspects of work to personal preferences in career opportunities compared to surveys which were conducted in the 1980s. To understand the conceptions of young people concerning work, standardised methods are not adequate because they ask for a ranking of job criteria. This contradicts our knowledge that the life course consists in mutual references between work, leisure, family and other fields of experience. To measure objective determinants of job choice and labour market entry is futile because the young person connects her/his experience in a dynamic process with systems of subjective meaning. As the study by Baethge *et al.* (1988) has demonstrated, a career that would conflict with private life is rejected. Many young people see their fathers' work situation as a negative role model. He does not even relax during holidays. Since the 1980s many studies of young people and work have observed a trend for life plans to be placed before job careers. A possible explanation is in the increased level of education, the higher labour market participation rates of young women, and an erosion of the traditional recruiting base for skilled workers, the so-called working-class culture.

For many young people, staying in the educational system is not primarily motivated by educational goals but by the threat of unemployment before or after apprenticeship. For example, the German post office used to be a reliable employer of young people who decided on a technical or a commercial apprenticeship. Most of its apprentices were attracted to a stable career. Today, the post office recruits only a small number of apprentices who started their training three years ago. A young man who had already finished another apprenticeship as a sales person without finding a job and who took the risk of starting a second apprenticeship with the post office comments 'We were trained for the dustbin'.

According to estimates of the Prognos Institute, Germany will have a growing deficit of several million jobs. This will affect not only the job opportunities but also the availability of apprenticeships. Big companies either reduce the recruitment of apprentices and trainees or develop new forms of job entry. A recent model has been introduced by Volkswagen: after apprenticeship there is a pre-recruitment process whereby a part-time job is turned into a 28- to 32-hour working week after three years. This partial integration into the labour force is a severe blow for young people who expect to have a full-time job to establish their independence.

Thus, there is much instability in the process of transition in Germany. According to a 1992 survey of the Bundesinstitut für Berufsbildung, many skilled workers are still in transition three years after completing their apprenticeship, contrary to their expectations. About 13 per cent of them are unemployed; only 42 per cent of the young skilled workers are employed in their occupation, but more than two-thirds of the young qualified women are employed in occupations for which they have not been trained.

PERSPECTIVES ON THE TRANSITION FROM UNIVERSITY AND THE *FACHHOCHSCHULEN* (HIGHER TECHNICAL SCHOOLS) TO EMPLOYMENT

In this section we draw on a study of first jobs into the social service sector, a sector that since the 1980s has shown a high rate of unemployment (Nagel 1993). These results are used to formulate two theses concerning the conditions for a successful transition from university education to work.

In the mid-1980s, the 'risk society' was characterised as a society in which a process of dissociation of peoples' personal identity from their professional roles had begun, with the result that these roles would no longer be the primary source for individuals' personal identity (Beck 1986). Not only has this interpretation proved incorrect but the following can be postulated. It is the close interrelatedness of the construction of personal and vocational biography that probably guarantees good standing in employment. We expect that those who develop an integrated perspective on professional and personal advancement will be the winners in a risk society. For them the risky passage into work will develop towards a stable and continuous career. By this we mean to say that the chances for 'survival' in the employment system seem to be especially good for those who consider work as an arena for the development of personal identity – an arena that is not in competition with private life but rooted in it and contributing to it.

Studies by Baethge (1991) have shown that such a subject-oriented approach to work is not only met in white-collar professions but to an increasing degree can be found with qualified blue-collar workers and even with untrained workers and those trained on-the-job.

Our second thesis is that this subject-oriented, highly individualistic conception of work is strongly related to a clear consciousness of the risks of modern occupational careers. Accordingly, as has been observed for social workers, measures are taken during their education at university or professional school to prepare the transition to work and to prevent risks that may arise at the beginning of this process. For this population unemployment has lost its threat; it is conceived of – *cum grano salis* – as an opportunity for further qualification and as a means of securing long-term career continuity. Unemployment is also seen as a period for regenerating physical and psychic energy.

A characteristic feature of this population of social workers is their way of presenting themselves as conscious, organised professionals, confident in their competence and qualification, who direct their life courses in an autonomous way. This relationship to the professional role can be described as 'engaged distance'; there is an identification with work and profession but it is not excessive. The pattern of action corresponding to this habitus can be considered a form of management of risks, i.e. the management of uncertainties. These uncertainties are treated as consequences of autonomous decision-making (Blanke 1990) and the consequences derive from the choice of an occupation which carries labour market risks or occupational diseases. Another example would be the consequences of decisions between unemployment or further education.

To prevent misunderstanding, it must be emphasised that the male or female manager of biographical and professional risks should not be compared to ruthless success-oriented actors nor the so called 'Alternativszene' and the informal economic sector. On the contrary, risk managers represent the model actors who are conscious of their role and are informed engineers of their life courses. They seek a position in the economic system, but they are not ready to accept a job at any price. They are engaged in their professional lives but do not accept self-sacrifice and self-exploitation.

SCHOOL-LEAVERS WITH MINIMUM QUALIFICATIONS

Finally, we examine a population that enters the transition to work with lowest-level school-leaving certificates and has little opportunity of finding employment or an apprenticeship: these are the students of the Haupt- and Sonderschulen (special schools). In a study based on quantitative and qualitative data on the transition process, Schumann (1994) has reconstructed the conditions for a successful status passage into apprenticeship. He points out that if members of this population do not obtain an apprenticeship on completion of school, they will only be successful in the long run if they enter preparatory training programmes run by the State. These programmes have to be accepted even if this means changing the field of specialisation originally chosen. To avoid marginalisation, it is important that these courses are followed by an apprenticeship. This is most likely if the young person's family and friendship network plays a supportive role and strengthens this ambition.

This relation between constancy in ambition and a supportive network during detours on the way to an apprenticeship is even more important when the individual experiences repeated failure. Total failure in obtaining any vocational qualification is most likely to occur when the individual gives up ambitions and cannot rely on any support from a social network. If such failure is accompanied by a reduction in ambition, it leads to acceptance of unskilled work or to a total withdrawal from the labour market.

BIBLIOGRAPHY

Allatt, P. and Yeandle, S. M. (1992) *Youth Unemployment and the Family: Voices of Disordered Times*, London: Routledge.

Baethge, M. (1991) 'Arbeit, Vergesellschaftung, Identität – Zur zunehmenden normativen Subjektivierung der Arbeit', in W. Zapf (ed.) *Die Modernisierung moderner Gesellschaften*, Verhandlungen des 25. Deutschen Soziologentages in Frankfurt am Main 1990, Frankfurt/New York: Campus.

Baethge, M., Hantsche, B., Peluk, W., and Volkamp, H. (1988) *Jugend: Arbeit und Identität*, Opladen: Leske und Budrich.

Banks, M., Bates, I., Breakwell, G., Bynner, J., Eissler, N., Jamieson, L. and Roberts, K. (1992) *Careers and Identities*, Milton Keynes: Open University Press.

Beck, U. (1986) *Risikogesellschaft. Auf dem Weg in eine andere Moderne*, Frankfurt: Suhrkamp.

——(1992) *The Risk Society*, Beverly Hills, CA: Sage.

Blanke, T. (1990) 'Zur Aktualität des Risikobegriffs. Über die Konstruktion der Welt und die Wissenschaft von ihr', *Leviathan* 1: 134–43.

Buchmann, M. (1989) *The Script of Life in Modern Society: Entry into Adulthood in a Changing World*, Chicago/London: University of Chicago Press.

Combe, A. and Helsper, W. (eds.) (1991) *Hermeneutische Jugendforschung. Theoretische Konzepte und methodische Ansätze*, Opladen: Westdeutscher Verlag.

Evans, K. and Heinz, W. R. (eds.) (1994) *Becoming Adults in England and Germany*, London: Anglo-German Foundation.

Fuchs-Heinritz, W. and Krüger, H.-H. (eds.) (1991) *Feste Fahrpläne durch die Jugendphase*, Opladen: Leske & Budrich.

Hamilton, S. (1990) Apprenticeship for Adulthood, New York: Free Press.

Hamilton, S. and Hurrelmann, K. (1993) 'Auf der Suche nach dem besten Modell für den Übergang von der Schule in den Beruf – ein amerikanischdeutscher Vergleich', *Zeitschrift für Sozialisationsforschung und Erziehungssoziologie* 13:194–207.

Heinz, W. R. (1991) (ed) 'Theoretical Advances in Life Course Research'. Weinheim: Deutscher Studien Verlag.

Heinz, W. R. (1995) 'Transitions in youth in a cross-cultural perspective. School-to-work in Germany', in B. Galaway and J. Hudson (eds.) *Youth in Transition to Adulthood: Research and Policy Implications*, Toronto: Thompson.

Heitmeyer, W. and Olk, T. (eds.) (1990) *Individualisierung von Jugend*, Weinheim/München: Juventa.

Lex, T. (1993) *Männlich, deutsch und fit – Determinanten des Weges ins Arbeitsleben bei benachteiligten Jugendlichen*, München: Deutsches Jugend-Institut Arbeitspapier.

Nagel, U. (1993) 'Hilfe als Profession', in L. Leisering, B. Geissler, U. Mergner and U. Rabe-Kleberg (eds.) *Moderne Lebensläufe im Wandel*, Weinheim: Deutscher Studien Verlag.

Rindfuss, R. C., Swicegood, C. G. and Rosenfeld, R. A. (1987) 'Disorder in the life course: how common and does it matter?' *American Sociological Review* 52: 785–801.

Schäfer, H. (1993) *Auf dem Weg ins Abseits*, München: Deutsches Jugend-Institut Arbeitspapier.

Schumann, K. (1994) 'The deviant apprentice: the impact of the German dual system of vocational training on juvenile delinquency', in J. Hagan (ed.) *Delinquency and Disrepute in the Life Course: Contextual and Dynamic Analyses*, Greenwich: JAI Press.

Willis, P. (1978) *Spaß am Widerstand. Gegenkultur in der Arbeiterschule*, Frankfurt: Syndikat.

THE RELATIONSHIP BETWEEN EDUCATION AND EMPLOYMENT IN GERMAN INDUSTRIAL SOCIOLOGY

New technologies, work organisation and training

Ingrid Drexel

INTRODUCTION

German Industrial Sociology has expanded considerably over the past two decades. It would of course be beyond the scope of this article to describe this process in its entirety. Selection is necessary, the aim here being to provide an overview of the 'hard core' of Industrial Sociology developed around the work of a handful of industrial-sociological research institutes.[1] Those areas in which Industrial Sociology overlaps with neighbouring disciplines, some of which avail themselves of industrial-sociological methods[2], will be excluded, as will the relevant work of other industrial-sociological institutes such as that of the Sozialforschungsstelle Dortmund (Social Research Institute, Dortmund) and that of ASIF (Arbeitsgruppefür Sozialwissenschaftliche Industrieforschung (Bielefeld)). The bias towards industrial-sociological research of a few research institutes is both unavoidable, given the limited space available, and necessary in order to examine the continuity and development of the specific problems addressed.

German Industrial Sociology is an empirical research discipline which works primarily with qualitative methods (company case studies, semi-standardised questionnaires). The problems and areas of study selected and the interpretation of the findings obtained are especially important to the definition of its contours. Therefore the summary characterisation of this particular research discipline which begins this article will be followed by an overview of selected studies with the aim of elucidating for non-German readers some of their most important premises and approaches, the questions posed and interpretations made as well as their development over the past ten to fifteen years.

THE SOCIAL CONTEXT AND SHARED PREMISES OF INDUSTRIAL SOCIOLOGY

The contribution of Industrial Sociology to the subject of education and employment has been shaped by some general social conditions which probably distinguish it from similar disciplines in other countries.

The first of these concerns the specific features of the education system, in particular the vocational training system and its structures for providing training and qualifications. The existence and special role of the Facharbeiter (skilled worker), Facharbeit (skilled labour) and the dual system are a central point of reference for Industrial Sociology. This can also be said of the particularly close relationship between learning and labour in German society as a whole, even going beyond the dual system itself. The third factor is the special significance of the concept of *Beruf* (profession) in German society. Originally defined by the persistence of relics of the guild system – a system which managed to survive both liberalism and capitalism – Beruf survived in a modernised form to influence firstly the training of artisans and later that of the industrial workforce as well. Between the two world wars and during the post-war period, employers and unions succeeded in modernising the dual system.

This background information goes some way towards explaining why the Facharbeiter is such a central figure in Industrial Sociology. The Facharbeiter is the yardstick against which all unskilled and semi-skilled workers are measured and has had an enduring influence as the ideal of 'qualified, competent, self-confident and autonomous labour force'. The particular strengths of other groups in the labour force tend to receive far less attention than those of the Facharbeiter. The so-called '*Beruflichkeit*' (professionalism) of labour, i.e. the tailoring of work to specific jobs according to the principle of professionalism coupled with the organisation of training according to the pattern of skilled labour is, as a rule, the socially desirable norm as far as Industrial Sociology is concerned.

Another significant factor affecting Industrial Sociology has been the political orientation of the second generation of industrial sociologists, who were influenced by '1968 and its repercussions' and followed the 'founding fathers' of the immediate post-war period. The political socialisation and search for identity of this generation, which was largely responsible for the expansion of Industrial Sociology, drove it to concretise its general political goals in a specific field of research, concentrating on company studies. The premise that the production process is central to general social and political development directed their attention to research into the internal functioning of enterprises and made their goal an improvement in working conditions, especially for blue-collar workers.

Third, it was this influence of the 1968-generation of industrial sociologists which, in the 1970s and 1980s, was made use of in a national programme for the 'humanisation of working life' – a programme which gave rise to a series of projects sponsored by the social democratic/liberal government to improve the technical, organisational and social aspects of working conditions. The projects of this and other public programmes provided companies with financial assistance from the government for implementing pilot projects with new technologies and new forms of work organisation approved by their works councils. Social scientists were increasingly called upon to take on not only the monitoring and promotion of such projects but even a certain amount of active intervention. Not only government bodies recruited this support, but employers, unions and works councils as well. These projects provided industrial sociologists with a broad range of work through which they could convey their normative goals.

Fourth, this widespread involvement of industrial sociologists in processes of concrete technical and organisational change familiarised them with corporate reality and enabled them to put their general reforming aims into practice and in doing so, allowed them to recognise the ambivalence of these aims. The price paid for this experience was, up to a point, the loss of Industrial Sociology's links with the social theories pursued in former years. The structural theories which predominated in the 1970s, bringing together the labour process and the valorisation process, later lost ground to more practical approaches concerned primarily with corporate action and power structures and micropolitics within the enterprise. In other words, these approaches were the result (among other things) of the considerable practical experience which so many industrial sociologists had acquired of the processes of innovation and negotiation in the workplace and of the role of individual and collective actors, as well as the power relationships within these processes.

Last, but not least, Industrial Sociology has of course been influenced by the institutional and financial framework provided for its research activities. Most industrial-sociological research takes the form of projects conducted by non-university research institutes, which are commissioned by public or (to a lesser extent) private bodies. The most important of these are the relevant ministries and the research council, the Deutsche Forschungsgemeinschaft, but there are various semi-public funding agencies as well. The only research to remain independent of such bodies is that conducted by the universities, whose research capacity is limited however and therefore has to be supplemented with external funds. The dependence of industrial-sociological research on public funding results in a relatively strong link between the questions it poses and the research interests of its sponsors, a concentration on current political problems and, above all, in an essentially empirical thrust.

The following sections will examine the consequences of these emphases and premises for research into the education and employment systems.

FIELDS OF RESEARCH: EMPHASES AND UNEXPLORED TERRITORY

Classical Industrial Sociology concentrates on labour, work organisation and technology within the company, starting and often ending at the corporate level. When approaching this subject, it can be said that the relationship between the education system and employment system – as a multidimensional relationship between two fields each with its own structure – is not a central and systematically researched field in this discipline. There are of course publications devoted explicitly to this topic – a few theoretical approaches dating mainly from the 1970s as well as various internationally comparative and empirical studies suggesting, examining and differentiating such approaches. Most industrial-sociological research, however, addresses the relationship between education and employment only in part, namely at the concrete level of work and training. Such research may take the form of investigations into the consequences of certain new technologies, organisational models and job changes in line with training requirements or inquiries into the barrier presented by inadequate training to the introduction of new technologies and/or organisational structures and the resulting need for additional training.

Whereas training itself is thus frequently a subject of industrial-sociological research, inquiries into its origin and development within specific institutions in general schooling, at university, in initial and continuing training systems, in company training departments, are often ignored. This is also true of the impact of these institutions on the qualifications produced. The development of the education system and its institutions is a subject for Educational Sociology. The division of labour between these disciplines thus cuts the interrelationship of the field of interest of this article into two parts, and Industrial Sociology has proved highly selective in using these findings of Educational Sociology.

There are also certain unexpected emphases and gaps within the field of Industrial Sociology. This is because for a long time research focused above all else on the industrial production process in large and medium-sized firms. Small industrial enterprises, the service sector, unskilled workers, public administration and the health sector were neglected as a result of this bias.

Even when inquiring into those fields of research in which training and the division of labour are interrelated – for example, into the different categories of labour constituted by differences in training and in status in the work process – an imbalance in the distribution of research work becomes apparent. Industrial Sociology was for a long time concerned above all with the Facharbeiter, especially in machine-building. It was not until demands were made for a humanisation of working conditions for unskilled and semi-skilled workers that these types of labour became a subject for research as well. White-collar workers, both in business and public administration, were likewise long neglected – a state of affairs which is quite astonishing given the tradition of the sociology of white-collar workers which has existed since the turn of the century, and the fact that most also receive their training within the dual system and therefore comply with the norms of professionalism and highly qualified Facharbeit.

The same can be said of middle-level industrial personnel. Although there has been no lack of research into white-collar technical personnel, the work that has been done is full of repetitions and omissions. It has concerned itself first and foremost with the *Industriemeister* (foreman), usually in the light of his loss of function or change of function (the so-called 'Meisterkrise') as a result of technical and organisational changes. There are very few studies devoted to the problems of recruitment and training of Meister, i.e. to questions relating to the education system. To a far lesser extent than in the case of the Facharbeiter, the *Ingenieur* (engineer) and the relationship between his training and work organisation has also been a subject of industrial-sociological research while the *Techniker* (technician) remains largely disregarded, despite the structural significance of this type of qualification in both the education system and industry.

DOMINANT ASSERTIONS OF THE PAST TWO DECADES IN RESEARCH ON TECHNOLOGY, WORK ORGANISATION AND TRAINING

The following section will outline the questions raised and central assertions made in some of those studies that deal with the relationship between the education and employment systems. Some international comparisons which explore this relationship more explicitly will then be examined in greater detail in the following section. The studies discussed have been selected for their exemplary nature and/or because of the impact they have had in this field.

The discovery of new production concepts – the optimistic turning-point of the 1980s and its consequences

In the mid-1980s a publication appeared which mobilised and indeed polarised debate more than almost any other work that had preceded it. This publication was a study by SOFI, the Institute of Sociological Research at Göttingen, of rationalisation processes in the machine-tool, automobile and chemical industries (Kern and Schumann 1984). The findings and central assertions of this study were that enterprises in the core manufacturing industries (to the extent that they were not affected by economic crisis) were in fact creating new production concepts. The basic tenet of these new production concepts was that the reduction of manpower to the minimum does not, of itself, bring about maximum profitability. On the contrary, restrictive use of labour in Tayloristic work organisation caused enterprises to squander an important productive potential. 'Inherent in the holistic organisation of tasks are not risks but rather opportunities; the qualification and professional autonomy of the workforce are productive forces which should be used better.' The outcome of this new rationalisation logic, according to the authors, was a 'paradigm shift in labour policy' obliging industry to rethink matters such as job design, training and personnel policy as well as manpower deployment (1984: 24).

As far as the consequences are concerned, Kern and Schumann see a repro-duction of the old dichotomy of 'risks versus opportunities'. For the 'winners', these new production concepts mean more interesting work, reprofessionalisation and hence greater opportunities for enhanced personal development and improved negotiating power. This group, however, is only one side of the coin. There are also the 'losers', those who are marginalised by the new production concepts, especially those who are less qualified and may be forced into unemployment.

What does this mean for the relationship between the education and employment systems? To summarise, it can be said that while qualifications and training have their place in the authors' theses and empirical findings, the terms are used only in a diffuse manner. Facharbeiter qualification and professionalised work are used as synonyms for 'good work'. In some places, newer forms of training and further training are considered a necessary consequence or indicator of new production concepts, an 'improvement in the labour supply' being regarded as a 'stimulant for the new production concept' (1984: 55ff.). Nevertheless, the interrelationship between develop-ments in the education system and those in the employment system is not itself a subject of interest in this book.

Kern and Schumann's publication gave rise to a wave of discussion. The first responses were overwhelmingly critical. Their assumptions regarding the quantitative relevance of their empirical findings, their theoretical inter-pretations as well as their prognoses and above all their political conclusions (cf. Malsch and Seltz 1987; Pries *et al.* 1990) all came under attack. In the following years, however, inquiries into the existence of the new production concepts, their quantitative significance and their consequences became an important focus of new empirical studies and led to the reinterpretation of old ones. Industrial Sociology had once again found a common theme, even if this had given rise to some very different viewpoints. Yet despite this, the Facharbeiter and work in the production process had once again captured the interest and attention of industrial sociologists.

The implementation of new technologies – the evolution of work and rationalisation of production

For a long time, the machine-building industry was widely regarded as the field in which production logic would prevent or at least impede the marginalisation of the Facharbeiter by Tayloristic work organisation. Therefore all the more interest was taken in the introduction of new technologies in this particular industry and the question of what would become of its highly qualified workers.

Various studies in the mid-1980s were able to shed new light on the debate and in doing so challenged the long-standing assumption that the evolution of workforce qualification is dictated by technological evolution (owing to the company's interest in exploiting it to increase profits). There was increasing recognition of the existence of not only technical and economic factors but social factors too, as well as the complex interrelationships determining the concrete organisation of technology and work. Lutz's so-called 'antideterminist thesis' became the slogan accompanying this 'turn in the tide' in Industrial Sociology, even if by no means all authors went as far as Lutz, who postulated a systematically 'open' relationship between technology and work.

One example of this new approach to the impact of new technology on work organisation and Facharbeit is the study by Hirsch-Kreinsen *et al.* (1990) on the introduction of computer-integrated manufacturing (CIM), which will be outlined here. After investigating the implementation of CIM in machine-building, the authors raised the question of the future of work in this industry. Their central thesis was that as CIM permits a separation of the development of labour and technology, so that the development of labour is, at least in principle, 'open', i.e. not determined by technology. This means that labour could well develop quite differently from technology. The authors found that the impact made by the introduction of new technology to a large extent depends on the implementation process, i.e. whether it is 'technology-oriented', 'open' or 'labour-oriented'. The authors then went on to elaborate three distinct rationalisation strategies, each with very different consequences for Facharbeit and its future prospects.

Here too, qualification crops up again and again, the future of Facharbeit being one of the central questions raised. The relationship between labour and qualification is considered in terms of both the importance of work organisation to the deployment of skilled labour and its ability to reproduce or destroy existing skills. Nevertheless, the relationship between labour and the education system is examined only from one point of view. Even if the authors assume that the supply of skills available on the market influences rationalisation strategies and job design, neither the evolution of the education system and its output, nor the concrete impact of the deployment of more highly qualified personnel in such enterprises is of interest to this empirical study.

The possibility of replacing Taylorism by new forms of control – destabilising old assumptions

From the mid-1980s onwards, the traditional equation of Facharbeit with (relatively) autonomous labour was increasingly questioned. This was the result of the critical debate on the new production concepts thesis, spurred on by the British labour process debate and increasingly differentiated investigations into the role of new information technologies in the work process. Old certainties with regard to Taylorism were thus destabilised.

Seltz and Hildebrandt (1985) had already introduced the concept of control as a specific – and perhaps even the central – determinant of work quality, pointing out that control could well increase in parallel to increases in the level of qualification and training.

The uncoupling of the level of qualification and training from the quality of work was presented with great cogency in Manske's study of the introduction of personnel planning systems (PPS) and company data capture systems (BDE) in machine-building (1990). One of the fundamental claims of this study was that the classic Taylorist principle of external control, which takes individual workers as its point of reference, becomes increasingly obsolete as the importance of what a single worker can achieve declines, as it is superseded by the temporal and material co-ordination of the entire work process. The second thesis propounded by this study was that Taylorist control can be replaced with the aid of new control techniques, by a bundle of control mechanisms rendering the precise regulation and hence dequalification of the worker superfluous, thereby permitting, indeed demanding, a certain degree of autonomy on the part of labour. 'Controlled, skilled labour' is thus put forward as a highly efficient solution to the problem of control.

> The Taylorist method of an extreme division of work and dequalification apparently no longer has to be applied in order to control and rationalise labour effectively. As far as the actual workers are concerned, this means that higher qualifications . . . do not necessarily mean more room to manoeuvre and better opportunities for the independent regulation of performance.
>
> (Manske 1990: 165–6)

This study destabilised one of the central premises of Industrial Sociology, namely that the deployment of skilled labour (assuming this deployment corresponds with the skilled workers' training) is a clear indicator of relative labour autonomy. At the same time, Taylorism loses its monopoly as a compulsive, control-intensive labour system and other forms become conceivable too. Although the study is not interested in the education

83

system *per se*, its undermining of old premises and its image of the correlation of higher qualifications and new control techniques does necessitate a rethinking of the relationship between the education and employment systems.

THE RELATIONSHIP BETWEEN THE EDUCATION SYSTEM AND EMPLOYMENT SYSTEM – THEORETICAL CONCEPTS AND EMPIRICAL EVIDENCE IN AN INTERNATIONAL COMPARISON

Even if it is generally acknowledged that corporate structures are determined at least in part by social institutions, above all by education systems, there are very few studies which actually provide concrete evidence of this. This would require the analysis of the relationship between the system of education with its structures and mechanisms on the one hand and the system of employment with its structures and mechanisms on the other.

International comparisons and research in these two areas of sociology which venture into neighbouring disciplines and the theoretical conceptualisation of this relationship have provided an important contribution to the examination of the connection between the education system and employment system. Therefore the studies discussed here were selected because they combine internationally comparative empirical investigation and theoretical considerations.

From the thesis of interdependence between the education and employment systems to the supply thesis

Of particular importance here is a study conducted by Lutz with the team from the Laboratoire d'Economie et de Sociologie du Travail (LEST) at Aix-en-Provençe in the first half of the 1970s.[3] This study examined personnel, training and earnings structures as well as the hierarchical and functional organisation of labour in comparable companies in France and Germany. What follows is first Lutz's interpretation of his empirical findings and then their conceptualisation in the perspective of the relationship between the education and employment systems.

Lutz first provides empirical evidence of the existence of considerable differences between French and German enterprises concerning the organisation of both work and the enterprise itself, with regard to the vertical and horizontal division of work and the formal structure of employee qualification. The French enterprises differed from their German counterparts in their extreme division of work between production and engineering departments and in their bureaucratic organisation (Lutz 1976).

To explain these differences, Lutz introduces the education systems and the structures of labour supply to which they give rise as a central variable.

84

France's education system, according to Lutz, is characterised by the growth of higher education (secondary and tertiary) and by the fact that virtually all initial vocational qualifications are provided by schools while in Germany it is the dual system of publicly standardised training in firms and schools which dominates. As a result of these differences, the distribution of the qualifications of the working population in both countries is structured very differently, being far more homogeneous in Germany. Companies are obliged to adapt to the specific structure of labour available in each country. Lutz summarises his detailed description of this adaptation process as follows: 'Each country has a basic pattern for the corporate deployment and utilisation of manpower, which corresponds to a large extent to its system of publicly organised or at least publicly regulated education and training' (1976: 130).

According to Lutz, these findings are neither consistent with the so-called subordination thesis, which regarded the education system as determined by the technical and economic requirements of the employment system, nor with the so-called uncoupling thesis, which postulated the dissolution of such a connection. As an alternative to these theses (which dominated debate in the 1970s), he propounded the idea of the 'interdependence of the education system and corporate labour policy' (1976: 132) which draws on the concepts of system theory. The education system and employment system are regarded as social sub-systems, to a certain extent capable of autonomous action as well as specific reactions aimed at safeguarding or restoring inner stability. Between the two sub-systems there is a system of mediation which can serve as a medium for the transfer of services, demands for innovation and stabilising effects, but which must also be sufficiently elastic to prevent certain solutions to problems having a destabilising effect on the other sub-system.

In later versions of this study, this thesis of the interdependence of the education and employment systems became the 'supply thesis', i.e. the thesis of a unilateral determination of the employment system by the education system.

> As [in France], a highly selective education system with strongly hierarchical levels and diploma is by far the most important, if not the only, source of vocational competence, the enterprise has no choice but to structure its work organisation in such a way that it can use the qualified school-leavers produced by the education system in accordance with the particular level and profile of their certified abilities and the expectations that these sanction.
>
> (Lutz 1976: 144)

The education system as an environmental factor affecting the use of technology – the thesis of the centrality of institutionally moulded corporate strategies

Sorge has proposed a concept of the relationship between the education system and corporate structures which is heavily influenced by economic theory and organisational sociology (Sorge 1985, 1986). This concept is also based on an international comparison, its subject being the introduction of microelectronics in British and German industry. Central to Sorge's approach is, on the one hand, the coherence of all social spheres and structures, which together produce a 'societal effect' (Maurice *et al.* 1982) and, on the other, the fact that the institutional and cultural features of a society (including vocational training) have considerable influence on its corporate structures and a high degree of historical continuity. This means that those developments which are specific to one country can be understood only from a socio-historical point of view.

The author first shows how the strategic orientation of corporate policy ensuing from the socio-economic environment and market developments can explain the use of technology and its consequences. A comparison between British and German industry is then used to show how their institutional conditions have led to different patterns of organising numerical control and different distributions of skill. Finally, the two composite causes are linked by the evidence Sorge provides to show that not only do institutional conditions determine the strategic orientation of corporate policy but that corporate policy also helps to create and change these same conditions.

It is against this backcloth, this complex model explaining the introduction of technology, labour organisation and qualification, that Sorge examines the role played by the education system. Basing his arguments on a socio-historical analysis of the history of vocational training in both countries following their (very different) departure from the guild system (Sorge 1985: 164ff.), he shows that in Britain, both the system of vocational training and corporate organisation have been characterised by the 'tendency to delimit what are felt to be autonomous spheres of activity. The underlying model of social categorisation and job design is that of the professions, i.e. a corporate entity which regulates access to particular activities and practice independently of firms and employers interests' (1985: 21). As a result of this, the social organisation of the British enterprise is more inclined than its German counterpart to disintegrate into separate professions, whereas in Germany, the Beruf concept relates to a broader skill base for working life, which is acquired by publicly regulated vocational training and examination. In British companies, one consequence of these institutional factors is a sharper division of labour than in Germany, taking the form of more specialised occupations and jobs. Not only is there a tendency to remove certain special functions away from the factory floor and the blue-collar workforce, assigning them instead to the engineering departments, but there is also a higher degree of horizontal differentiation between the various expert and management functions (1985: 24).

According to Sorge, CNC technology has been introduced in keeping with this pattern (1985: 24–5). British enterprises have been much less aware of and more hesitant about user-programming than their German counterparts. Programme-oriented functions thus tend to be situated off the factory floor. Nor has the possibility of user-programming proved a decisive criterion when it comes to the purchase of new machines. There have been attempts to improve the skills of machinists, but these have generally taken the form of company-specific further training measures without the development of a new occupational profile. In the Federal Republic, on the other hand, a generalisation of CNC programming skills has been encouraged in all the relevant vocational training courses. Because of this institutional environment German companies have been able to react to variations in their markets and to a more differentiated demand for products with a reduction in batch size.

> Given that they do not actually restrict a company's ability to take action, British institutional preconditions do not render this option impossible. Nevertheless, [British companies] are simply not designed in such a way that they can pursue success by product innovation and differentiation and by the economic exploitation of smaller batch sizes to the same extent as is done in the Federal Republic.
>
> (Sorge 1985: 26)

To summarise, Sorge comes to the conclusion that long-standing differences between German and British society with regard to the Facharbeiter tradition, to the creation and preservation of skills on the shop-floor as well as the economic exploitation of these skills, provide an explanation for the nature and extent of their response to the possibility of user-programming (1985: 25). His theoretical argument thus emphasises on the one hand the considerable importance of the market situation, of economic efficiency and corporate strategy, while at the same time showing that these have very different consequences in the countries studied as they build on those institutional preconditions which are peculiar to each country, among them the education system.

The relative autonomy of the education system and its ultimate determination by business enterprises – the concept of an asymmetrical dialectical relationship between education and employment

This article concludes with a report on a study by the author on the relationship between the education system and the employment system. Based on a theoretical explanation of the separation of work and education (Drexel 1980), a series of empirical investigations were conducted into these questions, including two international comparisons. What follows is first an outline of this theoretical concept, to the extent that it is relevant here, and then one of the aforementioned comparisons, the subject of which is the evolution of intermediate education and careers in France and Germany.[4]

The theoretical concept bases the existence of the education system and its relative autonomy on the necessity to remove all unproductive functions and especially training from the corporate production process in the interests of the valorisation of capital. These are established in society as functions in their own right. However, the education system's autonomy is limited above all by the fundamental asymmetry between the education and employment systems. It is the companies that make decisions about how to use and valorise skills, thus exercising an indirect influence on educational choices and, ultimately, on changes in the education system. This concept counters the thesis of the interdependence of the education and employment systems as two equivalent social sub-systems with the concept of a dialectical relationship between two asymmetrically interrelated spheres in which it is the companies which are ultimately determinant.

This theoretical concept was used for an international comparison of developments in intermediate-level skills and training schemes (i.e. the level between worker and engineer) in France and Germany (Drexel 1993). This comparison was based on case studies of comparable German and French enterprises conducted at the end of the 1980s (in co-operation with a team made up of various French research groups and headed by Méhaut) as well as on an analysis of the literature on past and present intermediate-level education and training and the labour categories (above all the technicians) to which they give rise. The central concern of the comparison was the access routes to middle-level positions in industry in each of the countries studied, i.e. both new and traditional training courses, career patterns and their developments.

There were two findings which are of particular relevance here. First, the education and employment systems and the relationship between them have developed very differently in the two countries studied, giving rise to specific patterns and a development logic peculiar to each. The point of departure for both countries was roughly the same, worker promotion to middle-level positions being the norm. It was against this backcloth that state and industry started to interpret the similar skill problems they were facing in the 1950s and 1960s in different ways, attempting to solve them by applying very different solutions. This gave rise to specific patterns of development in each country, which continued to influence the evolution of the systems right up to the end of the 1980s. The French pattern is characterised by sudden changes in the education system, by the initiation of changes at the top end of the scale of existing education schemes, by the creation of competition between initial and continuing training and the relative weakening of continuing training and the tendency of the younger generation to stay on longer at school. The German pattern is characterised by more gradual changes in the education system by improvements starting first at the lower levels of vocational training and occupational groups, by competition between traditional and new training courses, by the mutual reinforcement of initial and further training as well as the early entrance of well-qualified young people into the employment system.

The author analyses the process coherence of the French and German development patterns. She shows how these patterns have an increasingly regulatory, clarifying and reinforcing effect on each other, thereby gaining coherence and hence also their own dynamism in the causation of the resulting problems and typical attempts made to solve them. A 'country-specific development logic' (1993: 269ff.) becomes visible, and this logic has the power both to stabilise and to destabilise. The German development pattern has for a long time tended towards stabilisation, a 'positive circle' of stabilisation, whereas the French pattern has tended towards destabilisation or a 'negative circle', in which the results desired by the parties involved from the repeated creation of new training schemes were not obtained, and the destabilisation processes triggered were not wanted by anybody.

Finally, Drexel analyses some of the most recent counter-trends in both countries, 'course corrections' in France and the possible beginnings of a negative circle in Germany. This shows that even if it is becoming increasingly difficult for a society to break away from an established development logic, this does not mean that the direction taken is irreversible. It is precisely the perpetual reproduction of a particular type of development that causes problems to accumulate, building up the pressure required to push through new kinds of solution and hence a change of trend.

In addition to the differences between developments in the two societies, Drexel also analyses what they have in common, above all the astonishing continuity of worker promotion in both countries. The most diverse personnel and further training policies are revitalising traditional forms of worker promotion as well as creating new ones.

Finally, the consequences of these results for the relationship between the education system and employment system are analysed. For one thing, the supply thesis turns out to be unfounded. In both countries, the growth of middle-level positions did not develop in reaction to the emergence of intermediate-level training schemes and the supply of labour with immediate qualifications to which they gave rise. Rather it began either long before the growth of this supply (as in the case of France) or independent of this (as in the case of Germany). Nor has worker promotion been totally destroyed by competition from higher-level training courses permitting horizontal access to middle-level positions. Furthermore, the by no means insignificant continuity of worker promotion in France shows that business enterprises not only can but, to a certain extent, do withstand the pressure to structure themselves in line with the supply of manpower provided by the public education system. Above all, the findings of this study show that in their recruiting, deployment and payment systems, companies do indeed have a decisive influence on the types of education and training pursued. The deployment of personnel below their level of training, for example, is an inducement to others to stay on longer at school – developments to which the education system can respond only by creating new training schemes at a higher level.

The reciprocal reactions of the education and employment systems to their respective changes certainly do not mean that these social sub-systems are of equal weight even if they both contribute to the country-specific development patterns. Innovations on the part of the education system and corporate policies do not have the same power to influence the development process. Despite all the mechanisms with which the education system can confront companies, it is the latter which ultimately determine the development process and its results. The study shows very clearly the structural asymmetry at work here.

SUMMARY WITH A VIEW TO FUTURE RESEARCH

What conclusions can be drawn from this overview of the contribution of German Industrial Sociology to the analysis of the relationship between education and employment? How can progress be made in the research in this field? This article concludes with five propositions.

1 The relationship or, to be more precise, the complex structure of multiple relationships between education and employment, cannot be 'found' but instead has to be theoretically reconstructed. Investment in theoretical, methodological and (further) empirical work is required to this end.
2 Theoretical work is also required in order to be able to place the abundant but highly fragmented empirical findings now at our disposal within a larger framework and to identify outstanding questions.
3 Further empirical studies aimed at the totality of the relationships between education and employment and – above all – at the medium- and long-term development of these relationships are necessary. Historical analyses of the development of education systems as such are not enough. What is needed is a structured history of the relationship between corporate structures and personnel policy over a long period of time.
4 Methodological studies are necessary in order to create theoretically founded and at the same time operable designs for such studies. International comparisons are an especially effective way of clarifying both general and specific questions regarding the relationship between education and employment. Here too – indeed, here especially – well-

constructed designs are necessary in order to be able to define relevant questions which can be investigated empirically and to interpret their results coherently and in relation to the results of previous studies.

5 In the interests of both the accumulation and synthesis of our knowledge of the relationship sought, which requires a qualitative leap, Sociology must develop 'new production concepts' permitting a better utilisation of its potential. For one thing, the division of labour among the 'hyphenated sociologies' and between Industrial Sociology and the Sociology of Education in particular, will have to be overcome somewhat – purposefully, systematically and without stooping to eclecticism. Secondly, international co-operation will have to be intensified as it is just such co-operation which provides opportunities, indeed compels us, to reflect on the restrictions of our respective disciplines and to discard the blinkers imposed by our 'national spectacles'.

NOTES

1 The SOFI (Soziologisches Forschungsinstitut Göttingen e.V., the ISF (Institut für Sozialwissenschaftliche Forschung e.V., München), the WZB (Wissenschaftszentrum Berlin) and the Institut für Soziologie, Universität Erlangen Nürnberg.
2 Most of these are studies produced as part of the research into professional training institutionalised in the Bundesinstitut für Berufsbildung (Federal Institute of Professional Training) and the Deutsche Jugendinstitut (German Youth Institute), commissioned by the relevant ministries.
3 Lutz 1976; for a presentation of the (later extended) results of this search from a French point of view, cf. Maurice *et al.* 1982.
4 The second of these is a comparative analysis of the structural changes in German and Italian steel industry since the end of the 1960s and of the very different strategies adopted in these two countries (Drexel 1992).

BIBLIOGRAPHY

Drexel, I. (1980) 'Die Krise der Anlernung im Arbeitsprozess – betriebliche und gesellschaftliche Ursachen der Trennung von Qualifizierung und Produktion', *Soziale Welt* 3.
—— (1992) 'New production structures à l'Italiano? – similarities and differences in the West German and Italian steel industries', in N. Altmann, C. Köhler and P. Meil (eds) *Technology and Work in German Industry*, London/New York.
——(1993) *Das Ende des Facharbeiteraufstiegs? Neue mittlere Bildungs- und Karrierewege in Deutschland und Frankreich – ein Vergleich*, Frankfurt/New York.
Hirsch-Kreinsen, H., Schlutz-Wild, R., Köhler, C. and von Behr, M. (1990) *Einstieg in die rechnerintegrierte Produktion. Alternative Entwicklungspfade der Industriearbeit im Maschinenbau*, Frankfurt/Munich.
Kern, H. and Schumann, M. (1984) *Das Ende der Arbeitsteilung? Rationalisierung in der industriellen Produktion-Bestandsaufnahme, Trendbestimmung*, Munich.
Lutz, B. (1976) 'Bildungssystem und Beschäftigungsstruktur in Deutschland und Frankreich. Zum Einfluss des Bildungssystems auf die Gestaltung betrieblicher Arbeitskräftestrukturen', in Institut für Sozialwissenschaaftliche Forschung (ed.) *Betrieb, Arbeitsmarkt, Qualifikation*, Frankfurt.

Malsch, T. and Seltz, R. (eds) (1987) *Die neuen Produktionskonzepte auf dem Prüfstand. Beiträge zur Entwicklung der Industriearbeit*, Frankfurt/New York.

Manske, F. (1990) *Kontrolle, Rationalisierung und Arbeit. Kontinuität durch Wandel Die Ersetzbarkeit des Taylorismus durch moderne Kontrolltechniken*, Berlin.

Maurice, M., Sellier, F. and Silvestre, J.-J. (1982) *Politique d'éducation et organisation industrielle en France et en Allemagne*, Paris.

Pries, L., Schmidt, R. and Trinczek, R. (1990) *Entwicklungspfade von Industriearbeit. Chancen und Risiken betrieblicher Produktionsmodernisierung*, Opladen.

Seltz, R. and Hildebrandt, E. (1985) 'Produktion, Politik und Kontrolle', in F. Naschold (ed.) *Arbeit und Politik – Gesellschaftliche Regulierung der Arbeit und soziale Sicherung*, Frankfurt/New York.

Sorge, A. (1985) *Informationstechnik und Arbeit im sozialen Prozess. Arbeitsorganisation, Qualifikation und Produktivkraftentwicklung* , Frankfurt/New York.

——(1986) *Institutionelle Bedingungen und strategische Orientierungen des Einsatzes neuer Techniken*, Discussion Papers of Wissenschaftszentrum, Berlin.

7

LABOUR MARKET TRANSITIONS AND DYNAMICS OF TRANSITIONS IN GERMANY

Klaus Schömann

INTRODUCTION

This chapter reviews economic and sociological analyses of the labour market, focusing on transition processes in the labour market and the dynamics of mobility. It is based on two quantitative sources: the German Socio-Economic Panel (SOEP)[1] and the German Life History Study (GLHS).[2]

A great number of studies which deal with societal and economic processes either implicitly or explicitly take issue with various forms of transition processes. Besides the most basic process of entering the labour market (Schömann *et al.* 1991), or the school-to-work transition as it has become known amongst policy analysts, there is the equally important transition process into and out of unemployment or leaving the labour force (Pischner and Wagner 1991; Allmendinger and Brückner 1992). These transition processes have been subject to economic and sociological research for many years using longitudinal data.

Results suggest that transitions, entry as well as exit from the labour market, should no longer be considered as discrete options of being either inside or outside the labour force. These two kinds of transitions have been studied from the perspective of how more gradual transitions can be achieved either by means of initial training, apprenticeships on labour market entry or more gradual retirement from the labour force through a reduced number of working hours before retirement. From this perspective transitions become processes of their own kind with their own dynamics.

Labour market policies as well as policies directed towards the education system have both aimed to facilitate a smooth transition from education to work. Education policies, at least in Germany, have tried to prepare pupils at an early stage for the entry into the labour market by means of practical courses and even short periods of practical experience for several days and sometimes weeks within firms. On the other hand, labour market policies provide incentives to firms to facilitate transitions for members of disadvantaged groups. In some instances labour market policies provide training for skills which come close to the curriculum of the full-time education system.

The paper starts with an outline of a theory of labour market transition processes and then reviews longitudinal evidence of some selected processes and policy evaluations. The conclusion stresses the necessity for policy evaluation to be contextualised historically if conclusions are to be drawn that are valid for more than one country.

MORE THAN ONE LABOUR MARKET AND LABOUR MARKET SEGMENTS

Labour market processes and transitions

Our point of departure is the theoretical perspective that the labour market, unlike most other markets, does not consist of a single market. Theories of labour market segmentation and dual labour market theory (Doeringer and Piore 1971) distinguish a primary and secondary segment. Primary segment jobs are characterised by high productivity, good working conditions, stable employment patterns, high wages and a well-established system of initial and continuing training. Implementation of new technologies through training is a widespread practice in this segment. Firms are usually large, capital-intensive, highly unionised. Good working relationships are ensured by means of above-average wages, seniority rules and structured promotion ladders.

In contrast, in the secondary segment there is no stable employment, lower wages and few opportunities for initial and continuing training within or outside the company. The tasks to be performed are usually learned through a short training period and even when different tasks are performed the training is similarly minimal. Workers in this segment are recruited easily on the labour market so that the abundance of workers able to perform these repetitive tasks together with a low level of unionisation in this segment keep wages low.

The labour market is also characterised by a lack of job mobility between segments. Due to good in-company training in the primary segment, which is strictly limited to company members (Malcomsen 1984), promotion ladders are restricted to employees. Initial and continuing training therefore plays a crucial role in promoting occupational mobility in the labour market and in particular between labour market segments. Mobility between segments could be promoted through courses providing more general training to secondary workers so that their skill level, work attitudes and probably other 'secondary' characteristics perceived by employers could be overcome.

Secondary segment workers are obliged to seek training outside the firm, since they have no access to it internally. Despite their training efforts, upward job mobility is more likely to result from changing jobs than from internal mobility (Schömann and Becker 1995). Secondary segment workers aspiring to work in the primary segment will try to achieve this mobility through participation in training courses. Obviously the state might intervene in this process by providing additional training courses or through subsidies to secondary workers to encourage participation. Alternatively, the state could operate as a 'model employer' facilitating mobility between segments by developing special career tracks for employees previously employed in the secondary segment.

This view of the functioning of the labour market requires the existence of at least two apparently separate labour markets to be considered. In this perspective, the role of labour market policy consists of facilitating transitions between the two segments or facilitating entry into the primary segment. For the former West Germany, Lutz and Sengenberger (1974) elaborated an analysis of segmentation theory which distinguished within the primary segment a firm-specific labour market in large firms with high job-qualification standards, a craft-specific labour market in small firms with high qualification standards, and set this against a secondary segment demanding no or few skills either in small or large firms.

The vocational training system in Germany is considered to contribute to segmentation of labour markets, since those who receive occupational training constitute a group of people selected by firms who obtain qualifications that are specific for certain occupations. Technical qualifications are acquired jointly within and outside firms and hence facilitate transitions between firms without much friction (Blossfeld and Mayer 1989).

With respect to transition processes, the segmentation theory advanced by Stinchcombe (1979) has been adapted to the German context for the analysis of labour market transition and entry processes. Stinchcombe derives seven industrial segments on the basis of a cross-classification of a firm's position in the labour market, i.e. relying on skilled or unskilled jobs, and constraints on the firm due to its position in product markets, which function in a competitive or monopolistic manner. Empirical analyses for Germany have shown that this form of labour market segmentation is useful in explaining earnings differentials between industrial segments (Hannan *et al.* 1990) and differences in the use of fixed-term employment (Schömann and Kruppe 1993).

An additional dynamic perspective on the labour market has been developed by Schmid (1993) who distinguishes five different kinds of transition processes connected to the labour market. These are (1) mobility within the primary labour market: between and within segments; passages from one industrial sector to another; and passages from full-time to part-time work; (2) movements between unemployment and the labour market, including entry into long-term unemployment and the experience of repeated episodes of unemployment; (3) transition from the education system to the labour market; (4) transitions between the domestic sphere and the labour market, for example, periods of maternity leave followed by a return to employment; various types of sabbatical leave; (5) retirement or, in some types of labour markets, a progressive reduction in working hours in the period preceeding retirement.

Transitions defined in this way operate as bridges into the primary labour market and combine standard forms of employment with periods of other forms of activities. From a societal point of view these activities may be viewed as equally desirable – for example, higher education, training or caring for children or the elderly. Facilitating school-to-work transitions is achieved by various forms of financing, in one instance pupils take up an unpaid 'placement', while others use apprenticeship, which is a form of co-financing, as a means of entering the labour market. Those who experience more difficulties in finding jobs sometimes receive substantial state subsidies which finance skill acquisition or offer wage subsidies to employers with the aim of supporting their integration or re-integration into the labour market.

THE DYNAMICS OF LABOUR MARKET TRANSITIONS

Labour market transitions within the labour market (type 1, above) and between employment, unemployment and inactivity (types 2 – 5 above) are themselves embedded in dynamic processes of macroeconomic and macrosocietal change which evolve in time and space. Labour market segments defined through monopoly power in product markets may lose their competitive advantage, or industries relying on low-paid unskilled work might withdraw investment in one economy and move to production sites in countries with lower wages or less labour market regulation. Technological change and faster diffusion of advanced technologies could have implications for labour market transitions.

Another kind of societal change, such as a greater concern with ecological issues which might result in the development of production processes less damaging to the environment, could have an impact on the structure of the labour market. Similarly a preference for part-time employment or an increase in the numbers of women joining the labour force will create a new dynamic in labour market transitions.

The unification of East and West Germany, as well as the process of European integration – especially since the ratification of the Maastricht Treaty – have given a new dynamic to labour market transitions. These dynamics do not only influence transition processes within a country but, at European level, another 'player' has been added in the formulation and implementation of labour market policy.

TOWARDS A SOCIO-ECONOMIC ANALYSIS OF LABOUR MARKET TRANSITIONS

The availability of longitudinal data like the GLHS and the SOEP has contributed greatly to fruitful exchanges between economists, sociologists and political scientists on topics related to the labour market. Each year a rich data set is collected for the SOEP, with a core of basic information on employment, remuneration and family-related events and additional questions covering special topics, such as home environment, social origin, house work, transitions into retirement, assets, further education and training, time budgets, social networks and opinions on social policy.

The understanding of transition processes has gained from interdisciplinary exchange and debate on this common source of information. The falsification of hypotheses in the Popperian tradition has been among the major successes of the analyses based on longitudinal data. This has allowed some overly simplistic views about labour market processes to be discarded – especially those which could be described as having a single theoretical perspective, be it neo-classical, neo-Keynesian, structuralist or institutional in approach.

Users of this data source become part of a network who share information, facilitating interdisciplinary communication. Increasingly, cross-country comparisons are being added to this discussion.

LONGITUDINAL ASSESSMENT OF ENTRY INTO THE LABOUR MARKET

Prior to the availability of these longitudinal data, cross-sectional analysis predominated. Within the human capital tradition the interpretation of rates of returns to investment in education was derived on the basis of cross-sectional data. However, these analyses risk over or underestimating possible sources of differences in earnings between men and women.

The analyses in this review of results present longitudinal estimates based on the German Life History Data (Mayer and Brückner 1989). A representative sample of 2,171 West Germans from the birth cohorts 1929–31, 1939–41 and 1949–51 were interviewed. The data collection was carried out from October 1981 to May 1983. With the aid of a standardised interview, the survey collected data on the life course of these people with respect to social origin, education, occupation, family, housing etc., and in this way created a data set suitable for dynamic longitudinal analyses.

Using multivariate analysis Schömann et al. (1991) estimate differences in (1) the level of entry wages between men and women; (2) rates of return to education and changes over the years; (3) the extent of segmentation in the German labour market. Of particular interest is the information collected on monthly net starting and net finishing wages for each job-spell in a person's occupational career. On the basis of the data on hours worked on that job, hourly wage rates were calculated and deflated by the retail price index.

This study makes use of retrospective life histories. Interviewees were asked to reconstruct their life course with exact reference to time. Recollection errors are more likely the longer the time between the interview and the occurrence of the event. Methodological studies concerning the reliability of retrospective data show that mis-specification of equations is more likely to be a source of error than recall bias (Courgeau 1991; Schömann 1994).

Jobs were coded in terms of qualification standards necessary to perform certain tasks, using a system that has already proved useful in several empirical studies (Blossfeld and Mayer 1989), distinguishing between skilled and unskilled activities. Previous experience using this classification shows that the resulting category of 'jobs with low qualification standards' includes activities which, according to the theory of segmented labour markets, belong to the secondary segment.

The ensuing distinction between jobs with high qualification standards in large and small firms takes into account the fact that the Federal Republic of Germany has a highly developed system of vocational training, the dual system. The qualifications acquired can be used in a number of small firms while in large firms these qualifications tend to be firm-specific. However, the separation of jobs with low and high qualification standards in large firms also allows for the distinction between primary and secondary jobs within large organisational structures (Blossfeld and Mayer 1989).

In a second attempt to operationalise labour market segmentation, Stinchcombe's approach was applied. Stinchcombe (1979) defined industrial sectors using a cross-classification of two dimensions. The first distinguishes product markets where entry is restricted (by licenses, technical restraints or state monopolies) from open, competitive markets. The second distinguishes industries according to whether they rely on unskilled labour, skilled labour or whether positions are tied to property rights.

Carroll and Mayer (1986) defined seven industrial sectors:

1 traditional primary industries such as fishing and forestry (competitive, labour tied to property rights);
2 small competitive industries such as the retail trade (competitive, unskilled labour);
3 classical capitalist firms in commodity markets such as textiles and food processing (competitive, unskilled labour);
4 competitive industries such as construction (competitive, skilled labour);
5 large-scale engineering-based industries such as chemicals and machine tools (technical restrictions on entry, skilled labour);

6 professional service industries such as education and health (restriction by licensing, skilled labour);
7 bureaucratic service industries such as government and banking (state restrictions, skilled labour).

In a study of wages in West Germany since 1950 (Schömann *et al.* 1991) we found that labour market segmentation in relation to different sectors was most significant at the beginning of the occupational career for both men and women. Five major conclusions can be drawn from this work.

First, the analysis of longitudinal data shows that women have slightly higher earnings in first jobs than men, but for men wage growth is subsequently more rapid. The German Life History Data reveal that from 1950 until 1983 women mainly occupied jobs with few career prospects and slower wage growth.

Second, the differences in the impact of an additional year of education for men and women on the log of the starting wage is astonishing. At the maximum level of education – nineteen years of schooling, or university degree level – women obtained a wage of up to six times the value of those with only the compulsory minimum of education. The corresponding figure for men was three times. This demonstrates that the inequality of returns to education for the first job is twice as high among women compared to men. It also reveals the greater importance of higher education for women if they are to obtain high starting wages. This result is in line with studies by Helberger (1983) for West Germany and Bartel (1980) for the US.

Next, a statistically significant change occurred in the returns to education for both women and men between 1950 and 1975. The starting wage advantage of both men and women with higher education was halved compared to those with minimum years of education during the period of 1950 and 1975. This supports the view that educational credentials have the character of productivity indicators to employers, but the more people have them, the lower their value. The value of such a signal or filter is largely its ability to differentiate between otherwise similar applicants (Arrow 1973). If there are too many job applicants with the same credentials, additional filters are introduced to differentiate between equally qualified applicants.

Fourth, the second group of variables deals with labour market segmentation. The fit of the model for both men and women increased significantly after the inclusion of these variables. The estimated effects of education remain virtually unchanged. Primary industries (i.e. fishing, forestry and animal-related industries) are found to pay significantly less than all other sectors for both men and women. The other significant negative effect for starting wages is found for women in the intermediate professions in the service sector, including health and education. This is the sector of the economy in which most women find employment (Müller *et al.* 1983), and

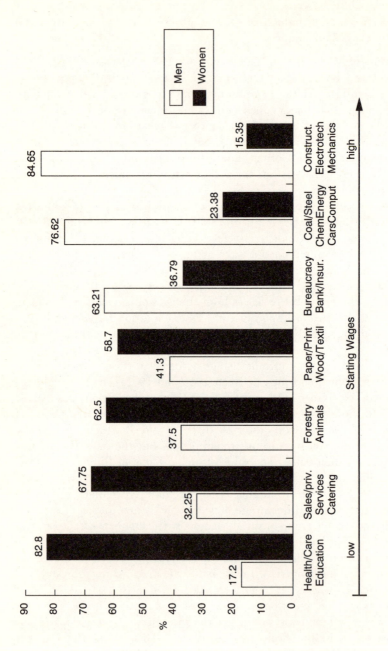

Figure 7.1 Distribution of women and men by sectors of activity according to starting salary

it pays them less than men at the beginning of their careers. High-wage craft- and engineering-based industries do not recruit many women.

Figure 7.1 shows starting salaries based on the industrial sector and the percentage distribution of women and men as observed in the German Life History Data. The well-paying segments are clearly dominated by male workers and women are particularly crowded into the low-paying segments. A clear policy implication of this is that increased educational efforts will not improve the relative position of women's wages unless the kind of course they choose also changes.

Finally, yearly changes in aggregate conditions did not have any impact on starting wages for men or women. The time trend reflects a tendency for women's wages to grow more quickly than men's, which indicates some narrowing of the wage differential between 1950 and 1983.

DO FIXED TERM CONTRACTS FACILITATE ENTRY INTO THE LABOUR MARKET?

Among the policies proposed to build bridges between full-time education and the labour market is the German Employment Promotion Act (Beschäftigungsförderungsgesetz 1985, 1989, 1994). This law increased the possibilities for recruiting employees for a fixed-term period. The argument for the introduction of this law was to stimulate more employment by alleviating legal restrictions. Despite this deregulation there was not an increase in the total number of these contracts. However, the law had some unintended side-effects on the composition of those in 'precarious' or 'atypical' forms of employment.

These effects have been studied by the Socio-Economic Panel Study for East and West Germany (SOEP), which addressed two questions. Who is most likely to be employed on a fixed-term contract? Do employees on fixed-term contracts earn less than employees on a more permanent contract?

Logistic regressions showed that the number of highly qualified staff in fixed-term employment has decreased over the years. This could be interpreted as evidence that since the introduction of the Employment Promotion Act (BeschFG 1985) more employees with lower qualifications have taken up jobs with fixed-term employment. In other words, this group now runs a higher risk of having a job for a limited duration. Between 1985 and 1991 in West Germany the tendency to apply fixed-term contracts to younger workers has increased. In East Germany this age selectivity is even more pronounced.

From a theoretical point of view this supports the perspective that fixed-term contracts are considered as a 'prolonged probationary period' for young labour market entrants. They are most likely to be employed in the first instance on a fixed-term basis and subsequently the probability of fixed-term employment decreases with age or general labour force experience. White-collar employees are among those with lower risks of fixed-term employment. Since these employees are closest to managerial positions in firms, it is in the firm's immediate interest to have a more long-term employment relationship with these employees.

Labour market segmentation has proved to be of some importance in analyses of the labour market in West Germany. Our results show that there is no difference in hiring practices in small and large firms, but the skill level required for the job has an impact on the probability of being employed on a fixed-term contract. In West Germany until 1988, and in East Germany until 1992, the higher the skill level, the lower the likelihood has been of being on a fixed-term contract.

The East and West German labour markets have already developed a number of similarities. Large-scale engineering industries such as the iron, steel, and chemical industries make significantly less use of fixed-term contracts. Similarly, competitive craft industries, i.e. jobs in the construction and electrical components industries, use fewer fixed-term appointments. This can be explained by the shortages of skilled labour in these industries until 1991.

To test the question of possible earnings differentials between fixed-term and permanent employees, cross-sectional earnings functions were estimated to compare results with previous studies using the SOEP data set. The effect for educational qualifications measured in years is positive and the size of effects is slightly below that estimated by Schwarze (1991). Effects of labour force experience show the usual non-linear positive effect whereby employees with more labour force experience have higher net hourly wages. White-collar employees, who have a lower risk of fixed-term employment, have higher labour earnings indicating the favourable position in both employment security and earnings of this group in West Germany.

Large firms, those with more than two hundred employees, pay significantly higher net hourly wages in West Germany. There are wage premiums to be gained when working in the occupation-specific labour market segment, but no additional wage premiums are awarded in internal labour markets. The historically high reputation of the *Facharbeiter* is still an institutional feature of the German labour market and is marked by high employment protection (fewer fixed-term appointments) and higher earnings which corresponds to high return to general training received. Recently qualified young people are likely to receive lower earnings.

Stinchcombe's classification of labour market segments (1979) shows that traditional primary industries such as forestry and agriculture pay significantly lower wages in both East and West Germany relative to the service sector — for example, banking, insurance and social administration. Industries classified as small competitive industries, such as restaurants, personal services and retail, also offer significantly lower wages than in services. In West Germany large-scale engineering industries, such as the iron, steel and car industries have above-average wages even after controlling for education and labour force experience. These findings are based on retrospective longitudinal data for the period 1950–1983 (Schömann *et al.* 1991).

A dummy variable was constructed to indicate whether the job was fixed-term or permanent. Fixed-term employment shows a negative and statistically significant effect on wages after controlling for other variables. Fixed-term contracts pay about 10 per cent lower net hourly wages in West Germany. This result supports the view that facilitating fixed-term employment not only reduces indirect labour costs in the form of lower redundancy payments, but also direct costs during employment on a fixed-term contract. This result does not hold for East Germany – which is still in a period of transition – where wage levels in general are substantially lower than in the West.

It can be concluded that the development of fixed-term employment enhances labour market segmentation. This corroborates the findings of Alba-Ramírez (1991) for Spain and Vissers and Dirven (1994) for the Netherlands. Evidence presented by Schömann and Kruppe (1993) reflects a consistent pattern of labour market segmentation in East and West Germany. Labour market segments that pay higher wages do not make great use of fixed-term employment. Industries which pay lower wages also make more use of fixed-term contracts. The combination of effects shows a further segmentation of the labour market towards a pattern of stable, well-paid jobs on the one hand, and precarious lower paid jobs on the other hand. The introduction of the Employment Promotion Act in 1985 did not reduce this duality but stabilised and even increased it in employment conditions.

DOES CONTINUING TRAINING[3] FACILITATE LABOUR MARKET TRANSITIONS?

Public policies on continuing training aim at facilitating transitions from the education system into the labour market as well as within the primary labour market. In addition, the further education and training of the unemployed is encouraged to increase the probability of re-employment. In this section West German further education and training policies since 1950 are evaluated (for a more complete analysis see Schömann and Becker 1995).

In Figures 7.2 and 7.3 age-specific further education rates for three birth cohorts are shown based on the GLHS. These rates are calculated as proportions of the labour force participating in further education at different points in time during the life course. These figures demonstrate the remarkable increase in participation in continuing training for subsequent birth cohorts. Younger cohorts show higher levels of participation from an early age and continue to do so at later stages during their life course.

The increase in youth participation can be explained by two

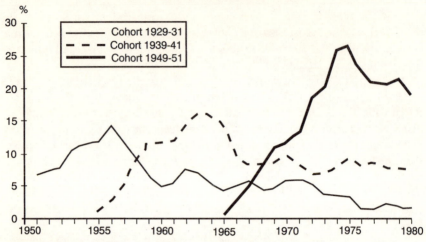

Figure 7.2 Participation rates of men in further education and training 1929–31,
1939–41 and 1949–51

developments. On the one hand there is easier access to government grants to finance higher education not only at university levels, but also partially to finance further education and training, while on the national level the Education Promotion Act (Bundesausbildungsförderungs-gesetz Bafög) which assisted financing of education and training was enacted in 1971. It led to increased access to continuing training for the more recent birth cohorts. Additionally, the Labour Promotion Act (Arbeitsförderungsgesetz AFG 1969) and the Vocational Training Act (Berufsbildungsgesetz 1969) increased the involvement of firms and public employment offices in continuing training. This led to the creation of many additional opportunities to participate in courses.

Age-specific education ratios of men and women reveal pronounced gender differences. Although participation rates increase both for women and men over consecutive cohorts, there remain differences in the level of participation at several stages over the life course. Only 1 per cent of women at age 25 in the cohort 1929–31 participated in continuing training. For the 1939–41 cohort, this ratio increased to 6 per cent and for the 1949–51 cohort to 12 per cent. For men at the same age in the 1929–31 cohort, there is already a participation ratio of 12 per cent which increases to 14 and 27 per cent for subsequent cohorts.

Across cohorts, there are remarkable gender-specific changes. For example, 2 per cent of women in the 1929–31 cohort who were 18 years old participated in continuing training while the ratio of the 18-year-old men in the same cohort is much higher (7 per cent). However, the following cohorts of young women are more likely than young men to participate. For 18-year-old women in the 1939–41 cohort, the degree of participation was

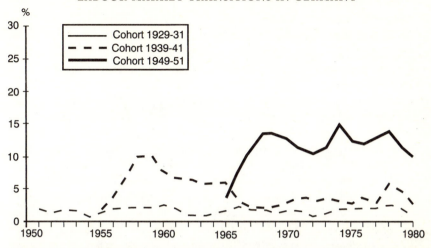

Figure 7.3 Participation rates of women in further education and training 1929–31, 1939–41 and 1949–51

about 10 per cent, similar to that of men. The ratio has increased to 13 per cent for women in the 1949–51 cohort, and has decreased to 8 per cent for men in the same cohort. These differences could be explained by structural change in the labour market (e.g. post-war conditions, technological change, or changes in female labour force participation rates and patterns) as well as by different educational and occupational histories of women and men which result in differences in subsequent occupational opportunities and earnings trajectories (Schömann 1994). In spite of the gain in participation in employment and education, women still participate less overall in continuing training than men.

Results based on Hazard Rate Models suggest that firms are more likely to offer participation in further education courses to employees who stayed with the firm for a longer period. Employees with a proven record of 'attachment to the firm' are considered to be less likely to leave the firm for another employer once they have participated, hence reducing the risk of the poaching of a firm's investment. The firm might also be offering successful participants on a training course faster internal career advancement or higher wage growth (Becker 1991; Schömann and Becker 1995). Following the signalling theory, the selection of a 'loyal' employee for a training course is to be understood as the signalling of the employer that the successful participant is very likely to be considered in case of job openings demanding a higher qualification level or a more productive workplace. Employees with longer periods of employment with the same employer are at the same time very likely to be employees working in primary segment jobs.

Jobs that can be classified as located in internal labour markets (highly skilled jobs in large firms) show the expected positive and significant effects of increased participation in further education and training. Those employees in skilled jobs in large firms are more likely to receive some form of training, which may be provided either internally or externally. It is within the firm-specific labour market segment that further education seems to play an important role in assuring both employees and employers of their long-term commitment to this work relationship. Participation in further education ensures for the firm high productivity levels from its employees, as well as career advancement for employees in highly regulated internal careers. Further education until the mid-1980s operated to confirm existing lines of labour market segmentation rather than making borders between labour market segments more transparent or enhancing their permeability.

In the late 1960s and early 1970s there was a period of broad consensus on the benefits of an increase in educational levels and the promotion of equal opportunity in West Germany. The Labour Promotion Act of 1969 reflects this consensus and offered substantial state assistance to employees with educational aspirations. To measure the influence of this law a period dummy variable was introduced. The results show a strong positive effect on participation in continuing training between 1969 and 1974.

Financial cuts to these state subsidised programmes from 1975 limited this expansion in continuing training (Sauter *et al.* 1984). Only twenty years later with the reunification of Germany can a comparable situation be found in the new federal states of Eastern Germany. The severe economic recession in 1993 and cuts to the training programmes in East Germany mean that despite greater needs for continuing training, measures to introduce it have had a shorter and less pervasive effect than during the period 1969–74 in West Germany.

Younger cohorts of women have benefited the most from this expansion when compared to older cohorts of women and their male counterparts of the same birth cohort. The size of the coefficient measuring the effect of education on participation in continuing training is almost double the size of the one estimated for men. This indicates that the education accumulation hypothesis is even more pronounced among women. As Schömann *et al.* (1991) and Schömann (1994) have shown, inequality in returns to education has been more pronounced among women than between men.

Following earlier results on women's wage profiles it is not surprising that at the individual level earnings, work experience and duration of employment with the current employer show no statistically significant effects on participation for the three cohorts of women, but labour market segments do. Women with jobs in an internal labour market have significantly higher participation in continuing training. Similarly, though to a lesser extent, women in the occupation-specific segment also have more possibilities for continuing training than those in open segments, in small or large firms. In particular, the public sector offers opportunities for women to train, retrain or improve their skills.

Strangely, the 'golden period' of the Labour Promotion Act has had less significance for women than for men. Despite the simultaneous pressure from the women's movement there was no significant increase in the participation of women in training courses within or outside the firm. The fact that it has largely bypassed women calls for decisive revisions of the guidelines for programme participation.

During the post-war period participation in continuing training has increased differences in educational attainment of employees rather than narrowed the gap between the highly educated and those with no or few educational credentials. The much-hoped-for equalising effect of increased access to continuing training has not prevented a further polarisation of educational qualifications over the life course.

Despite the negative effect of the duration of general work experience on participation, the longer the duration of employment with the same employer the greater the probability of participation in continuing training. This result corresponds to the findings by Groot *et al.* (1990: 8), where work experience prior to the current job had no effect on on-the-job training, but tenure within the firm showed a U-shaped pattern for the probability of participating in training. Similarly, our results suggest that firms are more likely to offer participation in further education courses to male employees who stayed with the firm for a longer period.

Following the interpretation of the effects of general education on the probability of participating in further education by Tuijnman (1989), Lynch (1992) and Groot *et al.* (1990), our evidence supports the view that in West Germany schooling and off-the-job training complement each other rather than serve as alternatives, as is the case for the Netherlands (Groot *et al.* 1990: 7). This is due to the dual system, which incorporates firm-based training into its general education system at an early stage.

Participation in continuing training, and the careers and earnings trajectories to which it leads, are determined to a large extent by cohort-specific effects, period effects, and labour force experience or seniority within the firm. Whereas young and better qualified birth cohorts had easier access to continuing training, older employees seem to be unwilling to participate, or are no longer selected for training courses. Our analysis highlights the necessity of disentangling cohort, period and age effects in analyses of components of occupational careers. The accumulation of education and gender-specific patterns of participation in continuing training allows us to conclude that it can increase inequality. Emphasis should be placed on the participation of women in training programmes in order to avoid the discriminatory practices which have dominated in West Germany between 1950 and 1983.

INTERNATIONAL COMPARISONS AND CONCLUSIONS

The theoretical perspective of labour market segmentation and data collection in several European countries have allowed labour market entry and its impact on wages to be analysed. Labour market segmentation was evident at first entry into the labour market in Poland in the middle of the 1970s (Schömann 1994). Labour market segmentation similar to that in West Germany is evolving in the transformation process in East Germany (Schömann and Kruppe 1993). Labour market segments offering higher wages also provide more job security and frequently better upward career mobility within firms through continuing training opportunities.

The comparison of fixed-term employment as a means of facilitating the transition from school to work across European countries has highlighted the need to study transition processes from a historical perspective. This means labour market institutions like the German apprenticeship system are understood only if they are judged against the context of the whole education system and labour market institutions which determine the 'opportunity costs' of enrolling into an apprenticeship. Insertion through fixed-term contracts has to be measured against the wider context of the system of employment protection, unfair dismissal legislation and collective agreements determining notice periods for dismissals in one country before meaningful comparisons of 'country models' of transitions from school to work can be made.

The aim of country comparisons should not be to abstract historical and institutional specificities. Rather they should take them into account in elucidating the social and economic conditions which enable or impede the adoption of models of the transition from school to work from other countries.

This chapter has attempted to provide a picture of the background conditions of transition processes and their dynamics in Germany. Therefore we conclude with a number of propositions concerning the factors behind the functioning of the labour market. Our analyses show evidence for the presence of labour market segmentation between major industrial sectors. Education policies which enhance the development of professional labour markets, such as the continuing training policies of the Labour Promotion Act (AFG) until 1975, have contributed to the maintenance of labour market segmentation rather than facilitating transitions between the segments. Employment policies, like the attempt to promote the use of fixed-term contracts, have strengthened the barriers between labour market segments with high earnings and employment security and those with low wages and precarious employment.

The importance of macroeconomic cycles for the integration of young people into the labour market has been demonstrated. Whereas wages at first entry into employment are little affected by these influences, the probability of finding a job has been adversely affected by low or stagnating labour demand. Marginal changes or adjustments of employment and training policies do not have the same ability to facilitate the insertion into the labour market as an employment-intensive economic recovery. Since economic downturns are frequently accompanied by cuts in public-sector expenditure, its high absorption rate of qualified labour market entrants is also reduced during periods of recessions. Neo-Keynesian economic policies which aim to create jobs should be complemented by employment policies that promote reliable bridges into employment or a redistribution of hours of work.

The successful completion of full-time education has become a necessary condition for a smooth and rapid transition from school to work but it is no longer sufficient to guarantee the success of this transition. With the increase in educational credentials in most European societies, labour market entry has become a more difficult transition. Selection into school or university has been replaced by a filtering process by firms of candidates whom they consider more suited to their objectives. For initial training through apprenticeships or continuing training through in-company courses, the common input provided by a high standard of general education is still at the core of the transition process in every society and provides its own dynamic for these transition processes.

NOTES

1 For a more detailed description of the design of the SOEP as a household survey compare Hanefeld (1987) and the Projektgruppe Panel (1990).
2 The samples of the GLHS are described in Mayer and Brückner (1989). In addition to the birth cohorts of 1929–39, 1939–41 and 1949–51, older and younger cohorts have been surveyed and an East German survey was conducted in 1991.
3 Continuing training is defined as the totality of general and vocational courses which are followed by people who have completed their training and have entered the labour market. This excludes courses of general interest and leisure courses.

BIBLIOGRAPHY

Alba-Ramírez, A. (1991) 'Fixed-Term Employment Contracts in Spain: Labor Market Flexibility or Segmentation?', unpublished manuscript, Universidad Carlos III de Madrid.
Allmendinger, J. and Brückner, H. (1992) 'The production of gender disparities over the life course and their effects in old age. Results from the German Life History Study', in A. B. Atkinson and M. Rein (eds) *Age, Work, and Social Security*, London: Macmillan.
Arrow, K. J. (1973) 'Higher education as a filter', *Journal of Public Economics* 2: 193–216.
Bartel, A. P. (1980) 'Earnings growth on the job and between jobs', *Economic Inquiry* 18: 65–84.

Becker, R. (1991) 'Berufliche Weiterbildung und Berufsverlauf. Eine Längsschnittuntersuchung von drei Geburtskohorten', *Mitteilungen aus der Arbeitsmarkt- und Berufsforschung* 24: 351–64.

Blossfeld, H.-P. and Mayer, K. U. (1989) 'Labor market segmentation in the Federal Republic of Germany: an empirical study of segmentation theories from a life course perspective', *European Sociological Review* 4: 123–40.

Carroll, G. and Mayer K. U. (1986) 'Job-shift patterns in the FRG: the effects of social class, industrial sector, and organisational size', *American Sociological Review* 51: 323–41.

Courgeau, D. (1991) 'Analyse des données biographiques erronées', *Population* 46: 89–104.

Doeringer, P. B. and Piore, M. J. (1971) *Internal Labor Markets and Manpower Analysis*, Lexington, MA: Heath & Co.

Groot, W., Hartog J. and Oosterbeck, H. (1990) 'Training Choice and Earnings', *Research Memorandum 9027*, Universiteit van Amsterdam.

Hanefeld, U. (1987) *Das sozioökonomische Panel Grundlagen und Konzeption*, Frankfurt/New York: Campus.

Hannan, M. T., Schömann, K. and Blossfeld, H.-P. (1990) 'Sex and sector differences in the dynamics of wage growth in the FRG', *American Sociological Review* 55: 694–713.

Helberger, C. (1983) 'Humankapital, Berufsbiographie, und die Einkommen von Männern und Frauen', *Sonderforschungsbereich 3 Arbeitspapier* 129, Frankfurt/ Mannheim.

Huinink, J., Mayer, K. U. and Diewald, Martin (1995) *Kollektiv und Eigensinn. Lebenserläufe in der DDR und danach*, Berlin: Akademie Verlag.

Lutz, B. and Sengenberger, W. (1974) *Arbeitsmarktstrukturen und öffentliche Arbeitspolitik*, Göttingen: Schwartz.

Lynch, L. M. (1992) 'Private sector training and the earnings of young workers', *American Economic Review* 82: 299–312.

Malcomson, J. (1984) 'Work incentives, hierarchy and internal labor markets', *Journal of Political Economy* 92: 486–507.

Mayer, K. U. and Brückner, E. (1989) *Lebensverläufe und Wohlfahrtsentwicklung. Materialien aus der Bildungsforschung*, Discussion Paper 35, Berlin: Max-Planck Institut für Bildungsforschung.

Müller, W., Willms, A. and Handl, J. (1983) *Strukturwandel der Frauenarbeit 1880–1980*, Frankfurt: Campus.

Pischner, R. and Wagner, G. (1991) 'Zwei Aspekte der Flexibilität beim Übergang vom Erwerbsleben in den Ruhestand', in R. Hujer (ed.) *Herausforderungen an den Wohlfahrtsstaat im strukturellen Wandel*, Frankfurt/New York: Campus.

Projektgruppe Panel (1990) 'Das sozio-ökonomische Panel für die Bundesrepublik Deutschland nach fünf Wellen', in *Vierteljahresschrift zur Wirtschaftsforschung* (2/3).

Sauter, E. *et al.* (1984) 'Berufliche Weiterbildung und Arbeitslosigkei', *Bundesinstitut für Berufsbildung, Materialien und statistische Analysen zur beruflichen Bildung* 47.

Schmid, G. (1993) 'Übergänge in die Vollbeschäftigung. Formen und Finanzierung einer zukunftsgerechten Arbeitsmarktpolitik', *WZB Discussion Paper*, FSI 93–208.

Schömann, K. (1994) 'The dynamics of labor earnings over the life course – a comparative and longitudinal analysis of Germany and Poland', *Studien und Berichte* 61, Berlin: Max-Planck Institute for Human Development and Education, Edition Sigma.

Schömann, K. and Becker, R. (1995) 'Participation in further education over the life course – a longitudinal study of three birth cohorts in the FRG', *European Sociological Review* 11 (2): 187–208.

Schömann, K., Hannan, M. T. and Blossfeld, H.-P. (1991) 'Die Bedeutung von Bildung und Arbeitsmarktsegmenten für die Arbeitseinkommen von Frauen und Männern', in K. U. Mayer, J. Allmendinger and J. Huinink (eds) *Vom Regen in die Traufe – Frauen zwischen Beruf und Familie*, Frankfurt/New York: Campus.

Schömann, K. and Kruppe, T. (1993) 'Fixed term employment and labour market flexibility, theory and longitudinal evidence for East and West Germany', *WZB Discussion Paper*, FSI 93–204.

Schwarze, J. (1991) 'Ausbildung und Einksommen von Männern – Einkommensfunktionsschättzungen für die ehemalige DDR und die Bundesrpublik Deutschland', *Mitteilungen aus der Arbeitsmarkt und Berufsforschung* (MittAB) 1: 63–8.

Stinchcombe, A. S. (1979) 'Social mobility and the industrial labor process', *Acta Sociologica* 22: 217–45.

Tuijman, A. (1989) *Recurrent Education, Earnings and Well-Being. A Fifty-Year Longitudinal Study of a Cohort of Swedish Men*, Stockholm: Almqvist and Wiksell.

Vissers, A. and Dirven, H. J. (1994) 'Fixed-term contracts in the Netherlands: some evidence from panel data', *WZB Discussion Paper*, FSI 94–212.

8

INSTITUTIONS AND THE MARKET

The basis of relations between education and work in Great Britain

Lucie Tanguy and Helen Rainbird

INTRODUCTION

In Britain, the relationship between education and training on the one hand and the organisation of work and employment on the other constitutes a lively field of research questions, but it is not one which is well integrated. In this, Britain hardly differs from the other European countries. It does differ, however, by the way in which research questions are posed in relation to the social issues from which they arise and the answers to them. The intensity of changes in political and social configurations over the last two decades has given rise to the concept of a rupture, which is still debated (see, for example, *Work, Employment and Society* special issue, 1990; Gallie 1988).

INDUSTRIAL DECLINE AND EMPLOYMENT RESTRUCTURING

Among these changes, first and foremost are those affecting the system of employment, work organisation and industrial relations. The decline of manufacturing employment has been particularly marked: there were only 5,432,000 employees in 1990 as opposed to 8,514,000 in 1970 and it now accounts for only 20.5 per cent of employment as opposed to 34 per cent twenty years earlier. The share of employment in services reached 66.5 per cent in 1991, compared to 64 per cent in France and 52 per cent in Germany. These shifts in employment have been accompanied by changes in the occupational structure. Between 1971 and 1991 the proportion of skilled manual jobs declined from 19 per cent to 15.5 per cent and unskilled manual jobs from 14.5 per cent to 10 per cent of the workforce. In contrast, the growth of service activities has increased the proportion of managerial and administrative grades from 11 per cent to 14 per cent, professional occupations from 6.5 per cent to 10 per cent and associate professional and technical occupations from 6 per cent to 8 per cent over the same period.

At least as significant has been the growth in part-time work, which rose from 18.6 per cent in 1980 to 23.4 per cent in 1992. It is found particularly in the distribution sector (35.7 per cent), services (37.5 per cent), health and education (45 per cent). Part-time jobs accounted for the whole of the 1.2 million growth in employment between 1980 and 1990 (Institute for Employment Research 1991). The growth of part-time work has mainly been amongst women, whose labour force participation has steadily increased.

Another major change in Britain has been the development of self-employment. The rise of this form of employment, representing 12.5 per cent of the workforce in 1992, was encouraged by government policies (for example, the Enterprise Allowance Scheme) and is characterised by the replacement of the employment contract by a contract for services. Many of the self-employed are found in the construction sector where they represent 40 per cent of the workforce. Here, the practice of labour-only sub-contracting on a self-employed basis represents a form of casual labour.

After a decrease in the first half of the 1980s, the unemployment rate is at the same level as it was at the beginning of this decade. It is to be noted that the unemployment rate among women is lower than that among men, respectively 9.2 per cent and 12 per cent in 1992 (Eurostat 1993). This feature, which distinguishes Britain from the other European countries, shows the unequal position of men and women *vis-à-vis* part-time work. This kind of employment represented 43 per cent of women in employment in 1990 as against 5 per cent of male employment for the same year. This category includes contracts for a range of hours, some of which fall outside the employment protection provisions. There are also discrepancies in enti-tlement to employment benefit which mean that married women do not always appear in the unemployment statistics. Overall 38 per cent of women receive unemployment benefits as against 76 per cent of men whereas only 28 per cent of married women receive it as against 77 per cent of married men (Labour Force Survey 1993). These are just some of the indicators of women's disadvantage in the labour market.

Labour market participation also varies by age. The unemployment rate among people under 25 is almost twice that of people over 25, respectively 15.9 per cent and 7.9 per cent for men and 11.4 per cent and 6.3 per cent for women in 1991. This measure of age discrimination accounts for only one aspect of the situation of young people since many do not appear in the unemployment statistics because they are part-time trainees under the provi-sions of Youth Training (YT). Thus comparison of unemployment rates between young people and adults in Britain and France for example (where unemployment rates among under-25-year-olds are 17 per cent for men and 22.6 per cent for women as against 5.9 per cent and 9.9 per cent for adults) demonstrates discrepancies.

Comparing the social position of young people of a given age-group within different societies therefore requires examining the connections between at least three conditions: schooling (in its various forms), economic activity (concerning status as an employee, apprentice or trainee) and unemployment. In Britain, as elsewhere in Europe, young people without qualifications are particularly hit by unemployment (Table 8.1). In contrast, those with good GCSE qualifications exhibit unemployment rates similar to and sometimes lower than those with a higher-level qualification (GCE, 'A' level, BTEC, City and Guilds).[1]

In Britain, unemployment, and especially long-term unemployment, is found essentially among manual workers. Higher and intermediate professions are less exposed to it, apart from women. By 1990, 79 per cent of the unemployed were skilled or unskilled workers, the others being in higher and intermediate professions. The former represent 54 per cent of the male population and the latter groups 45 per cent (White 1993).[2] The forms of unemployment are related to the social organisation of the labour market, which is often perceived as resistant to change. The strength of labour market divisions in this country can be seen in the expression 'workers have a trade, in contrast white-collar workers have a career', an observation that does not apply to women.

The economic changes outlined above have altered the forms of social stratification and the model of industrial relations, but to what extent can this be considered as a rupture? The system of industrial relations has been characterised by the significance of the workplace as opposed to sectoral-level negotiation, as in Italy, France and Germany, and the state has taken a weak role historically in the regulation of the employment relationship. The system is therefore built on customs, practices and unwritten terms which

Table 8.1 Unemployment rates by age and highest qualification in 1990 (Thousands of unemployed)

	16-19 years	20-24 years	25-34 years	16-59/64 years
Degree or			25	63
equivalent			2.8%	2.4%
Higher education			11	46
below degree level			2.2%	2.7%
GCE 'A' level or	46	75	104	383
equivalent	10.6%	6.3%	5.0%	5.2%
GCE '0' level or	71	63	94	292
equivalent	7.2%	6.6%	6.5%	5.7%
CSE (below grade 1)	24	42	45	137
	13.2%	11.1%	8.7%	7.2%
Other qualifications		19	24	137
		18.1%	8.3%	7.2%
No qualifications	99	104	193	774
	20.5%	20.1%	15.1%	10.9%
Total	250	325	501	1,835
	11.5%	9.1%	7.1%	6.7%

Source: Employment Gazette, March 1992. The age limit of economic activity is 59 years for women and 64 years for men. (The blanks represent fewer than 10,000 observations.)

have certain similarities from one place to another. This model has been weakened by the loss of influence of the unions in the 1980s. This has been due more to the closure of industrial establishments, where unionisation was strong, than to a loss of confidence of workers in the unions (Gallie 1988). In contrast to other European countries, they negotiate directly with the managers of their companies rather than through the intermediary of higher level organisations. The level of the workplace is significant not only as a site for collective bargaining but also for apprenticeship and training. Apprentices in manufacturing have normally had the status of employees and notions of skill have been tied to the exercise of job controls and demarcations at this level.

In this context, Industrial Relations has been established as a separate discipline within the Social Sciences. This research, often based on case studies, also draws on large-scale surveys. The Workplace Industrial Relations Surveys (WIRS) show the weakening of collective bargaining as an institution, the decline of 'closed shop' (which has been illegal since 1982) and the development of legal procedures in industrial disputes (Millward *et al*. 1992). These studies emphasise the persistence of shop-floor organisation and the role of trade unions (although appreciations differ according to authors, see for example Gallie 1988; Edwards *et al*. 1992).

Economic decline and the weak competitiveness of the economy have been linked to low levels of investment in vocational training in the policy debate. Historically, many young people have entered the labour market without obtaining formal educational qualifications. A number of reports and studies have emphasised the significance of low levels of qualification, for example *Competence and Competition* (NEDO/MSC 1984) and *Towards a Skills Revolution* (Confederation of British Industry 1989). Many of these reports refer to the strengths of the German training system and identify British employers' reluctance to invest in transferable skills where the returns to this investment are uncertain. In a model which integrates economic characteristics, patterns of work organisation and product market strategies, Finegold and Soskice have represented the British economy as based on a 'low skill equilibrium' (1988).

Recent training interventions by the Conservative government have been based on the notion of rational individuals, making decisions in a market. This is exemplified in Training Credits, a scheme whereby young people could make decisions on the basis of an entitlement to training. In order to give greater responsibility to employers for training, Training and Enterprise Councils have been set up at local level since 1988. These have replaced statutory forms of intervention. Their role is not the regulation of training as such, but rather the allocation of funding according to the outputs of training, in the form of National Vocational Qualifications. The focus on outputs is based on the notion that different institutions constitute a variety of forms of supply of qualifications, whose value can be measured on the market (Raffe 1992b). The following sections examine some of the radical changes which have taken place in education and training institutions in the last twenty years.

EDUCATIONAL POLICY AND PRACTICE

If it can be argued that the place of the school as an institution in society can be understood in terms of participation beyond the age of compulsory schooling, which all industrialised societies have fixed as the level socially necessary for each citizen, then school occupies a weaker place in Britain than it does in France. The expression 'participation in education' therefore cannot be translated as an equivalent to the French term *scolarisation*. Moreover, education beyond the age of compulsory schooling takes place in a range of different institutions (Figure 8.1). Indeed, the same qualifications, for example GCSE and GCE 'A' level, can be studied in Further Education Colleges and secondary schools. The Further Education Colleges in Great Britain are attended by young people and adults, who may be waged, unwaged or unemployed. The majority study for vocational qualifications, but others may study for academic qualifications. These courses are differentiated into non-advanced further education (below 'A' level standard) and advanced further education, which is considered as a form of higher education. These colleges provide various modes of study: full-time (20.5 per cent of the people registered in 1990–1), part-time day (39 per cent) and evening-classes (40.3 per cent). Out of the 1,964,000 students enrolled in Further Education Colleges in 1990–1, an unidentified number attend socio-cultural or personal development activities such as pottery, drawing and cooking.[3] A course may include people in search of promotion through vocational training and people who attend it as a personal goal. These colleges have had an important role for the expansion of education and training in the working class and in improving the qualifications of employed adults (Gleeson 1989). Their heterogeneity reflects the complexity of the British educational system.

The diversity of institutions and forms of education contrasts with the standardisation and integration of the school system in France. This diversity derives from the historical role of the local education authorities in the provision of education. In contrast to the state monopoly over qualifications in France, in Great Britain there are more than fifty organisations which award them.

The categories and nomenclatures used to describe educational phenomena are significant in this respect. They emphasise the significance of time as a unit for categorising and measuring different forms of education. The first distinction in the statistics is between full-time and part-time education. The latter has ceased to be used in France with the extension of full-time schooling beyond the compulsory minimum (although this is

116

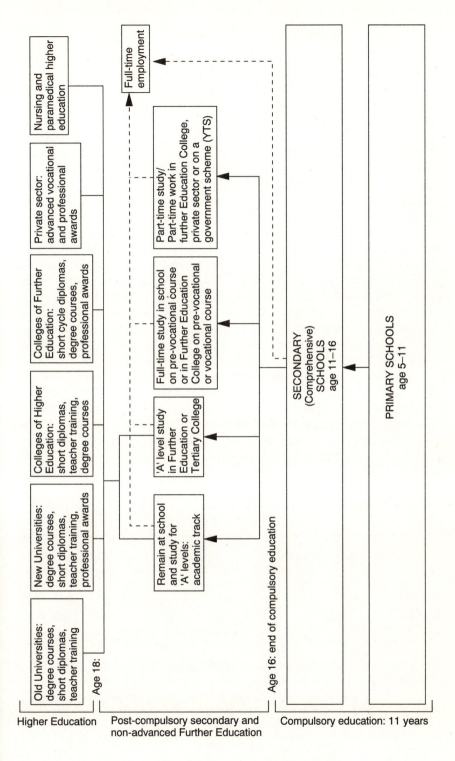

Figure 8.1 The education system in Great Britain

being modified with the development of work placements as part of educational courses).

The relatively weak development of educational participation post-16 shown in Table 8.2 has its origins in a number of factors. Amongst these are school's weak attraction for – and even rejection by – working-class families, deriving from economic factors (the anticipated costs and benefits) and cultural values. Vocational studies have low status and apprenticeship has constituted the main route into skilled manual work. The range of jobs and high relative rates of youth pay which, until recently, have been available to young people entering the labour market, have discouraged them from remaining in education (see Marsden's chapter in this book). Moreover, the specialisation of the school curriculum post-16 and the role of 'A' levels in providing access to higher education means that the broadening of curriculum is debated (see, for example, Finegold *et al*. 1990). Raffe (in this volume) stresses that age is the main factor structuring the education system: there is no system of 'redoublement' (repeating unsuccessful years of study). Indeed, the traditional age limitations on apprenticeship, the existence of guarantees and entitlements in terms of age,[4] have had the result that policy debates are also conducted in terms of age, notably for the 16–18 age group.

Because of the economic and occupational transformations mentioned earlier, there have been rapid changes in education and training. Between 1987 and 1991, participation in full-time education among 17-year-olds in England and Wales rose from 41 per cent to 58 per cent, increasing by 17 per cent in four years (*Employment Gazette*, July, 1993), showing a rapid change in attitudes towards education in a context where there is a declining demand for young people in the labour market.[5]

Table 8.2 Participation in full-time education and youth training, by age: UK January 1990 (percentage)

Age	16 year olds			17 year olds			18-year olds		
Sex	F	M	Total	F	M	Total	F	M	Total
School	37	33	35	24	22	23	2	3	3
Other forms of full-time education	21	14	17	18	13	15	20	18	19
All full-time education	58	48	52	42	35	38	22	21	22
YTS/YT	18	28	23	16	25	20	1	2	2
Others	24	25	24	43	40	41	77	76	77
Total	100	101	99	101	100	99	100	99	101

Source: Raffe (1992a).
Amongst the 19% of those studying full-time at the age of 18, about half are in higher education and half in further education.

The intensity of these changes is higher in England where the full-time education rate among 17-year-olds rose from 33 per cent to 49 per cent between 1987–8 and 1991–2 and that of 18-year-olds rose from 18 per cent to 28 per cent during the same period. Lastly, the share of general education ('A'/'AS' level) has increased over the last decade: only 20.8 per cent of 18-year-olds were in this kind of education in 1979–80 and 34.9 per cent in 1991–2. These percentages reach 18.7 per cent and 31.4 per cent respectively among 17-year-olds. Technical or vocational studies leading to a qualification issued by BTEC (Business and Technician Education Council) rose slowly, concerning 8.9 per cent of 16-year-olds and 8.1 per cent of 17-year-olds in 1991–2.

Yet, aggregate indicators conceal the division of the educational system into separate pathways and its high social selectivity. The distribution of 16- to 17-year-olds between education, employment and unemployment or Youth Training (YT) according to social categories is very evocative. The children of professionals are twice as likely to be in education as those of unskilled workers, as shown in Table 8.3. Employment and unemployment rates also show major differences between workers' children, service and sales personnel's children on the one hand and professionals' children on the other.

In Britain, education, training and employment are not as dissociated as they are in France. Young people may study, even on a full-time basis while holding a part-time job. In 1993, out of 913,000 16- to 17-year-olds 32.1 per cent had a job and 8 per cent declared they were looking for one. Out of

Table 8.3 Activity at 16–17 by characteristics and experience in England and Wales

Parents' Social Occupation Class (SOC)	Full-time Education	Full-time Job	YT	Unemployed	Others	Weighted Base
Professionals	86	6	6	2	1	1,361
Associate prof./tech.	76	12	7	3	2	904
Clerical and secretarial	66	16	11	4	3	780
Craft and related	51	21	19	7	3	3,114
Personal and protective services	56	21	13	9	2	857
Sales	57	20	14	7	2	617
Plant/machine operatives	41	25	21	10	3	1,641
Total	58	18	14	7	3	14,511
Boys	53	22	16	7	2	7,410
Girls	64	14	13	6	4	7,101

Source: Youth cohort studies, England and Wales, 1991 (weighted base 14, 151 16-year-olds on 31 August 1990), data communicated by David Raffe

119

387,000 young people of the same age-group attending part-time education, 284,000 (73 per cent) had a job and 75,000 declared they were looking for one (*Employment Gazette*, July 1993). Most of the former worked in distribution, hotels and restaurants, and half had sales positions. Most worked between 5 and 10 hours weekly, 28 per cent between 10 and 20 hours. Those attending part-time education worked in the same sectors but also in industry, as manual workers, and in administrative, service and sales occupations. Among them, 85 per cent worked over 30 hours weekly. Thus, they are closer to the situation of wage-earners than that of a pupil or student.

Higher education has been more élitist in Britain than in other European countries although participation has increased rapidly in recent years. In 1991 23 per cent of 18- to 21-year-olds attended university compared to 13 per cent in 1981 and 12 per cent of 21- to 24-year-olds compared to 7.5 per cent. The British higher education system provides students with the greatest opportunities to complete their studies since the rate of achievement varies between 98.5 per cent (University of Cambridge) and 91 per cent (Universities of Lancaster and Leicester). Higher education is not as debated nor as researched as education and training for 16- to 18-year-olds, who have constituted the main age-group for policies.

A whole range of reforms characterises the 1980s. These are expressed in the 1988 Education Reform Act, often viewed as a break with the 1944 Butler Education Act, which created a certain consensus over the educational system until the 1970s (Lawton 1992). The ERA reduced local authorities' influence over schools in favour of a degree of centralisation characterised by the initiation of a national curriculum, and the monitoring of students' attainment through national tests.

Attempts have been made to change the orientation of prevailing cultural models in schools through the introduction of technological and vocational education in curricula through the Technical and Vocational Education Initiative, introduced in 1983. This programme included a set of initiatives meant to give 14- to 18-year-olds work experience and to create close co-operation between education and industry. The changes thus initiated were analysed in terms of the development of the 'new vocationalism', a term which indicates the strength and scope of the attempted changes (Gleeson 1987).

The Education Reform Act gives parents greater power of intervention in school and grants schools more power regarding management of the funds they obtain directly from the State instead of the local education authority, and in the recruitment of pupils, teachers and head teachers. It has been analysed as a shift in school status and criticised because it has been elaborated in a market-led perspective (Lawton 1992). Thus increasing state intervention has been directed towards funding, management modes and outputs of educational institutions and not to the status and form of institutions since these are not considered to affect the quality of education.

Politicians argue that countries such as the United States, Japan, Germany and France succeed with very different educational systems. In short, the educational policies of the 1980s, strongly influenced by the search for economic efficiency, rest on the presupposition of a demand for competences in the labour market and on the resulting need to organise a flexible educational system. In recent years, these policies have sought to change the separation between general education and technical and vocational education by instituting a new qualification, the General National Vocational Qualification, equivalent to 'A' levels, that would allow access to university (National Commission on Education 1993). The scope, swiftness and strength of implementation of the changes initiated in the 1980s made some researchers assert that there was a new educational order, which they regarded as 'post-Fordist' (Ball 1990).

FROM APPRENTICESHIP TO THE YTS

If there is an acknowledgement of the need for reform regarding the definition of curricula, certification and, more generally, the need for 16- to 18-year-olds to receive training, there is controversy as to the location in which it should be conducted: educational institutions, apprenticeships or other arrangements. While the educational system has undergone major reorganisation, apprenticeship, the primary method of training for workers and technicians, has been undermined by the twofold pressure of industrial recession and political changes. Apprenticeship declined sharply in the 1970s. The number of apprentices decreased from 218,000 in 1970 to 147,600 in 1981, and continued to decline until 1990, reaching 53,600. The decline of apprenticeship has outstripped the decline in manufacturing jobs. Although it constituted a relatively high-status route into skilled manual work, it has never had the formalisation nor the generalisation of the German dual system. Outside manufacturing, it took an uneven form in the service sector, and was only found in the banks, the post office and telecommunications, and in hairdressing. In 1980, 37 per cent of boys and 8 per cent of girls aged 16 left school to enter craft apprenticeship and about 14 per cent of other leavers of the same age-group attended another kind of training in the company along with their first job (Keep and Mayhew forthcoming). If some kinds of control of knowledge and skills have been instituted by examining bodies they have never been an obligation or a norm. Time has been the primary social measure for acknowledging skilled workers' training through apprenticeship. Numbers of apprentices were controlled by agreements between unions and employers on the ratio of apprentices to skilled adult workers. High youth wages relative to those of adult workers constituted a form of restricting entry into skilled jobs, but did not specify the quality of training.

Apprenticeship was funded primarily by employers and the volume of training tended to fluctuate with recruitment, which varied according to the economic cycle. By the 1960s, this fluctuation, along with the problem of the 'poaching' of trained labour by employers who did not themselves invest in training, was seen as prejudicial to the economy. The 1964 Industrial Training Act made provisions for a more equitable distribution of the costs of training through the introduction of a statutory levy on wage costs. This was administered by sectoral training boards, organised on a tripartite basis which could, in turn, redistribute grants for training programmes achieving the required standards. Although they were not set up solely to support apprenticeship training, in practice this was often the main form of training supported. The sectoral-level powers of the boards were gradually eroded as the levy mechanism was weakened and direct state financing increased through legislation passed in 1974. This also set up a national labour market body, the Manpower Services Commission, which had a co-ordinating function. As youth employment rose in the 1970s and early 1980s, policy shifted from promoting counter-cyclical measures which maintained the volume of apprenticeship training, to schemes aimed at providing young people with training and work experience. The Youth Training Scheme, set up in 1983, was directed at employed and unemployed school-leavers aged 16 and, later, 17 as well. It provided trainees with a weekly allowance along with training and job placements in sectors and occupations where previously no structured training had existed. Table 8.4 shows the evolution of participation in Youth Training Schemes between 1983 and 1990. In the 1990s, declining job opportunities and the poor reputation of many of these schemes have contributed to the reinvention of 'modern apprenticeships' which are administered by the Training and Enterprise Councils (locally based, private-sector and employer-dominated bodies).

The unclear and changing terminology used to refer to training must be emphasised: for example, vocational training, work-based education, work-related learning. All these terms refer to a relatively undefined reality apart from the prevalence of work experience. The term 'apprenticeship' is not distinguished any more from the others in official statistics; 'training' does

Table 8.4 Percentage of young people on Youth Training Schemes

Age	16-year-olds		17-year-olds	
Sex	Boys	Girls	Boys	Girls
1983	92,000	78,000	35,000	30,000
	20%	18%	7%	7%
1986	136,000	97,000	20,000	18,000
	31%	23%	4%	4%
1990	104,000	66,000	114,000	61,000
	27%	28%	28%	16%

Source: Employment Gazette, data communicated by David Raffe, 1992.

not refer to a well-circumscribed activity whose boundaries with work are explicit.

The kinds of training young people are provided within the YTS (it was renamed Youth Training, then became Youth Credits) are much criticised and characterised as modes of socialisation in the workplace rather than modes of acquisition of knowledge and skills. The diversity and instability of these training schemes and their low social effectiveness in relation to their stated objectives gave way to state interventions giving more power to employers in relation to Youth Training.

Thus the criteria of certification and validation of achievements instituted in the system of certification of vocational competences (through the National Council of Vocational Qualifications) derive essentially from employers, and are often assessed by supervisors in the workplace rather than an external assessor. This competence-based approach is being applied to all vocational qualifications and is also greatly debated.

To conclude, similar developments can be identified in the general education system and in vocational training whereby national regulatory frameworks have been introduced, based primarily on certification. However, this mode of state intervention allows local scope for initiative in the organisation and in the definition of contents, that is to say, to employers in relation to training and to schools in relation to education. It therefore privileges a form of unification in terms of procedures of certification and allows strong divisions to remain in the institutional forms leading to university study, on the one hand, and the measures directed towards the majority of young people who will enter manual work, on the other.

All these changes underlie the orientation of research. In terms of general tendencies, it could be said that economists interested in the debate on economic efficiency focus their research on training in intermediate skills (for example, Ryan (ed.) 1991). This designation excludes unskilled work, for which there is no training, at one extreme, and managers and professionals, at the other, who have higher levels of qualification (Steedman *et al.* 1991). Sociologists are more engaged in a tradition of analysis focused on inequality and social class; amongst them, a number pose questions about polarisation in the social hierarchy and the constitution of an underclass (for example, Giddens 1973). This thesis has been discussed and refuted by others, including Gallie (1988) and Willis (1986) who point out that groups experiencing new social conditions are eminently heterogeneous and cannot be considered, on this basis, to constitute a new sub-proletariat.

MULTIDISCIPLINARITY AND ENGAGEMENT: A GENERAL CHARACTERISTIC OF THE SOCIAL SCIENCES IN BRITAIN

The orientation taken by the social sciences is the result of a set of configurations arising from the intellectual traditions of the academic community and the structure of scientific and public institutions (Wagner 1989). Research on the relationship between education and work, with which we are concerned here, is distinguished by its multidisciplinarity. It is composed of different disciplines and the approaches which have been developed are not strongly bound to specific academic disciplines. In part, this reflects the fact that in Britain Sociology, where this field could be located, has never had the status it has enjoyed in France and Germany.

According to Lepenies, the relatively late recognition of Sociology as an academic discipline is due to the fact that sociological thought was adopted in philanthropy and administration at an early date as well as in literary criticism (1990). Cultural Studies have often been presented as the discipline which has most influenced intellectual debates in Britain and abroad. Hoggart's *The Uses of Literacy* (1990) and Williams' *Culture and Society 1780–1950* (1961) are eloquent illustrations of this. This tradition, taught notably at the Centre for Contemporary Cultural Studies at the University of Birmingham, has generated much research on youth – especially working-class youth – and has contributed to our understanding of young peoples' relationship to work, the family peer groups and leisure. Even if this work has been strongly criticised and modified by feminists, as Chisholm argues in Chapter 11, it has produced work such as Willis' *Learning to labour* (1977) and Jenkins' *Lads, Citizens and Ordinary Kids* (1983) which have been influential in Britain and abroad. As Lepenies argues (1990), each society elects a leading discipline in each stage of its history. In Britain, Economics remains the discipline that best represents this.

Halsey (1988) interprets the weak status of Sociology as being due to its rapid expansion in the 1960s and 1970s. Westergaard and Pahl (1988) stress academics' lack of confidence in this discipline, resulting from Marxist criticism, on the one hand, and from the development of ethnomethodology, on the other, both of which have influenced the erosion of its intellectual territory. The fracture between theoretical and empirical research is another characteristic of this discipline (Bulmer 1988) which has had the effect of thematic specialisation.

Multidisciplinarity and specialisation have been accentuated in recent years with pressures deriving from policy debates and with the methods and time-scale of research funding (which is mainly on a short-term basis). These are factors inducing research on circumscribed themes and which do not contribute to the development of analyses within theoretical frameworks which are necessary to the accumulation of a body of knowledge. A report on the financing of research in the Social Sciences shows that 37 per cent is funded by central government, of which three-quarters is devoted to 'strategic' and 'applied research' according to the categories defined by the Organisation for Economic Co-operation and Development (Loder 1992). Research conducted in universities is financed by the Economic and Social Research Council (ESRC) and charitable trusts and foundations. These two sources account for 29 per cent and 16 per cent of the costs of basic research in the Social Sciences respectively. To give an indication of this funding, Education receives about 25 per cent of the total and more than half the spending on applied research, which has been focused on the definition of the National Curriculum and the transition from school to work (Loder 1992). These financial indicators demonstrate the dependence of university research in Britain. The fracture between empirical and theoretical research is therefore located within an intellectual tradition and the politicisation of research. These are reinforced by the methods of funding which promote short-term projects of a descriptive or evaluative nature where the need for information prevails over the need for knowledge.

At the same time, researchers have attempted to provide themselves with the tools necessary to escape from the subordination of their activities in this environment. They have done this by setting up networks and seminar series (those financed by the ESRC have been some of the most fruitful).

New journals have also been created, in addition to the established ones based on disciplines, and have grown out of Sociology and Economics. Amongst these are the *British Journal of Education and Work*, set up in 1987, which brings together research on the transition from school to work, and *Work, Employment and Society,* set up in 1980 and published by the British Sociological Association. The latter defines its aims as serving as a forum for the discussion of all aspects of work, employment, unemployment and their interconnections with wider social processes and social structures.

To conclude, it is also important to note the place occupied by Industrial Relations, which is taught in many British universities and has journals devoted to it (*British Journal of Industrial Relations, Industrial Relations Journal*), producing research of international reputation. This branch of the Social Sciences constitutes an intellectual tradition which has no equivalent in other European countries. It has contributed to the investigation of the changes which have occurred in the course of the 1980s and 1990s in the field of vocational training.

ACKNOWLEDGEMENTS

We are particularly indebted to David Raffe for helping us find our way through the labyrinth of British statistics. We are also grateful to the British Council and the Industrial Relations Research Unit (University of Warwick) for their financial support for this study.

NOTES

1   The CSE (Certificate of Secondary Education) certified exams were taken at the end of compulsory schooling. It represented the lowest level of academic attainment. The GCE 'O' levels (General Certificate of Education) were exams taken

by the most able pupils at the end of compulsory schooling. These exams were replaced by the GCSE (General Certificate of Secondary Education) in 1988. BTEC (Business and Technician Education Council, established in 1983), City and Guilds of London Institute (established in 1878) and RSA (Royal Society of Arts, founded in the late eighteenth century) are the three main certification bodies for vocational studies. GCE 'A' levels are taken at age 18 and the grades attained by (normally) three subjects taken determine acceptance for university enrolment.

2 By contrast, women with intermediate occupations represent 47 per cent of the total number of unemployed women while representing 52 per cent of women aged 16–59. These data from the 1990 General Household Survey were communicated by Michael White of the Policy Studies Institute, London.

3 These statistics are taken from the *Statistical Bulletin* 1992, 17, Department for Education and Science.

4 Until 1985 entitlement to social security benefit and housing allowances started at age 16. Entitlement now begins at age 18 and 21 respectively.

5 These data do not refer to Scotland and Northern Ireland, where educational policies and practices differ from those in England as well as between themselves.

BIBLIOGRAPHY

Ball, S. K. (1990) *Politics and Policy Making in Education: Explorations in Policy Sociology*, London: Routledge.

Benoît-Guilbot, O. and Gallie, D. (1993) *Le chômage de longue durée*, Paris: Actes Sud.

Bulmer, M. (1988), 'Theory and method in recent British Sociology: whither the empirical impulse?', *British Journal of Sociology* 3.

Confederation of British Industry (1989) *Towards a Skills Revolution. A Report of the Vocational Education and Training Task force*, London: CBI.

Edwards, P., Hall, M., Hyman, R., Marginson, P., Sisson, K., Waddington, J. and Winchester D. (1992) 'Great Britain: still muddling through', in A. Ferner and R. Hyman (eds) *Industrial Relations in the New Europe*, Oxford: Blackwell.

Employment Gazette, July 1993.

Eurostat (1993) *Labour Force Survey Results*, Office of the European Community, Luxemburg.

Finegold, D., Keep, E., Miliband, D., Raffe, D., Spours, K. and Young, M. (1990) 'A British "Baccalaureat",' London: Institute for Public Policy Research.

Finegold, D. and Soskice, D. (1988) 'The failure of British training: analysis and prescription', *Oxford Review of Economic Policy* 4.

Gallie, D. (1988) 'Employment, unemployment and social stratification' in Gallie D. (ed.) *Employment in Britain*, Oxford: Blackwell.

Giddens, A. (1973) *The Class Structure of the Advanced Societies*, London: Hutchinson.

Gleeson, D. (1987) *TVEI: a critical appraisal*, Milton Keynes: Open University Press.

——(1989) *The Paradox of Training*, Milton Keynes: Open University Press.

Halsey, A. H. (1988) 'A turning of the tide? the prospects for Sociology in Britain', *British Journal of Sociology* 3.

Hoggart, R. (1990) *The Uses of Literacy, Aspects of Working Class Life with Special Reference to Publications and Entertainments*, London: Penguin.

Institute for Employment Research (1991) *Review of the Economy and Employment*, Coventry: IER, University of Warwick.

Jenkins, R. (1983) *Lads, Citizens and Ordinary Kids: Working-Class Youth Life-Styles in Belfast*, London: Routledge.

Keep, E. and Mayhew, K. (forthcoming) *The British Vocational Education and Training System. A Critical Analysis*, Oxford: Oxford University Press.

Labour Force Survey (1993) *Results*, Luxemburg: Office for Official Publications of the European Communities.

Lawton, D. (1992) *Education and Politics in the 1990s: Conflict or Consensus*, London: Falmer Press.

Lepenies, W. (1990), *Les trois cultures, entre science et littérature l'avènement de la sociologie*, Paris: Editions de la Maison des Sciences de l'Homme.

Loder, C. (1992) *Support for Social Science Research: Setting the Scene*, London: Institute of Education, Centre for Higher Education Studies/Economic and Social Research Council.

Millward, N., Stevens, M., Smart, D. and Hawes, W. R. (1992) *Workplace Industrial Relations in Transition. The ED/ESRC/PSI/ACAS Surveys.* Aldershot: Dartmouth.

National Commission on Education (1993) *Learning to Succeed. A Radical Look at Education Today and a Strategy for the Future*, London: Heinemann.

National Economic Development Office/Manpower Services Commission (1984) *Competence and Competition. Training and Education in the Federal Republic of Germany, the United States and Japan*, London: NEDO.

Raffe, D. (1992a) 'Participation of 16–18-year-olds in education and training', *National Commission on Education Briefing* 3.

——(1992b) 'Beyond the "mixed model": social research and the case for reform of 16–18 education in Britain', in C. Crouch and A. Heath (eds) *Social Research and Social Reform; Essays in Honour of A. Halsey*, Oxford: Clarendon Press.

Ryan, P. (ed.) (1991) *International Comparisons of Vocational Education and Training for Intermediate Skills*, London: Falmer Press.

Steedman, H., Mason, G. and Wagner, K. (1991) 'Intermediate skills in the workplace: employment, standards and supply in Britain, France and Germany', *National Institute Economic Review* 136: 60–76, May.

Wagner, P. (1989) 'Les sciences sociales et l'Etat en Europe occidentale continentale: la structuration du discours disciplinaire', *Revue Internationale des Sciences Sociales* 122.

Westergaard, J. and Pahl, R. (1988) 'Looking backwards and forwards: the UGC's review of sociology', *British Journal of Sociology* 40(3): 374–92.

White, M. (1993) 'Le chômage longue durée en Grande-Bretagne', in O. Benoit-Guilbot and D. Gallie (eds) *Le chômage de longue durée*, Paris: Actes Sud.

Williams, R. (1961) *Culture and Society, 1780–1950*, Harmondsworth: Penguin.

Willis, P. (1977) *Learning to Labour: How Working Class Kids Get Working Class Jobs*, Farnborough: Saxon House.

——(1986) 'Unemployment: the final inequality – report on the Wolverhampton youth review', *British Journal of Sociology of Education* 2.

Work, Employment and Society (1990) Special Issue 'The 1980s: a decade of change?', May.

9

THE 'TRANSITION FROM SCHOOL TO WORK' AND ITS HEIRS

An analysis of a changing research field

David Raffe

RESEARCH ON THE 'TRANSITION FROM SCHOOL TO WORK' BEFORE 1980

In the 1960s and 1970s a substantial amount of research into the 'transition from school to work' (TSW) was carried out in Britain. It comprised a distinct field of study, recognised as such by most of its practitioners, even if the precise boundaries of this field may have been open to debate. It studied pupils in their last year at secondary school, young workers in their first year or two in employment, and apprentices and other young workers studying part-time in Further Education (FE) Colleges. Most of its subjects were working-class males who left school at the minimum age.

The typical transition study was a questionnaire survey of young people who were either about to leave school and enter employment, or who had recently done so. Some studies used additional data sources, for example interviews with employers, Careers Service records, and data from observation, group discussions or interviews with young people. Some studies used qualitative methods only. A few large surveys were used for TSW research, including the three British birth cohort studies based on samples born in 1946, 1958 and 1970, and a regular survey of school-leavers in Scotland which was established in 1971. However, most TSW studies were small in scale, observed a single cohort or school-leaver group, and drew their samples from a single college or a small number of neighbouring schools. Many contacted their sample only once, with any longitudinal data collected retrospectively; others followed up their sample members once or twice.

The longitudinal span covered by most TSW studies was short, rarely more than three years, and often much shorter. There were a few studies of the transition from higher education to the labour market, but this was a largely separate field of enquiry.

The TSW research is reviewed in more detail by Clarke (1980a, 1980b). Much of the research was policy-related, descriptive and only weakly underpinned by theory. TSW studies typically collected descriptive data on a range of topics: the preparation of young people for employment, guidance,

128

job search, the jobs entered, induction and training, the duration and stability of employment, and the attitudes and aspirations of young people. Some studies attempted to inform future policy, either by identifying needs (for guidance, education, etc.) that were not currently met, or by identifying 'risk groups' of young people in the greatest need of help.

However the TSW research did make some theoretical contributions. For example, sociologists such as Roberts (1968) developed a critique of the individualistic 'developmental' theory of occupational choice which influenced careers guidance; entry to the labour market, they argued, was determined less by free individual choice than by socialisation at home and school and by the channelling associated with the 'opportunity structures' facing young people. A related theoretical strand explored the relative roles of home and school in the socialisation process (Carter 1962; Ashton and Field 1976). Several TSW studies (for instance, Willis 1977) addressed theoretical issues about social class and the reproduction of social inequalities.

THE TRANSFORMATION OF THE TSW RESEARCH FIELD AFTER 1980

The pre-1980s research was premised on an education system in which a majority of young people left school at 15 (16 from 1973), most received little or no explicit education for employment, and such vocational education as existed tended to be part-time and for apprentices. It was also premised on a labour market in which full-time jobs were readily available to teenagers. It assumed the 'transition from school to work' to be a short, one-step process, capable of analysis in terms of a limited number of sociological dimensions (principally home, school and work, with work regarded as synonymous with employment). The concept was applied to a restricted group of people – typically low-attaining, working-class males.

These assumptions were overturned by the rapid rise in youth unemployment around 1980, by the introduction of new work experience and training schemes, by the development of vocational curricula in full-time education, by the prolongation of the transition process and, over a longer period, by the rise in educational participation rates. They were also challenged by developments in Social Science, including the growing influence of feminism and of holistic and life course perspectives in the Sociology of Youth. The former concept of 'transition from school to work' was increasingly acknowledged to be problematic; consequently the concept was no longer able to define a research field or give coherence to it.

The resulting changes in the research field – and the underlying continuities – are summarised in Figure 9.1. This provides a crude map of the pre-1980 research field and shows the main changes that occurred subsequently. The three circles in Figure 9.1 divide this research field according to the main subjects of study: young people about to leave school (e.g.

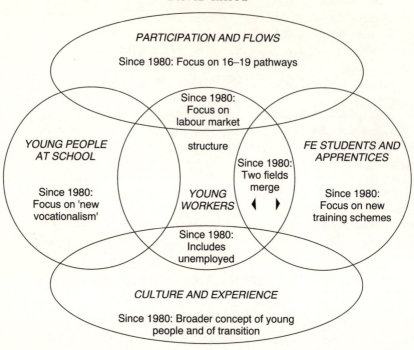

Figure 9.1 A map of the research field before 1980 showing developments since 1980

Thomas and Wetherell 1974); young workers who have recently made the transition (e.g. Keil 1976); and FE students and apprentices (e.g. Venables 1967). The three circles overlap, since many studies covered young people as they moved between these statuses. The two oblongs at the top and bottom of the diagram identify two main emphases within the research: a more quantitative emphasis on participation patterns and flows; and a more qualitative emphasis on the culture and experience of young people.

Each area of research changed after 1980. Research in the left-hand circle, on young people at school, was given a new focus by the introduction of new curricula – the 'new vocationalism', especially the Technical and Vocational Education Initiative (TVEI) – designed to prepare young people more effectively for work and adult life. The next area of research – 'young workers' – developed in three main ways. It broadened its focus to include the unemployed as well as young people in jobs; it spawned a significant strand of research on the structure of labour markets, to complement research on individuals' experiences in the labour market; and it merged with the next field of research (the right-hand circle in Figure 9.1), which had studied FE students and apprentices before 1980, but which now turned its attention to young people on work experience and training schemes such as the Youth

Training Scheme (YTS) and its predecessor, the Youth Opportunities Programme (YOP: 1978–83). It became virtually impossible to separate the study of the labour market from the study of the new schemes, partly because young people moved frequently between schemes and (un)employment, and partly because the organisation of the new schemes was so closely linked with the organisation of the labour market.

There was a continuing strand of largely quantitative, survey-based research on participation and flows (the oblong at the top of the diagram), but the concept of a one-step transition from school to work was replaced by a concept of 16–19 pathways (or routes), which involved a longer sequence of possible steps between a larger number of statuses (training schemes, college and unemployment as well as school and work). Finally, the research into young people's culture and experience (the bottom oblong) also developed. It examined young people's experiences of unemployment, covered a broader range of young people, including women and 'ordinary kids', and developed a more holistic concept of transition, exploring the links between education/labour market transitions and transitions in family, household and the private sphere.

THE HEIRS OF THE TSW RESEARCH TRADITION SINCE 1980

As a result of these changes, the TSW research has become more diverse in its aims and methods, and harder to represent as a single and coherent current of research. This may explain why there has not been (to my knowledge) a comprehensive literature review of the field since 1980, although examples of some strands of this research may be found in collections of papers such as those edited by Brown and Ashton (1987) and Gleeson (1990). The topography of the research has changed, and in Figure 9.2 I present again the post-1980 research but in terms of a different set of overlapping circles. These describe four main areas of research: research and evaluation on the new initiatives such as YOP, YTS and TVEI; the youth cohort surveys; labour market studies; and research on young people's experiences of, and reactions to, unemployment and training schemes. 'Representative' authors and studies are marked on the diagram. For reasons of simplicity, a fifth circle has been omitted from Figure 9.2: this represents the field of 'vocational education and training (VET) policy studies' which emerged towards the end of the 1980s. Below I describe each of these five areas of research.

Research on new policy initiatives

Work experience, training and education initiatives such as YOP, YTS and TVEI have brought in their wake a huge body of evaluation and research into their operation and their effects. Much of the research has been policy-led in

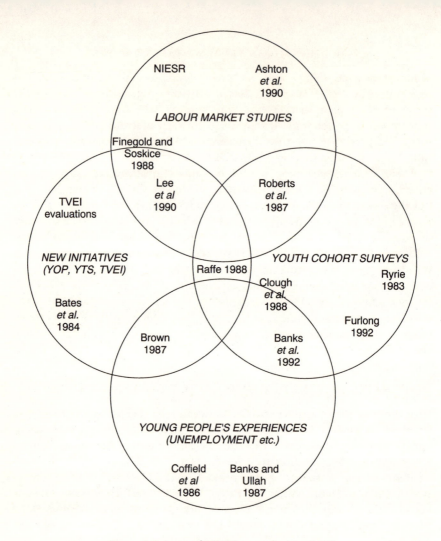

Figure 9.2 Areas of 'TSW' research since 1980

the sense that policy-makers have determined its agenda and methods: these have tended to be narrow, unquestioning of the broader social and political context, and vulnerable to short-term fluctuations in the policy environment. However, there have also been more radical critiques of the goals, assumptions and political rationales of new policy initiatives.

A wide range of methods, approaches and designs of research have been employed. Some studies have been small-scale and qualitative; others have been large-scale and quantitative, including studies based on the cohort surveys described below. Several disciplines and traditions of research have been involved. Studies of full-time education programmes such as TVEI have drawn on educational research traditions such as the study of curriculum and pedagogy, school-effects research and evaluation research.

(The evaluation of educational innovations, particularly formative evaluation to inform those introducing the innovations and to illuminate their practice and its context, is an important strand of research in Britain with a distinctive methodological and philosophical tradition). Research into part-time and work-based education or training has drawn on a variety of research traditions including ethnography, labour market economics and labour market studies. In the post-compulsory education and training system that has developed since 1980 the boundary between education/training and the labour market is very weak. This is reflected in the substantial fusion, noted above, between research on employment and the labour market and research on training schemes. An example is the study of YTS by Lee *et al.* (1990), who used concepts of segmentation drawn from labour market analysis to study the organisation and internal differentiation of training schemes.

It is impossible to summarise the conclusions of all this research, but two themes are important. First, in the early 1980s there were many rather simplistic critiques of the covert political aims of new policy initiatives and the ideological messages they were designed to promote; later analyses have been more sophisticated, and have stressed the extent to which policy objectives (covert or overt) become transformed in the process of implementation. Second, much of the research has found that the new policy initiatives have had little or no effect on their target outcomes, especially on more quantitative outcomes such as participation and attainment in education/training, or employment and earnings in the labour market.

Research on new policy initiatives reached a peak in the mid-1980s. It continues in the 1990s, in relation to newer policy initiatives such as compacts, City Technology Colleges and Training Credits, but it is on a smaller scale, and more of the research is conducted by management consultants. Among academic researchers this area has been partly displaced by VET policy studies, described below.

Youth cohort surveys

In Scotland, a national postal survey of school-leavers has been conducted since 1971; since 1977 it had been biennial and covered a sample of all young people leaving secondary school. However, the survey design – based on a single contact about ten months after leaving school – was inadequate to study the more prolonged transition process of the 1980s, or to monitor young people's choices between continued schooling and the new training schemes. In 1985 (following a large-scale pilot in 1984) it became the Scottish Young People's Survey (SYPS), and included a longitudinal survey which followed school year-groups over the three years after the end of compulsory schooling (from 16 to 19). In the same year the Youth Cohort Survey (YCS), an age cohort survey with similar design and objectives, was introduced in England and Wales. In 1987–9 surveys of young people aged

15–17 and 17–19 in four British towns, similar in some respects to the two national cohort surveys, were conducted as the centrepiece of the ESRC's 16–19 Initiative (Banks *et al.* 1992); there have been several other local surveys (e.g. Ryrie 1983).

An important feature of the two national surveys, the SYPS and the YCS, has been their regularity, with fresh cohorts contacted every two years in Scotland and every one or two years in England and Wales. They have been used to study period change as well as longitudinal change, for example to monitor changes in the labour market or to assess the impact of policy changes by comparing the young people affected with earlier cohorts.

Another important aim of the SYPS and YCS has been to monitor the progress of 16- to 19-year-olds along the new pathways available to them, through and between secondary school, FE College, training schemes, employment and unemployment. The surveys have been used to study the number and characteristics of people following each pathway, the factors influencing the choice of pathway, the destinations to which each pathway leads and the consequences of following one pathway rather than another (Raffe 1988; Clough *et al.* 1988). The Scottish survey has also collected extensive data on other transitions in youth, such as those involving family, households and peer group relations, allowing researchers such as Jones (Jones and Wallace 1992) to place education/labour market routes in a broader context. This more holistic approach is also exemplified by the ESRC's 16–19 Initiative, which has used a typology of career paths through education and training as a basis for studying the identity formation, social and political attitudes, and peer group and family relationships of young people.

It is instructive to compare the SYPS and YCS with other European surveys, such as the French Observatoire EVA (*Entrée dans la Vie Active*). The comparison not only highlights features of the British youth cohort studies, but also throws important light on characteristic features of the whole TSW field in Britain. At least three significant differences emerge.

First, despite the prolongation of the transition process and the rise in the average age of school-leaving, the SYPS and YCS, like most other British studies in this field, have hitherto stopped at the age of 19.

Second, the Observatoire EVA and other European surveys have focused largely on routes within the labour market, while the British research has focused more on routes within the education and training system. This partly reflects the British policy interest in levels of participation in education and training – the British surveys have been designed to study the choice *between* continued education and the labour market and the factors influencing participation in the new education and training pathways. It also reflects the weak boundary in Britain between post-compulsory education/training and the labour market; it is much harder in the British context to define pathways through education and training independently of pathways though the labour market.

Third, most analyses of the SYPS and YCS have been based on the whole age-group and have made comparisons within this frame of reference, for example of young people following different pathways. It is difficult to use the French Observatoire – in effect a suite of separate surveys of young people leaving different levels and sectors of education – for cross-sectional analyses of this kind.

Labour market studies

This sub-field includes studies of employers' employment, recruitment and training practices, and of the structure and organisation of the youth labour market. This research is discussed in detail in David Ashton's contribution to this study in Chapter 10, and here it is sufficient simply to note the substantial overlap with the other sub-fields discussed in this section.

Young people's experiences

Again, a detailed discussion is not required here since much of this sub-field is covered in Lynne Chisholm's contribution in Chapter 11. Of particular interest to the TSW tradition are the studies of young people's responses to unemployment and to schemes such as YOP and YTS.

VET policy studies

The end of the 1980s saw the emergence of a new area of research, which I shall call 'VET policy studies' (VET refers to Vocational Education and Training, a new acronym of the 1980s). I have not included it in Figure 9.2, partly because it emerged later than the other areas of research represented there, and partly because it would need to be represented in a different dimension, overlapping with at least the top three of the circles already shown.

The VET policy studies analyse the economy, employment, education and training and other social 'institutions' in order to specify the future policies which are required to promote a high-skills economy in Britain, and to identify factors which contribute to the success or failure of policy. In contrast to much of the research on policy initiatives described above, the VET policy studies aim to prescribe future policies, rather than simply to describe and analyse existing policies. Analyses of existing policies may nevertheless contribute to this because of what they reveal about the workings of the British system and the implications for future policy design. The VET policy studies also reflect a relative degree of consensus – at least compared to the earlier research on new initiatives – about the aims and broad parameters of policy.

This field can be described by reference to two of its most influential examples. Prais, Steedman and others at the National Institute for Economic and Social Research (NIESR) have conducted a series of studies comparing Britain with Germany, France and other European countries. One set of studies has compared levels of vocational skills and attainment in VET, finding them much lower in Britain than elsewhere; other studies have gone on to suggest that lower British skill levels contribute to the low-skill production and employment strategies of British employers.

The second example is the work of Finegold and Soskice (1988: 22), who present Britain as:

> trapped in a low skills equilibrium, in which the majority of enter-prises staffed by poorly trained managers and workers produce low quality goods and services. The term 'equilibrium' is used to connote a self-reinforcing network of societal and state institutions which interact to stifle the demand for improvements in skill levels. [These institutions] include the organisation of industry, firms and the work process, the industrial relations system, financial markets, the state and political structure, as well as the operation of the ET [education and training] system.

This analysis summarises much of the VET policy research. It suggests that a market-led training system merely responds to the demands of the low-skills equilibrium and thus reinforces it; the analysis encapsulates many researchers' criticisms of the UK government's growing reliance on market mechanisms to regulate education and training. It also exemplifies another feature of the VET policy studies: a focus on the socio-economic dimension – on institutions, structures and organisations at the societal level, and on history – rather than on the more psychological or cognitive dimension or on micro-level processes of learning and skill acquisition. I discuss this contrast between 'structures' and 'processes' in the following section.

As these examples suggest, the VET policy studies have displayed a strong interest in comparative research. The Warwick VET Forum, which played an important role in shaping this area of research, devoted its first national meeting to French research perspectives, with particular attention to *L'Introuvable Relation Formation-Emploi* (Tanguy 1986) and to the societal approach of Maurice *et al.* (1986). Several of the meetings that followed have had a comparative theme, and several books have compared British VET with Germany, France, the USA, Japan, Canada and other countries. Partnerships and networks have linked British researchers with colleagues in other countries, especially in Europe.

GENERAL CHARACTERISTICS OF THE FIELD

In this section I discuss some of the more persisting characteristics of the research field.

The role of government

Throughout this period, and especially in the early 1980s, the government has played a major role in defining the research field. Its most direct influence has been as a sponsor of research. The new policy initiatives of the early 1980s brought in their wake a vast increase in government-funded research and evaluation, and gave a major boost to the TSW field. The government has also influenced the field by defining much of its subject matter. A large proportion of TSW research has concentrated on new and usually transient policy initiatives; as a result broader and longer-term issues have sometimes been neglected.

Inevitably this powerful governmental role has caused tensions. The objectives of many government-funded policy studies have been narrowly drawn, and their contribution to the longer-term development of the research field has often been negligible. There have been tensions between the government's desire to manage and control the research field and the academic tradition of independence and criticism. My own experience is that these tensions have been strongest not in relation to the more abstract and radical critiques of policy but in relation to research which evaluates government policies in their own terms and which has the legitimacy of strong empirical evidence (Bell and Raffe 1991).

Weak definition of the field

The TSW field has always been weakly defined, especially after 1980 when the TSW concept itself became less able to define the field. Internally, it is fragmented, and best represented as a set of overlapping circles. Externally, some of its boundaries are weak; it overlaps with other circles – that is, neighbouring sub-fields such as gender studies, the economics of education, labour market segmentation and educational evaluation – to which many researchers owe their main allegiance. The weak definition of the TSW field partly reflects the role of the government in defining it. VET as an area of government policy has weak definition; its low political priority means that VET initiatives need to be linked with other issues such as unemployment in order to gain political support, and there have been frequent shifts in policy and priorities. No dominant paradigm or theory has emerged to unite the field. Theoretical development has been inhibited by the narrow specification of many government-funded research projects, and by their excessive and sometimes exclusive attention to current policies. The TSW field has been more multidisciplinary than interdisciplinary; different disciplines (often too many) have cohabited within the field, but only occasionally have they fused to support theoretical development. Other aspects of the organisation of academic research in Britain have contributed to the weak definition of the TSW field. These include the continued emphasis on disciplines in the academic reward system, the growing use of management consultancies for government research contracts and the small scale of most British research teams – there are no large players in the field such as BIBB (Bundesinstitut für Berufsbildung) or CEREQ (Centre d'Études et de Recherches sur les Qualifications). However, several developments in the late 1980s have promoted somewhat greater coherence in the field, for example, the foundation of the *British Journal of Education and Work* in 1987, the ESRC's 16–19 Initiative (1986–91) which linked researchers in several different institutions, the Warwick VET Forum and other seminar groups and networks.

Fusion between education and labour market research

One aspect of the weak definition of the TSW field is the close link between educational and labour market research. This reflects the particular character of education and training in Britain, especially for 16- to 18-year-olds. On the one hand, 16-year-olds have traditionally had to choose between full-time education and the labour market: those who have 'stayed on' have often missed age-restricted opportunities for training and employment. On the other hand, for those who leave full-time education at 16 there is a weak boundary between training and employment. Both factors have encouraged a research perspective which embraces both education/training and the labour market. The politics of training have also been important. During the 1980s the policy agenda was subtly and progressively altered, from a focus on youth unemployment to a focus on education and training; in the process many labour market (unemployment) researchers were recruited to the study of education and training.

Most occupationally related training occurs after a young person has entered the labour market, so it is not possible to study the 'fit' between training and employment by observing the occupational destinations of trainees. There is no British equivalent to the French research interest in *adéquation* (except perhaps in relation to higher education); to the extent that the 'fit' between occupation and employment is a subject of study, a more qualitative approach is followed.

The age-structuring of the research field

Many aspects of education in Britain – progression, entitlements and policy debates – are tightly organised in terms of age, and the research field is similarly age-structured. There is a weak boundary at 16, which has been partly eroded by research on the new vocationalism which covers both 14- to 16-year-olds and 16- to 18-year-olds. There is a stronger and persisting boundary at 18 or 19, reflected in the tendency for most longitudinal studies to stop at around 19 years. The weak – or restricted – longitudinal focus of British research is complemented by a strong cross-sectional focus. Studies tend to adopt the whole age cohort as their reference group, explicitly or implicitly. Nevertheless the short longitudinal span of British research has disadvantages which are increasingly recognised. Young people are observed in the labour market for a relatively short time, if at all, and inadequate measures of 'labour market outcomes' have been available to British researchers studying the effects of education and training. As a result of the boundary at 19 the TSW field has almost wholly excluded higher education; the links between higher education and employment have been a largely separate area of study. In the long term, the present age-focus may be incompatible with trends towards flexibility in post-compulsory education and training which (in principle) give students greater control over the pace and phasing of study and blur the boundaries between higher education, further education and training.

Structure and process

VET in the UK is comparatively strong with respect to processes: in other words, there are good examples of innovations in the curriculum and in methods of teaching, learning and assessment. But VET in the UK is weak with respect to structures: that is, the organisation, institutions and socio-economic context of British VET depress participation, reduce coherence and prevent innovations in the 'processes' of teaching and learning from being disseminated and incorporated in the national system (Gordon and Parkes 1992). Policy-oriented research has focused on areas of relative weakness, that is, on structures rather than processes.

The 'structural' emphasis in the British research is reflected in the current enthusiasm for comparative studies and in particular for macro and societal approaches. It is also reflected in the areas of research with which the TSW field has had relatively few links. There have been at least three such 'missing links'. First, research on the learning process has made significant progress in recent years (Berryman and Bailey 1992), but there has been little contact with the 'structural' research described above. Second, the TSW research has been substantially separate from research on the labour process and on the definition and deployment of skills in the workplace. In this respect the TSW research field mirrors the organisation of education and training in Britain – more directly influenced by the labour market than by the labour process. Third, there has been a strong British tradition of research into the 'hidden curriculum' and of evaluation of curriculum initiatives, but the TSW research has remained substantially separate from curriculum development, that is, its findings have not been major inputs into the design and implementation of new curricula. However, current developments are beginning to supply some of these missing links. For example, some researchers, influenced by post-Fordist conceptions of social and economic change, have begun to develop models for the 'curriculum of the future' which unify academic and vocational learning (Finegold *et al.* 1990; Young 1993).

FUTURE DIRECTIONS

In this paper I have described several areas of research which are all, in varying degrees, heirs to the TSW tradition that existed before 1980. As these areas continue to develop they move further away from the tradition which once united them, and increasingly incorporate the influence of other traditions of research. I conclude by extrapolating from current trends to suggest some future directions for research.

First, the interest in comparative and international research is reflected more and more in cross-national collaboration among researchers; British research is becoming more 'European' and is being exposed to other research traditions (such as 'post-modern' German Sociology, currently influential in Britain) which will influence its further development. Second, there is scope for further development of more holistic perspectives on youth and the life course, linking education and the labour market with family, household and other dimensions of young people's transitions and identities. Third, and related to this, the boundary at 19 years is increasingly recognised as inappropriate, and will continue to erode. Fourth, there is scope for cross-fertilisation between the socio-economic or 'structural' emphasis of British research and the study of the learning process – for example, in relation to such issues as the relative effectiveness of school-based and work-based (or dual) models of provision. Fifth, work in the 'VET policy studies' tradition is becoming more programmatic, and researchers are playing a more important role in defining visions for the future of education and training – this is reflected in the contribution of researchers to 'think-tanks' and to the independent National Commission on Education, and in research projects and programmes with such titles as *The Learning Society* and *Learning for the Future*. Finally, researchers will devote more attention to the practical aspects of implementing these visions at the level of the school, college or workplace, and to refining the visions in the light of this experience.

ACKNOWLEDGEMENTS

The financial support of the UK Economic and Social Research Council is gratefully acknowledged.

BIBLIOGRAPHY

Ashton, D. N. and Field, D. (1976) *Young Workers*, London: Hutchinson.

Ashton, D. N., Maguire, M. and Spilsbury, M. (1990) *Restructuring the Labour Market*, London: Macmillan.

Banks, M., Bates, I., Breakwell, G., Bynner, J., Emler, N., Jamieson, L. and Roberts, K. (1992) *Careers and Identities*, Milton Keynes: Open University Press.

Banks, M. and Ullah, P. (1987) *Youth Unemployment: Social and Psychological Perspectives*, Research Paper 61, London: Department of Employment.

Bates, I. *et al.* (1984) *Schooling for the Dole*, London: Macmillan.

Bell, C. and Raffe, D. (1991) 'Working together? Research, policy and practice: the experience of the Scottish evaluation of TVEI', in Walford, G. (ed.) *Doing Educational Research*, London: Routledge.

Berryman, S. E. and Bailey, T. R. (1992) *The Double Helix of Education and the Economy*, New York: Institute on Education and the Economy, Teachers College.

Brown, P. (1987) *Schooling Ordinary Kids*, London: Tavistock.

Brown, P. and Ashton, D. N. (1987) *Education, Unemployment and Labour Markets*, Lewes: Falmer Press.

Carter, M. P. (1962) *Home, School and Work*, Oxford: Pergamon.

Clarke, L. (1980a) *The Transition from School to Work: A Critical Review of Research in the United Kingdom*, London: HMSO.

——(1980b) *The Process of Occupational Choice: A Critical Review of Research in the United Kingdom*, London: HMSO.

Clough, E., Gray, J., Jones, B. and Pattie, C. (1988) *Routes Through YTS*, Youth Cohort Series 2, Sheffield: Manpower Services Commission.

Coffield, F., Borrill, C., and Marshall, S., (1980) *Growing up at the Margins*, Milton Keynes: Open University Press.

Finegold, D., Keep, E., Miliband, D., Raffe, D., Spours, K. and Young, M. (1990) *A British Baccalauréat*, London: Institute for Public Policy Research.

Finegold, D. and Soskice, D. (1988) 'The failure of training in Britain: analysis and prescription', *Oxford Review of Economic Policy* 4. (Reprinted in Gleeson (1990))

Furlong, A. (1992) *Growing up in a Classless Society? School to Work Transitions*, Edinburgh: Edinburgh University Press.

Gleeson, D. (ed.) (1990) *Training and its Alternatives*, Milton Keynes: Open University Press.

Gordon, J. and Parkes, D. (1992) *Strategies for VET in Europe*, London: Association of Vocational Colleges International.

Jones, G. and Wallace, C. (1992) *Youth, Family and Citizenship*, Milton Keynes: Open University Press.

Keil, E. T. (1976) *Becoming a Worker*, Loughborough University.

Lee, D., Marsden, D., Rickman, P. and Duncombe, J. (1990) *Scheming for Youth*, Milton Keynes: Open University Press.

Maurice, M., Sellier, F. and Silvestre, J.-J. (1986) *The Social Foundations of Industrial Power*, Cambridge, MA: MIT Press.

Raffe, D. (ed.) (1988) *Education and the Youth Labour Market*, Lewes: Falmer Press.

Roberts, K. (1968) 'The entry into employment: an approach towards general theory', *Sociological Review* 16.

Roberts, K., Dench, S. and Richardson, D., (1987) *The Changing Structure of Youth Labour Markets*, Research Paper No. 59, London: Department of Employment.

Ryrie, A. C. (1983) *On Leaving School*, Edinburgh: Scottish Council for Research in Education.

Tanguy, L. (ed.) (1986) *L'Introuvable Relation formation-emploi*, Paris: La Documentation Française.

Thomas, R. and Wetherell, D. (1974) *Looking Forward to Work*, London: HMSO.

Venables, E. (1967) *The Young Worker at College*, London: Faber and Faber.

Willis, P. E. (1977) *Learning to Labour*, Farnborough: Saxon House.

Young, M. (1993) 'A curriculum for the 21st century? Towards a new basis for overcoming academic/vocational divisions', *British Journal of Educational Studies* 41.

10

LABOUR MARKET APPROACHES TO THE STUDY OF THE RELATIONSHIP BETWEEN EDUCATION AND (UN)EMPLOYMENT IN THE UNITED KINGDOM

David Ashton

INTRODUCTION

In this paper the development of the labour market approach to the study of the relationship between education and (un)employment in the United Kingdom is examined. The first part examines the theoretical origins of the labour market approach, the types of issues it has addressed and highlights some of the differences in emphasis between the various research groups which have pioneered this approach in the UK. The second part concludes with a discussion of the achievements of the labour market approach and some of the new research questions it has raised.

The labour market approach emerged from the discipline of Sociology in response to the political and economic changes which brought the study of the labour market to the fore in the 1980s. Early studies of the transition from school to work had characterised it as being relatively unproblematic (Carter 1962; Ashton and Field 1976). They focused almost exclusively on the part played by social class and educational achievement in the reproduction of social class inequalities. These studies were part of a broader concern with identifying the determinants of social mobility. This meant that there was little systematic knowledge of the ways in which employers used the labour of young people, the type of socialisation they experienced at work, their chances of promotion and the routes they followed into the adult labour market. However, in the late 1970s and throughout the 1980s, economic and political changes combined to focus attention on the operation of the labour market. The decline of the manufacturing industry and the growth of the service sector resulted in a loss of the full-time skilled and semi-skilled jobs traditionally filled by males, and an increase in part-time jobs, filled primarily by females. Apprenticeships and traditional career routes into the labour market collapsed. The result, in the 1980s, against a background of mass youth and adult unemployment, was a radical restructuring of the routes young people followed into the labour market and their experience of (un)employment (Ashton *et al*. 1990). The government's response was to introduce the Youth Training Scheme and further deregulate the labour market. In this political context academic and government-sponsored research shifted to focus on the operations of the labour market.

THE LABOUR MARKET APPROACH

The concept of the labour market was introduced by British sociologists in the early 1980s to fill the vacuum in our knowledge about the structure of work opportunities which the preoccupation with identifying the determinants and patterns of social mobility had left. Work in the USA by radical economists, especially that of Doeringer and Piore (1971), challenging traditional notions of the labour market as used by neo-classical economists, had led to the development of the concept of a dual labour market. The concept of the dual labour market introduced the idea that there are two different labour markets characterised by fundamental differences in the behaviour of employers and workers. The primary market consists of a series of firm internal labour markets found among large employers. In such internal labour markets formal rules or customs determine issues such as who has access to which jobs, how people are promoted, the nature of pay differentials and the circumstances under which workers can be laid off. In general these are the higher paid jobs which offer workers some form of career prospects, training and job security. They are mainly filled by indigenous white males. Internal labour markets were explained in terms of the need for firm-specific investment in human capital in capital-intensive industries. The secondary market consists of jobs offered by smaller employers, often in labour-intensive operations where investment in human capital is unnecessary. The jobs are characterised by low pay, the absence of training and career prospects and high levels of insecurity and labour turnover. These secondary market jobs are generally filled by women, ethnic minorities and youth. Osterman (1980) had used this concept of a dual labour market to argue that youth in the USA entered the secondary market on leaving school, during a moratorium phase, before entering the primary labour market.

The early forms of dual labour market theory suffered from a number of deficiencies. They were static in character, providing an explanation of the fairly stable structure of pay and inequalities which existed in the USA in the late 1960s. There were problems about how well they could cope with the characteristics of labour markets outside the USA and especially their applicability to more dynamic circumstances. In addition, a number of empirical studies found much greater intersectoral labour mobility than dual labour market theorists had postulated (Rosenberg 1989).

For sociologists working in Britain in the late 1970s and early 1980s here was a set of theoretical ideas which sought to explain the differentiation of occupations and the relationships between them as socially constructed phenomenon rather than the product of abstract economic forces. They raised a new set of questions about the characteristics of jobs and their consequences for those who entered them: questions and issues which had been regarded as unproblematic by conventional stratification theory. Interest in the youth labour market was given added significance in the 1980s with the collapse of the demand for youth labour and mass unemployment. It was this context which provided the basis for the development of a British tradition of studies into the structure of work opportunities for youth and of young adults' experience of them.

THE DEVELOPMENT OF THE LABOUR MARKET APPROACH IN BRITAIN

In theoretical terms the development of research into the British youth labour market has been closely associated with the emergence of labour market segmentation theory. Segmentation theory was developed in the UK primarily by the Cambridge Labour Studies Group. These were labour economists based in the Department of Applied Economics at Cambridge University. This group was in turn part of a larger international network of scholars (primarily economists but also consisting of a number of sociologists) who formed the International Working Party on Labour Market Segmentation (IWPLMS). This network is concerned with developing a more adequate theoretical basis for the study of labour markets than that currently available in the form of the neo-classical theory (Wilkinson (ed.) 1981; Rubery 1978).

The IWPLMS was created in the late 1970s in the aftermath of the debate about the adequacy of dual labour market theory. It brought together scholars from the US such as Piore and Bluestone, with others from Europe such as Wilkinson, Ryan, Rubery and Sengenberger to foster collaborative research on the nature of labour markets. The American variant of dual labour market theory as developed by Doeringer and Piore (1971), with its emphasis on the establishment of firm-specific skills, still bore the mark of human capital theory. In the UK the Cambridge Labour Studies Group rejected this and took the historical development of the firm as a central determinant of labour market structures. Through their work they demonstrated that unions were able to create higher paid shelters in the labour market so that the existence of segmented markets could not be explained by simple reference to the interests of one class as a whole (Rubery 1978; Elbaum and Wilkinson 1979). They also argued for the importance of specific historical conjunctures and for the different interests of capital and labour to be taken into account, while still maintaining that technology and forms of work-group organisation were non-neutral instruments in the struggle between capital and labour. Their framework, which allows for a central theoretical role for inter-firm competition, has proved better able to handle the more dynamic environment created by the intensified competition found in world markets during the 1980s and early 1990s (Rubery et al. 1989).

The empirical studies produced by the Cambridge group examined employers' labour strategies under a range of different product market conditions, using case study methodology. Their results demonstrated the significance of inter-class competition and the range of dimensions along which companies can develop, each of which may have different consequences for labour organisation (Craig *et al.* 1982). They have also shown how unions, government regulation and household structures influence the organisation of labour markets (Rubery *et al.* 1989).

More recently Rubery has explored the impact of recession on women's employment and the impact of gender on the perception of skill (Horrell *et al.* 1990). The latter work, together with that of Burchell on the impact of unemployment and insecure work on the quality of life (Burchell and Rubery 1987) was based on the findings of the Social Change and Economic Life Initiative. Although the Cambridge group represented only one of the six teams they had a significant impact on the design of the study.

In the same way that sociologists examining the educational system had developed models which sought to explain its influence on the socialisation of young people, segmentation theory as developed by the Cambridge group provided a dynamic model of the determinants of labour market structures. Labour market behaviour could not be understood just by reference to the actions of individuals but is a consequence of the interaction of a number of groups with unequal power. The work of the Cambridge group provided a model of the range of factors which influenced final outcomes and conditions under which their relative power to determine outcomes changed. It perceived labour market outcomes as the product of conflict between employers, workers, trade unions and governments. The result is the differentiation of the labour market into clusters of jobs which provide different opportunities for mobility, training, payment and security. The actions of governments and employers in regulating the labour market and of workers, trade unions and professional associations in seeking to defend and enhance their position within it reproduce this differentiation through time. Consequently, the price paid for labour, the type of training provided, the opportunities for promotion and the movement of people into and within the labour market, are seen as products of the institutional structures which have been erected to safeguard the interests of the various parties, rather than of the rational actions of individual human beings, as in conventional economic theory.

Within the UK the work of the Cambridge group and of the IWPLMS in general has influenced to a greater or lesser extent all those groups which have adopted a 'labour market approach' to the study of the relationship between the education system and (un)employment. There are four clearly identifiable groups who have contributed to this 'labour market approach': Ashton *et al.* at the Centre for Labour Market Studies, Leicester; Marsden at the London School of Economics and Ryan at Cambridge; Lee and colleagues at Essex University; and Roberts at Liverpool University. However, this 'labour market approach', which takes the structuring of the demand for labour as the point of departure, rather than the experience of young people, remains the exception rather than the rule in British approaches to the study of the transition.

Roberts at Liverpool University

Within this 'labour market approach' all four groups have a different emphasis. Roberts *et al.* at Liverpool University have concentrated on exploring what he terms the 'opportunity structures' which confront young people at work and which he argues are largely responsible for determining the young person's life chances within the labour market. Of all the four groups Roberts has been the most pragmatic in his theoretical orientation and the least affected by the segmentation theory. However, his abiding concern with understanding the structure of the labour market has meant that his later work has been influenced by the work of the segmentation theorists. For Roberts, individual choices are relatively insignificant in determining the type of job the young person enters, the type of training they receive or indeed whether they get a job at all. What is crucial, he argues, is the type and availability of jobs in the locality – that is, the opportunity structure (Roberts 1975).

In the mid-1980s he developed his ideas by examining the relationship between the opportunity structures in three local labour markets and the experience of early school-leavers. He used a structured questionnaire to interview 308 employers and 854 17- to 18-year-olds who had up to 18 months experience of the labour market (Roberts *et al.* 1986). The three local labour markets were Chelmsford, a prosperous town in the south-east of England, Liverpool, a depressed town in the north, and Walsall, a town which suffered severely from the decline of manufacturing industry. His aim was to identify how the jobs available to young people were changing and what that meant in terms of the young person's experience of the labour market. The results documented the declining opportunities for unqualified young people and illustrated how employers were adapting government schemes to fit around their own recruitment and training practices.

As leader of one of the teams on the ESRC (Economic and Social Research Council) 16–19 Initiative, Roberts followed through a cohort of young 16- to 19-year-olds from school to work in Liverpool during the late 1980s. This documented the impact of the recession on young people's career tracks and illustrated how entry to the labour market had become more diverse, with some moving from school to unemployment, others from school through the YTS to employment and others entering employment direct from school (Banks *et al.* 1992). He also conducted a survey which documented the impact of discrimination on the labour market experiences of black youth.

More recently Roberts, together with Bynner of City University and Heinz from the University of Bremen, has been exploring how opportunity structures differ between societies through comparative work in England and Germany (Bynner and Roberts 1991). The methodology used was innovative in that the teams selected similar towns in the two countries, Liverpool and Bremen, to represent declining economies and Swindon and Paderborn to represent expanding economies. Within each town a sample of 160 16- to 19-year-olds were selected, matched in terms of their age, sex and career patterns. The results of this study are still being analysed but the early findings illustrate the difference in the ways in which the transition to the labour market is structured in the two countries and how profoundly this affects young people's view of the world, their confidence and attitudes toward work, and their experience of the labour market.

Marsden and Ryan

The other three groups all adopt variants of the segmentation approach as developed by the work of the IWPLMS. The work of Marsden and Ryan has been particularly concerned with identifying the impact of employers, unions and other labour market institutions on the price of youth labour and the points at which youths enter the labour market. Using data from the European Labour Force Survey they have shown how the institutional arrangements regulating the price of youth labour affect the number and range of opportunities available for them in each country. They have also made important contributions in furthering our theoretical knowledge of the reproduction of occupational and firm-internal labour markets and the part they play in structuring the transition to work and young adults' experience of it. For example, there is a current debate in the UK about whether or not the country would benefit from rebuilding the apprenticeship in order to use occupational labour markets as the main means for structuring the transition and training of young people, or whether the remaining occupational labour markets in the UK should be abandoned and reliance placed on firm-internal labour markets as the basis of future training policy.

In developing his work on occupational labour markets, Marsden has been influenced not only by the work of the IWPLMS but also by the team at the Laboratoire d'Economie et de Sociologie du Travail (LEST), at Aix-en-Provençe, with whom he worked in the 1980s. In methodological terms the work of Marsden and Ryan is distinguished by their concentration on comparative studies and their analysis of secondary data sets. However, their work is covered in Marsden's chapter in this book and will not be fully discussed here.

Lee *et al.* at Essex University

Lee's early work was developed in the context of the debates in the 1970s about the British system of social stratification. He made important contributions to our understanding of the part played by the apprenticeship system in the system of stratification. He highlighted the significance of skilled work in creating divisions within the working class, anticipating in some respects the later work of Rubery on the significance of unions in creating and sustaining pay differentials (Lee 1966). He also documented the part played by part-time vocational education in facilitating social mobility, especially for workers from working-class origins. In his later work, started in 1983 with colleagues at Essex University, he adapted a variant of the segmentation approach and produced a highly regarded analysis of the Youth Training Scheme (Lee *et al.* 1990).

His study covered the whole period of the Youth Training Scheme and examined how it fitted in with the local economy of a town in the south-east of England, how it affected the lives of the trainees, its impact on the behaviour of trainers, employers, careers officers and teachers. The research team used a combination of non-participant observation, postal questionnaires and interviews to record the setting up of the scheme, the movement of young trainees through it and into the labour market and the behaviour and attitudes of careers officers, employers and training providers. In terms of their methodology this group combined a quantitative study of employers, training providers and young people with qualitative work in the tradition of the Cultural Studies school, thereby integrating the two approaches. It was the most comprehensive study of the scheme undertaken in any one locality.

Officially YTS set out to improve the skills and job prospects of young people in Britain and to promote equality of opportunity by relying on employers and market forces. In fact what the authors show is that the scheme developed a commercial logic far more complex than the idea of market forces implies. To understand the working of the scheme the authors employed the concept of the 'surrogate' labour market. This concept was used to indicate how the scheme was created by a mix of employer action (market forces) and state intervention, thereby creating a substitute or surrogate youth labour market. This was segmented in the same way that the 'real' youth labour market was segmented, with some scheme placements leading to a high-quality training with the possibility of employment at the end but others offering no more than work experience with a minimum amount of training. This training was often seen as irrelevant by both trainees and employers. In this way the YTS reinforced forms of gender and class discrimination that already existed in the labour market and failed to make any inroads into the provision of greater equality of opportunity. It was seen as undermining the provision of vocational education in the local College of Further Education and as itself being undermined by the commercial logic of market forces. It failed to enhance the quantity of high-skill training and led to an expansion of programmes which consisted of low skilled and insecure work dressed up as 'training'. To a large extent the function of the scheme was to soak up youth unemployment.

Ashton *et al.* at Leicester University

The Leicester group at the Centre for Labour Market Studies (CLMS) (Ashton et al. 1990) have utilised theoretical ideas from Marx, the Cambridge Labour Studies Group and Elias to develop their approach to the study of the relationship between the educational system and the (un)employment system. They take as their central problem the need to understand the processes responsible for the reproduction and change of the institutional structures which characterise the transition from education to the labour market. In theoretical terms the focus is not on individuals seen as autonomous actors, but on the figurations people form in the process of reproducing each new generation of workers (Elias 1978a). Methodologically, this places less reliance on the single individual as a source of data and more on acquiring data from employers, government officials and others concerned in forming the structures which characterise the transition in each society.

The influence of the German sociologist Elias on the Leicester group has been important in two ways. First, in his attempt to resolve the agency structure problem, Elias argued that one of the central problems facing Sociology was the need to reconceptualise the problem of the relationship between the individual and society. In conventional terms, following Giddens, the problem is currently seen as that of reconciling the focus on individual behaviour (agency) as opposed to social structure (conceived of as independent of individual action) as the basis for sociological theory. In his attempt to move beyond the conventional approach to this problem, Elias developed what he termed Figurational Sociology (Elias 1978a). This led to a focus on both the institutional structures (the figurations formed by interdependent human beings) and the individual's experience of those figurations, as inseparable elements of any sociological analysis. In methodological terms this is manifest in a concern to explore both the experiential dimension of the transition as well as to study the impact of employers and other powerful groups in structuring the labour market. It is inconceivable from the perspective of Figurational Sociology to produce an adequate analysis without incorporating both aspects. For this reason the Leicester group continued to utilise both quantitative and qualitative methodologies when the methodological split referred to above occurred.

Second, Elias placed considerable importance on the processual character of human existence (Elias 1978b). It was this concern with identifying the processes of change which are currently transforming both the state and the economy that led the Leicester team to concentrate on the transformations of contemporary industrial societies and, through them, the youth labour market. In the economy, this included the globalisation of product markets, the shift from manufacturing to service industries and the impact of the new regional trading blocs such as the European Union. In the sphere of the state their attention has been on the impact of the EU on the constituent nation-states as Europe moves to a higher level of political integration associated with the emergence of a European state. All these processes are important in restructuring the economy and the state and therefore have implications for the organisation of the youth labour market and its relationship to the adult labour market.

The Leicester group used segmentation theory, especially as developed by the Cambridge group, as a means of exploring the structure of the youth labour market and its relationship to the adult labour market. Their concern has been to explore how employers' product market strategies influence their employment practices and how these, together with legislation, forms of certification, union agreements, training schemes and training institutions, influence the entry of young people into the labour market and their pattern of movement and experience of work once they are in it. The other source of their ideas was the work of Marx. From Marx came the concern to understand the processes whereby class structures are reproduced, both through the education system and the labour market. Here, as in the work of Lee, the education system is perceived not just as a mechanism for allocating people to their role in the industrial division of labour but in terms of its functions in legitimising the existing system of domination and socialising the next generation of workers.

Early work by Ashton and Field (1976) explored the role of the educational system in the reproduction of each new generation of young workers. This work was part of the wider debate among British sociologists in the 1970s and 1980s (see Jenkins 1983; Willis 1977; Brown 1987) as they sought to explain why working-class youth entered working-class jobs. Furlong has developed these ideas in the contemporary context and is examining the ways in which young people are adjusting their frames of reference to accommodate the realities of the opportunities available to them in the restructured labour market of the 1990s (Furlong 1993).

This early work on the experiential dimension of the transition served to highlight the lack of knowledge of the demand side of the equation. This led the Leicester group, in the late 1970s, to investigate some of the ways in which employers' actions influenced the recruitment, training and work experience of young people. Their central theme was to examine the ways in which employers' training practices, trade unions' agreements, internal labour markets and employer and worker beliefs act as barriers to some young people and provide opportunities to others. In short, the agenda was to investigate how the opportunities for young adults within the labour market differ and to explore the part played by employers and unions in reproducing those differences.

This was done through a comprehensive study of 360 employers in three contrasting labour markets during the period 1977–80 (Ashton *et al.* 1982). The three towns chosen for study were St Albans, which represented the more affluent south-east with its dependence on high technology industry and low levels of unemployment, Sunderland, a northern town in decline with high levels of unemployment as the old manufacturing industries collapsed, and Leicester, which had a broad industrial base and average level of unemployment. The focus was on employers' recruitment and training of 16- to 18-year-old school-leavers. The study demonstrated how opportunities for young people varied between local labour markets and how local labour market conditions affected employers' recruitment and training practices. It also revealed how employers used age, sex, training and promotion as mechanisms for segmenting their labour forces. Dual labour market theory was initially used as the basis for the research but, as the research revealed the inadequacy of that approach, segmentation theory was adopted as a more appropriate framework for the analysis of the youth labour market.

While this research was one of the first to explore the structure of opportunities facing young people in the labour market, in terms of Eliasian Figurational Sociology it remained an incomplete analysis. This was because it ignored the experience of young adults moving through the labour market and the part they play in reproducing and changing the overall figuration. To rectify this, the Leicester group embarked on a study of 1,800 young adults (18- to 24-year-olds) in contrasting local labour markets during the period 1983–4 (Ashton and Maguire 1986). The same three local labour markets were used, together with a fourth, Stafford, chosen to provide a better balance between white-collar and blue-collar workers in the total sample. The theoretical task was to explore the relationship between the two dimensions and to explore hypotheses derived from their earlier study of employers about the significance of age, gender and skill as factors which segmented the labour market. The results provided clear evidence of the segmentation of the labour market in terms of gender, age and skill. It provided firm evidence of the separation of the youth and adult labour markets and how young adults moved from one to the other. It also provided some of the first evidence of the existence of an underclass, that is, a group of young adults who over a four- to eight-year period had never experienced full-time employment and whose experience of the labour market was confined to one of sub-employment, moving from government schemes, casual employment to unemployment and back to government schemes.

Having identified the boundaries of the youth and adult labour markets and their segmented character the next task, from an Eliasian perspective, was to examine how processes of change were transforming the relationship between them. Segmentation theory had been utilised to identify some of the practices used by employers and unions to segment the labour market and it was clear that, with the perpetuation of high levels of unemployment and the radical changes that were taking place in the economy during the 1980s, the labour market for young adults, as distinct from school-leavers who were absorbed into YTS, was undergoing significant changes. The theoretical task was to identify which of the various processes of change, impacting on the economy and the state and affecting the labour market in general, were transforming the relationship between the youth and adult labour markets. The result was a project started in 1986 which involved interviews with 40 large UK-based employers together with an analysis of the labour force survey (Ashton *et al.* 1990).

The various processes of change which could be important in transforming the relationship between the youth (16- to 24-year-olds) and adult labour markets were to be identified through interviews with employers. These interviews were also to be used to identify the factors which influenced employers' decisions about the types of labour they used, how they used that labour and the circumstances under which they changed the type of labour they used. However, case studies of this type were of limited use in identifying the consequences of such changes for the youth and adult labour markets. If the research was to uncover the impact of processes of change (such as the globalisation of product markets, new technology and the relocation of capital) on the relationship between the youth and adult labour markets, other research techniques had to be used. To answer these questions, data from various sweeps of the Labour Force Survey was used. In methodological terms this involved integrating qualitative data from intensive in-depth interviews with employers with quantitative data from the Labour Force Survey.

Using shift-share analysis the researchers were able to differentiate the impact of the business cycle (recession) from that of the longer-term processes of change which were affecting the UK.[1] While the 1980–3 recession had been instrumental in producing the greatest increase in youth unemployment, the longer-term processes of change were gradually reducing the size of the labour market for 16- to 17-year-olds and changing the points in the labour market where young school-leavers were able to compete with adults. Thus the relocation of capital, especially the labour-intensive industries of textiles, footwear etc., was reducing the number of unskilled and semi-skilled jobs available for early school-leavers (both males and females); the decline of engineering industries was reducing the demand for (male) apprentices while the growth of part-time work in the service

153

sector was further reducing jobs for (female) school-leavers and replacing them with married women workers. The growth of administration and the professions was increasing the opportunities for older (18-years plus) school- and college-leavers with intermediate and higher level qualifications. New technology was transforming the type of skills required of young adults, providing those who had acquired keyboard skills at school with a competitive advantage in relation to older workers when it came to white-collar jobs. Overall the result was a continuous shrinkage of the labour market for 16-year-olds, both males and females, although the male segments were shrinking faster than those for female school-leavers.

The latest stage in the research process was to introduce a comparative dimension into the analysis (Ashton 1988; Ashton and Lowe 1991). This meant identifying the distinctive features of the relationship between the youth and adult labour markets in other societies (initially Canada). The task was to examine how far the processes of change which were restructuring the youth labour market in Britain were also transforming the youth labour markets in other industrial societies. According to Elias, the same processes of change would be affecting all industrial societies but their outcomes would differ in accordance with variations in the national context. In view of this, the task was to find out how far the outcome of these processes of change was the same in all industrial societies and the extent to which different national institutions responsible for regulating the transition were producing differences in the outcome of these processes.

They found that the same pattern of a general shrinkage in the opportunities for unqualified 17- to 18-year-olds was also evident in Canada. However, there were important differences, for example in the use of the apprenticeship system in the two countries. In the UK, age restrictions on entry have meant that it has been used to provide sheltered points of entry to craft training for school-leavers. In Canada this is not the case. There firms usually wait until the new 18-year-old entrants have been with the company for a number of years before investing in their apprenticeship. This means that there is a much narrower range of opportunities for 18-year-old leavers than is the case in the UK. Another interesting feature of the Canadian situation is that because of the longer period young people (16- to 24-year-olds) spend in education, and because many of them combine education with part-time work, the process of transition is more attenuated. This means that the education system is more capable of absorbing young people during the recession and therefore reduces the level of youth unemployment (Ashton and Lowe 1991).

THE ACHIEVEMENTS OF THE LABOUR MARKET APPROACH

The main achievement of the labour market approach has been to demonstrate the extent to which the labour market in general and the youth labour market in particular has been segmented in terms of age, skill, gender and ethnicity. Prior to the development of segmentation theory, while some academics acknowledged the existence of these barriers to employment, their impact in structuring the opportunities within the labour market had not been systematically taken into account.

Thus the segmentation approach has stressed the role of vocational education and training in structuring the movement of young people in the labour market. Schools are seen to play an important role in providing young people with ideas, beliefs and behaviours 'functional' for the type of work they enter in the labour market. The institutional form taken by training is also seen to play an important part in constraining the movement of young people into particular segments of the labour market. Apprenticeships and other forms of occupational labour markets do this in a number of ways: by leading the young trainee to identify with the occupation, for example, and by creating pressure on him or her to stay within the occupation in which they have been trained in order to capitalise on the investment made in their training. The certification requirements imposed by employers and unions function to exclude other workers from competing for these jobs, even within internal labour markets.

The specific form in which vocational education in the UK is provided also has important consequences for the ability of different groups to compete within the labour market. For example, in Canada vocational education is largely provided through the educational system, producing similar levels of educational attainment among males and females by age 18. Therefore, when competing for professional and intermediate white-collar jobs, both groups have equal credentials and this appears to have facilitated a higher proportion of females entering traditional male enclaves in these jobs. In the UK, females opt out of the system earlier to enter traditional female segments in clerical and allied jobs. One consequence of this is that rather than facilitating access to higher segments, their credentials only serve to 'lock' them into clerical and secretarial employment and fewer females in the UK are therefore in a position to compete with males for entry into the higher level professions. In this way the theory focuses on the mechanisms whereby vocational education and training reproduces the differentiation of the labour market through time into discrete segments.

Segmentation theory also emphasises the reciprocal influence of labour market structures on the educational system. For example, in Britain it highlights how historically the delivery of training through the employer and to a lesser extent union provision, left schools free to concentrate on academic education. The initial delivery of the Youth Training Scheme through employers had the consequence of reinforcing the British tradition of early school-leaving by offering young people a financial incentive to leave school at 16. With regard to government policy, while the segmentation approach acknowledges that this can be an important influence on the structuring of labour markets, it contextualises that influence and shows how the power of vested interests can be used to structure government interventions, as in the case of the discussion by Lee *et al.* of the youth training programmes (1990). More generally it has established the importance of work-related factors such as the local opportunity structure, the level of unemployment, firms' employment and recruitment strategies and training provision in structuring the transition to (un)employment.

Another area where it has made a significant impact has been in the study of unemployment (Ashton 1986). The existence of barriers to employment in the form of age, skill, gender and ethnicity has also made it more difficult for those who become unemployed to re-enter the labour market. The systematic tracing of the labour market histories of the unemployed has revealed the typical pattern of sub-employment and the disadvantages which this imposes on young people as they seek to re-enter full-time employment. Moreover, the nature of employers' recruitment practices, their attitudes towards the unemployed and their use of informal mechanisms for recruitment mean that the longer-term unemployed become geographically concentrated and develop their own culture. They mix socially with other unemployed people and drop out of the informal information networks through which news of job vacancies is transmitted among the employed.

Overall the labour market approach can be said to have opened up the 'black box' of the youth labour market to sociological enquiry. It has been instrumental in identifying the parameters of the youth labour market and the main contours of the segments which comprise it, and in examining the relationship between the youth and adult labour markets. In this respect it has provided an alternative model for the analysis of movement within the labour market to that of the 'status attainment' school. It has drawn attention to the need for an understanding of changes in the relationship between education and the labour market to take account of longer-term changes in the nature of capital, in the structure of competition between employers, in the relocation of capital between societies, in the impact of new technology and in the role of government intervention.

There are a number of questions which remain to be examined. Recent changes in the flows of young people through the educational system, in the role of government training programmes and in employers' demand for labour are continuing to transform the youth labour market in the UK. This inevitably means that the size and structure of the various segments which comprise the youth labour market in the UK are also changing. One aspect of this problem concerns the changing role of occupational and firm-internal labour markets in the socialisation of new workers, about which relatively little is known. As the apprenticeship system declines has this resulted in the decline of occupational labour markets within the UK or have alternative means been found for reproducing occupational-based skills within the education system? If the apprenticeship system has declined in certain industries, e.g. engineering, have employers developed alternative mechanisms for training within the context of their internal labour markets? We have already seen how the broader processes of economic change are reducing the size of the market for 16-year-olds, but there is also evidence within the UK that they are combining with political change to polarise groups within the labour market. As the size of the youth labour market shrinks, those young people who enter it with few or no educational qualifications are finding it increasingly difficult to obtain secure employment. One consequence is that many young adults are being confined to marginal positions within the labour market, generating the conditions for a possible new underclass. Reacting to new economic pressures from intensified competition, employers are making new demands on youth in terms of the qualities they seek, but relatively little is known about how these changes are impacting on different segments of the youth labour market. In terms of the relationship between the youth and adult labour markets, earlier research suggests that the labour market for young workers is diminishing, but relatively little is known about the impact of the latest recession in either accelerating or reversing this trend.

Other questions which remain to be explored are those concerned with the relationship between young adults' experience of household formation, housing provision, welfare benefits and their (un)employment experiences. It is clear that young adults' experiences and behaviour in all these areas are interdependent, but our knowledge of the nature of those interdependencies is still in its infancy.

CONCLUSION

In conclusion, the main achievement of the labour market approach has been to develop an understanding of the structure of the youth labour market, its relationship to the adult labour market and the ways in which it is being transformed, and how this varies between societies. One consequence of this has been a growing convergence among researchers in the Sociology of Education tradition and in the labour market tradition, in terms of their approach to the study of the transition. Questions of labour market organisation and their impact on the educational system now figure prominently in the work of Raffe and Bynner, while researchers approaching from the labour market tradition are more sensitive to the significance of factors associated with individual achievements and characteristics in their attempts to understand the behaviour and experience of young people in the labour market.

However, there is still a great deal of work to be done in establishing a more coherent approach among researchers to the study of the transition and more generally in terms of developing our understanding of the relationship between the education/training system, the labour market and young people's experiences in other spheres of contemporary life. At the level of international comparisons, in spite of the advances made through the 'societal approach', there is still no satisfactory conceptual framework available for the analysis of education/labour market relations. To develop such a conceptual framework is essential if we are to enhance our understanding of our own societies. The task becomes imperative if we are to establish a meaningful dialogue among the international community of researchers working in this area.

NOTES

1 Shift-share analysis provides an estimate of the extent to which the decline in youth employment, which occurred in the period 1979–84, was due to each one of three components: changes in all-age employment, changes in the industrial or occupational structure and changes in the proportion of youth to all-age employment. The first component, the change in all-age employment, provides an estimate of the impact of changes in the general level of demand (cyclical change) on the demand for youth labour; the second provides an estimate of the extent to which change is due to shifts in the industrial or occupational structure (structural change).

BIBLIOGRAPHY

Ashton, D. N. (1986) *Unemployment Under Capitalism: The Sociology of British and American Labour Markets*, Brighton: Wheatsheaf.
——(1988) 'Sources of variation in labour market segmentation: a comparison of youth labour markets in Canada and Britain', *Work, Employment and Society* 2(1): 1–24.
Ashton, D. N. and Field, D. (1976) *Young Workers: The Transition From School to Work*, London: Hutchinson.
Ashton, D. N. and Lowe, G. S. (eds) (1991) *Making Their Way: Education, Training and the Labour Market in Canada and Britain*, Milton Keynes/Toronto: Open University Press and University of Toronto Press.
Ashton, D. N. and Maguire, M. J., with Bowden, D., Kennedy, S., Stanley, G., Woodhead, G. and Jennings, B. (1986) *Young Adults in the Labour Market*, Research Paper 55, London: Department of Employment.
Ashton, D. N., Maguire, M. J. and Garland, V. (1982) *Youth in the Labour Market*, Research Paper 34, London: Department of Employment.
Ashton, D. N., Maguire, M. J. and Spilsbury, M. (1990) *Restructuring the LabourMarket: The Implication for Youth*, London: Macmillan.
Banks, M., Bates, I., Breakwell, G., Bynner, J., Emler, N., Jamieson, L. and Roberts, K. (1992) *Careers and Identities*, Milton Keynes: Open University Press.
Brown, P. (1987) *Schooling Ordinary Kids: Inequality, Unemployment and the New Vocationalism*, London: Tavistock.
Burchell, B. and Rubery, J. (1987) 'The experience of individuals in the labour market: determinants of their employment expectations and job satisfaction', *International Working Party on Labour Market Segmentation*, Turin: International Labour Organisation.
Bynner, J. M. and Roberts, K. (1991) *Youth and Work: Transition to Employment in England and Germany*, London: Anglo-German Foundation.
Carter, M. P. (1962) *Home, School and Work*, Oxford: Pergamon.

Craig, C., Rubery, J., Tarling, R. and Wilkinson, F. (1982) *Labour Market Structure, Industrial Organisation and Low Pay*, Cambridge: Cambridge University Press.

Doeringer, P. and Piore, M. J. (1971) *Internal Labor Markets and Manpower Analysis*, Lexington, MA: Heath & Co.

Elbaum, B. and Wilkinson, F. (1979) 'Industrial relations and uneven development: a comparative study of the American and British steel industries', *Cambridge Journal of Economics* 3.

Elias, N. (1978a) *What is Sociology?*, London: Hutchinson.

——(1978b) *The Civilizing Process*, Oxford: Blackwell.

Furlong, A. (1993) *Growing up in a Classless Society: School to Work Transitions*, Edinburgh: Edinburgh University Press.

Horrell, S., Rubery, J. and Burchell, B. (1990) 'Gender and skills', *Work, Employment and Society* 4(2): 189–216.

Jenkins, R. (1983) *Lads, Citizens and Ordinary Kids*, London: Routledge.

Lee, D. (1966) 'Industrial training and social class', *Sociological Review* 14(3): 269–85.

——(1981) 'Skill, craft and class: a theoretical critique and a critical case', *Sociology* 15(1): 56–78.

Lee, D., Marsden, D., Rickman, P. and Duncombe, J. (1990) *Scheming for Youth: A Study of YTS in the Enterprise Culture*, Milton Keynes/Philadelphia: Open University Press.

Osterman, P. (1980) *Getting Started: The Youth Labor Market*, London: MIT Press.

Roberts, K. (1975) 'The developmental theory of occupational choice: a critique and an alternative' in G. Esland, G. Salaman and M. Speakman (eds) *People and Work*, Edinburgh: Holmes McDougall.

Roberts, K., Dench, S. and Richardson, D. (1986) *The Changing Structure of Youth Labour Markets*, Research Paper 59, London: DE.

Rosenberg, S. (1989) 'Labor market restructuring in Britain and the United States: the search for flexibility', in S. Rosenburg (ed.) *The State and the Labor Market*, New York: Plenum Press.

Rubery, J. (1978) 'Structured labour markets, worker organisation and low pay', *Cambridge Journal of Economics* 2: 17–36.

Rubery, J., Wilkinson, F. and Tarling, R. (1989) 'Government policy and the labor market: the case of the United Kingdom', in S. Rosenberg (ed.) *The State and the Labor Market*, New York: Plenum Press.

Wilkinson, F. (ed.) (1981) *The Dynamics of Labour Market Segmentation*, London/San Francisco: Academic Press.

Willis, P. (1977) *Learning to Labour: How Working Class Kids get Working Class Jobs*, Farnborough: Saxon House.

11

IS THIS A WAY OF UNDERSTANDING EDUCATION–WORK RELATIONS?

Cultural perspectives on youth transitions in Britain

Lynne Chisholm[1]

Considering and illustrating the contribution of cultural perspectives to understanding education–work relations poses problems. We are faced with making sense of a relatively inchoate and fractured sub-field (called here 'youth transitions' research[2]), one whose boundaries are fluid and whose character is not wholly fixed. This does not necessarily mean that the study of youth transitions is underdeveloped. Rather, there are few theoretical sacred cows to observe and the empirical landscape is fast moving. The lack of objective certainty about what to include or exclude, and under which ordering principles to do so, carries unavoidable risks. On the other hand, it affords a certain luxury – a freer selection of anchor concepts and field structuring than might otherwise be the case.

This account opens by placing the recent history of British youth research on to the sociological and policy map. The Centre for Contemporary Cultural Studies (CCCS), at its zenith in the 1970s, became virtually synonymous with British youth research through to the mid-1980s. The culturalist perspectives it introduced existed alongside and at some distance from school-to-work research, whose macrostructural concerns and approaches could be more easily linked to the broader field of education–work relations. The 1980s saw a rapprochement between the two strands, prompted by the collapse of the youth labour market at the end of the 1970s. The outcome has been the development of youth transitions research, in which the influence of culturalist perspectives can be readily identified.

The second section of the chapter traces the development of cultural perspectives on youth transitions in Britain. The CCCS approach to youth research sets the scene, followed by examples of subsequent empirical research that carry forward its concerns into youth transitions research during the 1980s. The principle that guides this pathway is deliberate and simple. The analysis of gender relations delivered the driving theoretical edge in the youth research field as a whole during the 1980s. Therefore, work that focuses upon gendered youth transitions structures the argument.

This focus is carried over into the third part of the discussion. It illustrates how cultural perspectives have been applied to understanding gendered education–work relations in relation to processes of social reproduction and change. In this work, the concept of cultural codes – as originally elaborated by Bernstein (1977, 1993) – plays an important role. Cultural codes mediate between social structures and human subjectivities in the construction and reconstruction of social life. Contemporary writing on gendered transitions assumes relatively autonomous articulations between, on the one hand, firmly structured and interrelated gendered divisions of labour in the labour market and in the family and, on the other hand, girls' finely patterned positionings as active subjects in gender discourse. Reflections on the progress made by youth transitions research in the past decade and the problems that face us in the 1990s close the chapter.

YOUTH RESEARCH IN BRITAIN

British youth research is not a coherent intellectual field, nor a clearly recognised specialism. First, the policy portfolio 'youth affairs' is weak and fragmented, while funding specifically earmarked for youth research is scarce.[3] Second, field specialisms in sociology are typically synchronic. Privileging the analysis of positions and places, they divide up social life into discrete sectors (education, work, family) or groups (social class, gender, ethnicity/race). In contrast, diachronic specialisms (such as life course research), which focus on social processes and dynamics, are less well established. In consequence, sociological discourse characteristically produces bodies of knowledge that divide and fracture the public from the private, production from reproduction, structures from subjectivities. In particular, the tension between synchronic and diachronic modalities slips from view (Chisholm 1990; Cohen 1986). Effectively, privileging the analysis of social relations and of dynamic processes of transition demands that sociologists work against the grain of established theoretical furrows.

Contemporary youth research demands working against the grain. Sociologically, youth transitions are made up of a complex array of sites and social practices in which synchronic and diachronic principles of social organisation confront each other directly. The resulting tensions produce sets of contradictions with which young people must negotiate as they reposition themselves and are repositioned within generational divisions of labour structured by class, gender and ethnicity/race. The study of youth transitions as relational processes is thus oriented towards integrating the public and the private, production and reproduction, structures and subjectivities. Education–work relations are clearly a major element in the study of youth transitions. At the same time, post-1960s youth research in Britain has been strongly influenced by culturalist perspectives. These have consistently underlined the idea that, first, transitions between education and employment cannot be regarded in isolation from other dimensions of young people's lives and, second, patterns of transition between school and work represent more than the realisation of social chances and constraints. They also incorporate processes of production and reproduction of classed and gendered cultures and subjectivities. And so it has been argued, for example, that the 'new vocationalism' of 1980s Britain is of paradigmatic significance in understanding education–work relations today. The changing pathways between school and work not only affect the mechanics of youth transitions, but they also reform subjectivities in line with redefined social and economic requirements (Hollands 1991).

Until quite recently, the youth studies field was marked by a cleavage between 'school-to-work' research and 'youth cultural studies'. School-to-work research was anchored in synchronic perspectives: pupils in education are converted into workers in production. Youth cultural studies asserted diachronic perspectives: specifically located subjects constructing and reconstructing forms of cultural life and identities across time and space. The 1980s saw considerable rapprochement between these two research strands – in differently accented ways, they both study the structures and processes of youth transitions. Above all, in joining gender with generation (McRobbie and Nava 1984) the study of gendered transitions has powered this rapprochement. Quite simply, explaining and understanding girls' lives demands integrative principles of analysis.

Bringing cultural perspectives on youth transitions and the field of education–work relations into fruitful communication with each other continues to hold tensions. First, political and policy priorities mean that studying linkages between education and employment acquires an automatic legitimacy. School-to-work research is dominated by investigations into the structures of the youth labour market together with education, training and employment selection and recruitment mechanisms. It would be difficult to argue that cultural perspectives have been more than marginal to this endeavour (but see Ashton, this volume). Second, CCCS-style youth cultural studies had consciously distanced itself from the empirical and theoretical concerns of education and the labour market researchers. However, its work on youth sub-cultures and styles or (girls') family and domestic transitions did not offer immediate points of contact either. Would the two strands of youth research ever have seriously engaged with each other had Paul Willis not written *Learning to Labour* (1977)? Willis' study was about working-class white males, so it could indeed lock into a school-to-work research community that had bracketed class divisions into its understandings of youth labour markets – but that equally had steadfastly continued to bracket out gender divisions and had hardly begun to consider those grounded in ethnicity and race.

On the other hand, there is little doubt that the theoretical and method-ological effervescence of youth cultural studies has revitalised the study of education–work relations, certainly where youth and gender are concerned. Their contemporary influence can be charted at three levels. To begin with, adequate understandings of youth transitions require holistic and integrated perspectives. Education–work relations must be contextualised within estab-lished ways of life, within group and community cultures. Cultural and social biographical analysis is thus at least as important as institutional or system analysis: how do specifically located subjects and groups understand and deal with institutionalised imperatives and frameworks of possibility and impossibility in constructing the course of their lives and identities? Next, youth transitions studies favour smaller-scale and methodologically qualitative approaches. Research activity seeks here a solid empirical founda-tion for highly interpretative analyses. The value of an illuminative account which can set off a chain of metaphor and imagery is characteristic of the genre, which ultimately draws on the triple ancestry of literary criticism, critical social commentary, and Chicago School microsociology. This research style has in the past decade enriched the study of education–work relations, which traditionally favoured macrosociological, economic and hence quanti-tative approaches. Lastly, explicating the nature and the workings of ideologies in the production and reproduction of social relations, subjectiv-ities and cultural life became a core endeavour in British sociology from the 1970s to the mid-1980s. The application and development of these ideas in the 'bridge-building' field of research in the sociology of education undoubt-edly fostered their rapid infusion into the field of education–work relations during the 1980s (see Raffe, this volume).

By the mid-1980s youth cultural studies had moved into a different trajectory, increasingly interested in symbolic representation and imaginary relations *per se* (McRobbie 1991a). The growing popularity of post-structuralism (re)problematised terms such as reality and subjectivity altogether, which in turn placed question marks on the theoretical relevance of studying young people's real lives in the first place. The fundamental problem was that:

> the youth question was radically disconnected from young people; it became simply the site of a multiplicity of conflicting discourses; youth had no reality outside its representation. . . . In practice, the overwhelming focus [of the new wave theories] on the practices of leisure and pleasure . . . has tended to collude with the impact of the consciousness industries in ignoring the mundane worlds of family, school and work which most young people still inhabit.
>
> (Cohen 1986: 21, 24)

The collapse of the youth labour market returned these more mundane aspects of young people's lives back to the top of the agenda.

Education–work relations came to dominate youth researchers' concerns – in retrospect, too much so, it is now generally acknowledged. On the other hand, it might be argued that the very pressure of that collapse forced the process of rapprochement which has, in the early 1990s, forged a renewed youth research alliance. Events required a pooling of perspectives and methods to produce plausible and – above all – practically useful information about young people's plight in facing the transition between education, training and (un)employment. The study of youth transitions might be defined as the charting of continuities and discontinuities in the relationships between social and economic change and the social construction of the life course. As such, it makes a distinctive contribution to the field of education–work relations, although it remains the case – in my view – that on this terrain culturalist perspectives comprise the subsidiary discourse.[4]

CULTURAL PERSPECTIVES ON YOUTH TRANSITIONS

Youth cultural studies, which dominated youth research through the 1970s, took its initial lead in a critique of universalistic and ahistorical perspectives on youth as a social category.[5] CCCS-inspired writing powerfully argued that youth is not class-differentiated in nature, but that young people *per se* stand in a specific articulation with class structure. The precise quality of that articulation could be elucidated through researching youth (sub-)-cultures of different kinds (Murdock and McCron 1976). Investigation of youth sub-cultures came to be understood and practised as a form of class analysis. This view constituted a decisive theoretical moment in the direction taken by British youth research in the subsequent decade. Youth sub-culture was more or less conceptually identified with the forms taken by male working-class cultural representation and action. Explicit debate ensued over the question of whether, in theoretical terms, there could be such a thing as middle-class youth sub-culture (Clarke *et al.* 1976).

Despite *Learning to Labour*, the primary focus of youth cultural studies did not lie in youth transitions, and certainly not in school-to-work transitions. First, the cultural studies perspective defined youth as a social and cultural entity in its own right, not as an externally defined temporary lacuna between childhood dependency and accession to independent adulthood. Much research has therefore been directed at documenting and interpreting the meanings of fashions, life styles and social movements as distinctive features of autonomous youth culture (paradigmatically: Hebdige 1979; McRobbie 1988). Second, youth cultural studies has always underlined the significance of young people's lives outside school – and increasingly, outside and beyond employment. This was partly to counteract the idea that young people are only in transit between childhood and adulthood, or that they only exist in social and cultural contexts created and controlled by adults (schools and workplaces). As youth unemployment rose, so it became important to look at how young people construct their lives meaningfully without the prospect of paid work (summarising: Griffin 1993).

In addition, from the mid-1970s youth cultural studies had come under increasing criticism from within its own ranks on the grounds that girls' and young women's lives had been consistently marginalised and excluded from serious consideration, both theoretically and empirically (collating: McRobbie 1991b). In the first place, girls' (sub-)cultures were made invisible by the assumptions researchers held about what kinds of peer group activities indicated opposition to adult culture or resistance to (middle-class) cultural hegemony. In caricature, violent public disturbance counted, peaceful private withdrawal did not. But, in the second place, young women's lives are constructed within tensions and contradictions largely unknown or irrelevant for young men – between the public and the private, work and family, self-actualisation and sacrifice. The analysis of youth culture only makes sense if it is gender-specific. Gender-specificity implies not simply conscious recognition of gendered youth (sub-)cultures in themselves, but more essentially that youth cultural forms are fundamentally structured by gender relations, both materially and ideologically.

This is the origin of the concept 'culture of femininity' (McRobbie 1978) which was used to redress the marginal and stereotyped position of girls and young women in youth research by asserting the independence of girls' (sub-)cultures from those of boys, by providing a more realistic picture of female adolescent experience, and by demonstrating how gendered futures are socially constructed as girls approach the transition between school and paid work. Griffin's (1985) ethnography of working-class Birmingham schoolgirls (originally designed as the female counterpart to Willis' *Learning to Labour*) contended that it is ideological assumptions about what 'typical girls' are like that mask young women's actual experiences and attributes. Unlike Willis' 'gang of lads' constructions of working-class masculinity, Griffin was concerned to deconstruct the stereotypes of adolescent femininity that materially affected the quality of girls' transitions between school and (un)employment.

Willis' (1977) study of working-class schoolboys in the Midlands had concluded that they reproduced their own class positions through what he (unfortunately) termed a 'partially penetrating' understanding of symbolic distinctions between mental and manual labour. Mental labour signifies middle-class cultural values and activities, manual labour its working-class and ideologically oppositional counterpart. The schoolboys symbolised solidarity with their class-cultural community by valuing manual labour more highly than mental labour, in contradistinction to dominant hierarchies of social esteem and to objective rewards. But it was gender ideology that played the crucial mediating role in the boys' interpretation. They equated mental labour with femininity, manual labour with masculinity.

The reproduction of class relations and gender relations are evidently interrelated phenomena. However, in this kind of formulation gender relations took a subsidiary analytic role. Willis' analysis did not help to understand how girls learn to be women (note: Sharpe 1976) in the transition between schooling and the labour market (or how boys learn to be men, for that matter). The critical theoretical issue for the 1980s was to explore how gender and class relations – as relatively autonomous but equally significant analytic modalities – are produced and reproduced across youth transitions. The empirical focus lay especially on transitions between education and work, both because of high youth unemployment and, increasingly, in the light of changing labour market and occupational structures during the 1980s.

Sharpe's study of West London working-class schoolgirls had described their job aspirations as depressingly narrow and stereotyped.[6] But although almost all wanted to enter 'women's' jobs, few wanted to go into factory work, catering and similar lower level service occupations (which is where women workers were numerically most likely to be found). In her view, the girls' aspirations reflected the cultural symbolism of femininity combined with the extension of women's traditional roles into the market-place. Many women's jobs are imbued with the tasks of caring for and servicing other people, demanding self-sacrifice and offering few opportunities for self-expression. Beecham's (1980) study of East London schoolgirls also concluded that the culture of femininity restricted job expectations and posed motherhood as their main vocation in life, regardless of educational success (i.e. high-achieving girls equally aspired to 'women's careers').

Aspirations clearly have symbolic functions, and these are not simply or exclusively relevant for transitions into the labour market. Wallace's (1987) Isle of Sheppey study showed that young people of both sexes retained gender-appropriate job aspirations even though the local labour market offered few opportunities to anyone. But gendered job aspirations remained, acting as expressions of attachment to gendered identities. These identities can be realised and put to work in spheres of social practice that are effectively disconnected from education and production. The young women – and men – in this study had little alternative but to pursue independence and adulthood through domestic transitions, but the relative labour market equivalence between young women and men did not noticeably modify gender divisions in partner and family relations.

The clerical and caring jobs so prominent in girls' aspirations service others in an assisting capacity; clerical jobs emphasise respectability, caring jobs emphasise selfless dedication. In other words, such jobs are occupational expressions of the culture of femininity. Resistance inevitably means crossing occupational gender boundaries. Which girls are in a position to do so, and how do they come to understand 'femininity' in relation to their own identities and practices? 16- to 18-year-olds of both sexes studied by Aggleton (1987) had chosen 'A' level courses at college that reflected the values of their educated liberal middle class parents: academic rather than vocational specialisms, arts/humanities subjects rather than science/mathematics. But equally, subject choices were bound up with the expression of class-culturally-appropriate gendered identities. For the young men, this meant locating themselves somewhere between the 'brutish manliness' of Willis' lads (associated with manual jobs) and the 'essential impotence' of 'committed and industrious' non-manual workers (such as college teachers!). For the young women, it meant distancing themselves from both those girls who had already left the education system and those who were doing their 'A' levels at school rather than at college. The college girls saw themselves as having non-conformist aspirations, both in the sphere of domestic transitions (whereas early school-leavers envisage early family formation and motherhood) and in employment transitions (whereas girls staying on at school aspire to traditional women's occupations). Their self-definition as gender trend-setters rested on automatically disqualifying girls who were industrious, openly ambitious, interested in scientific and technical subjects, and so on.

My own study of inner London schoolgirls in the mid-1980s suggested that it is high-achieving girls from working-class backgrounds who are more likely to display these characteristics (Chisholm 1993). It is these girls who are more likely to cross occupational gender boundaries, less so middle-class girls such as those in Aggleton's study, who aspired to media and aesthetic–symbolic careers. Interestingly, girls from ethnic/racial minority backgrounds may also be readier to cross occupational gender boundaries. Mirzah's (1992) study confirms high-level aspirations and above-average examination success among black schoolgirls in London, who were strongly oriented towards upward mobility via education. They were also more likely to be occupational gender trend-setters than their white peers.

It seems clear that young women occupying different social locations position themselves differently within gender discourse (as ideology and practice). In turn, differentiated cultures of femininity are actively implicated in patterns of gendered educational–occupational transitions. In principle, the same argument might hold for cultures of masculinity, but to date few empirical studies have considered young men's transitions between school and work from this kind of perspective. Nevertheless, whether focused primarily upon the gender problematic or not, the development of youth transitions research has increasingly emphasised two features: the processes by which social positions are produced and reproduced in young people's lives, and the differentiated routes taken by these processes according to class, gender, ethnicity/race and regional locations as interactive factors.

CULTURES, CODES AND EDUCATION–WORK RELATIONS

Occupational segregation by sex constitutes a fundamental feature of the objective social worlds in which all children grow up. In constructing their own futures, they must take this 'fact of life' into account, even though they may resent it and/or present their aspirations as free choices. However, it is rarely necessary explicitly to marginalise and exclude girls from wide sectors of the labour market, or boys from the narrow range of 'women's jobs'. In a variety of ways, young people generally come to exclude themselves, well in advance of the actual transition between education and paid work. The range of the occupationally possible arises not only as a consequence of what people see around them, but also as a result of what is culturally thinkable. The structuring of the channels of transition through secondary education, vocational training, job recruitment and occupational socialisation is by no means neutral in these respects. In particular, its effects can be read off from the contraction in the range of girls' aspirations and expectations over time. But equally, cultural semantics provide sets of meanings with which girls juggle in coming to a decision about what they say they want to be. What they say is but part of what they mean; there is much they do not say, and sometimes what they might want to say cannot get out or is ignored when it does – and so fades away or becomes recontextualised. These processes affect boys too, but much less severely and with fewer negative consequences.

Cultural perspectives on youth transitions thus pay attention to under-lying structures of meaning, treat human subjectivities/identities as social phenomena and assert the significance of ideologies in the construction of social life. To illustrate how these qualities have been exercised in the field of education–work relations, this section focuses on the idea of cultural codes as applied to theorising the gender problematic and viewed from the different vantage points of education/schooling, training and paid work.

MacDonald's (1981) essay on schooling and the reproduction of class and gender relations synthesised the theoretical debate about imaginary versus real relations of (re)production more than any other single contribution. Historically, specific gender ideologies cannot be separated from the material bases of patriarchy and capitalism, she argued, even where their inter-articulation is fundamentally contradictory. Overtly and covertly, schooling transmits and legitimates sets of gender relations that are associated with the division between domestic and waged labour, which in turn serves to repro-duce social relations of production. This process is mediated by a gender code, which sets up categories of masculine and feminine as well as the boundaries and relations of power between them. There is no necessary one-gender code, but there may well exist dominant and subordinated codes which both reflect and generate struggles between groups at the ideological level. The gendering of school curriculum subjects and the ideological struc-turing of school knowledge provided examples to support this argument.

Feminist-oriented research on the ways in which the structures and processes of schooling reinforce existing gender relations has become a sub-specialism in its own right (Weiner and Arnot 1987).

This first strand of theorising the gender problematic in education–work relations takes the vantage point of education's role in social reproduction. Cockburn's studies of the social dimensions of skill and technology begin from the vantage point of paid work (see also Rainbird, this volume). Ideological and economic paradigms remain complementary, not competing, accounts. Studies of the printing trade (1983) and engineering (1985) showed that men's domination of machinery and technology is a product of social history, within the context of men's more general appropriation of the very concept of work itself. A deficit model of women becomes a foregone conclusion in a discourse where engineering is a cultural synonym for masculinity; it is hardly surprising that young women overwhelmingly reject any thought of entering such a firmly gendered occupational sector. New technological occupations acquire gender in a two-way process between the jobs themselves and the workers' genders (reminiscent of MacDonald's account of school subjects and pupils' genders). In other words, work practices are in themselves gendering processes that function at the ideological level to maintain gender divisions. In a subsequent study of the Youth Training Scheme (1987), these ideas were explicitly applied to gendered youth transitions between education and work. The price of resisting the realism of gendered training decisions on leaving school is too high, the effort required too great for the majority of girls, especially given the lack of positive support networks for doing so.

The theorising strands represented by MacDonald and Cockburn both attempt to give equal explanatory weight to material and ideological factors. Cohen's account (1986) of the cultural relations between education and work places the analysis of ideology firmly at the centre of attention: he was interested in uncovering the hidden grammars and symbolic meanings of historically specific class-cultural practices. Cultural codes here constitute subject positions through which contradictions, divisions and discontinuities come to be experienced as their opposites. In other words, using the 'deep structures of cultural hegemony', cultural codes 'weave webs of imaginary correspondence', enabling people to make sense of the social and personal disjunctions they encounter. Traditionally, the young working class undertook a cultural apprenticeship which was embedded in the inheritance of particular skills transmitted through the family, the workshop and the local community. Young men's cultural apprenticeship was defined through the acquisition and celebration of manual skills and macho workshop culture. In contrast, young women's cultural apprenticeship was mainly exercised through acquiring competences that were interpreted in domestic terms, even when these skills were used on the labour market. But interestingly, youth and female labour have historically been regarded as of equivalent economic and cultural value, i.e. as performing unskilled servicing tasks. In a consciously drawn parallel between male sexual and occupational apprenticeships, the crucial issue here is that young working-class men are accorded a female gender at work until they have shown themselves not to be incompetent and unskilled. The conclusions are straightforward and are not restricted to imaginary relations: girls can neither grow up nor can they be 'really' skilled anywhere else except in the home. However, as social and economic change has accelerated in recent decades, traditional forms of the gendered cultural apprenticeship have begun to disintegrate, producing a shift of emphasis towards a career code, based on the principle of achieved qualification and individual progress. But has this meant that de-gendering of education–work relations is taking hold?

Bates' ethnography (in Bates and Riseborough 1993) of young Yorkshire women on YTS community care courses is of particular interest in this connection, since she wanted to explore interactions between cultural factors and training systems in shaping young people's occupational paths. In a reformulation of Willis' research question, she asks how working-class girls today get working-class and gender-typed jobs. Community care was primarily a fall-back YTS option, and becoming a care assistant (working with old people, children and the severely disabled) is effectively an extended domestic career. Following an initial period of shock and distancing, most trainees adjusted their orientations and gradually became highly committed to becoming care assistants. In the form of a constraining moratorium, the institutionalised context of the YTS community care course reinforces and selects specific forms of gender socialisation found in particular kinds of working-class family milieux. Daughters learn to work hard, serving others and denying their own needs as they do so. The culture of being a good care assistant demands similar competences. The course tutors and, subsequently, the girls themselves engaged in a repeated screening process, aimed at changing or eliminating 'bleeding whining minnies' who could (or would) not realise the appropriate stance. YTS thus acts as a channelling bridge between two cultural terrains: family division of labour/socialisation practices and occupational cultures. Training is a process of contradiction and struggle, channelling and adjustment *en route* to a gender- and class-appropriate occupation and its culture.

The shaping and realisations of girls' contestations between resistance and accommodation in the transition between education and work have attracted considerable attention in 1980s youth research. My own research concluded that it is the symbolic dimension of occupational gendering that positions girls in the first instance, but it is real labour market factors that fix and realise these positions at the end of the educational day (Chisholm 1995). In making the transition from education to employment and from youth towards adulthood, girls are working at their vocation of becoming women, a social identity informed by a differentiated culture of femininity in which the anchor feature is that of sacrifice. Occupational choice processes can be viewed as strategies for dealing with structured contradictions in personal and social circumstances, which provide a backcloth of resources that girls may use in constructing their 'transition biographies'. These occupational expressions may contain elements both of accommodation and of resistance. In my schoolgirl sample, the most complex and vibrant education–work trajectories came from girls who were subject to a range of structurally framed cross-pressures associated with their gender, class and ethnic cultural milieu, family situation and strategy, and educational environment. Educationally successful working-class girls were those most critically conscious of existing gender relations in the family and at work, and they were more likely to aspire to non-traditional occupations.

Metz-Göckel (1992) has similarly proposed that it is working-class girls and women who potentially constitute an avant-garde group as far as changing gender relations are concerned. To begin with, paid work was always a taken-for-granted necessity in working-class women's lives but, second, the domestic division of labour is typically more highly gendered in working-class homes than in the homes of educated middle-class profes-sionals. In sum, working-class girls experience more intense tensions and contradictions in relation to gender divisions between home and work spheres. This offers greater potential for pressures to change the existing structuring of gender relations, but the potential can only be released via educational achievement which they seldom achieve.

In the process of educationally succeeding, however, girls (of whatever class background) acquire ideologies to explain that success, to legitimate their success in the face of other pupils' failures. When it comes to giving explanations for the patterns of gender relations that they can describe so well, educationally successful girls use ideas which essentially deny the contemporary relevance of structured social inequalities in the eradication of women's remaining disadvantage. In other words, they emphasise equal opportunities (not equality) within a framework of meritocratic individu-alism. Women's continued disadvantage, in this account, becomes attributable to a de-gendered individual failure. In sum, girls use the same kind of individualising ideology that explains and legitimates young people's educational success and failure to explain and legitimate girls' and women's educational and employment positionings. To feel that one can take one's fate into one's own hands is personally emancipatory, but it is not necessarily socially emancipatory. This is the contradiction and paradox at the heart of contemporary individualisation processes, from which girls and women may well benefit, but which are nonetheless ideological motifs whose de-coding is a more complex affair than ever.

CONCLUDING REMARKS

Cultural perspectives on education–work relations are perennially subject to a degree of reserve in the professional community as a whole. They regularly draw a number of (at times self-contradictory) criticisms: they are static and over-deterministic, unable to deal with social change; they underrate the significance of social and economic structures and institutions; they indulge in eternal circles, unable to move beyond abstract critical analysis; their attachment to qualitative and ethnographic methods produces interesting reading but lacks rigour. Cohen (1986), however, concluded that whilst breaking down the youth question into its constituent elements and recomposing these into a differential, historico-structural model of the life course may be an unfashionable theoretical project, it remained an essential precondition for any genuine advance. A decade later, the project has become rather more fashionable: the study of youth transitions as embedded in the revitalisation of life course theory and research has witnessed a growing popularity (see, for example, Buchmann 1989; Cavalli and Galland 1993; Heinz 1991).

The earlier youth cultural studies generally took young people's own cultural forms as privileged sites of observation and analysis. The focus lay on non-institutionalised settings and not on schools, training environments or at the workplace. The productive interaction between youth cultural studies, school-to-work research and sociology of education from the late 1970s to the mid-1980s spawned a generation of inquiries that returned to institutional settings but applied distinctive theoretical and methodological insights to their analysis. It is this cluster of work that might be said to constitute (or at least to embrace) cultural perspectives on education–work relations.

The active subjects of education–work relations are not only young people, but they are certainly importantly young people. The field has come to recognise that youth transitions cannot usefully be reduced to the transition between school and employment (or unemployment), and to pay much more conscious attention to specificities and processes rather than broad generalities and snapshot outcomes. One hypothesis might be that this development was spurred on towards the close of the decade through the problems raised by comparative research, which had begun to generate broader interest in the context of approaching 'Europeanisation' processes (Bynner and Chisholm, f/c). In the case of my own thinking, this replayed the theoretical irritations that many feminist researchers in the field had felt from the 1970s onwards as far as the integration of gender into our understandings was concerned. Quite apart from the straightforward neglect of gender and of girls/women in theory and research at that time, it seemed evident that established labour market theories and models of occupational structuring could not, as they stood, rise to the task at hand. Some feminist researchers worked at critiques of labour market and labour process theories, others sought to understand more about the internally differentiated processes by which girls are both placed into and 'choose for themselves' gender- and class-appropriate life plans – including, quite specifically, education, training, jobs and worklife trajectories. For my part, this led to using the idea of transitions biographies constructed through a sort of three-dimensional pinball machine of social space and time, structured by divisions and intersections. Active subjects – working with complex, fractured identities – must struggle within the structured and structuring contradictions of the pinball playing field. There is no pinball wizard (sic!): it is the subjects themselves who must visualise and negotiate the game. How they do so and the trajectories through gendered youth transitions that thereby arise were the questions to be asked.

New problematics continually present themselves, and the study of youth transitions is no exception. The issues raised by the interconnectedness of contemporary European social change mean that it is probably no longer quite accurate to continue the narrative as if it were part of describing the specifically and exclusively British field of education–work relations. Contemporary theories of social change demand that the concepts of reproduction and polarisation that have been so characteristic of British (and arguably French) perspectives had to be interrogated with those of individualisation and pluralisation, in order to communicate with continental European theory and research.[7] It is evident, in comparing different European nation-states simply using crude social demographic indices, that institutionalised transitions systems interact with established cultural practices to produce sharply differing patterns in historically specific economic and policy climates. Education–work relations comprise, at one and the same time, both an institutional and a cultural complex of arrangements and meanings, to which young people's own understandings and actions contribute and within which they must try to construct and negotiate their transition to independent adulthood and citizenship. Presently, it would appear that, acting together, these features are increasingly producing not only delayed and interrupted but also complexly fragmented youth transitions. Some field commentators would persuade us to reformulate the debates in terms of the classic post-modern condition – there are no relations as such, simply a cacophony of disconnected life events subject to no over-arching rationality. Youth transitions, on this account, disintegrate into a splintering crash at the frontiers of the European highway. The crisis in transitions, remarked one well-informed colleague[8] with characteristically dry humour, is not about the reduction in entry routes – it is about the complete absence of exit routes!

NOTES

1 This paper was written and published before the author joined the European Commission in 1996. It expresses her personal professional views and does not implicate official Commission policy positions or activities in any way.

2 'Youth research' as a whole is not a sub-category of the 'education–work relations' field, whose terrain we are attempting to map in this project. Youth research is an independent and interdisciplinary specialism, but its concerns frequently overlap with those that arise in the study of education–work relations. 'Cultural perspectives' as such are by no means the sole province of youth researchers in general, nor of the youth cultural studies strand in particular. However, culturalist approaches are well-established in youth studies.

3 However, the ESRC has now approved a new research programme, *Youth, Citizenship and Social Change*, to begin during 1997. The European Community action programme *Youth for Europe* also now makes provision for applied youth research funding. These initiatives are most welcome.

4 The ESRC-funded 16–19 Initiative was an interesting case in this context: whilst particularly concerned with education/training/labour market transitions and using large-scale survey methods, it equally facilitated a series of small-scale ethnographic studies which operated semi-autonomously (see Banks *et al.* 1990; Bates and Riseborough 1993). It has since given rise to valuable intercultural analyses (Evans and Heinz 1994).

5 'Youth cultural studies' has been exhaustively described and summarised in Brake (1980, 1985). In a critique of the ways in which the theme of 'adolescence' has been addressed in the twentieth century, Griffin (1993) illustrates the ancestry and core concerns of 'culturalist' youth research in general. The brief account of CCCS-inspired youth research that now follows draws on Chisholm (1990).

6 Aspirations are neither expectations nor destinations, of course, though the three are interrelated in indirect ways.

7 The literature in this field is now developing rapidly; see Chisholm *et al.* 1995; CYRCE 1995; Bynner *et al.* 1997).

8 Basil Bernstein, personal communication, December 1992.

BIBLIOGRAPHY

Aggleton, P. (1987) *Rebels Without a Cause. Middle Class Youth and the Transition from School to Work*, Lewes: Falmer Press.

Banks, M., Bates, L., Breakwell, G., Bynner, J., Emler, N., Jamieson, L., and Roberts, K., (eds) (1990) *Careers and Identities*, Milton Keynes: Open University Press.

Bates, I. and Riseborough, G. (eds) (1993) *Youth and Inequality*, Milton Keynes: Open University Press.

Beecham, Y. (1980) 'What girls think of school, teachers and work', *Schooling and Culture* 7: 11–19, spring.

Bernstein, B. (1977) *Class, Codes and Control* III, (2nd revised edition), London/New York: Routledge.

——(1993) *Class, Codes and Control* V, Barcelona: El Rouve.

Brake, M. (1980) *The Sociology of Youth and Youth Sub-Cultures*, London/New York: Routledge.

——(1985) *Comparative Youth Culture. The Sociology of Youth Culture and Youth Sub-Cultures in America, Britain and Canada*, London/New York: Routledge.

Buchmann, M. (1989) *The Script of Life in Modern Society. Entry into Adulthood in a Changing World*, Chicago: University of Chicago Press.

Bynner, J., and Chrisholm, L., (forthcoming) 'Comparative Youth transition research: methods, meanings and research relations, *European Sociological Review*, Vol. 14, No. 2.

Bynner, J., Chisholm, L. and Furlong, A. (eds) (1997) *Youth, Citizenship and Social Change in a European Context*, Aldershot: Avebury.

Cavalli, A. and Galland, O. (eds) (1993) *L'allongement de la jeunesse en Europe occidentale*, Paris: Actes Sud.

Chisholm, L. (1990) 'A sharper lens or a new camera? Youth research, young people and social change in Britain', in L. Chisholm *et al.* (eds) *Childhood, Youth and Social Change: A Comparative Perspective*, Lewes: Falmer Press.

——(1993) 'Adolescent girls and schooling: gender, youth and transitions', *Comenius* 52, Winter.

——(1995) 'Cultural semantics: occupations and gender discourse', in P. Atkinson *et al.* (eds) *Discourse and Reproduction*, New Jersey: Hampton Press.

Chisholm, L., Büchner, P., Krüger, H.-H. and du Bois-Reymond, M. (eds) (1995) *Growing Up in Europe. Contemporary Horizons in Childhood and Youth Studies*, Berlin/New York: de Gruyter.

Clarke, J., Hall, S., Jefferson, T. and Roberts, B. (1976) 'Subculture, cultures and class' in S. Hall and T. Jefferson (eds) *Resistance through rituals. Youth Sub-cultures in Post-War Britain*, London: Hutchinson.

Cockburn, C. (1983) *Brothers: Male Dominance and Technological Change*, London: Pluto Press.

——(1985) *Machinery of Dominance: Women, Men and Technical Know-How*, London: Pluto Press.

——(1987) *Two-Track Training. Sex Inequalities and the YTS*, London: Macmillan.

Cohen, P. (1986) *Rethinking the Youth Question*, PSEC Working Papers 3, London: University of London, Institute of Education, Post-Sixteen Education Centre.

CYRCE (Circle for Youth Research Co-operation in Europe) (ed.) (1995) *The Puzzle of Integration*, European Yearbook on Youth Policy and Research I, Berlin/New York: de Gruyter.

Evans, K. and Heinz, W. R. (eds) (1994) *Becoming Adults in England and Germany*, London: Anglo-German Foundation.

Griffin, C. (1985) *Typical Girls? Young Women from School to the Job Market*, London: Routledge.

——(1993) *Representations of Youth. The Study of Youth and Adolescence in Britain and America*, Cambridge: Polity Press.

Hebdige, D. (1979) *Sub-Culture. The Meaning of Style*, London: Methuen.

Heinz, W. R. (ed.) (1991) *Theoretical Advances in Life Course Research*, Weinheim: Deutscher Studien Verlag.

Hollands, R. (1991) 'Working class youth transitions: schooling and the training paradigm' in Education Group II (Cultural Studies Birmingham) (ed.) *Education Limited. Schooling and Training and the New Right since 1979*, London: Unwin Hyman.

MacDonald, M. (1981) 'Schooling and the reproduction of class and gender relations', in R. Dale *et al.* (eds) *Education and the State 2, Politics, Patriarchy and Practice*, Lewes/Milton Keynes: Falmer Press/Open University Press.

McRobbie, A. (1978) 'Working class girls and the culture of femininity', in CCCS Women's Studies Group (ed.) *Women Take Issue*, London: Hutchinson.

——(1988) *Zoot Suits and Second Hand Dresses: An Anthology of Fashion and Music*, London: Macmillan.

——(1991a) 'Moving cultural studies on: post-Marxism and beyond', *Magazine of Cultural Studies* 4: 18–21.

——(1991b) *Feminism and Youth Culture. From Jackie to Just Seventeen*, London: Macmillan.

McRobbie, A. and Nava, M. (eds) (1984) *Gender and Generation*, London: Macmillan.

Metz-Göckel, S. (1992) 'Bildung, Lebensverlauf und Selbstkonzepte von "Arbeitertöchtern". Ein Beitrag zur sozialen Mobilität und Individualisierung von Frauen aus bildungsfernen Schichten', in A. Schlüter (ed) *Arbeitertöchter und ihr sozialer Aufstieg. Zum Verhältnis von Klasse, Geschlecht und sozialer Mobilität*, Weinheim: Deutscher Studien Verlag.

Mirzah, H. S. (1992) *Young, Female and Black*, London/New York: Routledge.

Murdock, G. and McCron, R. (1976) 'Consciousness of class and consciousness of generation', in S. Hall and T. Jefferson (eds) *Resistance through Rituals. Youth Sub-Cultures in Post-War Britain*, London: Hutchinson.

Sharpe, S. (1976) *Just Like A Girl: How Girls Learn to be Women*, Harmondsworth: Penguin.

Wallace, C. (1987) *For Richer, For Poorer. Growing Up In and Out of Work*, London/New York: Tavistock.

Weiner, G. and Arnot, M. (eds) (1987) *Gender Under Scrutiny. New Inquiries in Education*, Milton Keynes: Open University Press.

Willis, P. (1977) *Learning to Labour. How Working Class Kids Get Working Class Jobs*, Farnborough: Saxon House.

12

THE SOCIAL CONSTRUCTION OF SKILL

Helen Rainbird

INTRODUCTION

The literature surveyed in this section covers three major areas of research which focus on training and skill. Within these areas there are some clearly defined currents of research in terms of theoretical approach and methodology, but others are less coherent. The extent to which they engage directly with a concern for training and education varies. This reflects a number of objective features of the British training system and its relationship to skill. The most important feature of this has been the role played by apprenticeship as the major method of training for employment in skilled work and its regulation by craft unions. Therefore, to talk of skill is to talk of the role of skilled manual workers and their unions in the workplace. In this respect, apprenticeship was one of a number of mechanisms whereby these unions maintained their control over the supply of skilled labour.

An apparently contradictory aspect of this relationship lies in the fact that although the workplace has been the primary site of vocational education, nevertheless skills acquired through it have been widely recognised in the labour market. Thus apprenticeship training produces 'transferable skills' in the sense that the fact of having served an apprenticeship and being union members guarantees workers' employability in an occupational labour market. This is despite the fact that formal instruction has never been a requirement for recognition as a skilled worker. On-the-job training and 'sitting next to Nellie' have been the norm. There are formal qualifications, but it has been the completion of a period of time as an apprentice ('time-serving') which has traditionally been the criterion for recognition of skilled status.

Since the workplace is the primary location for the provision of vocational qualifications, apprentices are normally employees and receive their off-the-job instruction in Colleges of Further Education or in specialist training workshops. Vocational qualifications are not normally attained through the school system, so educational achievements are the criteria for recruitment into manual work.

It is often argued that employers and unions colluded in limiting apprenticeship intakes through a variety of mechanisms such as age limits and agreements on ratios of apprentices to skilled workers, resulting in a relatively low proportion of workers attaining skilled status. As a consequence, apprenticeship has always constituted a route into high-status manual work. The majority of manual workers have received little or no formal training. Alongside this, workers have operated job demarcations, defining who can do what in the workplace, as a means of restricting the employers' prerogative.

Trade union organisation is based on the principle of occupational recruitment. Therefore within the same workplace, workers in different categories are organised in different unions and there may also be different bargaining units for skilled, unskilled and white-collar workers. The existence of multiunionism and multiple bargaining units in the company has the effect of limiting the occupational mobility of workers from one category to another. The restriction of certain types of work to apprentice-trained workers is linked to the establishment of wage differentials between skilled and unskilled workers.

The characteristics of the training system outlined above have consequences for the way in which research on the workplace and training have developed. Although there is a rich tradition of qualitative, empirical research in the workplace within the Sociology of Work and Industrial Relations, this has tended to ignore vocational education and training. It has been more concerned with concepts of skill, deskilling and workers' control, on the one hand, and a focus on the institutions of collective bargaining, on the other. In contrast, researchers who are directly concerned with vocational education and training have tended to focus their empirical work on the policy environment and institutional structures of training rather than the workplace itself. The bringing together of a perspective on training with studies of the workplace has yet to be accomplished on a significant scale.

THE CONCEPT OF SKILL

In Britain the concept of skill, and skilled work or workers is intimately bound up with the tradition of apprenticeship. It is therefore surprising to find that the concept of skill is rarely defined. There are two explanations for this. First, 'skill' is a natural category about which there is common cultural understanding, requiring no explanation. Second, it is a complex concept concerning the characteristics of individuals and the politics of the organisation of production. Thompson argues that 'skill is largely based on knowledge, the unity of conception and execution, and the exercise of control by the workforce. . . . But in most cases skill is measured less by a formal definition than by historical context and comparison. The central

starting point of many studies has therefore been the nature and transformation of *craft* labour' (1983: 92).

Despite this long-standing association with apprenticeship, Gallie (1988)
points out that some writers have recognised the changing nature of skill
and have incorporated broader notions of the exercise of responsibility and
judgement, alongside expertise derived from general education and on-the-
job experience in their understanding of the term. In addition, the concept
of 'tacit skill' refers to abilities acquired through experience rather than
formal training as is often the case with workers whose jobs are classified as
unskilled. In other words,

> there appears to be little consensus between analysts on what consti-
> tutes skill or how it should be measured. The term covers a number of
> distinct capacities which are difficult to compare directly. . . . The very
> complexity of the task of defining skill, however, makes it implausible
> that skill classifications in industry reflect in an unproblematic way
> some objective hierarchy. Rather, they are likely to be the product of a
> continuous negotiation between employers and employee, in which
> both relative power resources and prevalent cultural beliefs will influ-
> ence the grading structure.
>
> (Gallie 1988: 8)

THE MAIN CURRENTS OF RESEARCH

Worker organisation and skill in the workplace

The role of craft unions in controlling skilled labour markets has long been
recognised (e.g. Jackson 1984; Price 1980; Turner 1962). These writers have
attempted to distinguish the intrinsic skills required to perform jobs in
particular industries from the ways in which workers' organisations have
been able to operate monopolistic powers within the labour market. The
major mechanism for exercising this control has been through the restriction
of access to skilled jobs through the apprenticeship system. However, it is
extremely difficult to unravel the role of apprenticeship, which has been the
major institutional mechanism for providing training, from the way in
which craft unions have used it to maintain a scarcity of their skills. This
literature has been linked to debates on the nature of the labour aristocracy
and the historical analysis of trade unionism.

More recently, the labour process debate, developed in response to
Braverman's *Labor and Monopoly Capital* (1974), has examined the relationship between worker organisation and skill. Its primary concern is the extent
to which capitalists' need to control the production process results in the
separation of conception from execution and thus a process of deskilling.
Work in this tradition combines Marxist theoretical debate and qualitative

research conducted on a case study basis. There is a certain coherence in this strand insofar as there is an annual 'Labour Process Conference' which has produced a series of publications (Knights and Wilmott 1986a, 1986b, 1988, 1990; Sturdy *et al.* 1992), though the journals *Work, Employment and Society* and *Capital and Class* have also published papers in this field.

Vocational education and training are not examined in this discussion of skill, and questions of autonomy and control are sometimes conflated with technical abilities. Some writers have attempted to refute Braverman's thesis on the grounds that empirical studies of the introduction of technological change have resulted in the upgrading of workers' skills (Penn 1982; Penn and Scattergood 1985) or do not automatically result in deskilling but leave a range of options open (Wilkinson 1983). Other writers have argued that this is to confuse workers' subjective evaluations of how technological change affects their skills with the general tendency identified by Braverman for management to take control of the process of conception away from workers (Armstrong 1988). Jenson has pointed out that Braverman himself uses a romanticised conception of craft skill and that much of the analysis of skill is based on studies of male workers in manufacturing industry and cannot be generalised to the economy as a whole (1989).

Research conducted on new technology and published in journals such as *New Technology, Work and Employment* also addresses questions concerning how changes in work organisation and new technology affect the demand for skills, though it is not necessarily framed in terms of the same debate. Again, this strand of research rarely examines training directly.

Feminist critiques of labour market and labour process theories

Feminist writers analysing work and employment have found that many dominant theories of the labour market do not provide a satisfactory analysis of patterns of women's labour market participation and the discrimination they experience in the labour market. For example, human capital theory has difficulty in explaining why women's skills and qualifications are systematically attributed less value in the labour market than men's. Theories of labour market segmentation, in emphasising the ways in which employers and trade unions contribute to the stratification of the labour market, demonstrate how some sectors of the workforce (women and ethnic minority workers in particular) are excluded from those jobs deemed as requiring higher levels of skill and benefiting from more favourable conditions of employment (Rubery 1980).

In order to explain patterns of job segregation, the concept of the gendering of jobs and people has been developed (Cockburn 1985). Socialisation within the school system, both through educational choices and through the 'hidden curriculum', contribute to young people's career decisions. Processes of labour market segmentation therefore operate both before and after entry into the labour market. Young women, undergoing vocational training at a time when they are establishing their gender identity, may have particular difficulties in moving into male occupations. This is not just a question of subjective perceptions of the appropriateness of different types of gendered jobs, but also the ways in which work groups facilitate or hinder the acceptance and socialisation of young workers. Sexual bantering and harassment in the workplace contribute to the controlling of women's behaviour by men (Purcell 1988; Pollert 1981) and create sanctions on women moving into non-traditional jobs in male-dominated work groups. Women's relationship to technology and their ability to lay claim to jobs requiring higher level technical skills have also been examined (Cockburn 1985).

The concept of skill itself has been questioned. Phillips and Taylor argue that it is saturated with gender assumptions. They claim that the classification of jobs as skilled or semi-skilled has more to do with the sex of the worker than the training or ability required to do them (1980).

The relationship between masculinity, trade union organisation and the social construction of skill has been examined by Cockburn in relation to the print industry (1983). This is one of the most insightful analyses of the multifaceted nature of skill, meriting consideration in some detail. She identifies three different elements of skill.

> There is skill that resides in the man himself, accumulated over time, each new experience adding something to a total ability. There is the skill demanded by the job – which may or may not match the skill of the worker. And there is the political definition of skill: that which a group of workers or trade union can successfully defend against the challenge of employers or other groups of workers.
>
> (Cockburn 1983: 113)

In analysing the introduction of new technology in the printing industry, she argues that although the male compositors acquired new word processing skills, they felt deskilled in relation to the skills that they had accumulated over their working lives. In other words, although they continued to consider themselves to be skilled, in practice, their jobs were not. Nevertheless, the political definition of skill continued to play a role. It ensured that they were able to lay claim to a new field of work and thus remain in employment.

Cockburn points out that skill is not just a class political weapon but also plays a part in the power relations between men and women. Women's abilities and work have been valued lower than men's. 'It has been a two way process: women's inferiority has rubbed off on their activities and the imputed mindlessness of the activities has reflected on women' (1983: 116). Therefore, insofar as the male compositors found themselves doing work that was similar to the female job of typing, their sense of degradation of skills could also be measured socially, in the way they saw themselves in relation to other workers, and women in particular. The men were caught in a contradiction – either they had to acknowledge that they were totally deskilled or they had to admit that many women were as skilled as they were (1983: 117).

Finally, Cockburn distinguishes between individual and collective aspects of skill. The exercise of skill has a different meaning for the individual than the one it has for collective organisation.

> Skill for the collective employee of capital, manifest in the trade union, is, sadly, no more than a means to an organisational end. . . . There may be collective struggle *over* skill, but it is not necessarily *about* skill. It is about the value of labour power and control over production.
>
> (Cockburn 1983: 121)

The work in this field is not organised in one single coherent current of research although a number of papers have appeared in *Feminist Review*. Although training does not feature strongly in these analyses, some writers such as Cockburn have written on women and training (1987). Other studies by Payne (1990) and Clarke (1991) have focused specifically on women's access to initial and continuing training, linking it to the analysis of inequality.

'Competence' and the reconstruction of skill

The restructuring of the labour market and the institutions of industrial relations and training has been extensive under the Conservative government. Although the institutions of industrial relations have been significantly modified, the changes within the institutions of training have been the most radical (Keep and Rainbird 1995). The institutions of regulation have been abolished and the state has withdrawn from direct intervention in company policy, marking a transition from a tripartite to a neo-liberal régime (King 1993). In the new institutions set up at local level a model based on 'social partnership' has been eschewed in favour of domination by employer interests.

To what extent has government policy contributed directly, as opposed to indirectly, to the undermining of the paradigm of skill? First, trade unions have been systematically excluded from authoritative decision-making with respect to training since the Conservative government came to power in 1979. There has also been an explicit shift away from state support for the training of apprentices, which was characteristic of labour market policy in the 1970s. It has been replaced by schemes based on work experience such as the Youth Training Scheme. In fact, 'transferable skills' were redefined in official discourse. They no longer refer to apprenticeship training but to low-level work socialisation for the young unemployed.

The rationale for government thinking on training policy was linked explicitly to industrial relations reform and to the weakening of trade union restrictive practices. The reform of apprenticeship, through the setting of practical tests, accompanied the introduction of YTS in 1983. At this stage, the changes were concerned primarily with the way in which trainees progressed from youth to adult wages rather than the content of training (Rainbird 1990: 29).

However, to talk of a generalised rupture in the paradigm of industrial organisation is simplistic. The debate on flexible specialisation in Great Britain has had an influential critique which has argued that many of the developments hailed as advances on Fordism are reminiscent of productivity bargaining in earlier periods, amounting to little more than 'new wine in old bottles' (Pollert (ed.) 1992). The Workplace Industrial Relations Survey suggests that although there are indeed patterns of continuity in practices in manufacturing and in the public sector, it has been with the growth of non-union employment in the private sector that the greatest shifts have occurred (Millward *et al.* 1992).

Nevertheless, the old model of skill has been undermined by the decline in manufacturing employment. This has been accompanied by an even greater decline in the number of apprentices as few young workers were recruited and trained in skilled trades. Together, the decline in numbers of craft workers and the failure to train apprentices undermined the membership base of the craft unions. By 1990, numbers of apprentices stood at one quarter of the 1970 level (Keep and Mayhew forthcoming, table 5.14). Between 1979 and 1991, of the three biggest craft unions, membership of the Amalgamated Engineering Union (AEU) halved and that of the Electrical, Electronic, Telecommunications and Plumbing Union (EETPU) and the Union of Construction and Allied Trades and Technicians (UCATT) fell by one-third (Keep and Rainbird 1995). At the same time, the exercise of 'skill' in the workplace is under threat from the development of new forms of task and job flexibility which undermine demarcations between jobs and the spheres of influence of different trade unions.

If an emerging model of vocational education and training is to be identified, can it be located in the development of a new system of competence-based qualifications developed by the National Council for Vocational Qualifications? Although the foundations of this may have been laid in the publication of the 'The New Training Initiative' (Manpower Services Commission 1981) and were first introduced through the setting of standards for apprenticeship training, it has only been with the establishment of the NCVQ in 1986 that they have begun to be operationalised. At present there is little evidence of the impact of competence-based qualifications on the way in which jobs and skills are constructed in the workplace, although it is possible to theorise about their implications if they are widely adopted. They exist as a set of standards which have consequences for the practices of educational institutions and awarding bodies. They also serve as a means by which government departments gauge the performance of the Training and Enterprise Councils/Local Enterprise Companies in terms of qualifications awarded in relation to funding allocated.

In this section, two major areas of research are examined which analyse the nature of the rupture in the old paradigm of skill. The first of these focuses on studies which can broadly be defined as the political economy of training institutions and policy. The second focuses on the development of competence-based measures of assessment and, in particular, the educational debates that have taken place around them. There are few critical analytical studies of their implementation and consequences in the workplace. Both these areas of research have two important features in common. First, much of the work has been commissioned by government departments. It therefore tends to be highly empirical, directly policy-oriented and often uncritical. The availability of funding for work in this area has distorted empirical and theoretical knowledge in this field. Second, as a counterbalance to this, researchers have tried to make sense of these developments through critical analysis, though from a much less well-funded base. The work commissioned by government departments, particularly the Employment Department, is reviewed in official publications and the *Employment Gazette* and is not discussed here. The focus is rather on the debates that have been generated by the analysis of these developments.

The political economy of training policy and institutions

There has been a vast body of research conducted on government policy interventions in the field of vocational training, the contours of which are outlined in Chapter 8. This literature focuses on the interventions themselves, the policy-making process and the role of different interest groups within this, the stated objectives of policy and its consequences in practice.

The work in this area can be divided into five major themes:

The policy-making process   Researchers in Political Science have been interested in the relationship between government and the interest groups of labour and capital. They have been concerned, in particular, with the ways in which government delegates responsibility for policy development and implementation to representative organisations in areas where there is market failure and where the state itself can only intervene in a bureaucratic way. Training policy has been seen as a classic arena for the development of corporatist arrangements. In the early 1980s there were a number of studies which examined the policy-making process, in particular with regard to the development of the Youth Training Scheme within the Manpower Services Commission. The development of the Technical and Vocational Education Initiative (TVEI) was seen as marking the end of a consensual decision-making process. The abolition of neo-corporatist institutions has been marked by a decline in interest amongst Political Scientists in training policy and institutions.

Incongruity between policy statement and practice　A reading of many official statements would suggest that the British government shares many of the preoccupations of other European governments with regard to the upskilling of the labour force. However, researchers working on training policy have had to explain the disjuncture between the formal statements of policy and the effect of policies designed to deregulate the labour market and dismantle training institutions. Research in this field has focused on an attempt to decode formal policy statements. It has also sought to obtain empirical evidence on the practice resulting from policy interventions and, in particular, to examine young people's, teachers' and trainers' experiences of YTS and TVEI.

Models of other training systems　In the same way that Economists have used comparative international studies to emphasise the lack of competitiveness of the British economy and to argue for increased investment in training, so comparative study has been used by Social Scientists to demonstrate the greater effectiveness of other institutional systems. This macro-level focus has rarely been underpinned by rigorous comparative research, but uses other training systems as a point of reference for examining the shortcomings of the British system. The report *Competence and Competition* (NEDO/MSC 1984) is an example of this. Moreover, government itself has used selective understandings of different training systems to underpin 'policy borrowing'. Some elements of the Youth Training Scheme were introduced on the basis of a distorted model of the German 'dual system' (Keep 1991) whilst the United States has constituted a point of reference for the Training and Enterprise Councils and for schemes linking schools and companies.

Advocacy　A striking feature of the British literature on training is the number of writers advocating reform, either of institutions or of the curriculum. A number of writers have argued forcefully for greater regulation of vocational training. Finegold and Soskice's influential analysis of 'low skill equilibrium' is explicitly prescriptive (1988), but the research findings of Payne (1990), Senker(1992), and the National Commission on Education (1993) all form the basis for policy recommendations.

The 'good practice' model　This approach is found particularly amongst writers in Management Science and reflects the fact that many Business Schools are interested in disseminating the most successful business practices through their teaching programmes. There has been a debate in the

Management literature on the extent to which personnel management has been replaced by Human Resource Management (HRM), which integrates company policies towards the motivation and management of labour with corporate strategy. The debate itself focuses on the extent to which a distinctive approach to the management of labour is emerging and how such an approach might be characterised as opposed to more traditional approaches embodied in personnel management. Some of the literature on Human Resource Management is underpinned by rigorous empirical research conducted within the Industrial Relations tradition. Although it examines a range of strategies including pay and incentive systems, training and development particularly of key personnel (i.e. managers) are also considered. An underlying assumption is shift from personnel management's treatment of labour as a collective to HRM's treatment of labour on an individual basis.

There is no one journal publishing research in this area, though the *British Journal of Education and Work* and the *Oxford Review of Economic Policy* have published articles by a number of prominent writers in this field. The new *Human Resource Management Journal* publishes the management literature. Many of the important writings in this field have been published either as books or as collections of articles. The Warwick Vocational Education and Training Forum has played an important role in bringing together a network of researchers who are working in this field from a range of disciplinary backgrounds through its workshops, conferences and dissemination activities.

The development of a competence-based assessment system

Like 'skill', competence must be viewed as a concept which is historically and socially defined. Although there is a debate on the extent to which competence can include underlying knowledge, it is the definition of competence given by the National Council for Vocational Qualifications which is driving policy and the way in which standards are being developed. The official statement of the objectives of competence-based assessment is by Gilbert Jessup, Director of Research at NCVQ, in *Outcomes: NVQs and the Emerging Model of Education and Training* (1991). For each industrial sector, standards of competence are being defined by Industry Lead Bodies, which are dominated by employer interests although educational and union interests may also be represented by invitation. Although competences are being defined in relation to work-related rather than educational criteria, there has been little evidence to date of their adoption by employers. In contrast, the further education sector has been most active in implementing them because the funding of courses is linked to the students' achievement of NVQs.

The objective in setting up a new system of vocational qualifications was to make the system more transparent to employers and to build up a system of units of competence which will enable workers to progress from one level to another. Unlike other qualifications systems the process of learning is not important and the syllabus is not specified. Rather, it is the ability to perform to a prescribed standard which is assessed. Experience can also be assessed and can contribute to the certification of units of competence, known as 'accredited prior learning'. This means that competence can be certified in the absence of any formal training and instruction.

The development of NVQs and, in particular, the ability to certify accredited prior learning, has been greeted as having the potential to democratise vocational education and training. The fact that in theory, workers can progress from one level to another and that NVQs are intended to have wide currency in the labour market has also been seen as a mechanism for opening up access. However, this is to focus on the supply side of the labour market to the exclusion of employers' demand for qualifications processes of labour market segmentation which result in some workers receiving access to training and qualifications and the exclusion of others.

Criticism of competence-based assessment has come from different quarters. Prais has argued that there was no need to reform the system of vocational qualifications as the major problem was that too few people received training rather than a lack of clarity about their qualifications. He argues that the lack of written tests required to receive the qualifications and reliance on assessment by a work supervisor mean that procedures lack objectivity. Moreover, NVQ level 1 certifies competence at such a low level that it has no equivalent in continental European qualifications systems (1989).

Writers from an educational background have questioned the theories underlying the definition of competence and their inability to give weight to the process and context of learning and how knowledge can be transferred and used creatively in different situations. Marshall writes:

> The model is based upon blinkered and unsophisticated social theories and consequently also reflects these traits. The functionalist and behaviourist background has guaranteed that the model eventually produced is one-dimensional and prescriptive. There is no place for individuality, nor is there a place for any constructive contribution from the Trainee. The Trainee must remain passive and regurgitate the prescribed activities at the required time.

> (Marshall 1991: 62)

Others emphasise the inappropriateness of competence to the assessment of complex human activities and interactions. Ashworth and Saxton write:

> The individualism and lack of awareness of social context betrayed by the notion of competence is equally disturbing. But in general, we believe that 'competence' is the embodiment of a mechanistic, technically-oriented way of thinking which is normally inappropriate

to human actions or to the facilitation of training of human beings. The more human the action, in the sense of being unmechanical, creative, or sensitive to the social setting, the more inappropriate the competence of human action is.

(Ashworth and Saxton 1990: 24)

On this basis, they argue that competence-based assessment is appropriate only to the lowest level.

Given the shortcomings of competence as a construct for assessing human abilities, as identified by educationalists, what might its consequences be, applied to a work environment? Trade unionists have been quick to recognise the similarities between the statements of competence developed by NCVQ and job evaluation techniques (Rainbird 1993). Insofar as the development of standards of competence has been weighted towards employers' interests through the structure of representation on the Industry Lead Bodies, they are oriented towards meeting the current short-term requirements of the employer rather than future production requirements. This restriction is complemented by the use of the technique of functional analysis to define competences. Fuller points out that Taylorism is also based on functional analysis and, in this respect, the application of competence-based assessment in the workplace has the potential to reinforce and further develop scientific management techniques rather than supersede them with higher level skills (1993).

As yet, the debate on competence has mainly been conducted amongst educationalists, who have been most affected by the introduction of competence-based assessment techniques and have been concerned to develop a critique of the educational and social theories underpinning it. Many important contributions to the debate have been published in the *Journal of Further and Higher Education*. Other contributions have appeared in edited collections. Although there are some studies of the implementation of the assessment techniques in particular sectors this has not fed through to a development of workplace studies.

In order to assess whether a new paradigm has emerged to replace skill, we have to return to Cockburn's three elements of skill: that which resides in the individual, that which resides in the organisation of production, and that which resides in worker organisation. The way in which standards of competence have been drawn up suggests that they may be weighted against workers' interests and are unlikely to open up access to training for young and unskilled workers in a significant way. Nevertheless, it would be simplistic to take a deterministic view of this process. First, despite the shortcomings of the NVQ system, trade unions have seen the development of competence-based assessment as a means of extending bargaining strategies into new areas (Rainbird 1993). Their action in this area may have a transformative potential. Second, young people themselves are 'voting with their feet' as far as low-level training schemes are concerned and are staying on at school in increasing numbers beyond the age of compulsory schooling to gain additional qualifications. Third, the problems of implementation of a very complex system cannot be overestimated, especially where its usefulness and appropriateness are uncertain in the face of long-established systems (both formal and informal) of training, recruitment and work organisation. The old paradigm of skill appears to have been weakened in the face of multiple interactions between the systems of education and production but, despite the development of competence-based assessment systems, there is, as yet, no alternative to replace it.

CONCLUSION

The three currents of research identified in this paper represent a somewhat arbitrary drawing of boundaries and imposition of coherence. The paper does not claim to be exhaustive. Nevertheless, it will be clear that to talk about training in Britain involves prior assumptions about the historical and social context of the apprenticeship system and the nature of craft labour. Some of the most insightful analyses of the nature of skill have been made by feminist writers who have seen it in terms of the exercise of male and craft union power in the workplace whilst emphasising the benefits to the employer of the segmentation of the labour market. Whilst writers analysing the exercise of skill in the workplace rarely give training consideration, equally those analysing training policy and institutions rarely make explicit their assumptions about the nature of skill. The particularly British concern with the policies and institutions of training reflects researchers' need to understand the nature of transformations taking place in the way in which skills are constituted in the workplace and in society. The decline of a model of skill based on craft unionism is not trivial and, together with the narrowness of the emerging model of competence, contributes to the deep pessimism found in the writings of many researchers in this field.

ACKNOWLEDGEMENTS

The author wrote this whilst working at the Industrial Relations Research Unit, which is a designated research centre of the ESRC. She would like to thank Alison Fuller, Prue Huddleston, Annette Jobert, Ewart Keep and Lucie Tanguy for advice and comments on earlier drafts of the paper. It also benefited from the discussion at the workshop 'Education/Travail' held at the University of Warwick on 28 June 1993, for which the support of the British Council and the Industrial Relations Research Unit is acknowledged.

BIBLIOGRAPHY

Armstrong, P. (1988) 'Labour and monopoly capital', in R. Hyman and W. Streeck (eds) *New Technology and Industrial Relations*, Oxford: Blackwell.

Ashworth, P. D. and Saxton, J. (1990) 'On competence', *Journal of Further and Higher Education* 14(2): 3–25.

Braverman, H. (1974) *Labor and Monopoly Capital: The Degradation of Work in the Twentieth Century*, New York/London: Monthly Review Press.

Clarke, K. (1991) *Women and Training. A Review*, Research Discussion Series 1, Manchester: Equal Opportunities Commission.

Cockburn, C. (1983) *Brothers: Male Dominance and Technological Change*, London: Pluto Press.

——(1985) *Machinery of Dominance. Women, Men and Technical Know-How*, London: Pluto Press.

——(1987) *Two-track Training. Sex Inequalities and the YTS*, London: Macmillan.

Finegold, D. and Soskice, D. (1988) 'The failure of training in Britain. Analysis and prescription', *Oxford Review of Economic Policy* 4(3): 21–53.

Fuller, A. (1993) 'Changing the National System of Vocational Qualifications', Module 3, MSc in Training, Leicester: Centre for Labour Market Studies, University of Leicester.

Gallie, D. (1988) 'Introduction', in D. Gallie (ed.) *Employment in Britain*, Oxford: Blackwell.

Jackson, R. (1984) *The Formation of Craft Labour Markets*, London: Academic Press.

Jenson, J. (1989) 'The talents of women, the skills of men: flexible specialization and women', in S. Wood (ed.) *The Transformation of Work? Skill, Flexibility and the Labour Process*, London: Unwin Hyman.

Jessup, G. (1991) *Outcomes: NVQs and the Emerging Model of Education and Training*, Brighton: Falmer Press.

Keep, E. (1991) 'The grass looked greener: some thoughts on the influence of comparative research on the UK policy debate', in Ryan (ed.) *International Comparisons of Vocational Education and Training for Intermediate Skills*, Brighton, Falmer Press.

Keep, E. and Mayhew, K. (forthcoming) *The British System of Vocational Education and Training: A Critical Analysis*, Oxford: Oxford University Press.

Keep, E. and Rainbird, H. (1995) 'Training', in P. Edwards (ed.) *Industrial Relations in Britain*, Oxford: Blackwell.

King, D. (1993) 'The Conservatives and training policy 1979–1992: from a tripartite to a neoliberal regime', *Political Studies* XLI(2): 214–35.

Knights, D. and Willmott, H. (eds) (1986a) *Gender and the Labour Process,* Aldershot: Gower.

——(eds) (1986b) *Managing the Labour Process*, Aldershot: Gower.

——(eds) (1988) *New Technology and the Labour Process*, London: Macmillan.

——(eds) (1990) *Labour Process Theory*, London: Macmillan.

Lee, D. (1982) 'Beyond deskilling: skill, craft and class', in S. Wood (ed.) *The Degradation of Work? Skill, Deskilling and the Labour Process*, London: Hutchinson.

Manpower Services Commission (1981) *A New Training Initiative – An Agenda for Action*, London: Manpower Services Commission.

Marshall, K. (1991) 'NVQs: an assessment of the "outcomes" approach to education and training', *Journal of Further and Higher Education* 15 (3): 56–64.

Millward, N., Stevens, M., Smart, D., and Hawes, W. R., (1992) *Workplace Industrial Relations in Transition*, Aldershot: Dartmouth.

National Commission on Education (1993) *Learning to Succeed. A Radical Look at Education Today and in the Future*, London: Heinemann.

NEDO/MSC, (1984) *Competence and Competition, Training and Education in the Federal Republic of Germany, the United States and Japan*, London: NEDO.

Payne, J. (1990) *Women, Training and the Skills Shortage*, London: Policy Studies Institute.

Penn, R. (1982) 'Skilled manual workers in the labour process 1856–1964', in S. Wood, (ed.) *The Degradation of Work? Skill, Deskilling and the Labour Process*, London: Hutchinson.

Penn, R. and Scattergood, H. (1985) 'Enskilling or deskilling? an empirical investigation of recent theories of the labour process', *British Journal of Sociology* 36 (4): 611–30.

Phillips, A. and Taylor, B. (1980) 'Sex and skill: notes towards a feminist economics', *Feminist Review* 6.

Pollert, A. (1981) *Girls, Wives, Factory Lives*, London: Macmillan.

——(ed.) (1992) *Farewell to Flexibility?*, Oxford: Blackwell.

Prais, S. J. (1989) 'How Europe would see the new British initiative for standardising vocational qualifications', *National Institute Economic Review* 129: 52–3.

Price, R. (1980) *Masters, Unions and Men: Work Control in Building and the Rise of Labour 1830–1914*, Cambridge: Cambridge University Press.

Purcell, K. (1988) 'Gender and the experience of employment', in D. Gallie (ed.) *Employment in Britain*, Oxford: Basil Blackwell.

Rainbird, H. (1990) *Training Matters. Union Perspectives on Industrial Restructuring and Training*, Oxford: Blackwell.

——(1993) 'Grande-Bretagne. La politiques des syndicats à l'égard de la formation des salariés de bas niveaux de qualification', *La Revue de l'LRES* 13: 13–49.

Rubery, J. (1980) 'Structured labour markets, worker organisation and low pay', in A. Amsden (ed.) *The Economics of Women and Work*, Harmondsworth: Penguin.

Senker, P. (1992) *Industrial Training in a Cold Climate*, Aldershot: Avebury.

Sturdy, A., Knights, D. and Willmott, H. (eds) (1992) *Skill and Consent. Contemporary Studies in the Labour Process*, London/New York: Routledge.

Thompson, P. (1983) *The Nature of Work. An Introduction to Debates on the Labour Process*, London: Macmillan.

Turner, H. A. (1962) *Trade Union Growth, Structure and Policy*, London: Allen and Unwin.

Wilkinson, B. (1983) *The Shopfloor Politics of New Technology*, Aldershot: Gower.

13

THE APPROACHES OF ECONOMISTS TO THE RELATIONSHIP BETWEEN TRAINING AND WORK

The Case of Great Britain[1]

David Marsden

Much of the work of economists in Britain over the last twenty years on the relationship between education and work has concentrated on the problems of vocational training and the failings of the British system. The debate has been strongly influenced by the structure of the national system of vocational training, and especially by the decline of apprenticeship. For many decades, this had provided the main path to skilled jobs in industry and construction, and it was one of the few intermediate level skills that was recognised as transferable between firms.

In view of the low level of qualification of managers in many British firms, and the growing importance of services, not to mention the growth of women's employment, one might be surprised by the fascination apprenticeship has exercised. In contrast, relatively little attention has been given to the training of nurses or bank clerks.

To understand the obsession with apprenticeship would require a study on its own, but one can hazard a few reasons. It provided the bulk of the visible part of blue-collar training in the traditionally exporting branches of manufacturing. There was no functioning alternative. Hence the economic stake was high. It provided workers with a qualification which brought wide economic and social recognition. Hence its importance for workers and their trade unions. Finally, explaining its decline posed a serious intellectual challenge to the social sciences.

Unlike the training of nurses, which is mainly financed by the state, and that of bank clerks – financed by a small number of large employers who until the mid-1980s managed relatively closed internal labour markets – the apprenticeship system depended upon co-operation among a large number of employers, and on a system of cost sharing between them and their apprentices. In the case of nurses, to simplify a bit, the supply of training depends heavily upon government spending. In the second, it depended upon firms which managed employment systems which gave quasi-lifetime employment. In the case of apprenticeship, there is a complex market, a large number of actors, and government intervention has never been particularly successful. There was therefore a major economic problem, and neither the free market nor state intervention appeared to bring the hoped-for results.

This paper begins with a brief outline of the main concern which underlies the debate about training in Britain, namely, the loss of industrial competitiveness. It then passes to an analysis of the contribution by competitive theory, and its diagnosis of the problem (wage rigidity). It then turns to the non-competitive and institutional theories of trade union action, labour market segmentation, market failure, and the need for co-ordinating institutions. Towards the end, it looks at the problem of the structure of firms and of enterprise-internal labour markets. It closes with the current debate on government policy: whether we are witnessing the emergence of a new system of regulation of markets for vocational training.

EDUCATION AND ECONOMIC PERFORMANCE

There has been a widely held consensus that the inadequacies of the educational system have harmed the competitiveness of the British economy. This concern goes back to the end of the nineteenth century. Alfred Marshall (1920) warned his compatriots of the effectiveness of the German system for training engineers and skilled workers as compared with that in Britain.

More recently, these concerns have inspired a series of studies at the National Institute of Economic and Social Research by a group of researchers, notably Prais, Steedman and Wagner. At first, their work focused on the level of education as an indicator of the quality of factors of production in order to explain residual differences in productivity between countries (Prais 1981). Gradually, the focus shifted to comparative case studies of the quality of different training specialisms and the numbers involved, comparing Britain, Germany and France.

This group started with a series of statistical comparisons of the number of qualified persons (notably engineers and apprentice-trained skilled workers). In his international productivity comparisons, Prais (1981) found that differences in investment and economies of scale could not explain all the observed differences in productivity between Britain and other countries such as the United States and Germany. It seemed that the quality of human resources could explain a part of this residual. Other studies have confirmed a tendency in British manufacturing to specialise in the production of less sophisticated goods than those of their German or French competitors (Saunders 1978).

Prais therefore began a series of studies to delve deeper into this problem, and the team at the NIESR has shown there are major differences in the quality of human resources. The relationship they establish between these observations and international productivity differences do not prove the existence of a causal relationship, but it nevertheless seems plausible.

One of the most interesting studies undertaken by this group compares the training and utilisation of human resources in the manufacture of kitchen furniture. The British firms were forced to limit their production to unsophisticated kitchens because they had to work with a relatively unskilled workforce and use Taylorist organisational methods. In contrast, because of an abundant supply of skilled labour, the German firms were able to produce top of the range kitchens. This study, therefore, seemed to provide a concrete demonstration of how the lack of a supply of skilled labour constrained firms' commercial strategies and limited British firms to the production of low value-added goods.

These studies confirmed the existence and the seriousness of the problem. But the consensus stops at this observation. Is the problem the result of a blockage in the competitive process, as would be claimed by the supporters of the competitive view of markets for labour and human capital? Or is it the result of a failure of the competitive system itself, as is claimed by those holding institutional and corporatist theories of markets?

HUMAN CAPITAL AND EDUCATION

Human capital theorists are suspicious of complaints by firms of shortages of skilled labour. As Blaug (1971) pointed out, there is always likely to be a shortage of any good whose price is below its competitive equilibrium level. Thus, on observing a shortage, one should always ask whether the price mechanism is functioning properly, and whether there are any restrictions on competition. However, before developing this intuition, we should sketch out the main elements of the approach.

The human capital approach has its origins in the research in the US and Britain on the production of skilled labour in industrialised countries. The Robbins report (1963), which helped launch the expansion of higher education in Britain during the 1960s, was inspired by this philosophy. In the United States, Schultz and Becker, and in the UK, Blaug, Layard and Psacharopoulos developed the analysis of education as an investment process in human capital, drawing an analogy with investment in physical capital. If education raises the productive potential of workers, then firms will hire them up to the point at which the pay of such workers equals their enhanced productivity. This higher pay acts also as an incentive for individuals to invest in education.

According to this theory, a shortage of a particular kind of skilled labour should cause a rise in the rate of return on investment in the necessary training. In the long term, deviations from the competitive equilibrium will disappear owing to the entry of new people into the skill, and to substitution of other categories of labour (and capital) for those in short supply.

Hence the scepticism by a certain number of researchers of this school concerning the interpretation of work by the NIESR. They do not deny the

194

existence of shortages on the labour market. However, they would be sceptical of the conclusions drawn by Prais and his colleagues. If the shortage has existed for a long time, how can one be sure that firms really need these skills? Should one not also look at the demand for skills when trying to explain international differences in the availability of skilled workers among countries?

According to Blaug, one can learn little about potential shortages of skilled labour by means of questionnaire surveys of employers. It would be better to study the rates of return accruing to different types of training because the wage is a better indicator of what employers are prepared to pay in order to recruit categories in short supply.

There is no direct test of human capital theory. One can nevertheless measure the correlation between the level of education and earnings, which, in a competitive market, will indicate the value of employees to their firm, and hence their productivity. This correlation has been confirmed by a large number of econometric studies (for the UK see, for example, Layard and Psacharopoulos 1974). However, its interpretation raises a number of problems.

The first is raised by the theory of 'screening' according to which education serves primarily to screen or to filter out the abilities of future workers rather than contribute directly to their productive potential. This hypothesis can be tested: if education enhances productivity directly, then partially completed courses which were subsequently abandoned should attract at least some additional remuneration. The first year of a degree should attract a higher wage than 'A' level qualifications. In contrast, if the educational system is only filtering abilities, then only completed courses would attract higher pay. For the UK, Layard and Psacharopoulos' research supported rather the productive hypothesis.

The second problem is that the unexplained residual in the econometric analyses generally remains large. Of course, educational diplomas only represent a fraction of the total investment in education, and there are many forms of discrimination at work in labour markets (notably against women, whose diplomas are less rewarded than those of men).

The third is the very persistence of skill shortages in Britain. If there were a competitive market functioning as claimed by human capital theorists, then these shortages should disappear with time. However, for major categories of skilled labour, including those of engineering, new technology and in health services (notably nurses), these shortages persist even during periods of high unemployment.

One factor could however block the functioning of labour markets: the rules of collective agreements and custom. They can act in two directions. If they set too high levels of pay for apprentices, then the cost of training to employers will rise. If they reduce the wage of skilled relative to semi-skilled workers, then there may be insufficient incentive for workers to invest in skills training. Howard Davies, then President of the Confederation of British Industry (CBI), the British employers' organisation, drew attention to these factors in presenting his case for a 'social market' in training (1993).

THE COSTS OF TRAINING AS AN OBSTACLE TO SKILLS TRAINING

Investment in school and university education does not require a contribution from employers. In contrast, vocational training often requires a large financial contribution from employers. Initially, research in this area was inspired by the human capital approach. However, increased awareness of the blockages in these labour markets caused a shift of emphasis towards the dysfunctions of markets for vocational training.

Human capital theory predicts that an appropriate sharing of costs will be necessary. Usually, for investment in 'general' skills (those which are transferable between firms), trainees have to assume a large part, if not all, of the cost (Becker 1975). When employees leave the firm they take the investment with them, hence the lack of incentive for employers to fund training for general skills. According to Becker (1975), trainees will bear the cost by working for a wage below the value of their output during the training period. In this way, the employer is compensated for the training costs. Once the training is complete, the worker can command the full skilled rate of pay. Employers would be unable later to recoup the training costs by offering a wage less than the value of the employee's output because a rival employer could always tempt them away by offering the full skilled rate.

In contrast, for 'specific' (or 'non-transferable') skills, employers can assume a large part, and potentially all, of the training cost, because trainees cannot use the skills in question in other firms. Since quitting would probably lead to employment at a lower skill level and for lower pay in another firm, employees are more tightly bound to their current firm.

In reality, few skills are either purely general or purely specific. Understanding the basic rules of the workplace is necessarily specific, and yet crucial to being able to function effectively. Affective bonds with colleagues, and the organisation of one's private life around travel-to-work arrangements tend to tie workers to their current firm even when they have general skills. These bonds enable firms to invest to a certain extent even in general skills. However, one might consider that the supply of training places depends on the cost and profitability of such investments. Because vocational training depends in part on the investments made by employers, the relationship between these variables has major implications for the quality and quantity of vocational training.

A certain number of researchers have stressed the less favourable relationship between costs and returns on apprenticeship training in Britain compared with Germany. They have sought to explain thus the failings of skilled labour supply in Britain. In a comparison of Britain and Germany, Jones (1986) (formerly at the NIESR) showed that the overall cost of apprenticeship training was broadly comparable in the two countries. However, whereas apprentice pay accounted for about one-third of the total cost in Germany, it took up two-thirds in Britain. This difference of cost structure translated into a lower training content in Britain.

How was this to be explained? During the 1950s and 1960s there was a progressive increase in the pay of apprentices (and other young workers) compared with adults up until the mid-1970s (Wells 1983, 1987; Layard 1982). According to Wells (1983), towards the end of the 1960s there was a switch from a situation of excess demand for young workers under which competitive forces had drawn up youth pay, to one of excess supply. However, the increase in youth-relative pay continued owing to inertia in pay-setting institutions. Ryan (1987) also stressed the role of union action (a factor independent of the state of labour demand) as a cause of this increase. It seems therefore that the higher wage element of apprentice training costs in Britain arose from the action of non-competitive forces in labour markets.

Turning to the pay differential between skilled and semi-skilled workers mentioned by Davies, it seems that non-competitive forces have also been influential. Indeed, there was a compression of skilled/semi-skilled differentials through much of the 1950s and 1960s which did not begin to reverse until the late 1970s (Saunders and Marsden 1981). During the 1970s, then, one can observe a twofold influence of union policies and anti-inflation policies (which allowed bigger percentage pay increases for low-paid workers) on the pay structure. This compression would have reduced the attractiveness of skilled jobs, and thus the incentive for young workers to invest in apprenticeship training.[2]

Thus from both sides it seems that the signals from the price system were constrained, preventing labour markets from reaching their competitive equilibrium. However, the human capital story stops at these institutional factors. It points the finger at them, and urges their abolition, but it does not explain their nature and their origin.

NON-COMPENSATING WAGE DIFFERENTIALS, UNION ACTION AND ACCESS TO JOBS

Setting out from a non-competitive approach, Marsden and Ryan (1990) also stressed the importance of union action, but in doing so they sought to understand why unions (and skilled adult workers) should seek to raise the relative pay of apprentices (and young workers). Collective bargaining causes a departure of the wage from its competitive equilibrium level. This gap creates an incentive for employers to substitute capital and other less expensive categories of labour for those which gained from collective action (and which caused the appearance of a wage differential larger than that needed to 'compensate' for differences in working conditions and skill investments). Hence the need to control employers' utilisation of other categories of workers.

Overall, their hypothesis is based on the difficulty of controlling employers' utilisation of young trainees. Too low a wage for young workers (or apprentices) would be likely to result in employers substituting young workers for adults. In the case of apprentices, the danger is stronger because as they near the end of their training they can undertake a large number of tasks done by skilled adults. Indeed, in the past, the long duration of apprenticeship training served to reimburse employers for the cost of training during the first years (see Becker 1975, but also Elbaum 1991).[3]

For Marsden and Ryan (1986), apprentices' pay could be used to regulate the supply of skilled labour. In earlier times, unions sought to impose quotas on the number of apprentices (see Webb and Webb 1902). Once this ceased to be possible, they sought to limit supply by raising the price.

A very recent study of employer behaviour in engineering by Stevens (1994) shows that employers tended to treat apprenticeship training as an investment rather than as a source of cheap labour. This study suggests that the actions of unions and of government to strengthen the quality of apprenticeship have at least partially succeeded. The study also illustrated the difficulty of organising enterprise-based general training.[4]

LABOUR MARKET SEGMENTATION

Marsden (1990a, 1990b) sought to widen the critique of the competitive market approach, seeking to show that occupational markets are inherently unstable in contrast to the presumptions of the neo-classical approach of Hicks and Marshall, who tended to see occupational markets as the model of a competitive labour market (and the state towards which all labour markets would tend in the long term).

According to Hicks, an equilibrium is stable when it re-establishes itself after a small disturbance of prices or quantities. Suppose that the workers in a firm succeed in negotiating a pay increase above the competitive market level. This would cause a set of forces bringing the wage back to the competitive level: for example, the firm would lose market share because of its higher costs, or it might seek to substitute capital or other, cheaper, categories of labour. In the end, one should see a re-establishment of the competitive equilibrium.

In contrast, it can be shown that the equilibrium on which investment in general (transferable) skills rests in Becker's theory is not of this nature. The same is true of occupational markets which depend on this mechanism. Indeed, it can be shown that a small displacement from the competitive equilibrium can set in motion a series of processes which take one further away from it, and that in the absence of an institutional support, occupational markets are likely to degenerate into internal labour markets.

Suppose there is a displacement from the competitive equilibrium as a result of skilled workers negotiating a higher rate of pay. This would encourage employers to substitute cheaper categories of labour. For the skilled workers, the most dangerous category is that of trainees because these are in the process of acquiring the same skills. Thus, in the union–employer conflicts surrounding apprenticeship, important issues have been the length of apprenticeship and the utilisation of apprentices.

If the unions seek to control the utilisation of apprentices by raising their relative pay, then they block the mechanism by which employers shared the costs of providing general training (as is the case with apprenticeship). Once employers begin to bear these costs in a significant way, others will be tempted to poach their former apprentices, giving rise to a 'free-rider' problem. Such practices will tend to undermine occupational markets because, to protect their skill investments, employers will seek to reduce turnover of those they have trained. They have therefore a strong incentive to create an internal labour market.

Such vicious circles may be avoided if there are institutional structures enabling employers to share general training costs among themselves. It seems that the networks created and underpinned by the Chambers of Industry and Commerce play this function in Germany. These play an important part in vocational training, and create the channels through which informal peer group pressures can take effect to penalise free-riders. The problem in Britain is that such inter-employer networks have never been as strong as those in Germany and are now in decline.

Other researchers have also highlighted the problems posed by the structure of incentives for apprentice training (Elbaum 1991; Ryan 1993; Gospel 1993). These explanations relate to the decline of apprenticeship in Britain and the United States. Gospel (1993) seeks to qualify these studies using the example of the survival of apprenticeship in Australia thanks to a more favourable institutional framework.

THE CORPORATIST APPROACH

Whereas Marsden and Ryan stressed the problems of regulation, other researchers have pointed out the importance of 'neo-corporatist' structures as stabilisers of vocational training systems. Finegold and Soskice (1988), Crouch (1995) and Dore and Sako (1989) have sought to show the important role played by organisations of employers and of enterprises (notably in Germany and Japan).

Extending elements of the arguments of Marsden and of the NIESR group, Finegold and Soskice contrasted two types of equilibrium in the demand and supply of training. There may be a 'low skill equilibrium' in which firms are constrained by shortages of skilled labour to opt for unso-phisticated and often cheap products whose manufacture requires only a low level of skill. The choice of product and marketing strategy then conditions policies of skill utilisation and labour recruitment. Even if the educational system were to increase the output of skilled labour, there would be inade-quate job openings, and therefore little incentive for young people to invest in training. In the opposite case, that of the high skill equilibrium, an abun-dant supply of skilled labour enables firms to invest in the production of more sophisticated products using a high skill input. Once firms are estab-lished on such markets, the strong demand for skilled labour encourages young people to extend their training.

The stability of the high skill equilibrium is problematic for the reasons outlined by Marsden (1986) and developed by Finegold (1991). In effect, it depends upon co-operation among firms, and between workers and manage-ment. Awareness of the advantages of the high skill equilibrium is not sufficient for them to adopt the appropriate policies because other firms, which do not train, may seek to poach their skilled labour. Hence the need for neo-corporatist structures to underpin co-operation among firms and to reduce free-rider effects.

Where such structures are weak or non-existent, Finegold and Soskice propose strong state action to raise the level of basic education. However, this solution can only be partial, given the need for co-operative structures between firms.

TRAINING AND THE STRUCTURE OF FIRMS

Most of the research has focused on general training, whether or not financed by firms. However, a recent study for the Employment Department brought to light a level of employer training expenditures until then unimagined (Deloitte *et al*. 1989). This study sought to measure the cost of on-the-job training, including the time of trainees, of supervisors and skilled staff, and that of senior management. A study on this scale had never previously been undertaken.

Nevertheless, the researchers made a number of estimation mistakes revealed by Ryan (1991). Even allowing for these, however, Ryan's re-estimation showed that employers spent annually about 4 per cent of their wage bills on training. Even if these estimates remain debatable, they have served to highlight the importance of training outside the institution-alised channels and, notably, of on-the-job training.

We know much less about the behaviour of firms in the domain of specific training and the management of human resources. A certain number of studies have looked at firms flexibility policies for skilled labour at the enterprise level, including that of Atkinson and Meager (1986) which was vigorously criticised by Pollert (1988). The development of functional flexibility, discussed by Atkinson and Meager, could erode the skill categories which underlie occupational labour markets on account of the increased heterogeneity of skills. The development of functional flexibility is likely to reinforce internal labour markets, at least for the employees directly concerned. Atkinson and Meager envisaged the emergence of a dual model with an inner core of skilled staff working in a functionally flexible way, and a periphery of unqualified workers absorbing the fluctuations of business conditions. A number of more recent studies have questioned the nature of the 'core'. Some professions provide scope for numerical flexibility (accountants, legal advisers, information technology specialists etc.), while other less qualified groups are sometimes part of the core.

The main debate in Britain has hinged on the problem of transferable skills, and has neglected the problem of training in internal labour markets where problems of poaching and free-riding are much less important.

The estimates of the quantity of training within internal labour markets is very tricky. Soskice supposes that the level of investment is fairly low, which he attributes to the influence of financial markets (British and American) which demand short-term returns on investment.

However, the high level of spending by firms on training indicated by the Employment Department study (Deloitte *et al.* 1989) perhaps shows the extent of on-the-job training in Britain. It invites a comparison with Japan, particularly with the policies of large Japanese firms which depend on internal labour market conditions.

Dore and Sako (1989) and Sako (1991) turn the spotlight onto the structure of Japanese firms as a factor enabling long-term investment in enterprise-specific training. Employment stability creates a framework within which employers can invest in training without fear that others will poach their skilled workers. The diffuse relationships between firms and financial markets also facilitate a long-term approach to all investment decisions, including training.

Another study by Lam and Marsden (1992) underlines the constraints on skilled labour utilisation as a factor discouraging investment by employers. The Employment Department study showed that British employers invest a great deal, but if we believe the reports of skill shortages, it would appear that many firms find it difficult to profit from their investment. In the case of blue-collar skills, working practices impose serious constraints on skill utilisation. Lam (1994) shows that in the case of engineers, the segmentation of work within British firms imposes analogous limitations on the utilisation of engineers.

TRAINING AND INTERNAL LABOUR MARKETS

As far as training in internal labour markets is concerned, a series of studies of the careers of scientific workers (especially chemists and physicists) have shown that those who remain with their employer usually have a better career than those who leave for other firms (Creedy and Whitfield 1988a, 1988b). These observations are compatible with the existence of internal labour markets for these categories, confirming an earlier study by Mace (1979) on engineers in Britain.

These studies raise difficult questions for the analyses discussed earlier, for training in internal labour markets should be less exposed to the problems of market failure which have hampered transferable training. They illustrate the vigour of internal labour markets for certain categories of skilled labour, at least for those who have achieved a certain level of length of service within their firms.

There are two possible ways of reading these facts. According to the first, the previous research has concentrated on transferable skills, of which the obsession with apprenticeship would be an example, and they have neglected the training effort revealed by the Employment Department study.

According to the second, internal labour markets have not escaped the problems which afflict training for occupational markets. Indeed, if we take a certain number of studies of the organisation of qualified work, such as those of engineers, it is apparent that even though these may succeed in gaining a position on an enterprise-internal labour market after a few years, their work and their orientation remain profoundly marked by a professional or an occupational logic. A comparison of British and Japanese engineers by Lam (1994) shows that the work organisation of the former remains very segmented by department and by function, in strong contrast to the pattern found in Japanese firms. One could say that the British engineers retain their professional orientation and consider themselves first and foremost as engineers, and only then as members of a particular firm. Consistent with this orientation, Lam observed a very individualistic and random approach to on-the-job learning in the British firms, contrasted with the systematic pattern in the Japanese firms.

The engineers' links with the labour market outside the firm, and with a profession spanning many firms, mean that British employers cannot rely upon long-term labour stability. Indeed, Lam's study showed a relatively high rate of labour turnover among the young British engineers. Such labour instability would reinforce the pressures towards short-term planning of training that emanate from financial markets, justifying what Soskice referred to as 'financial Taylorism'.

For the moment, there is no consensus on these problems. The estimates of training investments are too uncertain and debatable. Even if one accepts Ryan's re-estimates of the Employment Department calculations, a similar study remains to be undertaken for other countries whose estimates to date have been much less exhaustive. However, if one accepts the existence of serious under-utilisation problems of skilled labour as highlighted by Lam and Marsden (1992), there remains a high degree of waste of training investments in Britain.

The work of Ashton, Maguire and Spilsbury (1990) reveals the terrible consequences for young workers who do not obtain any initial vocational training. Those who are excluded from skilled jobs experience great difficulty later in gaining access to internal labour markets because of a sharp stratification. According to their study of the first jobs of young workers, internal labour markets have little to offer those without any educational or vocational qualifications. They are thus excluded from both internal and occupational labour markets.

ANALYSIS OF RECENT GOVERNMENT POLICIES

Despite a debate which has stressed the deficiencies of markets for vocational training, since the early 1980s the government has pressed for greater deregulation of labour markets and training provision (Ryan 1993). It abolished the institutions set up to co-ordinate employers' training efforts and to revitalise apprenticeship training in 1964. It sought to give individual employers more choice as to the content of training, and it allowed the apprenticeship system to decay. Despite the desire to build a new system of vocational training upon the foundations of the Youth Training Scheme, and subsequently of Youth Training, it has sought to cure two ills – the inadequacy of training and youth unemployment – with the same remedy. As a result, the training system has been badly discredited in the eyes of employers as the young people leaving it are stigmatised.

At the end of a recent study, Ryan (1993) asked whether we could see the emergence of a new system of vocational training. The government has been concerned about the poor quality of many training places and the low level of attainment of many school-leavers. The new system of National Vocational Qualifications is intended to provide a framework for quality control. The Training and Enterprise Councils, where employers have a leading role, have the task of organising vocational training at the local level, and to co-ordinate the action of firms. Can we see the emergence of a new corporatist structure able to sustain the training efforts of employers? The recent proposal to merge the TECs with local Chambers of Commerce (although much weaker than the German counterparts) would be an indicator of a move in this direction. However, the results of the first research on the TECs suggests caution (Bennett *et al.* 1992). The theoretical question raised with this initiative is whether the state can organise employer networks which it could then cast off and allow to develop independently. The experiment will be significant for many countries which, like Britain, do not have the German tradition of intermediate level corporatism.

One can also ask whether the NVQ system will enable a new kind of labour market qualification to develop, different from those of apprenticeship and of internal labour markets. Will qualification-based labour markets combining a mix of theoretical and certified on-the-job training emerge? The NVQ system could provide the transparency of such qualifications. Will we move towards a system of labour market qualifications which resemble more closely those of nurses or teachers than traditional apprenticeships?

CONCLUSION

The approach of labour economists in Britain to the problems of vocational training has been strongly marked by the decline of the apprenticeship system which, during the industrial revolution and industrial maturity of that country, provided the anchor for blue-collar skills training. The good health of the German apprenticeship system shows that the decline of the British system cannot be explained by technological obsolescence.

A system of transferable skills has a number of advantages compared with skills which are recognised only by the firm in which they have been created. Among these one should count the greater ease with which workers can find jobs at the same level of skill when they change firms. This reduces the human cost of unemployment, increases the scope for redeploying labour between firms and reduces the amount of scrapping of human capital when workers are made redundant. According to Marsden and Ryan (1990), in Western economies where lifetime employment is less widespread than in Japan, transferable skill systems also facilitate the access of young workers to skilled jobs. One can only hope that what replaces apprenticeship eventually will ensure skill transferability.

The contribution of labour economists, despite the differences of approach among them, has been to emphasise the problems of co-ordination among the actors in the field of training. The labour market remains a critical arena within which such co-ordination takes place because the number of actors and the diversity of their interests are great. How should one organise vocational training and entry into working life in such a way that workers' aspirations, the needs of employers and those of society can be satisfied? The state has only a limited power to initiate, but it cannot claim to know the needs of firms in any depth. Nor can it claim to know the desires of young and other workers. It can help to create a framework within which workers and employers interact, and it can oversee the balance of power between the actors. It can also keep an eye on the wider consequences of their action for society as a whole. However, one of the lessons of the German system is that the effectiveness of the institutional framework stems from its belonging to the actors concerned, to the employers, with the strong support of the unions and works councils, and that they accept responsibility for making the system work.

The merit of the economists' contribution is to have studied the problems of co-ordination in depth. Their failing is probably to have focused too much on apprenticeship, where these problems remain very serious, and to neglect other kinds of training, such as that of internal labour markets, which have been very little researched (Lam 1994), and those of other categories of workers such as nurses, technicians and information technology staff. These may hold more lessons for the future in view of their larger component of theoretical training. A closer look at these may also reveal complex problems of co-ordination among the actors.

NOTES

1 This chapter was written before publication of an important new collection of articles by labour economists on training which develops many of the themes in this paper. See Booth and Snower (1996).
2 Because the cost of apprenticeship to young workers would have been reduced by the rise in apprentice pay, a smaller differential for skilled over semi-skilled workers should be needed. However, both movements arose from non-competitive pressures, and so there is no reason to expect them to compensate for each other.
3 Becker distinguishes two types of enterprise-based training: the first is 'specific' to the enterprise, and the second is 'general' in the sense that it can be used by many other firms. In the case of specific training, the firm can accept the full cost of training because the trainee cannot use it in other firms. It is non-transferable, and there is correspondingly less risk that the employee will take the skill elsewhere. In contrast, in the case of general training, the firm is unwilling to take on the cost because of the danger of other firms poaching the employee once training is complete. Nor can the firm hope to regain its investment by offering a wage below the value of the employee's output once training is complete because another firm can always afford to offer the full value. Becker therefore argues that the cost of training for general skills will be paid for during the training period by means of a wage below the value of the trainee's output. This is the form of cost sharing seen in apprenticeship rates of pay. In practice, the low wages of apprentices often do not fully compensate employers. Hence the difficulty of ensuring an adequate volume of training in a competitive framework.
4 This study draws on doctoral research on a much wider scale.

BIBLIOGRAPHY

Ashton, D., Maguire, M. and Spilsbury, M. (1990) *Restructuring the Labour Market: The Implications for Youth*, Basingstoke: Macmillan.
Atkinson, J. and Meager, N. (1986) *Changing Working Practices: How Companies Achieve Flexibility to Meet New Needs*, London: National Economic Development Office.
Becker, G. S. (1975) *Human Capital: A Theoretical and Empirical Analysis, With Special Reference to Education*, Chicago: University of Chicago Press.
Bennett, R., Wicks, P. and McCoshan, A. (1992) *TECs and LECs: Early Development*, Department of Geography Research Paper, London: London School of Economics.
Blaug, M. (1971) 'La signification de la corrélation Education-salaire', *Revue Economique* 6: 913–42.
Booth, A. and Snower, D. (eds) (1996) *Acquiring Skills: Market Failures, Their Symptoms and Policy Responses*, Cambridge: Cambridge University Press.

Creedy, J. and Whitfield, K. (1988a) 'Earnings and job mobility over the life-cycle: internal and external processes', *International Journal of Management* 9(2): 8–16.

——(1988b) 'The economic analysis of internal labour markets', *Bulletin of Economic Research* 40(4): 247–69.

Crouch, C. (1995) 'Organised interests as resources or as constraint: rival logics of vocational training policy', in C. Crouch and F. Traxler (eds) *Organised Industrial Relations in Europe: What Future?*, Aldershot: Avebury.

Davies H. (1993) 'A social market for training'. Social Market Foundation/LSE Public Lecture, 1.6.93.

Deloitte, Haskins & Sells (1989) *Training in Britain: A Study of Funding Activities and Attitudes*, London: HMSO.

Dore, R. P. and Sako, M. (1989) *How the Japanese Learn to Work*, London: Routledge.

Elbaum, B. (1990) 'L'Evolution de l'apprentissage en Grande-Bretagne et aux États-Unis depuis les XIXème siècle', *Formation Emploi* 31: 72–84, July-September.

——(1991) 'The persistence of apprenticeship in Britain, and its decline in the United States', in H. Gospel (ed.) *Industrial Training and Technological Innovation: A Comparative and Historical Study*, London: Routledge.

Finegold, D. (1991) 'Institutional incentives and skill creation: preconditions for a high skill equilibrium', in P. Ryan (ed.) *International Comparisons of Vocational Education and Training for Intermediate Skills*, London: Falmer Press.

Finegold, D. and Soskice, D. (1988) 'The failure of training in Britain: analysis and prescription', *Oxford Review of Economic Policy* 4(3): 21–53.

Gospel, H. (1993) 'Whatever happened to apprenticeship training? A British, American, Australian comparison', unpublished paper, University of Kent.

Jones, I. (1986) 'Apprentice training costs in British manufacturing establishments: some new evidence', *British Journal of Industrial Relations* 24(3): 333–62, November.

Lam, A. (1994) 'The utilisation of human resources: a comparative study of British and Japanese engineers in the electronics industries', *Human Resource Management Journal*, spring.

Lam, A. and Marsden D. W. (1992) 'Shortages of qualified labour in Britain: a problem of training or of skill utilisation?', *Vocational Training*, Berlin: CEDEFOP, spring.

Layard, R. (1982) 'Youth unemployment in Britain and the US compared', in R. B. Freeman and D. A. Wise *The Youth Labor Market Problem: Its Nature, Causes and Consequences*, Chicago: National Bureau of Economic Research, University of Chicago Press.

Layard, R. and Psacharopoulos, G. (1974) 'The screening hypothesis and the returns to education', *Journal of Political Economy* 82 (5): 985–98.

Mace, J. (1979) 'Internal labour markets for engineers in British industry', *British Journal of Industrial Relations* 17(1): 50–63, March.

Marsden, D. W. (1986) *The End of Economic Man? Custom and Competition in Labour Markets*, Brighton: Wheatsheaf.

——(1990a) 'Institutions and labour mobility: occupational and internal labour markets in Britain, France, Italy, and West Germany', in R. Brunetta and C. Dell'Aringa (eds) *Labour Relations and Economic Performance*, London: Macmillan.

——(1990b) *Marchés du travail: limites sociales des nouvelles théories*, Paris: Economica.

Marsden, D. W. and Ryan, P. (1986) 'Where do young workers work? Youth employment by industry in various european economies', *British Journal of Industrial Relations* 24(1): 83–102, March.

——(1990) 'Institutional aspects of youth employment and training policy in Britain', *British Journal of Industrial Relations* 28(3): 351–70, November.

Marshall, A. (1920) *Principles of Economics*, London: Macmillan.

Pollert, A. (1988) 'The "flexible firm": fixation or fact?', *Work, Employment and Society* 2(3): 281–316, September.

Prais, S. J. (1981) *Productivity and Industrial Structure: A Statistical Study of Manufacturing Industry in Britain, Germany, and the United States*, Cambridge: Cambridge University Press.

Robbins, Lord (1963) *Higher Education: Report of the Committee under the Chairmanship of Lord Robbins* (Robbins Report), Cmnd. 2154, London: HMSO.

Ryan, P. (1987) 'Trade unionism and the pay of young workers', in P. N. Junankar (ed.) *From School to Unemployment? The Labour Market for Young People*, London: Macmillan.

——(1991) 'How much do employers spend on training? An assessment of the "Training in Britain" estimates', *Human Resource Management Journal* 1(4): 55–76.

—— (ed.) (1991) *International Comparisons of Vocational Education and Training for Intermediate Skills*, London: Falmer Press.

——(1993) 'The institutional setting of investment in human resources in the UK: in search of mass education', Paper for the RAND/EAC/IET Conference on Human Capital Investment and Economic Performance, Santa Barbara, November 1993.

Sako, M. (1991) 'Institutional aspects of youth employment and training policy: a comment on Marsden and Ryan', *British Journal of Industrial Relations* 29(3): 485–90, September.

Saunders, C. T. (1978) 'Engineering in Britain, West Germany, and France: some statistical comparisons of structure and competitiveness', *Sussex European Papers*, Brighton: University of Sussex.

Saunders, C. T and Marsden, D. W. (1981) *Pay Inequalities in the European Community*, Sevenoaks: Butterworth.

Stevens, M. (1994) 'An investment model for the supply of training by employers.' *Economic Journal*, 104: 424, May: 556–570.

Webb, B. and Webb, S. (1902) *Industrial Democracy*, London: Longman.

Wells, W. (1983) *The relative pay and employment of young people*, Department of Employment Research Paper 42, London: HMSO.

——(1987) 'The relative pay of young people', in P. N. Junankar (ed.) *From School to unemployment? The Labour Market for Young People*, London: Macmillan.

14

EMPLOYMENT, EDUCATION AND TRAINING IN ITALY

The role of the regions, employers' organisations and unions

Annette Jobert

In the area of employment and education, Italy has experienced evolutionary, rather than revolutionary, change over the past fifteen years. There have been substantial changes in employment, notably in the service sector owing to the higher number of women in the workforce, an increase in unemployment rates as a result of economic recession, a marked tendency for young people to continue studying well beyond the minimum school-leaving age and an increase in vocational and continuing training. For the most part, however, the main features of the employment and education systems have not been subject to radical change. The analysis of these systems and current academic interest in this area seem to be conditioned by various aspects of the Italian situation which form the 'specific collective experience', to borrow the expression coined by Bonazzi (1992). Regarding education and work, three factors seem to have had a particular influence on the policy debate and research themes: geographical diversity based on a strong collective identity at regional level, the influence of trade unionism and the system of industrial relations, and the weakness of state initiatives and co-ordination in this area.

EMPLOYMENT AND UNEMPLOYMENT: AN ENTRENCHED, LONG-STANDING NORTH–SOUTH DIVIDE

Growth in women's labour force participation and the service sector

In 1992, Italy had slightly more than 57 million inhabitants, 63 per cent living in the northern and central regions and 37 per cent in the Mezzogiorno (southern Italy). The active population numbered 24.2 million, of which 62.5 per cent were men and 37.5 per cent were women. The proportion of women active in the labour force is constantly rising (37.8 per cent in 1991 for women aged between 15 and 64) yet still remains substantially lower than in most other European countries.

The structure of socio-professional categories has undergone a far-reaching transformation over the past ten years. According to an initial type of classification adopted by ISTAT (the Italian Institute of Statistics), highly qualified occupations, comprising members of the liberal professions, technicians and scientists, have enjoyed substantial growth, rising from 12.9 per cent of the total in 1981 to 21.2 per cent in 1992.

On the whole, the academic standard of the active population is low: in 1992, 65 per cent (68 per cent of men and 59 per cent of women) had an academic standard equal to, or less than, the school-leaving certificate awarded at the end of compulsory schooling, which is usually obtained at the age of 14. There is a marked distinction in educational levels between economic sectors and occupational groups: 79 per cent of the population employed in manufacturing and 91 per cent of manual workers have obtained the certificate awarded at the end of compulsory schooling; in contrast, 71 per cent of executives and white-collar workers have attained at least the *diploma* awarded at the end of secondary schooling at age 19 (equivalent to 'A' level standard). Despite concerted efforts to increase participation in full-time education and to raise the level of qualifications, this lack of basic education in the vast majority of the active population is considered one of the main features of employment in Italy. Awareness of this phenomenon is not new and is illustrated by the institution of the '150 hours' in Italy in the 1970s (see Meghnagi, this volume). However, in the present economic and social context (limited growth, restructuring, the rise of unemployment), this question is again of topical interest and fuels an important debate, not only on the need to enhance continuing training but also on the most appropriate methods and curricula to be adopted.

Unemployed Italians: young people, women, southerners

The available statistics (source: ISTAT) clearly highlight the following characteristics of unemployment in Italy. The overall unemployment rate in 1992 was 11.5 per cent (Centre–North: 7.1 per cent; South: 20.4 per cent). For men, the average unemployment rate was 8.2 per cent, representing 4.4 per cent in the Centre–North and 14.8 per cent in the South. The unemployment rate for women was an average of 17.3 per cent (Centre–North: 11.2 per cent; South: 31.6 per cent). For people under the age of 30, the unemployment rate was 25.3 per cent. For men, this represented 20.6 per cent, for women: 31.3 per cent. For southern men this rose to 35 per cent and for southern women to 54.9 per cent. In other words, 70 per cent of the unemployed are under 30 and 45 per cent of them are looking for their first job. These proportions have been more or less stable for the past ten years.

The Italian job market is characterised less by the rate of unemployment – which is comparable to the rates in other European countries such as France and Great Britain – than by the profound disparities in terms of region, age and sex. In the northern and central regions, unemployment of men is practically at the minimum level: 4.4 per cent in 1992, while young women in the Mezzogiorno are virtually excluded from the job market with unemployment at 55 per cent. Even so, these statistics reflect just part of the current situation and there exist forms of unemployment not taken into account in official figures, as we shall see in relation to workers in the *cassa integrazione*, or included on 'mobility lists' (some 200,000 in 1992).

The scale and entrenched nature of the North–South divide (Calza Bini 1992; Villa 1992) have long fuelled the reflections of many economists and sociologists and explain their involvement in research programmes and public initiatives intended to promote the economic development of the Mezzogiorno. A large number of first-wave studies emphasised a quantitative imbalance in their examination of unemployment, focusing their analysis on company requirements and structural factors. The tendency since the early 1980s has been to develop analytical structures that take greater account of individuals and the meaning they attribute to work, and to place more emphasis on the diversity of career paths (see Calza Bini, this volume). We also notice a shift in the categories studied. After focusing on the situation of young people at the end of the 1970s in a context of social upheaval marked by the 'youth movement' and related to public initiatives aimed at easing their integration into the world of work, there is now a wider spread of interest given to different categories, among which women and immigrants hold an important place. The decline in the population, as well as the demise of the youth movement, are not unrelated to this development.

The effect of educational levels on unemployment

In the 1970s, when it became apparent that the economic system was unable to provide jobs for school-leavers with qualifications equal to the diploma, the study of the relationship between education and employment acquired a particular significance. In a country where the academic standard of the population was still extremely low, this situation was considered even more intolerable because economic growth was strong and the adoption of new technology seemed to create a demand for more highly qualified employees. Debates on the nature and causes of this mismatch between supply and demand gave rise to a major area of research. In fact, at the beginning of the 1980s, one-third of unemployed people had obtained at least the diploma, with the proportion rising to almost 40 per cent in 1992. This figure exceeds 50 per cent among 20- to 29-year-olds, an age-group representing 54 per cent of all unemployed people, i.e. 1.5 million (CENSIS[1] 1993).

These statistics should not conceal the fact that more than 60 per cent of unemployed people in 1992 had obtained at least the school-leaving certificate at the end of compulsory education at age 14. Further studies and the attainment of qualifications at intermediate level (*diploma*) or higher level (*laurea*, or university degree) represent no guarantee against unemployment for young people, especially in the South. Nevertheless, they make it easier to find a permanent job after the age of 30, although this integration also depends to a large extent on the individual's social background (ISFOL 1989). The employee has frequently obtained a qualification higher than required by the position he or she actually holds, but this deskilling is perceived more in terms of the graduate's expectations and aspirations than through formal recognition in collective agreements of the value of qualifications on the job market. This formal recognition is less common in wage classifications grids in Italy than in other countries such as France or Germany.

'The Italian model of unemployment'

The various analyses are in agreement on the main cause of unemployment in the South. This is the result of the chronic lack of job opportunities arising from the low level of economic development, especially of manufacturing industry, whilst the supply of labour continues to increase. The latter is due to the reduction in agricultural employment and to the slowing of migratory flows to the North. Mingione stresses other factors such as 'the overall poverty of the southern employment system characterised by inefficient services, vote-catching palliatives and organised crime'(1991). The extent of the divide between the Centre–North and the South can be seen in employment policies, namely in the provision of separate programmes for the South and in the unequal applications of national initiatives (as in the case of work and training contracts, mostly used in the Centre–North).

Pugliese (1993) characterises an Italian model of unemployment as follows:

- a particularly high rate of unemployment among young people;
- an extremely high proportion of the unemployed seeking their first job;
- the large number of unemployed women (a statistic which is, in fact, underestimated as many southern women see little point in signing on as unemployed);
- the significance of long-term unemployment (more than one year) particularly amongst women and young people who make up 68 per cent of the total;
- a high geographical concentration of unemployment.

According to this author, a national model can be identified since the main features of unemployment have long been closely linked to macrosocial variables and, in particular, to the Italian system of industrial relations. Collective agreements regarding job security which create high protection for permanent employees in industry (men, for the most part) may, in one sense, be considered a victory of the working class, but they also express the patriarchal and family nature of Italian society.

BETWEEN RIGIDITY AND FLEXIBILITY: THE REGULATION OF THE LABOUR MARKET AND THE MAIN FEATURES OF EMPLOYMENT POLICIES

The power of the Italian trade union movement, evident in the definition of employment standards, is based on three factors: first, a strong base of 10.7 million members in 1992 (this includes a growing proportion of retired people representing a union density of 40 per cent); second, an increasing tendency to joint action on the part of the three confederations – *Confederazione Generale Italiana del Lavoro* (4.6 million), *Confederazione Italiana dei Sindacati del Lavoro* (3 million), *Unione Italiana del Lavoro* (1.4 million); and, third, the capacity to intervene at all levels (company, local and regional level, sectoral and professional branches, 'interconfederal' level). When faced with a crisis, the unions and employers prefer centralised forms of regulation at sectoral and interconfederal level, engaging directly in the dynamics of political exchange. In the past, this centralised regulation sought to preserve and enhance purchasing power through the wage indexation system, to control employment through the strict application of rules governing recruitment and redundancy and strict legal limits on atypical forms of employment (short-term contracts or part-time work, which is still relatively uncommon) and the operation of 'social shock absorbers' such as the *cassa integrazione* [2]. At present, the trade unions are directly involved in identifying global solutions aimed at curbing inflation and at maintaining the competitiveness of Italian industry. This is the goal of the agreement of 23 July 1993 which, after the suppression of the wage indexation system, established a new framework for incomes policy and new rules for collective bargaining.

A large number of studies devoted to the black economy or to industrial districts demonstrate that the existence of strict rules governing working conditions represents just one aspect of a situation marked by the influence of informal kinds of regulation. In the industrial districts where small companies predominate the analyses underscore the social conditions underpinning their development such as the existence of networks, political traditions and the acquisition of training in social and community networks rather than in educational establishments (see Calza Bini and Capecchi, both in this volume).

Initiatives promoting the employment of young people

Since the end of the 1970s, a number of initiatives have been adopted to promote the employment of young people, some designed exclusively for the

Mezzogiorno[3]. In many respects these initiatives are identical to those adopted in a great many other countries confronted with the problem of unemployment among young people. (For example employer's exemption from social security contributions, fixed-term contracts, training requirements). In other respects, they are distinctive. This is true of the definition of the category 'young people', which is particularly wide and includes all members of the population aged from 14 to 29, sometimes extending to 32. The designation of this group of beneficiaries of employment measures as 'young people' also expresses the social fact that children live with their parents for a long time (Cavalli and Galland 1993). A number of these measures are also distinguished by the link that their initiators have tried to establish between the types of employment and the aspirations of young people to work on a self-employed basis or in a co-operative (see Giovine, this volume).

Studies show that these measures have had little impact on the creation of new jobs in the private sector, particularly in the Mezzogiorno. Between 1987 and 1990, 500,000 work training contracts were issued but were used mainly by companies in Central and Northern Italy to recruit new staff that they would have taken on in any case when the economy was recovering. Since 1991, the numbers of contracts have been halved (230,000 in 1992). From the point of view of training, the impact of these measures has been even more negative, but very few studies carried out in the 1980s were devoted to this aspect and its relationship with employment.

The exacerbation of unemployment in Italy and the sharp increase in benefits paid under short-time working provisions led to the adoption of new measures to improve the employment situation. Some of these, such as the introduction of starting salaries at less than the sectoral minimum and the legalisation of temporary work, undermined the model of the wage relationship that the unions had been able to impose and preserve for thirty years. They have fuelled a passionate debate within the trade union organisations, which tried to improve their content and to supervise their implementation, rather than combat them.

THE DIFFICULT REFORM OF THE EDUCATIONAL SYSTEM

The Italian educational system presents great contrasts. On the one hand, it does not seem to represent a major preoccupation in the debates of Italian society, in the general population or amongst politicians. This is demonstrated by the decision not to raise the age of compulsory schooling from 14 and the fact that the reform of higher secondary education launched at the beginning of the 1960s has still not been completed. On the other hand, the increase in the percentage of children in full-time education (90 per cent of young people stay on at school beyond the legal minimum age), the curricula reform movement and the profusion of experiments in teaching methods all suggest that the situation is changing radically. They testify to the vitality of a system which is not limited by its inability to change at an institutional level.

The extension of schooling and its limits

Compulsory full-time education lasts for eight years, five years in primary school and three years in secondary school (*scuola media inferiore*). Higher secondary education (*scuola media superiore*), which starts at age 14, includes a number of routes of study: vocational institutes (three–five years of study), technical institutes (five years of study), teacher training colleges – where students follow a four-year course for primary school teaching – and high schools specialising in science, classics and art (five years of study). The diploma is awarded at the end of the five-year secondary cycle, and is usually taken at age 19. Until very recently, higher education was characterised by its uniformity: a single subject (the university) and a single level of studies (the *laurea*) (Benadusi 1992). The laurea is obtained after four–six years of study. Other diplomas (*laurea breve*) awarded for short courses of study (two or three years) were introduced more recently, but still remain relatively undeveloped (see Figure 14.1).

The effects of the extension of full-time education are mostly visible in the change in the percentage of children in full-time higher secondary education (aged 14–19 years) which rose from 44 per cent in 1971 to 72.3 per cent in 1993, the increase being particularly sharp in the last ten years. Almost 90 per cent of the pupils in their last year of middle school enrol for a course of higher secondary education. In 1989, 44.5 per cent of an age cohort attained the diploma. In 1993, the proportion reached 56.4 per cent.

In 1992 there were 1.5 million university students, representing a 30 per cent increase over the previous five years. The number of women students is increasing, with female students exceeding male students in 1991. Since 1969, university tuition has been free, which results in approximately 70 per cent of secondary school students entering university. This proportion has remained relatively stable since the end of the 1980s. However, less than one-third of the students enrolled in the first year obtain a university degree after five years, making Italian higher education one of the least efficient in Europe.

The distribution of pupils among the different routes of study in higher secondary education has changed very little over a long period. The predominance of the technical and vocational schools has been maintained and 42 per cent and 21 per cent of students respectively enrolled here in their first year in 1993.

Pupils' choices between the different schools are largely determined by their social origins. A study based on a survey of a representative sample of almost 1,300 young people who had obtained the diploma in 1986 in the

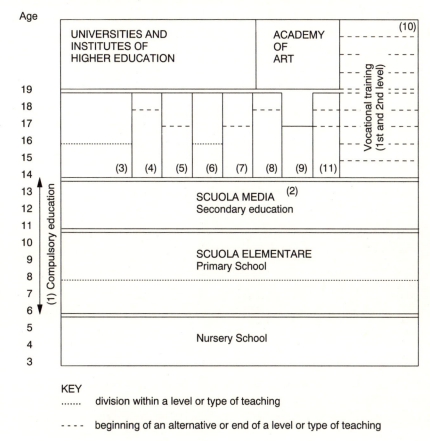

Figure 14.1 System of education and initial training in Italy

Lazio region (Buffoni 1993) shows that although 31.4 per cent of the pupils in higher secondary school come, on average, from families of a low academic level, this is true for more than half of the pupils in the vocational institutes but for only 14 per cent of pupils in the classical and scientific high schools. The surveys of students' entry into active life organised by ISFOL also highlight the importance of the type of school, correlated to the social origin, in the decision to continue into higher education and subsequent examination success. Approximately 80 per cent of the *laureati* in Economics and Arts and approximately 70 per cent of graduates in Engineering continued their secondary studies in high schools, which accept just one-quarter of secondary school students (ISFOL 1993).

The notions of 'drop out' – used to describe students excluded from the school system – and that of *dispersione scolastica* – which covers a whole series of closely related situations (abandoning studies, repetition, failure, falling

Compulsory education (1)

High school specialising in classics or science (3)

High school specialising in art (4)

Art school (5)

Technical instiute (6)

Vocational insitute (7)

Teachers' training college (8)

Training college for nursery teachers (9)

Apprenticeship (11)

WORK TRAINING CONTRACT, VOCATIONAL TRAINING
(1st AND 2nd LEVEL)

SECONDARY EDUCATION (2)
(MIDDLE SCHOOL - *SCUOLA MEDIA*)

PRIMARY EDUCATION
(PRIMARY SCHOOL - *SCUOLA ELEMENTAIRE*)

NURSERY SCHOOL

Figure 14.2 The education system in Italy

behind one's age-group, irregular school attendance) – are two notions widely used by sociologists investigating the mechanisms of selection and inequality generated by the system of education and training. In the 1970s, the drop-out phenomenon was studied within the wider context of academic selection which formed one of the main currents of research at that time. Subsequently abandoned by sociologists, it was examined through specific surveys commissioned by the Ministry of State Education. In the middle of the 1980s, CENSIS indicators measured 'educational risk' and 'academic handicap' in order to allow the identification of 'priority education areas'.

The scale and persistence of such phenomena explain the continuing relevance of these questions and their focus, in particular, on the first three years of higher secondary school, particularly in the technical and vocational institutes. Geographical differences also play a significant role even if to a lesser extent than in employment. In the South (despite the impressive progress achieved over the past twenty years), the percentage of children in full-time higher secondary education is 6 to 7 points lower than in the rest of Italy, and the number of students dropping out of the school system is higher.

The absence of educational policy

The education system has been democratised through the institution of a single middle school in 1962 and was projected to continue with the reform of higher secondary school. This widely debated reform was never adopted and came to be considered a typical case of *non decisione politica*, to quote the title of a collection of papers edited by Benadusi in 1989. The reason for this blockage can be attributed to the absence of a body of civil servants independent of the government and capable of pushing through reform on the basis of principle rather than the political advantage of the party in power. Since the end of the Second World War in particular, the Ministry of State Education has always been controlled by the Christian Democrat Party. This party was not interested in launching a process of reform, but aimed to avoid compromising its coalition with parties whose education policies differed from its own (the Socialist Party especially). Moreover, it did not want to undermine the status of a number of private Catholic institutions with which it has links and which ran some of the vocational training centres. These institutions were hostile to reform and did not wish to lose their autonomy (Benadusi 1989a, 1989b; Capecchi 1993).

The importance of these political factors should not lead us to neglect other factors of a cultural and social nature. The belief that education currently commands a minor place among the preoccupations of the Italians and in the public debate is widely shared, even if this appears to be contradicted by families who encourage their children to pursue their studies well beyond the age of compulsory schooling. The indifference expressed regarding this question would go a long way to explain the powerlessness of the political and institutional system to undertake reforms on a subject considered of minor importance. This has not always been the case. Benadusi argues that after the end of the Second World War, there was neither a popular movement in favour of educational reform nor a widespread progressive and egalitarian ideology. This situation changed in the second half of the 1960s and the movement which developed lasted longer in Italy than elsewhere (1989b). This period, during which the school became a school for the masses, is marked by the intensity of the debates surrounding this institution. The thinking, deeply influenced by educationalists and psychologists, focused in particular on the curriculum and the social model conveyed by it, i.e. that of the middle classes. This educational model is held responsible for the negative reactions towards school on the part of young working-class people, their high drop-out rate and the fact that many of them were held back to repeat a year of study. This debate was amplified by the publication in 1967 of the *Lettera ad una professoressa* from the Scuola di Barbiana whose influence was felt far beyond Italy itself (Fischer 1992).

Despite the absence of institutional reform properly speaking, the Italian educational system has long been developing experimental approaches. This is how the reform of secondary education is currently being implemented in technical and vocational institutions, tending to introduce a common core syllabus lasting two years. Many people criticise this 'permanent logic of experimentation', to borrow the expression used by the CENSIS (1992), which tends to generate disorderly changes in the system.

As emphasised by a number of authors, the place of school in society cannot be assessed merely in terms of the policies applied to it. School can be the vector of major social transformation, as shown for the Mezzogiorno by Moscati (1992). His analysis is based on the distinction between two types of function fulfilled by the school. The manifest functions, in his opinion, consist in supplying recognised academic qualifications that provide access to local jobs, chiefly in the tertiary sector and civil service, or allow recruitment into the traditional higher social strata related to the liberal professions. The latent functions include emancipation (for girls, in particular) and resocialisation. They concern non-traditional processes of social integration, the provision of elements of collective identity other than those related to membership of a family or clan, and the creation of opportunities to take part in the modernisation process. Contradictions exist between these different functions and provide an explanation of why certain students continue their studies to a high level and why others 'drop out' when confronted with an initial problem, an attractive offer on the labour market. There is considerable variety in behaviour according to the cultural level of the families. Moscati argues that in order to keep young people in the school system and in vocational training, it is necessary to recognise the importance of latent functions. It is therefore necessary to draw the appropriate conclusions whether this is in terms of assessment standards, which he considers excessively high, or in the diversification of training courses.

VOCATIONAL AND CONTINUING TRAINING: A CENTRAL CHALLENGE

Several institutions operate in the area of vocational training: the school system through vocational institutes in primary and secondary education, which accept 19 per cent of the pupils in higher secondary education; the regions, which possess considerable expertise in this area; and companies, through apprenticeship, work training contracts and continuing training. The three training systems, each highly independent, coexist and compete with one another, as is the case for the school system and the system organised by the regions.

The training system managed by the regions

A law passed in 1978 transfers the competence regarding vocational training from the state to the regions. If the planning of training is the responsibility of the region, its management may be delegated to the provincial and local government, leading to a highly decentralised system.[4] The regions have considerable autonomy as far as the organisation of training is concerned. This includes the definition of qualifications, training syllabuses and even assessment procedures which are independent of national standards. The regions have no financial independence and the greater part of their resources are derived from the European Social Fund, complemented by the state budget (Giovine 1991).

The vocational training activities managed by the regions are extremely varied in nature, depending upon the people to whom they are addressed. These are:

- early school-leavers aged 14 to 18, who can attend first level training programmes, generally of two years in duration. These play a vital role in the socialisation and 'recovery' of drop-outs from the school system;
- young people aged 18 to 25 in possession of the diploma, who may join second level training programmes often aimed at the acquisition of intermediate qualifications that were not provided in the educational system before the creation of the laurea breve;
- training courses for adults aimed at a relatively mixed public, including workers whose jobs are under threat of redundancy, unemployed people and even heads of small companies.

In 1993, the regions planned courses for about 350,000 trainees. The first level courses accounted for 37 per cent of the total, the second level courses (which have grown rapidly) for 20 per cent and the courses for adults for 42 per cent (ISFOL 1994).

The decision to give the regions the main responsibility for training has won general approval in Italy because it is founded on the widely held view that the regional level is the most appropriate to local labour market conditions and, consequently, most able to define appropriate training programmes. Criticism focuses more on the organisation of the system, which is considered excessively fragmented and frequently inefficient in terms of helping trainees to enter the job market.

Today, the same name given to a training course can cover a syllabus and lengths of training that vary considerably and, likewise, different names can apply to common curricula. The absence of shared terminology and referents, even within the regional framework, and the use of certification systems which are not recognised at a national level, make the comparability of the systems virtually impossible (Giovine 1991). Heterogeneity is maintained, or reinforced, by the fact that vocational training is provided by a wide variety of bodies, both public and private. The latter, in their majority, may have links with religious institutions, trade unions or employers' associations. It seems that the proliferation of organisations and the diversification of the supply of both public and private training (and it is difficult to determine whether these factors are due to an increase in the types of beneficiary), make it even more difficult to bring supply in line with demand (Moscati 1992).

The functioning of the regional training systems tends to reinforce differences in the labour markets between regions. In the Centre and North, where the job markets are relatively dynamic, the vocational training systems operate fairly well (Capecchi 1993), while in the South, characterised by weak demand, they function badly. All the failings of the system are concentrated in the latter: extreme fragmentation, poor accountability, high cost but – despite this – an inability to spend the sums granted by the European Social Fund, and low efficiency despite a higher proportion of trainers than in the Centre and North. In the South, the curricula are of a low standard and the qualifications have little currency, which is a barrier to occupational mobility. In brief, it is a system whose main function is that of *parcheggio* (a parking lot), to adopt the expression used in the 1970s to describe the role of the educational system as a whole.

These characteristics of the regional vocational training system in Italy emphasise the urgent need for reform which, in the opinion of the majority, should set out to define a system of national certification, to develop and clarify the assessment procedures and the content of training courses, and to establish co-ordination between the different institutions involved in training.

Training in companies and the commitment of unions and management

Vocational training in companies takes a variety of forms: apprenticeship, work training contracts, in-house training. The oldest form is that of apprenticeship, which was instituted by a law passed in 1955 under pressure from the trade unions. At the end of the 1960s, Italian firms employed some 800,000 apprentices. Their numbers gradually declined during the 1980s owing to the rise in educational levels and competition from work training contracts. However, with 500,000 apprentices in 1992 (ISFOL 1993), apprenticeship still represents the main form of entry into employment for 14- to 19-year-olds, chiefly in artisanal industries (which account for three-quarters of the total) and in the Centre–North region (90 per cent of the total). This form of labour market entry has been frequently criticised for providing industry with cheap labour without demanding an effective input from companies in terms of the training which is required by law. Trainers on these programmes have not been studied to the same extent as graduates from secondary or higher education.

At present vocational training does not constitute a right granted to all employees. At the beginning of the 1970s, the trade unions reached collective agreements at sectoral level which made provisions for employees to benefit from 150 hours of paid general training. These 150 hours were intended to enable employees to acquire basic education and were also used to enhance the level of knowledge and awareness of workers about the operations of the economy, the situation of women, and health and safety in the workplace (Meghnagi, this volume; Capecchi 1991). The implementation of this right, which was supported by many intellectuals, represented a major achievement of the trade union movement during the 1970s and many studies were devoted to it. From the middle of the 1980s, it was less used due to the raising of the school-leaving age, but also because of a certain lack of interest on the part of the trade unions. In the 1990s, the provisions of the agreement on 150 hours of study are again the subject of debate, focusing more on vocational training than on basic skills.

The growing interest of unions and management in vocational training and their determination to become more deeply involved in its definition and implementation were given concrete form in an interprofessional agreement signed on 20 January 1993 between the Confindustria (the Italian confederation of private sector employers) and the three union confederations. Through this agreement, the signatories aimed to achieve a three-fold objective: to influence the reform of the 1978 framework law by specifying the main orientations and priorities they jointly attributed to training; to co-operate actively in the development and functioning of the training system, through the creation of new institutions; and to have their autonomous role recognised in these matters.

The vocational training system seems to be entering a new phase characterised by large-scale changes. Comparative research on vocational training for workers (Campinos-Dubernet and Grando 1988) showed that Italy, like Great Britain, was based on a competitive training model characterised by weak institutionalisation. In Italy, the 1955 law on apprenticeships was never applied, there is no examination at the end of apprenticeship. There is a great variety in training provision depending largely on the companies and labour market and a weak involvement of the social partners both at sectoral and national level. The determination to reform the regional training system, to strengthen and supervise training provided under work training contracts, the search for coherence between the various institutions working in this field, the commitment of unions and management evident in the 1993 agreement and, more generally, the vast discussion launched on the education and training system indicate new orientations which, in time, could favour the emergence of a new model of training.

This perspective on developments in education and work allows features characterising the Italian situation to be highlighted. The first of these concerns the heavy involvement of the trade union confederations and the employers' organisations in public debate and in the search for solutions to the problems facing the country. The second lies in the strength of the regional dimension, although there remains a demand for the state to take on a stronger role in co-ordinating and indicating policy. Finally, this is a field in which major changes are occurring, sometimes more evident in practice in companies than in national policy initiatives.

NOTES

1 The CENSIS, created in 1984, may be defined as an observatory of social change in Italy. It makes an annual report on the changes taking place notably in the area of education and training, the mechanisms of redistribution, employment policies and local development. The data presented in the CENSIS studies, often based on official statistics, are frequently used in research work and its analyses are used as a basis of reflection at the CNEL (*Consiglio nazionale dell' economia del lavoro*), which is a consultative body for the local authorities, trade unions and management.

2 The employees involved in the *cassa integrazione* system are exempt from working yet retain their legal link with their companies and the greater part of their salaries, largely financed by the state. This system has enabled manufacturing companies to implement restructuring and redeployment schemes without having recourse to large-scale redundancies (Maruani *et al.* 1989).

3 Set up at the end of the 1950s, the SVIMEZ (Association for the development of the Mezzogiorno) and the FORMEZ (Centre of Training and Study for the Mezzogiorno) are bodies for economic and social study and intervention with a view to promoting the policy of developing the Mezzogiorno. In the past, they were important forums for reflection on the links between training, economic development and employment. The role of these bodies has declined considerably in recent years following the crisis in public intervention in the Mezzogiorno.

4 The ISFOL (*Istituto per lo Sviluppo Della Formazione Professionale dei Lavoratori*, Institute for the Development of Vocational Training of Workers) was set up in 1973 to take charge of vocational training and to help the regions to shoulder their new responsibilities in this area. The ISFOL, acting alone or in co-operation with other institutions (universities, trade unions, bodies set up by the European Union, etc.), covers quite a vast field of study: employment policies and labour markets, professions and qualifications, training courses and entry into active life, and the definition of methodological instruments devoted to training and its appraisal.

BIBLIOGRAPHY

Altieri, G. (1992) 'Disoccupazione e differenze di genere', in P. Calza Bini (ed.) *La disoccupazione*, Naples: Liguori.

Benadusi, L. (ed.) (1989a) *La non-decisione politica*, Florence: La Nuova Italia.

——(1989b) 'La politica scolastica: processi di riforma a confronto', in R. Moscati (ed.) *La sociologia dell'educazione in Italia*, Bologna: Zanichelli.

——(1992) 'I diplomi di primo livello in Italia e in Europa', *Sociologia e ricerca sociale* 37.

Bonazzi, G. (1992) 'Lo stato dell'arte nella sociologia economia italiana', in L. Gallino (ed.) *Percorsi della sociologia italiana*, Milan: Angeli.

Buffoni, F. (ed.) (1993) *La condizione giovanile nel Lazio, origini sociali, itineri scolastici, destini lavorativi dei diplomati*, Milan: Angeli.

Calza Bini, P. (ed.) (1992) *La disoccupazione, Interpretazioni e punti di vista*, Naples: Liguori.

Campinos-Dubernet, M. and Grando J. M. (1988) 'Formation professionnelle ouvrière: trois modèles européens', *Formation Emploi* 22, Paris: La Documentation Française.

Capecchi, V. (1991) 'Scuola, lavoro, classi sociali', *Inchiesta*, October–December.

——(1993) 'Ecole et formation professionnelle en Italie', *Formation Emploi* 44, Paris: La Documentation Française.

Cavalli, A. and Galland, O. (eds) (1993) *L'allongement de la jeunesse*, Paris: Actes Sud.

CENSIS (1992) *26° rapporto sulla situazione sociale de paese 1992*, Rome: Angeli.

—— (1993) *27° rapporto sulla situazione sociale de paese 1993*, Rome: Angeli.

Fischer, L. (1992) *La sociologia dell'educazione in Italia*, Turin, unpublished report.

Giovine, M. (1991) *La programmation des actions de formation au niveau régional*, ISFOL, Rome: Report for the Commission of the European Communities.

ISFOL (1989) *Percorsi giovanili di studio e di lavoro*, Indagine Isfol sull'entrata dei giovani nelle vita attiva, Milan: Angeli.

——(1992, 1993, 1994) *Rapporto Isfol 1992, 1993, 1994*, 'Formazione, orientamento, occupazione, nuove tecnologie, professionalità', Milan: Angeli.

Maruani, M., Reynaud, E. and Romani, C. (1989) *La flexibilité en Italie*, Paris: Syros.

Mingione, E. (1991) 'Le figure dei disoccupati nel contesto economico-sociale', in G. Altieri (ed.) *Tra Nord e Sud*, Rome: Ediesse.

Moscati, R. (1992) 'Il sistema formativo nel Mezzogiorno: funzioni manifeste e funzioni latenti in contraddizione', *Polis* 2.

Pugliese, E. (1993) *Sociologia della disoccupazione*, Bologna: Il Mulino.

Villa, P. (1992) 'Donne de Sud: fuori casa dove? Un "introduzione al dibattito"', *Politiche del lavoro* 20.

15

ANALYSIS OF RESEARCH IN THE SOCIOLOGY OF EDUCATION: 1960–1990

Luciano Benadusi and Paolo Botta

This paper is devoted to a critical and comparative analysis of the studies and research carried out in Italy on the relationships between the extension of schooling, the economic system and employment. We shall consider the main lines of study followed in the past forty years by researchers who, approaching this field from various angles, have respected heuristic principles by basing their approach on specific theories or have highlighted and analysed empirical phenomena which had largely been ignored until then.

The first two sections present a number of approaches which either focus mainly on the positive role of education in economic development or, alternatively, criticise its role. The first approach, which was adopted by researchers in the 1960s only to fall out of favour for a long period, is once again enjoying considerable popularity in more recent research. The second approach, which first appeared in the late 1960s and early 1970s, has acquired a considerable following in the 1980s.

The third section will examine more recent lines of study which have principally focused on the emergence of new phenomena. In the following two sections, we shall consider two specific research themes: inequalities of opportunity in education and employment, and educational policies concerning the relationship between training and employment. We shall conclude with a brief presentation of the themes which, in our opinion, deserve greater attention on the part of sociologists of work and education.

EDUCATION AS A FACTOR OF DEVELOPMENT AND THE RAISING OF QUALIFICATIONS

In 1961, SVIMEZ,[1] a research institute specialising in the problems of the Mezzogiorno, published a study entitled *Mutamenti della struttura professionale e ruolo della scuola. Previsioni per il prossimo quindicennio* (Changes in the employment structure and the role of the school. Forecasts for the next fifteen years). This was an important publication because, as Moscati (1989) has confirmed, it gave rise to a series of non-pedagogical studies on the education system in Italy, highlighting the relationship between economic development and the wider availability of education and training. This approach, based on sociological research of technico-functional inspiration and on economic studies founded on the theory of human capital, attributed central importance to a positive view of this relationship and, as such, sought to provide answers to questions related to the future demand for trained workers. SVIMEZ, in fact, articulated the concern that Italy might be facing a quantitative and qualitative shortage of trained labour to satisfy the needs related to the country's economic development. In substance, this approach tended to distance itself from the 'humanistic' concept of school and the time-honoured traditions of teaching and to emphasise the economic function of education, seen as a 'fundamental factor for progress' (SVIMEZ 1961: 79).

The SVIMEZ viewpoint was severely criticised in the 1970s in the light of later socio-economic developments as well as with the development of new ideological perspectives. Only in recent years has the idea that education and training are key factors of economic development re-emerged, based partly on the new popularity of the theory of 'human capital' and partly on the definition of post-industrial society as 'knowledge-intensive'. At the same time, the implications of the new post-Fordist paradigms for the organisation and the skill content of work gave rise to specific analyses.

Despite the existence of different theoretical frameworks, there now exists in Italy a general consensus about the importance of the extension of education and the need to adapt qualifications to development needs. This is evident in a great many studies devoted to these questions, for example, the research published in a recent issue of the journal *Il Mulino* (no. 346, 1993), devoted to schools, and the article by Moscati (1992) which analyses the reasons why it is necessary to raise academic levels in the Mezzogiorno. Another instance of this approach is a recent study of youth unemployment (Sarchielli *et al.* 1991) which underlines the scarcity of training resources for young people in Italy's southern regions. The macrosociological research into the imbalances in academic standards between Italy and the other European countries, but also between central/northern Italy and southern Italy, have led to the conviction that it is vital to reinforce the educational policy for economic and social reasons.

Linked to the relationship between education and employment and the growing needs for qualification, another current of research has gained primacy, based at the point of intersection between the Sociology of Work and the Sociology of Organisations. It focuses on the emergence of new professions and occupations and their importance for post-industrial Italian society with its emphasis on the so-called 'flexible economy', calling for flexible technology and the ability of companies to adapt to rapid changes in their operating environments. Given this decentralisation and flatter organisational structures, companies must set up what Butera has called 'the network company', based on outsourcing and a structure similar to that of a living organism rather than the prevailing 'clockwork' model, as in the title of his book (1984). According to this author, Italy has seen the end of Taylorism, which required a handful of specialists and large numbers of unskilled workers. Industry's current needs are different. Given the decline in the number of blue-collar jobs, companies now require higher academic standards from their workers; they also need larger numbers of trained technicians and highly qualified professionals. Other researchers who have studied this question, notably Prandstaller (1989), borrow the idea developed by SVIMEZ in the early 1960s of an increasing demand for qualifications in the labour market. Their approach differs in its qualitative rather than quantitative and future-oriented focus on the process whereby new professions are created and traditionally unskilled or semi-skilled activities become more 'professionalised' (i.e. the emergence of 'semi-professions').

A CRITICAL VIEWPOINT

In the years following its publication, the SVIMEZ report attracted considerable criticism – especially in the 1970s – because of the levels of unemployment noted among people with academic qualifications. Although this had not attained the levels it reached in the 1980s, especially in the Mezzogiorno, it caused numerous authors to focus on the existing labour market imbalance between the supply and demand of skilled labour. This led them to conclude that schools played the role of a 'parking lot' for the potential unemployed who, because they could not find work, enrolled at schools or universities as a way of filling in time.

This line of research can in turn be sub-divided into two different approaches. One tends towards a Marxist position, emphasising how school serves the needs of the 'capitalist' system and its divisions of labour (Emma and Rostan 1971). The perspective of those who have adopted this kind of analysis is clearly expressed in the following quotation: 'The contradictions in the relationship between school and work, and between school and the social divisions of labour, are . . . the reflection, within the educational establishment, of the fundamental contradictions between the development of capital and the development of the forces of production' (Emma and Rostan 1971: 171). A second approach, more theoretically refined and free of the ideological bias of the first, is put forward by authors such as Barbagli (1974) and Paci (1973), who focus in particular on the imbalances between supply and demand in terms of qualifications but from the opposite point of view to SVIMEZ.

Barbagli (1974) shows a negative correlation between the spread of education and economic development. He observes that the percentages of people going on from lower to upper secondary school, and from secondary school to university, are not higher in the more industrialised regions of the North but in the relatively undeveloped Mezzogiorno where schools do largely function as 'parking lots'. This contradicts the arguments of the human capital theorists who see a positive link between education and development. In the 1974 study, Barbagli also presents an extensive historical analysis, unusual for a sociologist, of the evolution of the relationship between school and the labour market, highlighting the endemic character of unemployment among qualified people in Italy.

One of the merits of Barbagli's study is that it focused attention on the issue of unemployment among the academically qualified which, in subsequent years, became the centre of concern as youth unemployment increased. The main limitation of his study is probably its failure to give sufficient attention to people's ability to control their own training trajectories and position on the job market, even in contexts characterised by widespread unemployment and underemployment of young people. Even at that time, young people's decision to pursue their studies was not just a matter of filling in time but was largely motivated by preferences that may not simply be reduced to the mere desire to adapt to a given situation. This was made clear, for example, by another study (Botta 1981) carried out in the Mezzogiorno just a few years after the publication of Barbagli's book. In fact, Barbagli's work strongly reflects the cultural climate of the time, which made it difficult for social scientists – often fascinated by structuralist approaches – to give proper weight to the preferences of the actors themselves. By the 1980s this was no longer the case.

A more recent interpretation of the relationships between education and the labour market is offered by Gambetta (1990), describing the results of different research projects on school careers, in which he lays equal emphasis on structural and subjective factors. Like other authors before him, he shows that the 'output' of education, in economic terms, varies with the students' social origins but he considers that the way students from different social classes reach decisions depends not only on economic factors but also on factors that may be described as 'sub-cultural'.

While Barbagli's analyses are characterised by a dominant historical approach, Paci's study (1973) is of a more 'synchronic' nature. On the basis of a sociological interpretation of statistical data related to work and education, Paci attempts to determine the imbalance between economic development and the spread of education, borrowing Marxist terminology to identify a 'relative overpopulation of educated people'. Paci focused attention on the 'upward thrust' by lower social classes towards higher levels of education, giving rise to an oversupply of intellectual workers in terms of employment possibilities.

It is obvious that both Barbagli's and Paci's arguments were developed in the context of an industrial society where the demand for qualified workers remained modest and any growth in education was seen as creating an imbalance or as a waste of resources. Different issues prevail today in a context which is not free from contradictions but where post-industrial transformations greatly increase the need for higher levels of education in the workforce and for a larger number of managers.

In this area, the study carried out by De Lillo and Schizzerotto (1982) on the relationship between education and employment is also of considerable interest. Through the secondary analysis of official statistics using a log-linear model, these authors focused on change over time in the education/work relationship. They asserted, although the data on which they based their conclusions is now partially obsolete, that educational upgrading had been modest in Italy and there was little evidence of an increase in the minimum educational qualifications required to practise particular professions. Unlike other countries, Italy experienced an increase in unemployment among academically qualified people owing to their unwillingness to accept jobs inappropriate to their qualifications. Employers were also reluctant to hire overqualified workers, because of the attendant risks of demotivation, salary pressures and labour conflicts liable to arise from the phenomenon of over-education. Another interesting feature of this study is that it shows how degrees or diplomas are valued differently according to the segment of the labour market involved, with the liberal professions, managerial and white-collar occupations on the one side and entrepreneurs, self-employed workers and blue-collar occupations on the other.

The issue raised by Barbagli is a real one. In the years following his study, the imbalance between the supply and demand in employment became more apparent and, in the late 1970s, other lines of research began to present a more complex and articulated view of unemployment among academically qualified people.

THE DISCOVERY OF DIFFERENCES: THE PATH FROM SCHOOL TO WORK

The context in which these issues were being assessed changed in the late 1970s and, especially, in the 1980s. In the latter period, the shift from an industrial to a post-industrial society became perceptible in Italy, despite the presence of a great many contradictions. The decline of Fordism, industrial crises and corporate restructuring were all evidence of a new scenario in which all sectors of society were modernised, bringing with this an increasing cultural level, even in the country's least developed regions. This development also comes in the wake of the rationalisation process resulting from the 'upward thrust' of the lower classes mentioned above (Paci 1973), and from new cultural aspirations. Particularly important were the changes noted in people's attitudes towards work which, perhaps more than anything else, indicate the shift, as Inglehart put it (1983), from materialist to post-materialist values. It is well known that to attribute this kind of interest to work means laying greater emphasis on its intrinsic aspects. This, in turn, influences the nature of the labour supply to the extent that people are seeking interesting work enabling them to pursue their goals of self-fulfilment. This is all the more the case, the higher the level of academic qualification. Many young people, unable immediately to find the job they desire, eventually accept casual employment. This is sometimes compatible with continued studying, but, in doing so, they reduce their ambitious. All this is consistent with the characteristics of the 'flexible economy' mentioned above.

It is obvious that not all the young people entering the job market are driven by aspirations such as these. Such ambition is more characteristic of those who already possess, as Bourdieu has argued, a certain amount of economic, social and cultural capital. The major discovery of research conducted in the 1980s was precisely the realisation of this difference: there are many routes into work and they are determined by objective factors (local job opportunities, the family's socio-economic status) as well as subjective ones (level of education, cultural aspirations).

Our understanding of these routes made considerable progress in the 1980s thanks to the contributions of Capecchi (1980, 1985) who identified several types of routes followed by young people, first within the education system itself and subsequently between leaving school and finding a permanent job. At that time, the scientific community was convinced of the need to proceed by making distinctions, analysing reality in the absence of preconceived ideas.

Two major differences emerge as far as our research perspective is concerned: a difference between university graduates and other young people and a difference between the sexes. The emphasis today, however, is not so much on the rate of graduate unemployment but rather on showing, through international comparisons, the small percentage of those who actually obtain their degrees owing to the large number of college drop-outs. Without unduly exaggerating the phenomenon of graduate unemployment, which has not acquired the same proportions in northern and central Italy as in the Mezzogiorno, it is necessary nevertheless to distinguish between types of graduates.

It is important to recognise the 'difficult transition from school to work', described by Sarchielli *et al*. (1991). These individual routes, transitions and interconnections between school and work are now becoming the subject of specific research within various fields of study generally conducted using the survey method. The three most important approaches are now summarised.

The research current focusing on the paths followed by young people after leaving school

Apart from Capecchi's research referred to above, the Entry into Active Life (EVA) survey has been carried out by Istituto per lo Sviluppo della Formazione Professionale dei Lavoratori (ISFOL) among students who had earned lower or upper secondary school diplomas or vocational training certificates.

Greater attention is now paid to the strategy adopted by the young people in question, to their attitudes and preferences, with the adoption of approaches, far removed from the economic motivation of the 1970s, which concern the construction of individual and collective identities. This research confirms that the possession of some sort of educational credential offers advantages in the job market, even if it fails to guarantee rapid occupational insertion and employment corresponding to the young person's training.

Research examining young people's attitude to work, and the youth situation in general

At the end of the 1970s, when there was a worsening of youth unemployment in the Mezzogiorno, a survey was carried out among young people aged 20–29 in southern Italy (Botta 1981). After examining the validity of traditional issues concerning the situation in the South, this research analysed the career routes of young people. Its starting-point was not the output of the school system but the complex and structured reality of young people. In the South as well, university graduates were relatively privileged, notwithstanding problems regarding certain types of degrees and specific occupations. At the same time, secondary school graduates were having difficulties because of the rigidity of the system, which prevented them from accepting work outside the service sector.

Ten years later, another study was conducted on the long-term unemployed in the Mezzogiorno, making a clear distinction between the routes followed by young people according to the type of diploma obtained. The least-educated young people were in a less favourable position than the others because they were employed, to a large extent, in casual manual work. The quality of career routes improves, therefore, with the general rise in academic level, even if these routes are also influenced by other variables including local job opportunities, social origin and family relationships (Botta 1991, 1992).

At the same time, CESPE[2] carried out two surveys among young people in Tuscany and Umbria (Carmignani and Pruna 1989, 1991). This research showed that in these regions casual work represented a transitional stage before finding a permanent job, in contrast to the situation in the Mezzogiorno where, for many, it was a more or less permanent condition. In all regions of Italy, a medium-to-high level of education increases the likelihood of avoiding unemployment and the long-term recourse to casual labour, even if a large number of studies highlight the difficulties encountered by male and particularly female secondary school graduates in finding a job in the Mezzogiorno.

Many research contributions tend to emphasise the importance of these routes and share Ribolzi's assertion that 'technological transformation . . . has changed the very concept of a working career, giving prevalence to the idea of a "route" instead of a "post"' (Ribolzi 1988: 186).

The studies carried out on young people in the 1980s, amongst which the most important are those by IARD (AAVV 1984; Cavalli and De Lillo 1988; Cavalli 1990), also addressed young people's relationship to work, but without examining in any detail the complex links between education and employment, as is evident in the fact that attitudes towards school and attitudes towards work were analysed separately. This research highlights the complexity of the transition from school to work and, in certain cases, emphasises young people's ability to lend meaning to their own school experience and to give it what might be termed a 'personalised' value with reference to expectations which are not exclusively related to work (Scannagatta 1984).

A specific line of study focused on university graduates

Research focusing on this population confirms the differences between the career routes followed even within a highly privileged segment of the labour market, because of difficulties encountered by some of them in finding a job. Among more recent studies, Jannaccone Pazzi and Ribolzi (1987) and D'Alessandro (1991) focus on cohorts of graduates and their experiences, which are analysed in terms of the characteristics of the organisations or industrial sectors in which they are employed (e.g. manufacturing companies). These studies highlight the diverse strategies followed by the individuals and the variety of problems they encounter in finding jobs, which are related not only to the subject of their degree but also to factors such as social origin.

Several conclusions emerge from the work in these three research currents. First, unemployment among young people with academic qualifications does exist but it chiefly concerns high-school graduates in the Mezzogiorno. Second, young people follow a range of routes from school to work and these reflect individual strategies which are not simply the expression of economic and socio-cultural change. Third, a diploma or degree is useful for finding a job, but it is not enough by itself – there are also other prerequisites, both subjective and objective. Fourth, a diploma or degree is less useful in the South than in the North, but in southern regions it unquestionably confers certain advantages on those who have it over those who do not. Fifth, people with little education inevitably end up caught in a web of marginalisation as far as work is concerned and, even if they find their first job rapidly, they are likely to find themselves repeatedly unemployed or underemployed.

Finally, despite the statistics showing that, in Italy, the highest rates of unemployment are found among young people holding intermediate or high level school certificates or diplomas, it should nevertheless be considered that education and training are worthwhile in terms of employment, at least in a medium- or long-term perspective. At the same time, it should also be recognised that Italy suffers from a serious lack of job opportunities and that the chronic failure to redress this situation compromises the effectiveness – from the point of view of employment – of the different policies designed to raise young people's level of instruction.

EDUCATION, MOBILITY, INEQUALITIES

Another line of research on the Sociology of Education in Italy is concerned with the relationship between academic levels and individuals' position in terms of social stratification or class structure, bearing in mind intergenerational mobility and inequality of opportunities. This type of research takes into account two main orders of relationships: first, the relationship between social origin (understood as the parent's occupational status and/or level of education) and the diplomas or degrees earned by the children, and, second, the relationship between the children's educational level and/or social origin and their occupational status on entering the job market (initial status and/or status achieved after a number of years).

In both cases, it is a matter of measuring the intensity of the relationship. In the case of occupation attained, it is a question of measuring the relative influence of the two causal variables (social origin and academic level). The concept of equal opportunity as used here corresponds to the degree of statistical independence between social origin and level of formal education, as well as between social origin (given an equal level of formal education) and occupational status. Any divergence from statistical independence is taken to be symptomatic of the influence of variables which Parsons called 'ascriptive', whereas if the principle of equality operated, inequalities could only be attributed to individual merit (such as academic achievements, which are not considered to be related to social origin). In this same perspective account is taken not only of inequalities linked to social origin but also of inequalities linked to other 'ascriptive' variables, such as gender and place of residence.

In order to obtain these measurements, the researcher must have access to statistical data enabling a reconstruction in summary form of individuals' academic and occupational careers, starting with the social origin of the family. This data is not provided by the periodic surveys carried out by Italy's national statistics institute, the Istituto Nazionale di Statistica (ISTAT). It can only be obtained through *ad hoc* surveys conducted on samples of the working population (either in its entirety or grouped by age).

Relatively little research has focused on social mobility and it has often been confined to a local scale. Recently, however, there has been renewed interest in such surveys, spurred by the work presented at the International Sociology Association (ISA) session devoted to social stratification and by other comparative research in this field – such as the so-called Casmin project.

The most extensive study on social mobility ever conducted in Italy was carried out in 1985 on a national sample of more than 5,000 individuals, both men and women, aged 18–64 (Barbagli *et al*. 1988). The stratification of social classes used in this study is substantially the same as that used by Goldthorpe in his study of social mobility in England (Goldthorpe 1987) and subsequently adopted by the Casmin project (set up in 1988) mentioned above. Several articles have appeared concerning the relationships between social origin, level of formal education and ultimate occupational status as well as their development in time and space, the latter referring to geographical regions of Italy (Schizzerotto 1988; Cobalti 1988; Cobalti and Schizzerotto 1993).

The research data were analysed by various, yet largely homogeneous, statistical methods – from the simple use of odds ratios to linear log and logit models. The results demonstrate that social origin has a strong influence on academic success, which is constant over time (except that children from families in rural districts in recent generations have been less disadvantaged in obtaining the diploma awarded at the end of the cycle of compulsory education). This influence is comparable amongst boys and girls, and in the North and South.

Social origin has a significant influence on ultimate occupational status, even given the same level of formal qualification. The latter, if taken separately, has an even stronger and more constant influence over time. Inequalities in academic opportunities, as well as inequalities in job opportunities, are fundamentally stable over time. Inequality of opportunity between the sexes tends to decline, while those linked to place of residence are relatively stable, though contradictory. A comparable study carried out in the Emilia Romagna region produced results largely consistent with those referred to above (Cobalti 1988). Different results, however, appeared from a secondary analysis of ISTAT statistics on school attendance, carried out by Gattullo (1989), which showed an overall reduction in inequalities of education between young people from families of differing social and cultural status. Finally, a study conducted using data from the last two censuses (Benadusi 1993a) yielded results intermediary between those of Schizzerotto and Cobalti on the one hand and Gattullo on the other, and highlighted greater equality in the lower secondary school system, which was attributed to the 1962 reform (through the introduction of comprehensive schools). In contrast to research based on data from surveys on social mobility, the last two studies mentioned above did not cover the entire trajectory from school to occupational career.

LUCIANO BENADUSI AND PAOLO BOTTA

EDUCATIONAL POLICIES

One might imagine that the unemployment problems of secondary school graduates could partially be mitigated by a reform of the upper secondary school system designed to take account of changes in the labour market. No such reform has occurred. Instead, the Italian political establishment, which nevertheless managed to complete a reform of the lower secondary school system in record time, has distinguished itself by its 'political non-decision', to quote the title of one of the few Italian research papers on this subject (Benadusi 1989). The scarcity of studies on educational policies in general, and an even scarcer number on their relation to employment problems, can be attributed to the fact that this field has mainly been dominated by educationalists, whose approach tends to be normative rather than analytical/descriptive. Although the upper secondary school reform has not yet taken place, it has to satisfy demands for a thorough overhaul and, in particular, to enhance equality of opportunity, to increase young people's participation in full-time education by increasing the minimum school-leaving age, and to promote better integration between education and the labour market. At the same time, a better co-ordinated distribution of responsibilities between the schools and the system of vocational training is needed.

Barbagli has provided an extremely cogent analysis of the reform of lower secondary education, which he describes as 'a successful initiative of the underprivileged classes' and which may be considered the reason for a better adaptation of the manual workforce to the needs of the economic system. Apart from this, there has been virtually no political action to promote a better balance between the supply and demand of the workforce.

Italy's inability to reform its upper secondary school – this reform is again being submitted to parliamentary approval (as so often in the past), yet risks being shelved now that the deadline is close[3] – has not only failed to encourage the schools to meet the needs of the economic system but has further complicated the relationship between the two systems. The traditional rigidities, linked to the class-biased character of Italian schools, are now exacerbated by a fragmentation of academic qualifications (with the appearance of new vocational or technical diplomas), which are rapidly outdated by the constant evolution in technologies and occupational roles.

With regard to university studies, the greatest need for reform lies in the differentiation between levels of instruction. The recent introduction of new diplomas (*laurea breve*, awarded after a short course of study in higher education), which eliminates one anomaly in the Italian education system, should respond to a constantly growing demand for intermediary credentials to bridge the gap between the technicians formerly trained in technical institutes and university graduates. It should also help to alleviate the serious problem of university drop-outs (only one-third of the students enrolling in their first year actually obtain their degree after five years). Among the various research papers on the system of higher education in Italy, we can mention the contributions of Benadusi (1993b), Jannaccone Pazzi and Ribolzi (1991), Bruno *et al.* (1989), Avveduto and Moscati (1992).

NEW AVENUES OF RESEARCH

To conclude, we would like to mention a number of issues in sociological studies devoted to education and work which have been even more neglected than the themes related to educational policy. These are now beginning to emerge as a result of researchers' new preoccupations and current changes in social reality and public policies.

The first of these concerns an examination of the effects of educational action, not only in terms of economics and employment but also in terms of civil society and the ethical and political dimension. From this viewpoint, it would be possible to examine the role of the school in contexts characterised by Mafia-style criminality and culture as is already the case in certain parts of the Mezzogiorno where compulsory school attendance is not respected. The second is to do with the development of microsociological analyses focusing on the educational structure (schools, classes) and on the individual career routes from school to work taken within specific contexts. The third concerns the development of thinking about in-service training and, more generally, about the process of individual and collective apprenticeship within organisations. Finally, the problem of academic and career guidance is being examined, with research focusing particularly on the role played by young people's families (whose influence is greater in Italy than in other countries owing to the lack of public action to facilitate the transition from school to work). The impact of this situation on the discrepancy between the job-seekers' academic qualifications and the job opportunities is being analysed, as well as its impact on the processes of intergenerational reproduction of social status.

It is to be hoped that research into educational policies will develop alongside sociological studies on these new themes, resulting in the establishment of a solid theoretical base for future research.

NOTES

1 *Associazione per lo Sviluppo del Mezzogiorno.*
2 *Centro di Studi sulla Politica Economica.*
3 At the time of publication, this risk had, in fact, materialised.

BIBLIOGRAPHY

AAVV (1984) 'Giovani oggi. Indagine Iard sulla condizione giovanile in Italia', Bologna: Il Mulino.

Avveduto, S. and Moscati, R. (1992) *Oltre la laurea*, Milan: Angeli.
Barbagli, M. (1974) *Disoccupazione intellettuale e sistema scolastico in Italia (1859–1973)*, Bologna: Il Mulino.
Barbagli, M., Capecchi, V., Cobalti, A. (1988) *La Mobilità sociale in Emilia Romagna*, Bologna: Il Mulino.
Benadusi, L. (1989) *La Non Decisione politica*, Florence: La Nuova Italia.
——(1993a) 'Diseguaglianze educative: un "assagio" sulle variazioni nel tempo e nello spazio', *Sociologia e Ricerca Sociale* 42.
——(ed.) (1993b) 'L'istruzione superiore di primo livello in Italia e in Europa', *A. F. Forum*, Milan: Angeli.
Botta, P. (1981) *Non lontanto dai padri. Ricerca del posto, solidarietà, adattamento, nell'esperienza dei giovani meridionali*, Rome: Edizioni Lavoro.
——(1991) *La Lunga Attesa. Lavoro, non lavoro e società nell'Italia meridionale*, Rome: Edizioni Lavoro.
——(1992) 'Una ricerca sulla disoccupazione e il precariato di lungo periodo nel Mezzogiorno', *Sociologia e Ricerca Sociale* 38.
Bruno, S., Linder, U., Cattarucci, M. (1989) *Università e istruzione superiore come risorse strategiche*, Milan: Angeli.
Butera, F. (1984) *L'orologio e l'organismo*, Milan: Angeli.
Capecchi, V. (1980) 'Lavoro e condizione giovanile', *Problemi della Transizione* 4.
——(ed.) (1985) *Prima e dopo il diploma. Percorsi maschili e femminili*, Bologna: Il Mulino.
Carmignani, F. and Pruna, M. L. (1989) *Occupazione e disoccupazione giovanile in Toscana*, Florence: Osservatorio sul Mercato del Lavoro Regione Toscana, Fondazione Cespe.
——(1991) 'I giovani, il mercato, il lavoro. Una ricerca in Umbria', *Politica ed Economia* 6.
Cavalli, A. (ed.) (1990) *I giovani del Mezzogiorno*, Bologna: Il Mulino.
Cavalli, A. and De Lillo, A. (1988) *Giovani anni '80*, Bologna: Il Mulino.
Cobalti, A. (1988) 'Istruzione e occupazione', in M. Barbagli *et al. La Mobilità sociale in Emilia Romagna*, Bologna: Il Mulino.
Cobalti, A. and Schizzerotto, A. (1993) 'Inequality of educational opportunity in Italy', in H.-P. Blossfled and Y. Shavit (eds) *Persistent Inequality: Changing Educational Stratification in Thirteen Countries*, Boulder, Colorado: Westview Press.
D'Alessandro, V. (1991) *La sfida del titoli e la ricerca dei posti*, Milan: Angeli.
De Lillo, A. and Schizzerotto, A. (1982) 'Diseguaglianze educative e diseguaglianze occupazionali: il caso italiano (1951–1971)', in S. Capello, M. Dei, M. Rossi 1982.
Emma, R. and Rostan (1971) *Scuola e mercato del lavoro*, Bari: De Donato.
Gambetta, D. (1990) *Per amore o per forza*, Bologna: Il Mulino.
Gattullo, M. (1989) 'Scolarizzazione, selezione e classi sociali tra scuola secondaria superiore e università', *Scuola e Città* 40.
Goldthorpe, J. (1987) *Social Mobility and Class Structure in Modern Britain*, Oxford: Clarendon Press.
Inglehart, R. (1983) *La rivoluzione silenziosa*, Milan: Rizzoli.
Jannaccone Pazzi, R. and Ribolzi, L. (1987) *I nuovi Laureati, Il Sole 24 ore*, Milan.
——(1991) *L'università flessibile*, Milan: Etas.
Moscati, R. (1989) 'Tendenze della sociologie dell'educazione: confronta tra l'Italia e la realtà straniere di riferimento', in R. Moscati (ed.) *La sociologie dell'educazione in Italia*, Bologna: Zanichelli.
——(1992) 'Il sistema formativo nel Mezzogiorno: funzioni manifeste e funzioni latenti in contraddizione', *Polis* 2.

Paci, M. (1973) *Mercato del lavoro e classi sociali in Italia*, Bologna: Il Mulino.

Prandstaller, A. (ed.) (1989) *Le nuove professioni nel terziario. Ricerca sul professionismo degli anni '80*, Milan: Angeli.

Ribolzi, L. (1988) 'La formazione come credenziale per l'occupazione: i giovani che si affacciano sul mercato del lavoro', in L. Pusci (ed.) *I giovani in Europa*, Naples: Tecnodid.

Sarchielli, G., Depolo, M., Fraccaroli, F. and Colasanto, M. (1991) *Senza lavoro*, Bologna: Il Mulino.

Scannagatta, S. (1984) *Giovani e progetto sommerso*, Bologna: Patron.

Schizzerotto, A. (1988) 'Il ruolo dell'istruzione nei processi di mobilità', *Polis* 2.

SVIMEZ (1961) *Mutamenti della struttura professionale e ruolo della scuola. Previsioni per il prossimo quindicennio*, Milan: Giuffré.

16

YOUTH EMPLOYMENT AND PUBLIC ACTION IN ITALY

Marinella Giovine

In 1977, the first coherent programme on youth employment appeared in Italy. To gauge the impact of these measures detailed studies were conducted on its direct effects on the beneficiaries as well as on the contextual variables which influenced the programme's conception and management. It was the first, and practically the only, case in Italy's history of integrated research on the condition of young people, their expectations and motivations regarding work as well as the situation of and forecasts for young workers on the labour market.

This notorious 'Act 285' gave rise to intense debate, stirring up a bitter controversy involving unions, employers, government and opposition parties, with particular emphasis on the presumed or real ineptitude of sociologists, economists and public administrators. Only young people themselves played no active part in the debate. Despite growing unemployment, the youth movement of the 1960s and 1970s had almost totally died out, especially sections concerned with marginalisation from work.

After the 1977 programme, no further comprehensive youth employment scheme was adopted in Italy apart from partial measures whose main goals were not the entry of young people into the workforce. It is difficult to say how much the various decisions, or rather 'non-decisions', were influenced by the absence of protests by young people, the failure of the 1977 programme or, more simply, by the Italians' lack of confidence in what is called 'active labour market policy'.

With the benefit of hindsight, certain issues which accompanied the debate concerning Act 285 now seem to belong to another age, another way of thinking and to outmoded ideological approaches. Nevertheless, to a great extent, the basic facts of the problem remain unchanged. Unemployment affects approximately 1.9 million young people aged between 14 and 29, particularly in the South and, notably, it is young people with an average to high level of education who encounter the greatest problems of finding work. At present, though, politicians and academics have other priorities.

THE FIRST YOUTH EMPLOYMENT PROGRAMME IN ITALY
(ACT 285/1977)

Unemployment among young people in the 1970s

In 1977, young people aged between 14 and 29 looking for work exceeded the one million threshold and the unemployment rate had risen from 12 per cent to 23 per cent in the space of ten years. This was equal to twice that of France and four times the unemployment rate in Germany. The composition of the population of young job-seekers, by level of education, was substantially different from that of the active population as a whole. The development model drawn up for Italy at the time of economic expansion in the 1960s had produced its effects when employment was rising rapidly and, above all, when the pace of investment was extremely strong.

During these years of growth, such trends fostered the belief that the demand for educated labour would rise in proportion to the increase in the level of capitalisation of the economy and to the rise in income concomitant with every development process, made possible by a massive accumulation of capital. In the second half of the 1960s, Italy experienced both a decline in this movement of accumulation as well as restructuring processes accompanied by a drop in employment (Bruno 1978). As a result, employment failed to rise as strongly as expected and there was no particular upskilling of jobs.

Until 1968, the majority of the unemployed were people who had worked before losing their employment. Then people looking for their first job started to outnumber the unemployed, in the strict sense of the word. This situation of 'crowding' caused by young people entering the labour market became particularly acute at the beginning of the 1970s. As early as 1971, people looking for their first job accounted for 60 per cent of all unemployed people in Italy compared with 17 per cent in France and 4 per cent in West Germany. There are many reasons explaining the disadvantage of young people on the Italian labour market. In southern Italy, the high birth rate in the 1950s and 1960s was a decisive factor.

With regard to the overall situation in Italy, research was carried out by Frey (1980) on the problems of young people's employment, based on analysis of data from the Italian national statistics agency (ISTAT), the Ministry of Labour, and the results of surveys carried out among employers and organisations concerned with recruiting young people. Frey's study shows how insufficient demand for labour is translated into youth unemployment. Resistance by employed workers results in a very limited 'rate of replacement', or turnover, by voluntary departure. Another negative factor, partly eliminated in more recent collective bargaining agreements and legislation, is thought to lie in the identical unit labour cost for young people as for adults.

In Italy, measures to promote jobs for young people concern persons aged up to 29, and have recently been extended up to age 32. This anomaly in comparison with other countries in the European Union is a result of the long waiting period young Italians experience before starting their first job. In southern regions in particular, there was a significantly high rate of unemployment among young people in the 25–29 age-group, and even for the 25–32 age-group. In substance, at least in terms of job promotion policies, the young population tends to be identified with first-time job-seekers.

In the 1970s, the least-educated young people had fewest problems finding work, although it was generally manual labour or work requiring no skills. In some regions there were even shortages in the manual labour market, partly because of the decline in the migratory flow from the South to the industrial regions of the North. In the South, meanwhile, there was a rising trend in the percentage of the population pursuing advanced levels of education.

There was much discussion at that time of young people's 'rejection of manual labour', even by those with low or intermediate levels of education. They were not rejecting manual labour in general, but farm work and unskilled industrial labour in particular (Barbagli 1974).

Surveys carried out at the time on young people's work expectations showed that they prioritised job stability and the type of tasks to be performed, with preference for jobs involving low degrees of supervision and physical effort (Gorrieri 1977). Both these factors took precedence, in young people's scale of values, over the prospects for earnings and career advancement. This concern for security alongside an absence of aspiration to occupational improvement or mobility, generated a high propensity to seek civil service employment which, as we shall see, constituted the unintended effect of the 1977 youth employment programme (ISFOL-CENSIS 1977).

The ISFOL-CENSIS survey was carried out on a sample of approximately 2,000 young people aged 15–24, including employed workers, students and people seeking jobs. The investigation covered many aspects of young people's attitudes and expectations concerning work. The results show that the stability of the job was their main preoccupation. It would nevertheless be a mistake to interpret this demand as an expectation of waged employment, because a large proportion of young people expressed a preference for self-employment, particularly in the form of a partnership or co-operative.

In the group studied, of whom a large proportion were still students, a preference emerged for some type of skilled work. The young people believed that the functions assigned to a job should be strictly correlated with the worker's type and level of education. This belief generated a preference for white-collar or administrative work, which was considered to be 'more highly qualified' than any form of manual labour, even of a skilled worker.

Not withstanding the high level of youth unemployment, it was thought in the 1970s that it had not yet acquired a structural character and that it would improve as a result of three factors: rapid economic recovery, a decline in the number of new job-seekers following the drop in the birth rate and the trend to remain in education and training. However, insufficient account was taken of this third factor. The higher level of education, together with a greater sense of well-being, would lead in subsequent years to a significant increase in the number of women going to work, in every age-group. Observers had also underestimated the potential of the economic system to increase its own rate of productivity.

The cultural context and social pressures

Between 1968 and 1977, a series of measures were taken to increase the access of young people to universities. In 1977, the economic recession was accompanied by a crisis in employment. For the first time the phenomenon of unemployment of the highly qualified appeared. Access to university studies had been opened to massive numbers of young people from the new middle classes who were unprepared for the possibility that a university degree could be of limited value in job-seeking.

The introduction of various forms of access to university studies had been a response to the 1968 student movement. A mix of administrative inertia and extremist egalitarian–permissive pressures had helped to create a sort of 'quarantine' between adolescence and the age of maturity, which corresponded to the period of university study. At that time it was still not possible to speak of a 'university for the masses'. It is nevertheless certain that, in 1977, more than in 1968, the university population included young people from social classes previously excluded from higher education. Beyond their membership of different social classes, university students found themselves faced with grave uncertainties about career prospects and job openings, although it was not for the first time in the country's history. To some extent they shared this experience with the most marginalised layers of the urban population.

The jargon of those years showed a frequent recurrence of terms such as a 'pockets of hidden unemployment' or a 'parking lot', referring to the expansion of the student population, particularly at university level. There was then, and there still is today, some resistance to the idea that studying is a 'good thing in itself', either for the individual or the community, and that extended education can help to give all young people, irrespective of their social origins, more equal chances of finding a job.

The student movement of 1977 originated in a sort of 'anticipated proletarianisation'. Not knowing if they would find work, students felt justified in behaving like the future unemployed. De Masi argues that because the unemployed worker is not a stable proletarian but a proletarian in a precarious situation, many of the unemployed identify themselves more with the marginal masses and reserve army of labour than with the aristocracy of the working class, primarily represented by the Communist Party (1978).

While the 1968 protests had begun in the North (Universities of Trento, Turin, Milan), those of 1977 began in the South (Palermo, Naples) – in other words, in the regions that had suffered most from the social and economic recession. At the University of Rome in 1977, the struggle against the prevailing social and political system involved all the social strata who were not protected from the recession and not represented at a political level: the unemployed, young workers employed in casual labour, women, and the university students themselves.

There was talk at the time of a deep fracture in society, between the employed, or 'integrated' portion of society, and the unemployed and marginalised groups who demanded change. There were also internal conflicts between various groups within the movement over issues such as the contradiction between the 'personal' and the 'political', and between individual needs and organisational momentum (AAVV 1978, 1979).

Although the movement of 1977 did not express new, coherent theories, there were nevertheless certain recurrent themes: a criticism and rejection of traditional politics, a need to link the 'personal' and 'political' and a demand for community control over conditions of working and studying. There was a rejection of the conception of work as an end in itself and of education as a 'parking lot'. 'Southerner, young, secondary school graduate, out of work' became the standard identikit for recognising the socially excluded Italian at the time, the unknown element with explosive potential in Italian society (Bocca 1977). This condition was seen as most propitious to the type of individual rebellion that can supply the springboard for dangerous reactionary movements. Such rebellion was considered capable of feeding violence and constituting a difficult testing ground for the traditional workers' parties, which despite everything had been successful in the political elections of 1976 (Lerner *et al.* 1977).

Following the activities of extremist groups in early 1977, the trade unions, among others, launched an appeal not to confuse the actions of extremist groups with the well-founded demands that the younger generation were addressing to politicians.

Nevertheless, much criticism was directed at the actions of trade unions and the Left for defending the system of 'guarantees' designed to maintain the status quo. They were accused of supporting the creation and consolidation of a new social class, that of the 'employed', including broad areas of parasitical employment in the civil service. Pirani argued that they would thus 'institutionalise a rigid society in which the majority of young people, whose education only constituted a disadvantage, would put pressure on the closed group of the employed' (Pirani 1977).

It was in this climate that the law was passed for the first universal programme on youth employment. It was a political response to a protest that was probably louder and more visible than widely shared in the consciousness of young people. The resulting measures were quite modest. Nevertheless it would be misleading to seek a cause-and-effect link between the inadequacy of the 1977 programme and the dramatic episodes of violence which occurred in the next few years.

Content, applications and results of the programme

The origins of the law on youth employment had begun long before the events of spring 1977, but parliamentary activity was probably stimulated by the student disorders and the explosion of the so-called 'autonomous student movements'. Two years previously, there had been a flurry of proposals put forward by academics, politicians, trade unions and consultants, aimed at solving the problem of unemployment among young people. These proposals fell into the category of 'active labour market policies', because a recovery of employment was considered unlikely given the difficulty of adjusting the mechanisms regulating demand for labour. In other words, it was decided to create temporary employment through specific public programmes.

The main measures contained in the law were as follows:

- the establishment of special job placement lists for young people;
- the promotion of the recruitment of young people in non-agricultural employment (excluding the civil service) by providing economic incentives (this meant increasing them in southern Italy) to employers who hired young people on permanent jobs and creating on-the-job training schemes. The latter involved training contracts of up to 12 months, wages reduced in proportion to the time spent in training, for which employers received an hourly based subsidy (this was doubled in the South);
- promoting farm co-operatives for young people, with a fixed monthly allowance per person for a 24-month period to bring previously uncultivated lands into cultivation, to process agricultural products and to manage technical services for agriculture;
- temporary hiring of young people in the public sector connected with existing social programmes run by public authorities. This was organised in the form of fixed-term contracts for people on special lists or through agreements between public authorities and youth co-operatives for 'works of public utility', for which each young person received an allowance for 12 months.

The number of young people registered on the special job placement lists reached 900,000 by the end of 1979; young people who found work in this way numbered around 80,000. Fewer than a quarter were hired in the private sector and more than 60,000 young people were therefore added to the

243

workforce in public administration. Private companies primarily hired young people on fixed-term contracts. Fewer than 6,000 were hired under the training contract scheme and only a few hundred were offered permanent jobs.

The creation of special lists for the placement of young people seeking their first job made the extent of latent youth unemployment explicit, as registration of this category had been hidden in the general statistics on unemployment. This enabled a clearer analysis to be made of the specific characteristics of youth unemployment. For example, it emerged that the proportion of young women finding work was very low, even in the most highly developed regions. Those registered on the special lists were almost equally divided between men and women, and 62 per cent of all subjects had pursued secondary or higher education.

The creation of the special lists was one of the most controversial provisions of Act 285 because they proved to be an 'instrument of notoriety', i.e. merely demonstrating the extent of the problem, given the inability of the employment offices to find jobs for the young unemployed with employers. Companies also failed to respect the enrolment order when looking for new recruits and preferred to find young workers through the ordinary lists.

When the law came into effect, it ignited fierce debate on the phenomenon of young people's perceived 'rejection of work'. Indeed, the job queuing system had resulted in a certain percentage of jobs being refused by young people, and of young candidates being refused by employers because the procedure was so rigid.

The measures adopted were intended to reduce the disparity between supply and demand in the labour market through favourable tax treatment of the costs of hiring young people. However, they failed to take account of the qualitative difference between the labour supply and demand and neglected to foresee the influence that the control mechanisms of the labour market would have on their operation.

The cultural reference framework was also largely erroneous. It should have been seen that economic growth was moving away from a work socialisation model based on the dual need for work and subordination to an employer. This model had been valid in Italy during the two post-war decades but no longer applied in the 1970s (Bruno 1980).

The programme further failed to take account of the difference in work expectations between young people in the South and those from the more developed North. Only the former consistently included a proportion of the long-term unemployed. While youth unemployment in the South was a structural phenomenon, in the North-Central regions it had a short-term economic character, as was demonstrated by employment trends in subsequent years.

Certainly, at the time, young people and their families were less prepared than they are today to see their hard-earned degrees failing to gain recognition in the job market, or to be rewarded in terms of the remuneration and quality of work until later phases of their careers. Business organisations, for their part, showed no willingness to change their methods of organisation as a consequence of the new measures to adjust to the special characteristics of these newly hired young people. Small firms used 'assisted' hiring to meet their short-term needs. Few larger companies took the trouble to set up effective training schemes (and, even then, did not change their basic internal organisation). In reality, in the private sector, the temporary subsidy for each newly hired young person represented the government's response to employers' demands for a reduction in the labour costs of young workers through favourable tax treatment of social insurance. This put the burden for the costs related to job training on the state.

Training contracts were attractive to companies for two other reasons. They were fixed-term contracts (a type of employment not otherwise permitted at that time) and, as critics pointed out, it amounted to a 'prolonged trial period.' There were also those who saw the youth training aspects of Act 285 as an ideological operation aimed at distracting attention from the distribution of labour demand, by focusing instead on the training issue. The training contracts were not very successful at that time, but were reviewed, revised and adopted in later youth employment programmes.

The provisions in the law related to agriculture appeared to be the most 'idealistic' and unconnected to a purely economic logic. The cultivation of 'previously uncultivated' lands by youth co-operatives appears paradoxical today given the European Union's set-aside incentives to farmers for every hectare of land left fallow. The measure seemed to satisfy young people's emotional, rather than rational, aspirations. They believed in the co-operative model and the possibility of establishing a life style alternative to that of urban living (ISFOL-CENSIS 1977). The incentive payments per worker under the law were certainly insufficient to launch farming enterprises with market potential, and did not even provide a minimum subsistence income to individual beneficiaries. In other words, the measure would have helped to increase agricultural underemployment, which was already widespread, particularly in the South. In addition, it was foreseeable that the co-operatives would not have been able to receive the technical assistance needed to implement and manage agricultural development programmes, as the law gave little or no consideration to this aspect. The sociologists and social 'engineers' who helped to develop the programme therefore had the right instinct – to the extent that it was based on the real motivations of young people – but 'forgot' to ask economists what a commercial enterprise really was. This funding mechanism provided per capita incentives which increased the numbers of young people on the programme rather than supplying the new enterprises with capital, equipment and know-how.

Even the part of the programme related to 'works of public utility' originated in a vague sociological analysis, flawed by an excess of idealism. The theory was to create a 'job corps' to be employed in socially useful activities. Here again, however, the programme failed to take account of the fact that young people, particularly in certain geographical areas, were not willing to accept any kind of unqualified or temporary jobs. The scheme might have worked, if the young people had been specifically mobilised through a co-operative-type structure and felt 'motivated' and 'involved' in social objectives which went beyond the requirements of working and earning a living. This did not happen, and the measures that were implemented generated aspirations and then demands for civil service jobs. Other factors were also underestimated. Insufficient recognition was given, for example, to the difficulties faced by the public sector, and particularly local authorities, who were expected to orient the activities towards fields in which they would not be competing with the private sector. In the case of socially useful projects, the demand was only for temporary or casual labour and, more often than not, unskilled workers. However, these activities could have offered real opportunities for training, if they were run by groups of young people capable of achieving a team spirit through a critical appraisal of the ultimate objectives of the projects and of the functions they were asked to perform. This could have occurred in a number of fields of activity, such as environmental protection, energy conservation, literacy teaching for adults, conservation of archaeological sites and social work.

The youth people's co-operatives and the works of public utility were inspired by the principle of activating a 'secondary' labour market in response to short-term economic conditions. This was achieved by creating jobs that did not compete with those that would have been generated spontaneously by normal demand, and at relatively low cost to the state.

The model was largely inspired by work programmes adopted in the United States to assist groups that were disadvantaged, due to the operation of segments of the labour market distinct from the primary sector. In times of recession, these groups are obviously the first to be affected by unemployment, and rather than counting on attempts to stimulate labour demand, it has been deemed preferable to create jobs directly through public channels, thus favouring these secondary segments of the labour force. 'Works of public utility' are typical in these types of programmes. The objective is to act on structural unemployment, but only in line with economic cycles. That is, only when the state of the economy is such that this structural unemployment may become dangerous to society.

The transposition of measures conceived in the USA to Italy did not take account of the national differences in the specific groups composing this secondary work force. In the 1970s, youth unemployment in Italy did not have the ethnic and racial connotations present in the United States but it included, as it still does today, young people, women, and residents of the underdeveloped South. All these groups are 'queuing up' to enter the primary labour market, given their relatively high levels of education and their consequent work expectations.

The role of the social partners

The ineffectiveness of Act 285 became apparent in its first few months in force. Companies proved reluctant to submit to the rigid hiring rules imposed by the law. The special lists measures were then amended to allow companies greater flexibility in recruiting so that they did not have to pay the young applicants the wages, established through collective agreements, which corresponded to their qualifications. These changes had little impact. Two of the law's underlying hypotheses were ignored in practice. These were, first, that companies had to show an increased demand for labour, if they were given these incentives and, second, that the gap between labour supply and demand should be met through the training contracts.

The hypothesis concerning young people's unwillingness to accept manual labour was disproved, for they would accept jobs that were under-paid and took no account of their qualifications, in exchange for a stable position and a permanent contract. Even from this point of view, the law was a failure in that it maintained the traditional guarantee-oriented hiring model and offered insufficient compensation to companies in terms of economic incentives and partial derogations to the usual legal requirements on hiring and the management of the labour force.

The initiatives conducted under Act 285 revealed the inadequacy of the institutional framework governing the labour market but failed to spark a real, thoroughgoing overhaul of public intervention in this sector (Arrigo 1983).

The programme also failed to take account of the special nature of the situation in southern Italy (Benedetti *et al.* 1977). Greater economic incentives would certainly not stimulate companies in the South to do more hiring, since that measure was mainly available to large companies with little presence in the industrial structure of the Mezzogiorno. Indeed, doubt emerged as to the appropriateness of setting up a national programme when it was only in the South that the problem of youth unemployment was so apparent and of a structural nature.

Another aspect deserves mention: for its implementation, Act 285 del-egated the planning and implementation of the law to grass-roots organisations and local authorities. It also recognised the competence of the regions to interpret and respond to local needs and the potential for the development of employment.

The regions, especially in the most disadvantaged areas of the Mezzogiorno, demonstrated their ineffectiveness in both programming and co-ordinating the interventions. For their part, the grass-roots organisa-tions demonstrated excessive fragmentation, the youth movements and associations of the unemployed failed to co-ordinate with each other, and even the trade unions were unable to play a co-ordinating role. Notwithstanding the claims by some leaders at the time, the trade union movement in Italy has never really demonstrated any inclination to assume responsibility for the problems of young people seeking work. At the bargaining table with employers, preserving existing jobs and salary levels has always meant sacrificing demands for jobs for new recruits as well as in-service training for workers.

In point of fact, continuing professional training and work experience programmes have been used in collective bargaining agreements as no more than a distraction to conceal objectives of an entirely different nature from the development of human resources. The trade unions lost an important opportunity to broaden their role in relation to the whole of the labour force when they prioritised their role of supporting and guaranteeing the maintenance of employment.

THE LEGACY OF ACT 285 AND YOUTH EMPLOYMENT POLICIES IN THE 1980s AND 1990s

Act 285 was the only experience in Italian history of a comprehensive programme to promote youth employment. Because of its unsatisfactory results, the measure was quickly set aside – except for the management of its unexpected effects – which included the slow absorption into the civil service of a large number of the programme's beneficiaries.

Unfortunately, along with the negative aspects, many of the valid ideas that had inspired the programme were also set aside. Among these was the attempt to establish job training programmes managed by a tripartite partnership between employers, trade unions and regional authorities. Conversely, some of the programme's errors have been intentionally ignored, such as the ineffectiveness of economic incentives to companies to stimulate hiring. Furthermore, Italy still lacks effectively operating bodies and agencies capable of matching labour supply and demand, and of undertaking measures at local level aimed at specific groups of unemployed who have problems entering the world of work.

Employment policies are still directed at overly broad segments of the population (categorised only by age and sometimes by sex), which are conducted at great expense in terms of energy and resources. As a general rule, they fail to recognise the needs of those for whom unemployment is assuming a chronic and dramatic dimension. Rarely have any of these measures been subjected to adequate monitoring, even for the purpose of evaluating their impact or the coherence between the (often substantial) resources spent and the results obtained. This absence of evaluation is also a result of their considerable fragmentation.

Different bodies, such as the job placement agency, the labour market observatories and the regional job placement agencies, as well as all the services responsible for providing employees with information and guidance, virtually all appear inadequate, with the exception of a few local successes (Strati 1985).

In the late 1980s, apart from the CFL scheme (Contratti di formazione e lavoro, or on-the-job training contracts), other programmes were developed which aimed at promoting youth employment (Giovine and Bulgarelli 1988). Some were based on the experience of the 1970s. This, in particular, was the case for the law adopted in 1986 for the 'Development of Youth Enterprise in the Mezzogiorno'. This set out to achieve the following:

- to create new enterprises in the country's most disadvantaged areas, along with the development of an 'entrepreneurial mentality';
- to grant 'realistic' levels of financing to those enterprises, which were not determined in advance or according to a formula but which actually correlated with the capital requirements and operating needs of each new company;
- to include among the company's staff, people who had no work experience, as well as those possessing the appropriate skills to ensure the success of the investment;
- to provide the young entrepreneurs with a wide range of material services, essential to effective use of the economic incentives (training, consultancy, etc.);
- to set up specific evaluation committees which were competent to assess the projects submitted by aspiring entrepreneurs, in order to ensure that incentives were awarded only to projects which had a real chance of success. The number of enterprises created under this Act 44 was not substantial, but it can be accurately concluded that the measure attained the more important objective of increasing young people's awareness of the possibilities of self-employment.

In the Mezzogiorno, indeed, it is important to correct a widespread opinion that work primarily means a guaranteed, salaried job, preferably in the civil service (Pugliese 1982).

The 'works of public utility' were another feature reinstated by the 1986 law, but on a completely different basis given the consequences of Act 285. This time, legislators carefully avoided any form of hiring of young people that might open a door towards later claims to admission to civil service jobs. The state therefore entrusted the management of young people and projects to companies and co-operatives in the private sector.

Above all, the problem of creating some kind of voluntary organisation which could look after the needs of special categories of young people has yet to be solved. An organisation of this kind is needed above all for those in the Mezzogiorno who are marginalised from the labour market and from any form of participation in society.

Nevertheless, many things have changed in the labour market since the 1970s. Regulatory measures designed to protect employed workers have gradually decreased and, even in Italy, the percentage of young people seeking employment is tending to decline a little in relation to unemployment in general.

SOME CONCLUSIONS

The phase Italy is going through now is somewhat similar to that of the early 1980s. The industrial system is again using all the instruments facilitating the dismissal of redundant staff. At the same time, the social partners have agreed to extend on-the-job training programmes and the incentives linked to them, from the age of 29 to 32. These measures will really only become operational in the event of an economic recovery, at which time companies will have to recruit new workers and young people will again be obliged to accept unfavourable wages, job classifications and conditions agreed during the present recession.

The measures which since the 1980s have had the greatest impact, even if it is not immediate, on the hiring of young people and which will continue to do so in the foreseeable future, are those which facilitate the departure of adult workers. Except for measures developed with respect to workers who have been made redundant, no major comprehensive measures are planned within the framework of so-called 'active labour policies.' This is partly because such policies would be costly to the state, at a time when government decision's are subordinated to the reduction of the public borrowing.

Despite certain changes in Italy in the 1980s and early 1990s, the growth in unemployment continues to hit young people most severely. But now youth unemployment is only sporadically analysed as a separate phenomenon, unlike the 1970s. The focus of attention of political decision-makers, trade unions and employers, and even researchers, has shifted to other 'disadvantaged' categories of the population, perhaps because of their greater capacity to arouse public opinion or generate conflict (these include women and immigrants, for example, although for different reasons). Studies of 'the condition of young people' have become less frequent in recent years, and work, or the lack of it, has been given less weight among the variables used in interpreting this situation.

On the whole, it can be said that there is no longer a perception of a single 'youth question', but instead, a multitude of youth questions, one for every field of possible social problems, each treated separately (drug addiction, school failure, physical and mental handicaps). More generally, it can be said that there has lately been among researchers a tendency to give secondary importance to the structural variables likely to offer partial explanations of young people's attitudes and orientations. Yet it is obvious that social class, regional identity, nuclear family characteristics and labour market segmentation still represent determining factors of even the smallest dimensions of 'everyday life', which has been the preferred focus of the most recent studies. Broad opportunities for benefiting from leisure-time activities, the ability to establish personal relationships outside school and work, have neither replaced nor dampened young people's expectations with respect to work.

The most recent 'transversal' national survey (IARD 1993), conducted among 2,500 young people aged 15–29, showed that in their scale of values, work occupied third place after the family and friendship among youth in North–Central regions, while it ranked second among youth in the Mezzogiorno.

Admittedly, it would be simplistic to attribute all social problems concerning young people exclusively to the lack or inadequacy of work. A great many surveys demonstrate that at least part of youth culture is oriented towards seeking one's own identity beyond one's involvement in work. The question which then arises is whether we are dealing with a freely chosen rejection of work by young people or the consequences of their real or feared marginalisation. Many studies of youth in the 1980s revealed that they perceived work as a means of survival and accepted it grudgingly as a fact of life.

It is nevertheless difficult to assert that our society has evolved to a point where it is generally possible to build life plans without taking work into consideration. It is more probable that exclusion from work means, in most cases, a risk of exclusion from organised society and therefore the loss of the primary prerequisites for building a life project. This is true, at least, for the present generation.

BIBLIOGRAPHY

AAVV (1978) *I giovani e la crisi degli anni '70*, Rome: Editori Riuniti.

——(1979) *Movimento '77. Storia di una lotta*, Turin: Rosemberg e Sellier.

Arrigo, G. (1983) 'Disoccupazione giovanile ed intervento pubblico in Italia', in D. De Masi (ed.) *Giovani e lavoro*, Milan: Angeli.

Barbagli, M. (1974) *Disoccupazione intellettuale e sistema scolastico in Italia*, Bologna: Il Mulino.

Benedetti, S., De Santis, G. and Frey, L. (1977) *La sottoccupazione del Mezzogiorno*, Milan: Angeli.

Bocca, G. (1977) *La Repubblica,* 15 February 1977.

Bruno, S. (1978) *Disoccupazione giovanile e azione pubblica*, Bologna: Il Mulino.

——(1980) 'Condizione giovanile ed azione pubblica: tre anni dopo', *Osservatorio ISFOL 3*.

Calvi, G. and Marbach G. (1983) *Giovani laureati e qualità del lavoro*, Milan: Angeli.

De Masi, D. and Signorelli A. (1978) *La questione giovanile*, Milan: Angeli.

Frey, L. (1980) *Le problematiche del lavoro giovanile e le sue prospettive negli '80*, Milan: Angeli.

Giovine, M. and Bulgarelli, A. (1988) 'Il lavoro dei giovani', in *ISFOL Strumenti e ricerche*, Milan: Angeli.

Gorrieri, E. (1977) *Il trattamento del lavoro manuale in Italia e le sue consequenze*, Turin: Fondazione Agnelli.

IARD (1993) *Giovani anni '90* (ed. A. Cavalli, D. De Lillo, Bologna: Il Mulino.

ISFOL-CENSIS (1977) 'Atteggiamenti dei giovani nei confronti del lavoro', *Quaderni di formazione ISFOL* 38–39.

Lerner, G., Manconi, L. and Sinibaldi, M. (1977) *Uno strano movimento di strani studenti*, Milan: Feltrinelli.

Pirani M., *La Repubblica*, 4 March 1977.

Pugliese, E. (1982) *I giovanni tra scuola e lavoro nel Mezzogiorno*, Milan: Angeli.

Strati, F. (1985) *Lavorare oggi*, Florence: Le Monnier.

17

CONNECTIONS BETWEEN COLLECTIVE BARGAINING, JOB TRAINING AND EDUCATIONAL RESEARCH IN ITALY

Saul Meghnagi

Educational research in Italy in the post-war years has steadily progressed from a philosophical approach to one which, while not ignoring the importance of this aspect, has become more scientific and empirical. This process, strongly influenced initially by psychological and social research carried out in the United States and northern Europe, is related both to the democratisation of education and to the link between job training and industrial reconstruction. In the wake of the destruction caused in the Fascist era and the war, the country had to build democratic structures from scratch and to recreate its entire economic infrastructure.

In the 1950s and 1960s, there was widespread debate about the school system, resulting in the establishment of the *scuola media unica*, or standardised lower secondary school system, in 1963. Despite this, the situation with respect to training remained largely unchanged; vocational training was then still considered as an auxiliary form of schooling aimed only at children who dropped out of academic classes before the minimum school-leaving age, and was seen as inferior to the 'noble' track of pre-university preparatory education. Serious discussion about the separation between academic education and job training seems to have developed only in the 1970s, with the advent of a long period of confrontation between trade unions and company management. This phase laid the groundwork for the present trade union policies on this issue and has had significant repercussions on Italian institutions and, more gradually, on the approach of researchers. In the teaching field at that time, experimental research, in parallel with the philosophically based work mentioned above, was essentially limited to studies on the education of young children. Only marginal attention was given to job training, which was treated as a practical matter rather than a proper subject for study and evaluation.

This paper proposes to present, in the context of their historical development, the main aspects of educational research on the relationship between work and training in Italy. It takes account not only of the debate between academic researchers, but also the confrontation between labour and management. This approach is adopted not merely to place the research examples in context but to provide evidence of the dialectic between the two worlds of academic research and collective bargaining, a duality which has characterised the vocational skills question in Italy. In view of this aim, the paper is divided into two sections. First, it examines issues arising in the early 1970s in connection with collective bargaining in Italy, which caused a change in educational research on job training, starting with some important studies on adult education. Second, it reviews studies conducted in the 1980s and 1990s on the learning process, which have caused a major change in educational research. While including references to research carried out in other countries, the field of study is limited to the current situation in Italy.

LABOUR NEGOTIATION, ADULT EDUCATION AND VOCATIONAL TRAINING IN ITALY 1970

The Origin of the '150 hours' Policy

Workers who, either for personal reasons or in connection with their work, wish to pursue courses at a publicly supported or legally recognised institute, have the right to enjoy paid study leave, which shall be paid for a number of hours over a three-year period.

The number of workers absent at any one time from the company or production unit in order to exercise the right to study leave may not exceed two per cent of the total work force.

Paid study leave may be requested up to a maximum of 150 hours per person per three-year period, and may be used within a single year, provided that the total number of hours in the course which the worker intends to pursue is at least double the number of hours requested as study leave.

This is a translation of an extract from Article 28 of the national collective agreement for the metalworking industry of 1973. It paved the way for a large number of workers to pursue retraining through what is still commonly known as the '150 hours policy'.

To find the scheme's origin, one need only look at the manifesto of demands voted in October 1972 by the national conference of the Italian metalworkers' union, with respect to the renewal of sectoral agreements. Along with two more traditional objectives (standardised equal rates of pay for apprentices and measures for those combining work and study) it included for the first time a demand for a contractual guarantee of a certain number of hours granted for training.

The most striking aspect of this was not the demand for paid leave as such, but the fact that it was included under the heading of the *inquadra-*

mento unico (single wage classification framework), which was the keystone of the entire manifesto. This framework essentially involved a single classification system covering both blue-collar and white-collar workers, a new division of roles and job functions which was different from the traditional system. This called for a drastic reduction in the number of wage categories with the elimination of the lowest ones, and greater job mobility, as the first steps towards a restructuring of the workforce in a way that differed from the traditional ideology of employers.

In the political debate that accompanied this struggle in the winter of 1972 and spring of 1973, the goals of the inquadramento unico were summed up as follows:

- to refuse to consider the traditional organisation of the means of production as a scientifically and objectively determined certainty, unchangeable for all time – thereby calling into question the entire industrial system;
- to lay the groundwork for greater solidarity and higher educational qualifications among the workforce at each plant, within a united trade union structure based on personal participation and development of each individual's capacity to understand the production process;
- to devise a plan to overcome the stratification and hierarchisation of the labour force, the under-use of individual capacities and the lack of qualifications of a large number of workers;
- to extend a new dimension to work which would facilitate greater integration in the production process;
- to assume an unquestionable right to personal cultural growth, as a means towards greater power within the company and more conscious participation in society;
- to demand, for this purpose, appropriate resources for learning and studying about economic, social and political processes.

Training therefore came to be conceived as a means of upgrading the labour force, empowering people to move to higher job levels and escape from routine, low-grade, monotonous drudgery.

On the basis of these general predetermined objectives, the union established certain lines of action. The 150 hours did not have to be used for training related to the job; in particular, the contract specified that for any courses organised by companies themselves for their own purposes, the workers attending should be given additional paid leave, not deducted from the 150 hours. The 150 hours did not have to be used for training related to the trade union; for this, companies had to grant special union leave or, in some cases, could use holiday periods. The 150 hours had to be used for the cultural improvement of all workers, through the acquisition of new cognitive skills and the development of their collective store of knowledge, organisation and experience, and should therefore allow them to study subject matter not traditionally taught in school.

Priority was given to remedial education for people who had not completed lower secondary school, not only to give them the certificate of qualifications they needed to escape from the bottom of the job scale, but also, more importantly, to provide them with the basic skills they would need in order to continue with any further training and to set up the conditions for a first step towards changing the methods and relations of production.

The unions concentrated on basic education, creating certificates equivalent to lower secondary education. In negotiations with the government, they persuaded the authorities to set up such a programme, with courses to be taught in state-funded schools, entirely free of charge, and with a recognised certificate to be awarded after 350/400 hours of study (12 hours per week for 30 weeks). Course teachers conducted an examination based on the same course material the students had studied.

In parallel, the unions turned to the universities, asking them to organise courses of varying length on economic, social and technical issues, closely connected with the real work experiences of the people who requested them. These courses were often linked with the trade union struggle, focusing on such issues as workplace safety, and the *scala mobile* (the wage indexation system).

Two other fields of action emerged. The first focused on a remedial campaign for the section of the population who were illiterate and unable to go directly into the programme mentioned above; the second was aimed at those who had completed compulsory schooling (through the 150 hours scheme for example) and who wanted to go on to higher levels of education.

The educational weakness of the country's adult population was more serious than statistical forecasts had predicted. Census data show that in 1971, 76 per cent of the Italian population over six years old had not obtained a lower secondary school certificate. Of these, 27.2 per cent were considered to be literate (able to read and write at an elementary level) but had no formal school certificates at all, while a further 5.2 per cent were illiterate, these figures in themselves being indicators of a very serious problem. Initially the 150 hours scheme had been envisaged as a mechanism for the collective mobilisation of workers, upgrading the labour force, empowering people to move up the job ladder and creating a better understanding of the production process. It soon became clear that the scheme was just one component in a long-term project to carry out some necessary intermediate steps.

Among other things, it became urgent to provide a secure legal basis for the right to paid study leave, through a law which would define the conditions for basic skills education for adults through the courses equivalent to lower secondary school; alongside this were measures to promote literacy classes and access to upper secondary school.

256

The 150 hours policy, which began as Article 28 of the national metal-workers' contract in 1973, in time came to be adopted, in a modified form, as a part of nearly every collective bargaining agreement. Within three years, paid study leave had been won not only by the major industrial unions (metals, textiles, chemicals, etc.) but also in other industrial sectors (food, printing, paper industry workers), the tertiary and services sector (hospital workers, local authority workers), and had even spread into agriculture (farm hands). In practice, virtually all workers were covered.

The structure of the remedial courses, their geographical distribution and the motivations of the students, were different from that initially imagined. The courses attracted not just industrial workers but a broad range of adults, including casual labourers, unemployed people and housewives, whose access to education had been favoured by the unions' 150 hours initiative. This had a significant consequence: the main motivations for registering were not political, cultural and socialisation factors, as had been assumed on the grounds that more education would help people have a better understanding of what goes on at work. Instead, the practical reason that the certificate could be used as a qualification for a better job was more important.

The widespread use of the scheme throughout Italy and the diversity of participants' aspirations for social mobility and education transferred the 150 hours framework from an experiment concerned with workers' job training to one which developed into general basic skills education for adults.

It therefore became necessary to define course contents and teaching methods suited to the whole population, while preserving the essential elements of the 150 hours scheme (free training in state-funded schools, with teachers paid by the state, the courses managed and controlled jointly by unions and management, with a teaching approach based on student-centred learning), opening access to higher education for those at the top and creating appropriate structures for literacy teaching for those at the bottom. There thus sprang up a flood of significant research papers in the educational field (for references, see Pagnoncelli 1989) which addressed not only the 150 hours scheme and adult education, but also, in a wider sense, the problems of the broader social skills of adults other than job training.

This emphasis on a conception of training strongly linked to collective bargaining focused on basic skills produced a phenomenon specific to Italy, namely, a richness of research on the education of adults, in contrast to the stagnation of research on job training and occupational qualifications.

STUDIES OF THE CURRICULUM

Studies in this area at first dealt with the conceptual models for teaching based on behavioural objectives, and then addressed wider issues related to curriculum contents and structure. The need to consider the curriculum requirements for adult education grew out of the realisation that the goal was not only to make formal education available to population segments who had previously been excluded, but also to guarantee the effective acquisition of the required skills. For this purpose, adult education needed to form connecting bridges between theoretical knowledge and practical application, between general education and job training, between classroom exercises and real concrete situations.

Adult education is often confronted with motivations for learning which are outside the scope of the formal educational system and which pose unaccustomed problems. It was not by chance, then, that in parallel with a growing demand for education at all age levels and a trend towards more intensive formal schooling, there was simultaneously a decline in strict standards and an impoverishment of the contents of educational institutions. In an ever more complex situation, existing teaching structures seemed incapable of undertaking a serious, coherent programme to combine general education with the development of job qualifications, or of reforming their own operating methods. Faced with these demands, adult education took on a strategic character. But it needed to be expressed in a variety of levels and settings. Adult education, as such, has to be flexible in adapting to people's educational backgrounds, yet extremely strict in analysing and assessing the variables that come into play in operation. While rigidity cannot be imposed on the teaching methods or determination of contents, because of the risk that students will abandon their studies, there still needs to be careful management based on clear theoretical foundations. For this reason, alongside the analysis of the teaching and learning process, it became important to study the ways in which a cultural and political programme could be translated into a specific educational plan, for a particular use, in a given context.

It became necessary to address curriculum issues, even if only in a partial way, to re-establish the balance between social and economic needs on one hand and educational objectives and contents on the other. Unfortunately, previous research on curriculum development had been chiefly concerned with the school system and education of young children. Nevertheless, although research on the education of children was more advanced and coherent than that on the education of adults, the latter was certainly further ahead in terms of relating curriculum contents to concrete realities, assessing the impact of living standards on the learning process, and considering the role of experience and its significance at various levels of individual maturity.

Adult education, in the broad sense, therefore came to be considered an essential aspect of vocational training programmes, company training, trade union training, and courses for political or cultural purposes. This was extremely important because it built on people's accumulated experience, while at the same time, it sought to transmit specific contents in a logical and systematic way. This confirmed the need to avoid a split in research on the learning process in children as opposed to that in adults, especially with regard to analysing the forms that structured contents might take in the development of the individual learner, and the transformation of those contents over time. This is the background for research on the relationship between the curriculum contents and the work environment.

Research on the adult education curriculum in the 1970s and 1980s, which set out to analyse the relationship between educational goals and their translation in practice, clearly demonstrated the narrowness of the separation between so-called basic education and job training. This is an aspect of the question which merits closer study here. A multidisciplinary study (IRES-CGIL 1985) confirmed how, in general, occupational skills are based on more than just technical abilities (*abilità*). It provided support for the theory that new technologies would accentuate this aspect, and that the learning skills needed for understanding processes of innovation could not be left solely to basic skills education, company training or trade union classes, but required a combination of approaches.

With regard to course contents, the boundaries between these types of training are in fact less clear, because of the speed of developments and the spread of the skills needed to cope with them in a balanced way. Here one can well understand the relationship between basic education and job training, between the course contents and the learning processes.

For this reason, educational research (including that on adult education) should spell out the relationships between the development, transmission and acquisition of knowledge, and between the functions of language and the forms of activating the various cognitive resources; it should go into the methods of organising and transmitting knowledge; it should expand on the way in which the mind processes information and the role of memory. Particularly important is the study of the relationships between consciousness, cognition and metacognition, with specific attention to the latter aspect, whose analysis, even though still partial, appears likely to show interesting developments.

RESEARCH ON JOB TRAINING AND PROFESSIONAL SKILLS

The impact of adult education on job training

The studies of the learning process in adult education have had a significant impact on research on job training in Italy. This occurred particularly in the 1980s in the face of a growing demand for more highly trained staff to cope with social changes and new production methods, and the recognition of the limits of a system of qualification based on an educational approach which was based on measurable performance.

As a result, a need emerged for deeper analysis of the forms through which learning occurs. It is obvious that the complex cultural growth of any individual cannot be analysed in its entirety through tests which, by their very nature, have a limited character. Furthermore, there are kinds of knowledge which, with respect to the performance of specific skills, may be necessary conditions but not sufficient in themselves, and it is obviously impossible to measure the full outcome of a teaching activity, even when it is carried out as intended.

With respect to the teaching of vocational qualifications, where the theoretical approach has been based on the analysis of tasks, these matters raised various questions concerning the how, where and when to build a training programme capable of preparing people for specific activities without falling into the trap of fragmentation of isolated skills with no general purpose and significance. There were also questions concerning how to provide people with useful skills in a short period which would still be able to evolve with changes in the environment as time went on. When the adult education problem was posed in these terms, the continuity and interrelationship between basic education and job training became obvious. It also revealed a field of study common to the two spheres, through the use of the term *competenza*. This term, in its most recent usage (for a broader examination of this, see Meghnagi 1992), refers to the development of conscious knowledge with which one seeks to understand the relationship between concretely observable actions and the forms in which experiences and conscious knowledge are assumed and used to produce choices and decisions. In this field, Bruner (1966/7) made a significant contribution to later developments by hypothesising that individual ability and cognitive activity occur through a process of discovery and invention using materials and tools developed through science and culture. Through this process, the individual defines styles of thought, modes of analysis of reality and diverse forms of expression and of exercising skills.

These studies led to consideration of the reciprocal connections and integration between the subjective and objective aspects of reality, beyond their simple 'interaction'. They consequently emphasised experience as the acquisition of knowledge which is dependent on the cultural environment. Thus the notion of learning changed: instead of being seen as simply the reception and rote memorisation of facts, learning came to be understood as a cognitive activity characterised by the development of information, the use of strategies, the testing of hypotheses and the tendency to go beyond the limits of the intermediate data. The acquisition of knowledge (learning) is the result of complex paths, the comprehension of which requires an examination of the cognitive and mental processes, bearing in mind the realities in which they take place. The contexts of life and work must be considered as settings where experience and unstructured knowledge are absorbed and developed.

The learning process, if we accept the theories described here, must be seen as a mental activity in which individuals reconstruct and redevelop their own particular relationship with reality, using general or occupational knowledge in connection with specific contexts and for precise requirements. This approach demonstrates the complexity of the relationship between structured knowledge and previous experience. In order to identify if particular knowledge has been assimilated, it is necessary to understand how other external knowledge is organised in the scheme of perception and cognition, and how it influences behaviour, knowledge and values.

Every action or observable manifestation uses skills and capacities which are the result of complex mental processes, even when the action is simple. The knowledge underlying skill may not be easily traced back to scholastic or academic categories.

Cognition and cognitive development interact with each other through experience acquired in various contexts. This favours the connection of the new with that which is already known, according to methods of cognitive processing that depend, among other things, on the frame of reference within which the person gives meaning to the contents of experience. The memory, in this process, plays an organising function, both general and individual.

Producing knowledge on the basis of experience and the contribution of new knowledge means supplying the cultural and instrumental references to elements in the individual's past, so that they rise to a higher level of generalisation. From this viewpoint, the outcome of the learning process, based on experience and the progressive elaboration and organisation of knowledge, is attributable to experiences centred in social reality and experiences related to work.

THE ACQUISITION OF KNOWLEDGE: A CONSTRUCTIVE AND ACTIVE LEARNING PROCESS

One of the most interesting features of research in the cognitive domain, which is focused on the processes of treating consciously known information, as distinguished from research in the behavioural field, which deals with the analysis and action of that which is immediately observable, is due, among other things, to the difference in the way they interpret the relationship between research and its application in the educational setting (Pontecorvo 1984). In the behavioural approach, operating methods are characterised by the definition of a learning model based on studies realised in controlled experimental conditions, and the application of this model in other learning situations which differ in terms of the students, the operating conditions, the contents, the task assignments and, above all, the number and dimension of uncontrolled or uncontrollable factors. In the cognitive domain, although there is no single model which would take account of the different ways in which individuals learn, there is a wide range of research which describes the learning process (acquisition of skills), in an attempt to explain how knowledge is organised, retrieved and used. Here we are dealing with the results of studies conducted on complex processes and tasks, related to the formation of concepts, linguistic comprehension and production, problem-solving and, in general, skills which are not extraneous to those taught in an educational setting.

Studies in the cognitive sphere (for references, see Boscolo 1986) focusing on the learning process emphasise its constructive nature, according to which the acquisition of the skill to perform a more or less complex task takes the form of a connection between this skill and others present in the individual's long-term memory. Knowledge is thus constructed in a form which is influenced by the way in which the previous knowledge is structured, through a process which is different from simple recording or reception.

Learning is also shown to be active, in addition to constructive. It is in fact the result of a process based on a strategy, on a method of confronting a task and pursuing an objective, on a form of control of the broad process of information codification, transformation and storage, on an activity and a dynamic which permit the assumption of elements of new, previously unknown information whose acquisition also causes changes in existing knowledge. What emerges from this attempt to map the learning process is the emphasis on the particular characteristics of the learners, the organisational forms of their knowledge, the strategies employed and the ways in which they make use of their capacities and skills.

From all this there arises a redefinition of the notion of competence (specific or general) as the outcome of a conceptual process which is translated into a given operational form, by a process through which the manifestation of new knowledge or skill changes the previously existing mental organisation. Described in these terms, the notion of competence covers both the ability to perform a particular task or solve a problem, and the processes which enable such performance.

For this reason, while it is possible to evaluate a single example of task performance, it is difficult to appreciate the full complexity of a capacity, which is built up from a combination of learning processes in formal and informal situations, at different times and in different settings. It is also necessary to take account of the value systems which support the acceptance of innovations, membership of an occupational group, the ability to express cognitive resources of various types which precede the action and decision-making processes and which determine the quality of an individual task performance. For this purpose, competence can be described through reference to a discipline, an operational practice, a course curriculum, a field of experience, a sector of activity, or the context of action. It can be defined on the basis of the capacity for a 'correct' response, in situations where only one right answer is possible, the capacity to 'interpret' or 'explain' issues on which it is possible to express opinions and value judgements, and the capacity for 'efficient' solutions, where it is a matter of intervening in specific situations (such as a car mechanic's ability to identify and repair a fault in a car, or a doctor's ability to diagnose and treat an ailment).

Research using this approach, (see Ajello *et al.* 1992) has nevertheless shown that none of these aspects alone is able to explain and entirely account for the competence connected with the management of knowledge, the use of an ability or the exercise of an occupation. These are all dependent on subjective and objective variables, the effective margins for autonomy and the capacity to manage a situation, the forms in which it is possible to perform a given task, and the models of authority and divisions of responsibility existing in the organisational context.

The process of constructing competence is not linear but involves bringing together elements from various sources internal and external to the subject, to form connections with each other to produce knowledge and abilities. It is inevitable and proper that, for purposes of educational research, this path should include areas of possible formal intervention, of a didactic character, concerning abilities specific to a given discipline or profession. Thus, if done properly, the testing of acquired skills through the examination of explicit and objectively measurable performances is certainly appropriate. It is worth repeating, however, that it is wrong to consider job training as external to the broader process of education and the development of individual knowledge. On the contrary, the acquisition of a competence must be considered a constituent element, for all practical purposes, of the individual's cultural and educational assets.

For this reason, the relationship between the individual who knows and the reality which is known can be defined by reference to Dewey's notion of 'transaction', to reaffirm the operational and interactive values of competence. Memory is the vehicle with which the heritage of collective and individual knowledge is preserved, organised, selected and protected, and is thus revealed as the mechanism which regulates competence.

Expertise is considered as the result of knowledge acquired through experience which is consolidated through processes of action and decision, the totality of abilities possessed and tested in problem-solving, and of the capacity for assessment and decision-making when encountering new or unforeseen situations. In this regard, limiting our illustrations to the field of occupations, it can be readily seen that the complexity of the work context increases the difficulty of describing and formally recognising the acquisition of a skill, which becomes limited merely to testing individual task performance.

In this field, the accepted approach is to consider occupational competence as composed of a kind of knowledge which links the individual's activity to a wider process of activity in the organisation. For this purpose, attention has been given not only to the phases of individual activity but also to those of the activity required by the organisation. This analytical approach takes into account the totality of planned activity and the concrete forms of individual action, how competence is characterised by a combination of actions planned on the basis of general objectives projected into particular accomplishments. In this framework, competence can be defined as contextual, linked to the field of action, and 'strategic' with respect to the possible forms of decision and intervention.

This hypothesis is supported by research done in the 1960s and 1970s on artificial intelligence and expert systems. In these studies, attention was focused on fundamental information-processing capacities of individuals, behaving more or less intelligently in situations where they lack any specialised knowledge and expertise. In more recent years, research has gone further into these issues (see Glaser 1987), seeking a better understanding of the structural characteristics of various fields of knowledge, the mechanisms of decodification of the problem, the comprehension of forms and models of its recognition (i.e. by a given individual), and the processes involved in decodifying difficult and unstructured ideas. Each individual builds his or her own competence and knowledge through a process not limited solely to contacts with material or symbolic reality but also involving social mediation by individuals having equal or greater expertise, who offer matter for further reflection, analysis and reasoning. This interaction, composed of dialogue and possibly contradiction, is a determining factor in the acquisition of competence. In this respect, the linguistic–cognitive exchange plays an essential role.

Recent studies in the psychology of learning (for references, see Pontecorvo 1990) have analysed the relationships between elements of development attributable to the precise chronological order in which certain contents of conscious knowledge occur, to avoid creating temporal discontinuity, and show that elements of competence cannot be broken down according to a rigid sequential relationship. As a result an individual's knowledge needs to be tested on the basis of what he or she knows, as opposed to what he or she does not know.

Each individual, in fact, reprocesses information received from the surrounding environment, reorganising it as a function of broader hypotheses, operating through strategies which are not always identifiable or predictable in an orderly process of 'teaching–learning'. This is connected to the debate in the adult education field on the relevance of contexts of life and work, to the increasing demand for new knowledge and cognitive processes producing changes in previously existing knowledge (Susi 1989). Recent experiments (Schwartz 1989), in confirming this learning theory, have demonstrated that it is possible to act effectively to achieve significant competence acquisition among subjects having low levels of formal schooling. This has been done by starting from the assumption that, whatever the individual's level of schooling and basic competences, a set of competences has always been acquired which can serve as the basis for educational intervention.

264

Social interaction, which supports the individual at the emotional level, allows the person not only to share difficulties and problems with others, but also to analyse questions, to communicate, to make observations, to express points of view, and thus to proceed using the contributions of others to construct the framework necessary for further learning and for the organisation of experiential data.

Expertise is considered as contextual. It is a form in which declarative skill is highly proceduralised and automatic, and in which there is a series of trial-and-error techniques for the solution of very specific problems.

This notion of expertise consists of intervening schemes of information which are situationally linked, with speed, flexibility, and with mental models which allow access to a larger set of data and its manipulation. This general definition allows scope to go into the merits of various levels of expertise, considering their specific implications and understanding how the expertise is acquired and operates. Experts and non-experts have different ways of organising their knowledge. For experts, this involves declarative knowledge, based on concepts and contents, as well as procedural knowledge, linked to precise rules of action and capable of controlling its own problem-solving process, turning back and stopping to think and even modifying what has been asserted previously if it conflicts with what has occurred afterwards. Non-experts mainly have declarative knowledge, which prevents the use of more general rules for problem-solving. Carried to extremes, it can be stated that the difference between experts and non-experts is not only the presence of concepts necessary to problem-solving, but in their methods of organisation and procedure.

Research on expertise, i.e. on 'being expert', is clarifying the ways in which experts organise and use information. In particular, Glaser and Chi (1988) argue that experts mainly excel only in their own field, that they perceive the most significant elements in their field of observation, that they are much faster than non-experts in the use of skills in their field, and that they solve problems rapidly with few errors. In addition, they have a better short-term and long-term memory, they see and represent a problem in their field at a deeper and more principled level than beginners, they invest a great amount of time in the qualitative analysis of problems, and they have a strong capacity for self-testing. The experts' capacity for self-testing reflects their greater underlying knowledge, and is contextually linked, allowing them to predict the difficulty on the basis of principles rather than on elements of little relevance.

Experts convert the problem into another structure previously encountered. This conversion takes time and in turn gives rise to a new representation of the problem, a representation which includes sub-problems and partial solutions. The non-expert spends little time in the phase of redefining the initial problem and goes immediately to attempts at partial solutions of particular problems. The non-expert's representation is constructed in very little time, and lacks an historical dimension.

Being an expert also means being able to explain one's own expertise in various ways at diverse levels, knowing how to give concrete examples and how to address a problem, even one that is vaguely defined, by representing it in other ways so as to be able to formulate interpretative hypotheses and proposed solutions, and knowing how to explain the nature of a problem and justify the reasons for one's choices, actions and decisions.

Expertise can be defined (Meghnagi 1989) as a competence based on special knowledge, and general expertise is the result of knowledge which can be managed and applied in many fields. Nevertheless, having knowledge is not enough to make one an expert: expertise exists only if the knowledge is used in a given way, in an appropriate form, in the right place. In this sense, expertise is a contextualised form of knowledge, where the context determines its effectiveness, the way in which it is manifested and applied, and its specific usefulness.

RECENT TRENDS

Studies on skills learning and expertise have recently had significant impact in Italy in the context of collective bargaining. In July 1993, a job training protocol was signed between *Confindustria* (the Italian federation of private sector employers), and the *Confederazione Generale Italiana del Lavoro* (CGIL), the *Confederazione Italiana dei Sindacati del Lavoro* (CISL) and the *Unione Italiana del Lavoro* (UIL), the main Italian trade union confederations. This document forms the basis of current negotiations on this issue.

The protocol provides, among other things, that management and labour assume a joint and continuing responsibility with respect to vocational training. This involves promoting legislative reform of the training system to promote innovations, introducing measures for combining work place-ment and study and setting up a system of continuing education, financed by a specific state fund. It also proposes the promotion of initiatives through bipartite organisations. With regard to this aspect, strategic importance is given to actions aimed at the systematic analysis of training needs.

The gathering of forecasting information will be done through a survey, which will have the purpose, at the regional level, of supplying the informa-tion needed for the programming of training activities and, at the national level, of establishing the overall directions of the system of job training. The survey is intended to be the instrument both of primary information and of testing the feasibility of establishing a system of job training needs analysis, in the form of an official report to be made available to, among others, the National and Regional Employment Commissions.

The permanent system of training needs analysis proposed by the protocol, promoted and managed by unions and employers, will guide training provision. The guidance would be implemented by defining the quality of the demand for particular job categories, stipulating the basic knowledge required for specific job functions and appropriate skills, and would also classify skills in terms of 'critical needs', 'emerging needs' and 'needs in decline'. A national group of experts in specific fields, chosen by common agreement between the contracting parties, was charged with proposing a feasibility plan to submit to the public authorities for the financing of the initiative. The protocol constitutes the first comprehensive agreement between employers and unions on job training since 1973, the year when the metalworkers' collective bargaining agreement included the landmark provision for paid training leave.

The 1993 protocol is in line with the general perspectives of the 1973 agreement but there has been a significant change in the balance of power. In 1972, the trade union demand for paid training leave was the result of a confrontation between labour and management, and job training was the object of a confrontation with the public authorities. In 1993, however, employers and unions joined forces to obtain changes in the state educational system to make it more open to the world of work, to improve the transition of young people from school to work and for the retraining of employees.

It is inevitable that, during implementation of the protocol, differences will emerge between the parties to the agreement on the forms that policy should take. There nevertheless appears to be full agreement between them on the ineffectiveness of the national system of vocational training and on the mechanisms for intervening to change it. This involves a recognition of the centrality of the work context, and of classes in basic education as productive fields for vocational qualification. An apprenticeship programme, well financed and culminating in a certificate of qualification, would generally tend to exclude any type of low-grade dead-end work. There is agreement that the establishment of a national system of definition of job qualifications and certification of training is required, through some means of skills testing or approval of training programmes. This would require meeting specified criteria, which would be the basis for the financing of any job training activity proposed by institutions in or out of the state system. This requires practical forms of collaboration between employers and unions on all elements of job training, conducted in or out of the workplace. If apprenticeship and adult education are to be accomplished through recognised programmes in approved settings, and if the experiment is to yield nationally formalised results, the educational process requires ongoing agreement and dialogue between various forces in society. Finally, connections need to be established between structures of academic and occupational guidance on one hand, and structures of job placement and career mobility on the other hand. If work is the setting for training, and if training is an instrument for qualification of the labour force, then the agencies responsible for this purpose must guarantee their support, both for work itself and for training.

In connection with all this is the programme of needs analysis which has been proposed to the Ministry of Labour, and, more generally, research on job qualifications, particularly on specialised skills, which is being carried out on the basis of findings of broader studies referred to above and recalled here.

BIBLIOGRAPHY

Ajello, A. M., Cevoli. M. and Meghnagi, S. (1992) *La competenza esperta*, Rome: Ediesse.

Boscolo, P. (1986) *Psicologia dell'apprendimento scolastico*, Turin: Utet.

Bruner, J. S. (1966/7) *Verso una teoria dell'istruzione*, Rome: Armando.

Glaser, R. (1987) 'Thoughts on expertise', in C. Scooler and W. Schair (eds) *Cognitive Functioning and Special Structure over the Life Course*, Norwood, NJ: Ablef.

Glaser, R. and Chi, M. T. H. (1988) 'Overview', in M. T. H. Chi, R. Glaser and N. J. Farr (eds) *The Nature of Expertise*, Hillsdale, NJ: Lawrence Ibaum.

IRES–CGIL (Istituto ricerche economiche e sociali–Confederazione Generale Italiana del Lavoro) (1985) *Qualificazione Professionale e contenuti della Formazione, Rapporto di Ricerca* Romei Ediesse.

Meghnagi, S. (ed.) (1989) *Analisi complementare all'attivazione di azioni sprerimentali in materia di orientamento scolastico e professionale*, Rome: Chirone 2000 (unpublished).

——(1992) *Conoscenza e competenza*, Turin: Loescher.

Pagnoncelli, L. (1989) *Sistema formativo ed educazione degli adulti*, Turin: Loescher.

Pontecorvo, C. (1984) 'I processi di acquisizione della conoscenza a scuola', in B. Vertecchi *La scuola italiana verso il 2000*, Florence: La Nuova Italia.

——(1990) 'Introduzione', in AAVV *La continuità educativa dai quattro agli otto anni*, Florence: La Nuova Italia.

Schwartz, B. (1989) 'Le nuove qualifiche', Istituto Ricerche Economiche e Sociali, Rome: unpublished.

Susi, F. (1989) *La domanda assente*, Rome: La Nuova Italia Scientifica.

18

INDUSTRIAL DEVELOPMENT AND TRAINING POLICIES

A regional approach

Vittorio Capecchi

Reports of the Commission of the European Community and Jacques Delors' recent White Paper all concur that the reduction of unemployment and the guarantee of acceptable levels of competitiveness for the European regions depend upon higher levels of education and training both within and outside the workplace. Has this always been the case? If today the political and cultural positions prevailing in the United States and Europe enjoy an almost universal consensus, certain aspects were the subject of profound disagreement only fifteen or twenty years ago. This disagreement did not simply derive from governments and different political parties, trade unions and business associations but also from militant sociologists and economists belonging to left-wing coalitions set up after the student and worker unrest of 1968.

The aim of this chapter is to explain the changes in attitudes during this period through an analysis of the relationship between industrial development and training policies, notably within the framework of a regional approach, and the contribution made by gender research to the renewal of these issues.

INDUSTRIAL DEVELOPMENT AND TRAINING POLICIES IN THE 1970s

The framework for the interpretative models proposed in the 1970s cannot be separated from developments specific to Italian Sociology. Indeed, it should not be forgotten that Sociology was rejected by the Fascist state, which retained a single chair in this discipline at the University of Florence. In the post-war period, Italian Sociology could be characterised by:

- a marked American influence (particularly that of Merton and Lazarsfeld at the University of Columbia): in the 1960s, students wanting to obtain the *libera docenza*, the university diploma enabling them to join the teaching profession, were obliged to prove that they had stayed in the

United States and that they were familiar with the most recent American sociological research;

- the divisions between sociologists were linked to the origin of their universities – secular for Ferrarotti, Pizzorno, Pagani and Sartori, Catholic for Ardigo and Alberoni – and between the functionalist/technocratic approach and the analysis of social phenomena in terms of class conflict;
- there was a strong link between sociologists and economists through the creation of the journal *Inchiesta*: instead of focusing exclusively on ideology and politics (like the other European journals at that time), *Inchiesta* immediately engaged in a debate from the very outset on the mechanisms governing the labour market and economic development, with contributions from a great many Italian economists (Graziani, Meldolesi, Brusco, Ginzburg, Salvati, Frey, etc.);
- after 1968, there was considerable support from the trade unions in terms of encouraging research – the unions, firmly rooted in the workplace through works councils, were not content with merely promoting the struggle for increased salaries or shorter working hours but were also interested in issues such as health and safety, access to training for all and the new forms of work organisation;
- the regionalisation of research;
- lastly, the work of researchers and militant feminists published in reviews such as *Inchiesta* was significant in criticising traditional representation of work (Guerra and Pesce 1991).

All these characteristics, which developed within a particular politico-cultural environment, explain the choices made in the first research and debates in the Sociology of Education, the Sociology of Work and Economic Sociology.

Two models for interpreting school and social change

The first model considers that technological innovation plays a central role in changes in the school system to the extent that it determines reforms of the curriculum and changes in the organisation of different occupations and types of work while requiring an appropriate training system. It is therefore necessary to reform the education system and the system of vocational training if we want to adapt to technological change. The value of the different structures of training, research and production is linked to their greater or lesser ability to adapt to the trends of technological progress.

In contrast, the model based on class and class conflict assumes that changes in the school system are chiefly the result of struggles born of the conflicts between the different social classes. The principal objective of this second model is the struggle against inequalities, whereas the technocratic model leads to an overall defence of the status quo.

While most sociologists in the United States tended to accept Talcott Parsons' functionalist/technocratic model, the situation in Italy, just after the period of student unrest, was quite different. There is no doubt that the research and analyses devoted, in particular, to an interpretation of the school system based on the class and class-conflict model encountered greater success than work based on other theories. Between the 1960s and 1970s, Don Milani's book against academic selection, *Lettera a una professoressa*, and the first sociological research on teachers, *Le vestali della classe media* by Barbagli and Dei, enjoyed a consensus within the sociological community. These works offer us a common interpretation of the Italian school system which, through the teachers it employs, transmits the knowledge of the middle classes, marginalises the members of the working classes and maintains social inequality.

The relationship between industrial development and training policies

Before confirming whether there actually is a relationship of this type, it is first important to recall the way in which industrial development is interpreted in the United States and in Italy. In the United States, interpretation is chiefly based on the large corporation engaged in mass production and on the concentration of research in large state and privately funded laboratories. Books such as *Monopoly Capital* by Baran and Sweezy (1968) and *The New Industrial State* by Galbraith (1972) – which differ considerably from the ideological point of view – nevertheless agree when they assert that no industrialisation process can take place outside the concentration of industry and research.

Similarly, in Italy, in the 1950s and 1960s, it was assumed that industrial development was linked exclusively to large manufacturing facilities, and industrial policy focused on the concentration of research into publicly funded structures, such as ENI (National Fossil Fuel Company), or on the transfer or creation of large industrial complexes (in the petroleum and chemical sector, for example) in southern Italy and on the islands. In the 1970s, however, this policy started to attract criticism and the large industrial complexes were seen as 'cathedrals in the desert'.

The attention paid to the large corporation and to mass industrialisation encouraged researchers to consider that the Taylorist/Fordist model was also to be found outside the workplace, where it could be studied by the empirical method. In the 1970s, it was not only used to interpret the relationships within the world of work but also relationships between production and consumption, between automation and the organisation of labour, and between industrial development and training policies.

From the point of view of the large corporation, how was the relationship between industrial development and training policies interpreted? The answer is very simple. The condition for industrial development was the availability of a limited number of specialists (engineers and highly specialised technicians) capable of co-ordinating the mass of work entrusted to workers required to execute routine tasks.

According to this model, secondary school was of no crucial importance. Vocational training was not considered an issue of public concern or as an element of regional development but merely as a problem to be solved by large corporations. In the final analysis, care was taken essentially to maintain the academic standards of the universities and institutes of higher education from which industry recruited its senior managers.

In the United States, in the 1970s, books were published with emblematic titles such as *Education and Jobs: The Great Training Robbery* by Berg (1970) and *The Overeducated American* by Freeman (1976). Continuing one's education to degree level is little more than a fraud: young Americans are overeducated. This model of interpretation was also adopted in Italy where, at the end of the 1960s, the percentage of pupils in their final years at secondary school was about 30 per cent. Forecasts projected this would rise to approximately 50 per cent for the 1980s. When still only 30 per cent, people were already speaking of 'long full-time education' and the 'university of the masses' and these figures and the forecasts published in *Inchiesta* were analysed, with disquiet, in essays forming the first analyses of the Italian Sociology of Education. What was the reason for this type of evaluation?

The explanation was provided in books such as Barbagli's work *Disoccupazione intellettuale e sistema scolastico* (1974). The characteristics of the Italian industrial system and, in general, the more highly industrialised societies, seemed to make unemployment among the academically qualified inevitable. It was considered that after an initial phase of reconstruction the production system emerging at that time would be based on a small number of skilled jobs, leading to high unemployment among the newly qualified people who would be obliged, at times, to make do with work requiring no academic qualifications.

The first empirical research, conducted in various regions of Italy on technico-industrial institutes, revealed certain data whose interpretation resembled that suggested by Barbagli. People with academic qualifications were likely to find themselves unemployed. The lengthening of education represents a 'parking lot', the objective of which is to postpone entry into the labour market. It is necessary to continue studying only because one acquires a relative advantage over those who have completed shorter training courses. Undoubtedly, there existed an inflation in diplomas but, as Bourdieu (1978) pointed out, those who enter the labour market without academic qualifications are, in fact, the principal victims of this inflation.

In fact, it was incorrect to apply the same interpretation to unemployment problems that differed in quantity and quality. Research carried out on the professional openings for the academically qualified (Capecchi 1983) demonstrated the absurdity of this generalisation. This judgement is probably valid for the Mezzogiorno (even if this is not always the case) but certainly proves to be inappropriate when applied to regions such as Emilia-Romagna. Indeed, regions such as these have attained extremely high levels of industrial development, a fact that is all the more surprising as it was unforeseen. In the 1970s, they managed not only to absorb all the graduates from secondary education (including those from technico-industrial institutes) but also to show that high-school graduates could move from waged employment to an activity as entrepreneurs.

By observing the way in which Italian sociological analyses in the 1970s interpreted the relationship between industrial development and vocational training, a tendency can be observed of generalising conclusions on the basis of results obtained from different studies. The American theories to which researchers tried to adhere failed, however, to stand up to more precise regional analyses.

First steps towards a regional analysis of socio-economic development

Unlike the Paris-based centralism characterising French research, Italian Sociology is not focused on a particular university area. This encourages the relocation of sociological researchers towards different regions and enables a periodical, such as *Inchiesta*, to draw inter-regional comparisons. Among the Italian trade unions, the FLM (the metalworkers' union) represented a major intellectual forum in the 1970s, stimulating research into the working conditions in factory workshops and in small- and medium-sized companies. The success in securing the '150 hours' agreement gave wide currency to the idea that a basic education must be given to all those hitherto excluded from it.

The fact of intervening in zones other than the large industrial cities of Milan or Turin led researchers to analyse the industrialisation processes outside large corporations. The first regional analyses also appeared at this time, testifying to the co-operation between economists and sociologists. These analyses encouraged them to debate for the first time the role of small companies in the central/northern and southern regions of Italy (Capecchi *et al.* 1978). At the heart of this debate, Graziani's analysis is significant because it links the failure of small companies to spread in the South to the type of industrial policy chosen for that part of the country. In the Mezzogiorno, there was a tradition of small- and medium-sized companies linked to the food, wood, furniture and clothing industries. Their weakness derived from their commercial organisation and allowed regions such as Emilia-Romagna to take the lead. These regions, enjoying a rich community tradition derived from agriculture, were able to equip themselves more rapidly as far as the manufacture and marketing of products were concerned and consequently managed to move ahead of the companies based in the South, including those in the food sector. The policy advocating the transfer of large industrial complexes to the South neglected the needs of small- and medium-sized companies and thereby encouraged the failure of industrial development.

Bagnasco's book *Le Tre Italie* (1977) summarises a number of the earlier regional analyses. He argued that to understand industrial development in Italy, it was not sufficient to refer to the large corporations in the industrial triangle, nor to oppose the industrialised North to a South devoid of companies of all sizes. Indeed, between these two zones there appears a third Italy characterised by a diffuse industrialisation and a host of small enterprises. It brings together in one zone two groups of regions which are very different politically: the 'red' regions (where the Communist party enjoys a strong presence) such as Emilia-Romagna and Tuscany, and the 'white' regions (where the Social Democrats have a strong presence) such as the Veneto region.

In the 1970s, a new current of research emerged which examined the mechanisms of regional industrial development by focusing on the work done by women. The research carried out by sociologists such as Balbo, Zahar and May analysed the role of women both within the formal economy and within the informal, non-monetary economy. The sociological and economic analyses of home-working and women's activities which did not appear in the statistics were incorporated into a framework of a more controversial and complex nature. By way of illustration, the special issues of *Inchiesta* cover the following subjects: 'The Condition of Women', 'The Double Shift and the Female Labour Market', 'Women, the Double Shift and Discrimination'.

Studies of small companies and women's work made it possible to develop the first regional analyses of industrial development. These proved to be more complex than the traditional analyses based on the observation of the large companies.

In the 1970s, this work was linked neither to research on the school system nor vocational training. In the area of training policies, interest was focused on the failure of the reform of the school system. The role of the school was analysed as a place of selection and exclusion of children from working-class families through the implementation of a cultural indoctrination through books exalting the values of the ruling classes.

The comparative study of Bologna and Naples by Capecchi and Pugliese (1978) represents one of the rare studies to compare the analyses of the politico-economic situation with data concerning schooling and attitudes to the ways in which the school systems and training systems operate. This concerns analyses which simply bring together the various components of socio-economic development without really linking them together. In order to define the closer relationships existing between industrial development and training policies, it was necessary to wait for a change in methodological approach, which was not to emerge until the second half of the 1980s.

INDUSTRIAL DEVELOPMENT AND TRAINING POLICIES IN THE 1980s AND 1990s

In the 1980s and 1990s, Italian Sociology became institutionalised and organised into disciplinary sub-groups based upon a number of journals and points of reference. The research co-ordinated by the trade unions played a less important role than it did all through the 1970s and the cultural initiatives (such as the right to 150 hours of education) were then abandoned overall. American cultural hegemony weakened and the contacts between European Sociologies and the European Economic Community research structures intensified.

The different models for interpreting school and social change

The two models (functionalist/technocratic and class conflict) which had dominated debates in the 1970s were confronted by a different scenario in the 1980s and 1990s. The technocratic model enjoyed wide circulation, with many journals devoted to Organisational Sociology, which considered the Japanese school system a point of reference. Some European and American sociological research which took account of the social-class model offered more critical appraisals of this training system (Capecchi 1993c).

Despite its critical capacity, the social-class model failed to develop a hypothesis for alternative training in Europe. Consequently, within the different European training systems, initiatives of a contradictory nature could be seen. On the one hand, there was greater selection of young people by reducing the number of options in subjects allowing the development of critical skills. On the other hand, initiatives in remedial work and the orientation of pupils encountering difficulties at school resulted in the introduction, even within technical/vocational education, of questions related to environmental protection and health and safety.

These new analyses constitute an epistemological break and go beyond the mere confrontation of the two models. The texts written by women within the new culture of gender difference developed by Irigaray were addressed to male researchers to reveal how the ostensibly different technocratic and social-class models concur, in fact, on a fundamental point: their masculine nature, which underlies a logic of expulsion/assimilation of the female sex.

An essay by Guerra and Pesce (1991) traces in detail the innovations introduced by the research carried out by women over the twenty previous years while referring at the same time to the relationship between cognitive processes, work and gender differences. The innovations in question are profound theoretical innovations capable of generating spin-offs at the political level.

The interpretation of the relationship between industrial development and training policies

Today, the interpretation of the relationship between industrial development and training is completely different from that of the 1970s. The objective of bringing 80 per cent of an age cohort to the level equivalent to British 'A' levels is a matter of consensus in public debate and sociological research. How has such a reversal of interpretation been possible?

The Japanese training strategies offer us the first explanation for this radical change in direction. Japan, for more than fifteen years, has managed to bring 90 to 95 per cent of each age cohort to 'A' level standard, thereby disproving the American and European analysis and forecasts prevailing in the 1970s. Not only were Japanese unemployment rates extremely low but its industrial and technological development successfully challenged the United States and the strongest European countries.

The mechanisms of international competitiveness and their effects on unemployment, which is increasingly structural in Europe, lie at the origin of the second explanation. Differences in wages between the different national labour markets have two effects on the employment level: (a) products whose quality is poor or average, manufactured in countries where salaries are up to five or six times lower, become competitive in Europe and lead to company closures; (b) the European countries are then tempted to invest in the low-cost facilities in these countries, thus reducing the possibility of creating employment in Europe. To this reduction in jobs is added 'technological' unemployment linked to productivity gains both in manufacturing and service industries.

The creation of new jobs becomes a key objective which can be attained only by creating a host of new products and services whose technical quality is high or average, provided that small- and medium-sized companies are the principal beneficiaries. The importance given to the promotion of diffuse and technologically advanced activities and the fact of not being exclusively interested in the development of large companies justifies the increase in the demand for people with academic qualifications or with higher level training of a more or less specialised nature.

The third explanation simply consists in a growing awareness of the existence of models of industrialisation which differ from the mass production model evident in the crisis of the Taylorist/Fordist model.

The analyses focusing on alternative types of industrialisation, notably those of Piore and Sabel (1984) and Sabel and Zeitlin (1985), emphasise that since the beginning of the first industrial revolution there has not been a single type of industrialisation based on the large, mass production factory.

In the United States as in Europe, the industrialisation model was based on flexible specialisation, the manufacture of specialised and flexible goods according to the demands of the customer, implying an organisation based on sub-systems or districts of small- and medium-sized companies.[1] This type of production differs from the model of mass production and the methods associated with Taylor and Ford. Flexible specialisation needs skilled workers with high intermediate level technical qualifications. It is therefore vital that a large number of people arrive on the labour market equipped with diplomas and valid skills in vocational training and not merely 'credentials', as Collins put it (1977).

At the same time, the principles of 'lean production' organised on the basis of the methods developed by Toyota spread even in large, mass production factories. With these methods, it is not only the organisation of the flows of information and merchandise within the factory that changes but also workers' activities in production. In the United States, in the 1970s, automation in the workshops of large factories was based on the notion of fool-proof machines, adapted for idiots. In contrast, within Japanese factories, the principles developed by Toyota stressed quality control at every phase of the production process and recognised the participation of workers in workshop innovations. In this system, workers starting out in the factories must possess knowledge at the level equivalent to 'A' level.

A fourth explanation enjoying wide currency in the United States and in Europe promotes the idea that in periods of structural unemployment it is very important for young people to obtain qualifications. Thanks to the transversal skills acquired, they adapt to changes in occupation (and from salaried employment to freelance activity), and to the alternation between spells of unemployment, study and work.

Since the 1970s, the role of work and the temporal nature of the training/work relationship has changed in the United States and Europe. A life-long job has been replaced by a series of different occupations, just as initial training has become continuing education interrupted by the exercise of several occupations. In order to gain access to this continuing education, it is necessary to start with a sufficiently high level of education and transferable knowledge.

In the United States and Europe, a final explanation (most frequently overlooked despite its importance) consists in linking the increase in the number of high-school graduates with the increasingly high percentage of young girls continuing in full-time education in secondary schools and whose number now exceeds that of boys. Initially, the extension of education was interpreted using the metaphor of the 'parking lot'. Within this, the training pathway was considered weaker and consequently offering fewer job opportunities. Since then, research has proved the existence of a cultural choice and the desire to acquire a body of knowledge on the part of young women wishing to pursue their education even in situations where job opportunities are uncertain, as in southern Italy. According to Pesce, women's access to training can be interpreted as a transmission of feminine models of instruction from one generation, and from one social class, to another (1990).

This change in horizon emphasises the need to set up structures for those who encounter difficulties in studying and who opt out of the school system before obtaining their *diploma*. Two kinds of action are envisaged: to make a substantial difference between the curricula (in the United States, prestigious high schools exist alongside schools offering services of a substantially lower quality, and the same duality characterises secondary schools in Japan) or, alternatively, to set up a multitude of institutions for vocational orientation or remedial institutions for young people in difficulty (as is the case in France).

In the 1970s, the importance of two research fields, macroeconomics and corporate economy, left an analytical vacuum between the study of the large national economic mechanisms and that of the large company. Today, we speak more of regional economics, and the availability of a large amount of European research emphasises the emergence of a 'Europe of regions' that cannot be reduced to an analysis in macroeconomic terms. The research programmes organised by the EEC-FAST in Brussels or the ILO in Geneva tend to emphasise the region as a framework of research and it is in this direction that Sociology must move if it is interested in the relationship between industrial development and training policies.

A regional approach to the relationship between training policies and industrial development

The interpretation of the relationship between industrial development and training policies in the context of greater numbers of academically qualified people not only raises problems concerning the organisation of the pathways of vocational orientation and remedial support. It is also a question of identifying, in a given region, the training courses vital to the development of entrepreneurs.

The training strategies leading to the diploma and the post-diploma qualifications are prioritised uncritically today and have been seen as the answer to the problems of unemployment and new enterprise creation while, in the 1970s, they were viewed with caution. But questions concerning the nature of training policies and industrial development remain. New avenues of inquiry are opening up to sociological and economic research to provide answers to these questions.

How can this research make its contribution to the achievement of these objectives in a given region? What type of research is capable of promoting the optimal relationship between training policies and industrial development?

Emilia-Romagna represents the privileged area for two annual reports compiled on behalf of a regional research institute: *School, Vocational Training, University and the Labour Market* and *Quality of Hiring and Demand for Professional Profiles on the Part of Businesses in Emilia-Romagna*.

Certain research shows that it is necessary to adopt two levels of analysis. The first is the history of industrial development and, more generally, the history of the development of companies in the region, differentiating between the pathways taken by men and those taken by women. The second consists in comparative analyses between regions and countries in order to identify the interdependence between technological innovation and social innovation. Different studies have emphasised that the Emilia-Romagna region is characterised by industrial development based on flexible specialisation compared with the other Italian regions whose older industrialisation was marked by the large companies using mass production methods (e.g. Fiat). Emilia-Romagna, from the beginning of the century until after the Second World War, may still be considered according to official statistics as a predominately agricultural region. During the three censuses of 1901, 1931 and 1951, the active farming population was in the region of 65 per cent, 61 per cent and 52 per cent respectively, while the national average was 62 per cent, 52 per cent and 42 per cent. These same statistics emphasise rapid industrialisation during the twenty years following the end of the Second World War. In 1971, the people employed in industry already accounted for 43 per cent of the active population (this had increased from 25 per cent in 1951) and chiefly worked in the mechanical engineering industry.

How was it possible to achieve this accelerated industrialisation process, dominated by mechanical engineering companies specialising in flexible machines capable of meeting customer's specifications (for example packaging machines, machine tools, woodworking and textile machinery) but also by social mobility into entrepreneurial activities? The reconstitution of the historical factors is highly significant, emphasising the role played by the male/female relationship within the agricultural family structure as well as that of training policies and specialisation in mechanical engineering, clothing, agro-food, ceramics and construction industries.

The organisation of farming in the Italian regions varies considerably. The official statistics emphasise the importance of agricultural activities in the first half of the century, and group Emilia-Romagna with the Mezzogiorno. This fails to explain that, in the farming community of Emilia-Romagna, about 70 per cent of families possess knowledge of business administration in their own agricultural area as well as proto-industrial experience (there is a large number of weaving looms). The spread of the sharecropping contracts in Emilia-Romagna resulted in different experiences in agriculture, both for men and for women, from those in the southern regions where, for both sexes, the most widespread activity was farm labouring.

The research carried out by Pesce (1990) has shown that within these

Emilian families, women with experience of administration and authority are the guardians of the initial proto-industrial experience. Indicative of this is the fact that at the beginning of the century, from 1904 to 1925, a woman from the Emilia-Romagna region, Argentina Altobelli, was head of the national secretariat of the *Federterra* (the federation grouping together agricultural labourers and sharecroppers' activities). Born in a parish in the province of Bologna, she worked throughout her trade union activity for the creation of technical schools for women.

The transition of culturally dynamic entrepreneurs based in agriculture to specialised engineering activity did not come about naturally, but through a conscious strategy between the second half of the nineteenth and first half of the twentieth century aimed at transferring theoretical knowledge of mechanics in secondary technical institutes, whose role was extremely active.

This is illustrated by the example of the development of the mechanical engineering industry in Bologna (Capecchi 1990b, 1993b). Noting the decline of the silk industry at the end of the eighteenth century, two Bologna academics connected to the university (the physicist Aldini and the economist Valeriani) went to France and England to see the most important innovations in mechanical engineering for themselves. Their objective was to prepare teaching materials useful for setting up a school for the sons of artisans. At their death in the early nineteenth century, the two scholars left their teaching materials and patrimony to the *commune* of Bologna. Towards the middle of the nineteenth century it built, with the agreement of the university and the companies of the city, a technical school specialising in training its students in the use and design of machine tools. The development of the mechanical engineering industry during the first half of the century and its expansion between 1950 and 1970 were managed by graduates from the Aldini-Valeriani schools.

If the mass production model based on the assembly line does not allow the worker to become an entrepreneur, the flexible specialisation type of industrialisation, organised in sub-systems comprised of small- and medium-sized companies, calls for a close collaboration between the academically qualified specialised worker and the entrepreneur technician. In this way, this type of industrialisation encourages workers to set up their own companies.

Women have no access to the training provided by the technical schools teaching technical drawing, but follow their own course of training. Women introduce their administrative skills in the new enterprises. Pesce has described how they bring to this flexible specialisation-based industrial model the feminine social character which developed within a peasant family as a mode of production, capable of meeting the differentiated demands of the members of the family and community (1990).

The organisation of these theoretico-practical skills in the area of mechanical engineering within the training system, of which men are the main beneficiaries, therefore lies at the heart of the development of the Emilian mechanical engineering industry. In contrast, the female pathway, focusing more on entrepreneurial activities in the textile and clothing sector, did not enjoy the same legitimacy conferred by the school. The analysis of this second course of training shows that the technical schools for girls placed less importance on theoretico-technical subjects, and thereby neglected to provide women with entrepreneurial skills. However, the transmission of knowledge was carried out directly and often outside the institutional training structures.

This analysis of the highly differentiated training pathways followed by male and female students enables us to move away from the traditional analysis. The presence of a majority of young men in the technical and vocational institutes preparing for industry was indicated in the concept of a strong career route, while the presence of a majority of young women in the technical and vocational institutes oriented towards tertiary sector and services was conceptualised in terms of a weak career route. It is nevertheless vital to consider that these pathways are both strong to the extent that the general tertiarisation of production activities has favoured the training routes followed by women, but often without recognising their value.

This historical analysis makes it possible to confirm the importance of a close and continuous link between the value attributed to career routes at different moments in time (the clothing industry in Emilia-Romagna is traditionally linked to the manufacture of straw hats exported at the beginning of the century to distant countries) and the introduction of knowledge useful to the new entrepreneurial activities.

Under these circumstances, how can research be organised from a methodological point of view? It is obvious that it is becoming vital to move out of the Emilia-Romagna region to observe what is happening in Europe, in the United States or Japan. But what point of view should be adopted to observe the other regions?

The research carried out by Capecchi et al. (1987) and Capecchi and Pesce (1992) on behalf of the European Commission has resulted in the identification of an Emilian regional approach adapted to the analysis of the most technologically advanced centres in Europe. The specific nature of the industrialisation in Emilia-Romagna is linked to a context in which the presence of the University of Bologna has favoured the creation of intermediary structures making it possible to apply technologies developed elsewhere, notably in mechanical engineering. Today, the technological innovation of the electronic, data-processing and communications sectors is based in Japan and the United States. The nature of the investment excludes the creation of innovation centres in the Emilia-Romagna region, characterised by co-operation between a large number of players but also by the absence of large companies capable of investing the sums necessary to create powerful research centres.

Consequently, from an initial standpoint, the technological innovation centres are considered as centres for the transfer of the results of these experiments. A second point of view makes it possible to consider the mechanical engineering sector in Emilia-Romagna as the centre of development of entrepreneurial activities, within which the rationale of flexible specialisation has been focused on the satisfaction of differentiated requirements of various types of industry. For example the packaging industries in Bologna meet the needs of the mechanisation of the food, pharmaceutical, tobacco, tea and cosmetics industries. In a word, flexible machines are produced for other industries.

Capecchi and Pesce have emphasised the existence in Europe of two 'maps' of technological innovation (1992). The 'map' of centres of strong innovation is oriented towards a rationale close to the technocratic model, and the 'map' of technological innovations is linked more closely to social innovations. This second structure highlights the Scandinavian experience, omitted from the first map, and also represents an important reference model for the European regions, envisaging technological development linked to social development.

The plan to reorganise the training system promoted by the Bologna commune (Capecchi 1993d) provides us with a good illustration of how the training system can interact with industrial development. The following action plans were put forward:

- first, the creation of a vocational guidance and support programme capable of taking account of the range of projects concerning young men and women;
- second, the organisation of a more vocationally orientated curriculum before and immediately after the diploma. (This would affect first level vocational training, technical and vocational institutes, post-diploma courses, short university courses and second level vocational training.)

The second aspect of this included a strategy aimed at strengthening the existing routes between training–work–entrepreneurial activity and account was taken of the different routes followed by men and women. The problem is to ensure that training courses take account of their relationship to waged work and to potential entrepreneurial capacities by developing courses in theory and new technologies. It also included a strategy aimed at the transfer of new knowledge within academic courses to facilitate the spread of the new routes contributing to entrepreneurial training. The research mentioned above shows that in the Bologna region, both the male career route focused on technico-industrial skills and the female career route centred on skills related to administration, commerce and services have been separated for too long. A whole series of new forms of competence and new entrepreneurial routes now depend upon the ability to link these courses closely together, allowing synergies to develop.

These proposals envisage synergies deriving from the use in education of the new communication technologies (hypertext, multimedia teaching tools, virtual reality, etc.), the application of new technologies to personal care (knowledge required for the construction of electro-medical devices or home-based diagnostic facilities), the use of the most up-to-date methods applied to enhancing the autonomy of the elderly and disabled, the setting up of new technologies for the protection and enhancement of the natural environment, which are linked to technology related to social communications and research.

Each of these proposals calls the existing training structures into question, because they break the separate rationales of traditionally male or female training routes while demanding a transfer of technological and applied knowledge to industry. In fact, it amounts to a medium-term strategy compatible with social and technological, male and female traditions. In order to establish the link between the enhancement of the existing career routes and the introduction of new knowledge for new career routes, it is vital to analyse male and female knowledge and the way in which they are consolidated, not in terms of strong or weak characteristics but as different forms of knowledge which should communicate with one another.

NOTES

1 The research focusing on Emilia-Romagna is analysed in detail in Capecchi (1989, 1990a); Capecchi and Pesce (1993).

BIBLIOGRAPHY

Bagnasco, A. (1977) *Le Tre Italie. La problematica territoriale dello sviluppo economico italiano*, Bologna: Il Mulino.

Baran, P. and Sweezy, P. (1968) *Monopoly Capital*, Harmondsworth: Penguin.

Barbagli, M. (1974) *Disoccupazione intellettuale e sistema scolastico in Italia, 1859–1973*, Bologna: Il Mulino.

Berg, I. (1970) *Education and Jobs: The Great Training Robbery*, New York: Praeger.

Bourdieu, P. (1978) 'Classement, déclassement, reclassement', *Actes de la Recherche en Sciences Sociales* 24.

Capecchi, V. (1983) *Prima e dopo il diploma: percorsi maschili e femminili*, Bologna: Il Mulino.

——(1989) 'Petite entreprise et économie locale: la flexibilité productive', in M. Maruani, E. Reynaud and C. Romani *La Flexibilité en Italie*, Paris: Syros.

——(1990a) 'A history of flexible specialization and industrial Districts in Emilia Romagna', in F. Pyke, G. Becattini and W. Sengenberger *Industrial District and Inter-firms Cooperation in Italy*, Geneva: International Labour Office.

——(1990b) 'L'industializzazione a Bologna nel'900' in W. Tega *Storia illustrata a Bologna* 18/IV and 9/V.

——(1993a) 'Ecole et formation professionnelle en Italie', *Formation Emploi* 44.

——(1993b) 'Industrializzazione flessibile e modello emiliano. Storia dell'industria meccanica bolognese dal 1900 al 1992', in Institut de recherche economique sur la production et le developpement *Industrie et territoire, les systèmes productifs localisés*, Grenoble.

——(1993c) 'Scuola e formazione professionale in Giappone, Stati Uniti ed Europa', *Scuola e città* 4.

——(1993d) *Sinergie per un sistema formativo integrato*, Comune di Bologna.

Capecchi, V. and Pesce, A. (1992) 'Innovation technologique et innovation sociale', in Conférence-consensus Fast (ed.) *Science, technologie et cohésion de la Communauté*, Brussels.

——(1993) 'L'Emilie-Romagne', in V. Scardigli (ed.) *L'Europe de la diversité*, Paris: CNRS Sociologie.

Capecchi, V., Pesce, A. and Schiray, M. (1987) *Nouvelles technologies et vie quotidienne*, Brussels: EEC.

Capecchi, V. and Pugliese, E. (1978) 'Due città a confronto, Bologna e Napoli', *Inchiesta* 35–36.

Capecchi, V. *et al.* (1978) *La piccola impresa nell' economia italiana*, Bari: De Donato.

Collins, R. (1977) *The Credential Society*, New York: Academic Press.

Freeman, B. (1976) *The Overeducated American*, New York: Academic Press.

Galbraith, J. K. (1972) *The New Industrial State*, London: Deutsch.

Guerra, E. and Pesce, A. (1991) 'Lavoro e differenza sessuale', *Inchiesta* 94.

Pesce, A. (1990) 'L'altra Emilia Romagna', in Pesce, A. (ed.) *L'altra Emilia Romagna*, Milan: Angeli.

Piore, M. and Sabel, C. (1984) *The Second Industrial Divide*, New York: Basic Books.

Sabel, C. and Zeitlin, J. (1985) 'Historical alternatives to mass production: politics, markets and technology in nineteenth-century industrialization', *Past and Present* 108.

19

SOCIO-ECONOMIC APPROACHES TO THE LABOUR MARKET

Paolo Calza Bini

The relationship between education and work in labour market research in Italy has been studied more from the point of view of the market's quantitative imbalance than in terms of the qualitative aspects of the processes involved in the social construction of competence and skill. In this chapter some of the principal studies devoted to the Italian labour market will be described. This is a research field in which there is a fruitful exchange between sociologists and economists specialising in work and employment. This research has helped to establish a body of knowledge about education/employment processes and about the social construction (or destruction) of skill in the labour market(s) — a term understood in this chapter in its broader sense as the world of work and its interrelations.

Among the great many socio-economic studies devoted to the vast labour market research area, the emphasis will be on contributions of a more empirical nature focusing on two key aspects: the importance acquired by this theme over the past few decades and its development over time, and the originality of its contribution to scientific thinking.

There exists a relationship between, on the one hand, the factors encouraging scientific debate to focus on current social and economic phenomena and, on the other hand, a distancing of scientific, sociological and economic paradigms following the emergence of scientific reflection based on temporal sequences.

In practice, this relationship has been sufficiently strong to bring researchers and their public to focus their efforts on specific issues during extremely short periods, and generating useful synergies in the process. The 'fashion effect', however, has made it impossible to establish a sufficiently stable foundation for these discoveries, intuitions and innovations, with the effect that part of the research findings may be lost along with a breakdown in continuity as far as these themes, methodological approaches and attempts at theoretical construction are concerned.

Two main thematic currents will be presented in these pages: the first concerns the work focused on territorial diversity, the decentralisation of production and the black economy; the second focuses on the social groups more affected by unemployment, namely, young people and women.

With reference to the labour market and the relationship between education and employment, a number of questions are highlighted in these studies. First, there is the presence of many segments of the labour market which are partially isolated from each other as a result of societal factors. These govern technico-organisational options, the structure of labour costs and the place of training in the composition of the labour markets. The presence of segments determines the allocations and relationships distinguishing these markets into their formal/informal, primary/secondary, internal/external aspects and makes any attempt at a neo-classical interpretation both simplistic and uncertain. Second, there exist several types of 'logic of rationality' or, as Boudon (1987) puts it, 'right frames of mind' among the actors in different 'societal' situations (Fordism, public enterprise, small or microenterprise, the regional specificities of Italy, industrial districts, networks of small- and medium-sized industries). Third, within a given country several 'societal' models are present, a consequence of the differentiated modes of operation of educational and training institutions, and also a consequence of different economic performance (see previous point). Fourth, consideration must be given to the presence/absence of social interaction and networks constituting resources or deprivations, practices and customs, constraints or resources, and, fifth, to the diversity and plurality of the social construction of identities and projects and the consequent reactions between the sexes, generations, territorial, social and professional identities. Finally, there is the analysis of economic relationships and changes in the content of qualifications, and the underestimation of the vocational skills acquired in the cognitive accumulation of interactive processes and in the experience of everyday life.

TERRITORIAL DIVERSITIES, MARKET PLURALITY AND THE SOCIAL CONSTRUCTION OF PROFESSIONAL SKILLS

The socialisation of professional knowledge in the 'Third Italy'

Although there has always been an interest in Italy in the social constructions and structures of production that distinguish one region from another, particular progress was made in this area in the 1970s. Since unification, the discussion of North–South dualism had been dominated by experts specialising in the problems of the Mezzogiorno. However, their interpretation was sharply focused and stressed the differences and inequalities between the North and the South (for example, scholars adopting divergent ideologies such as Croce, Gramsci, Sturso, Salvemini and Rossi-Doria). Socio-economic dualism has not only failed to decrease with political unification, it has also characterised and influenced the entire logic and praxis of Italian history from unification up to the present day, and even impeded and exacerbated (relatively speaking) the problems of developing the depressed areas of the Mezzogiorno. Similarly, for the past hundred years, there has existed a dualism in the viewpoints and interpretations contained in scientific research, testifying to differences in identity and cultural sensitivity between the Mezzogiorno specialists and other Italian experts. This explains the intensity of the debate about the role of territorial differences in all social relationships. The problematics of socio-territorial diversity and the different cultural models involved were widened and considerably enriched in the 1970s and 1980s with the development of research into territorial articulation and the different forms of organisation based on flexible specialisation, with studies devoted to small enterprises (Brusco 1975), the industrially developed regions known as the 'Third Italy' (Calza Bini 1976, Paci 1975), industrial zones (Becattini 1987) and the discussions based on middle-range empirical research (Bagnasco 1988). These analyses, and their conclusions, have given rise to an important debate about theoretical models, but have also led to the gradual decline of interest in social inequalities in industrial organisation and in the different forms of territorial reality. This neglect has had negative and perverse effects for appreciating the major macro differences which are the most significant to the country's economic and social situation (Mingione 1990, Pugliese and Altieri 1990). Indeed, in the 'Third Italy' human capital resources represent one of the key factors in the social construction of the model which is both based on and supports this particular mode of development (Calza Bini and Castellucci 1990). Social and class-based inequalities persist in these regions even if a whole series of social mediations tend – even when they are illusory – to attenuate the social contradictions linked to inequality.

In the Mezzogiorno, territorial and class inequalities have seriously impeded solidarity, cultural integration, the accumulation of knowledge and the appraisal of skills. The state, the business community and the social and political élites (not only in southern Italy) are largely to blame for the lack of awareness of the need to develop social and community solidarity, socialisation, the accumulation and sharing of experience and productive knowledge. The obstacles to the creation of local community links imposed by the law of silence and the violence of the Mafia are an illustration. Other examples are the impoverishment of human capital brought about by migratory processes and its impact on the labour force, and the negative effect on the entrepreneurial spirit of the policies aimed at setting up hubs of industrial activity which merely created 'cathedrals in the desert'.

It seems that no account is taken of the relationship between education and employment in the various development models of the 'Three Italies' (Bagnasco 1977). Moreover, this relationship is particularly underestimated in many studies of the success of the 'Third Italy' and the failure of the South. In practice, this relationship is considerably influenced by socio-territorial differences, especially regarding the educational aspect of socialisation through work and the acquisition of skills. It is worth noting that a uniform school system produces different results in different contexts and with different individuals. In addition, production systems, with specific organisational and professional characteristics, require adequately trained and socialised personnel. Finally, the socio-territorial systems may produce more or less consistent effects on the development of a work culture and qualification.

The originality of Italian work on flexibility (productive decentralisation, small enterprises and industrial districts) has largely fuelled the international debate, even if this debate has focused more on the 'enterprise models' than on the characteristics of employment and social inequalities at the origin of this research. The interdependence developing within the education/work relationship then becomes a resource generating social differences depending upon whether it tends to enhance or to diminish human capital. Insufficient account has been taken of this dimension in certain reappraisals of the facts and of the Italian contributions to the theories of flexible specialisation and flexibility (Regini and Sabel 1989).

The internal organisation and the active networks of small enterprises, their concentration in market niches and in industrial districts in the 1970s and 1980s have been consolidated through day-to-day activity, demonstrating their organisational specificity from the point of view of their size, of the qualities of the entrepreneurs and of the network of their relationships. The small enterprises in these areas are characterised by the ability of their operatives to be autonomous and to forge relationships with the market and institutions. The application of the knowledge, qualification and skills of the workers is frequently developed in everyday relations and spreads amongst them, constituting the strength of the company.

The creation of industrial districts is also the consequence of complex and specific processes of social and economic interactions, resulting from the social relationships of production. These social relationships are related to the crisis of the Fordist-Taylorist model of production as well as to the survival and transformation of other territorial and organisational models. These models, the Marshallian industrial districts, specialised productive co-operation, are typical of the production processes of small-scale enterprises manufacturing semi-finished articles and offering special services and work (Bellandi 1996; Calza Bini et al. 1996).

In this situation, education for work develops much more through the social environment of the community or family, which share experience and know-how, rather than through the more institutional providers of education. In fact, this is a process of interaction among several elements and there is no single causal relationship explaining it.

The novelty of this approach, in increasingly complex social contexts, lies in the search for ideal–typical models capable of explaining how these processes function in a situation characterised by greater diversity, in terms of population, culture, traditions, experience and products. In order to obtain an overall picture on which to base a discussion of the problem of the role and latent capacities of the education/work relationship in small enterprises, it is important to note that technology – in its technical, dimensional, applicational and innovative aspects – is directly stimulated, and often produced, by everyday social life and, consequently, by the producers themselves who may, at one and the same time, be both users and actors.

Favaretto's research (1988) has shown that the capacity to be actors in technological innovation has acquired new momentum in the past two decades with flexible specialisation and the development of industrial districts. It has also led to a change in the scientific models used to understand the development of technology and innovation. The existence of sectoral differences presents a major problem of analysis and interpretation. Differences between sectors – or even sub-sectors using different technologies and methods of production – are so numerous and varied that it is difficult to interpret them in an aggregated form, especially when considering educational and training processes. The picture becomes even further complicated if the analysis takes account of the interpretation of all the differences based on the territories, their socio-cultural characteristics and productive relationships.

Today, each territorial productive sector draws on accumulated experience in the mix of resources, organisational and socio-cultural models, and it is important to guard against making simple but misleading generalisations about these specific forms of education in, and through, work.

The concept of *professionalità*, the application of accumulated experience, encompasses not only the handing down of past traditions and present-day inventions. It is also the effect of a 'mix' between individual and collective memories of know-how acquired in the exercise of an activity over a longer or shorter period. *Professionalità* also varies depending upon collective memory, its capacity and modes of organisation and appropriation; it depends too upon the knowledge and the problems of everyday life shared by clearly defined circles.

The aspects of innovation resulting from the development of qualification in the everyday practice of work frequently depend, therefore, on the particular combination of the elements constituting this 'mix' (and are, consequently, applicable in a more or less intermittent fashion).

RESEARCH IN THE 1980s: THE IMPOVERISHMENT OF HUMAN CAPITAL AND THE RISE IN UNEMPLOYMENT

Two principal factors stimulated and influenced the renewal of academic interest in unemployment in the 1980s. These were the seriousness of unemployment and its quantitative expansion not only during periods of economic recession but also in periods of economic growth, rising to record levels in Italy in the 1980s, and the fact that unemployment affected new categories – young people and women with no experience of work.

Labour market analyses produced results showing the socio-economic causes (and, in particular, the implications of structurally weak and fluctuating demand) and the diversified, complex and unpredictable behaviour of social actors in periods of turbulence and change brought about by the market and the state. Economists considered Keynesian and neo-classical explanations in an attempt not only to reappraise critically the causes of unemployment (voluntary and involuntary) but also to introduce variants into the models capable of providing a better, more realistic explanation of socio-economic phenomena. Sociologists opposed structuralist views and behaviourist views and differed over the interpretation of the characteristics of labour supply and the factors explaining the behaviour of social actors affected by the phenomenon of unemployment. In particular, it was a question of elucidating the following paradox: unemployment was increasing, even when economic demand was favourable, but was not leading to an exacerbation of the social conflict. Studies of the 'black' economy and of the new codes of behaviour adopted by young people and women, showed that the increase in the numbers of working women was the result not only of demographic factors linked to the baby boom but also to a new female culture.

By comparing regional variations, the new focus on empirical research has highlighted the territorial concentration of unemployment among women. This research emphasised the way in which the rate of female unemployment was underestimated in the poorly developed Mezzogiorno because the participation of women in the labour market was still extremely small. This was due to cultural factors and to structures particularly affecting the economically weak social classes whose social condition created discouragement rather than incentives to enter the world of work (Altieri 1993).

The work carried out by researchers on unemployment among the *cassaintegrati*[1] in the North, denounce (and justly so) the relatively privileged conditions enjoyed by this category of the unemployed, some of whom, at least, have the 'good fortune' and the resources to find a place in the labour market more or less rapidly. In these regions, the flows of people entering the labour market are not zero (even when companies are shedding staff and the number of available jobs is shrinking). There are in general, substantial reserves of parallel, or 'underground' work offering opportunities of (albeit casual) employment.

In contrast, in the South, the structural weaknesses of the demand for labour, the families' underprivileged social conditions, the absence of employment prospects for young people and women, depress the social environment to such an extent that they relegate the question of differences – even the most sophisticated – between the conditions of total or partial unemployment to a position of secondary importance. The major concern is the emergence of mass unemployment with its immediate and future social repercussions for one or several cohorts of young people and its effects on the depreciation of the human capital of local economies. These social phenomena generate differences of opinion in academic interpretation and in the recommendations formulated for the policies guiding state intervention.

The findings of empirical research confirm the existence of extremely large disparities. A number of important studies were carried out by teams of sociologists and economists. Research on the *cassaintegrati* shows the influence of the workers' resources and social networks on their living conditions and possibilities of professional reinsertion. These studies focus on the way in which unemployed people, who have already had work experience, can attempt to escape from this condition. Research on Fiat's *cassaintegrati* in Turin, drawing its inspiration from Granovetter's model of the role of social networks, shows that it is the scope rather than the intensity of social networks that favours access to information and reinsertion in the labour market (Bonazzi 1989). In Piedmont, other research concentrates on the way context affects reactions and the forms of adaptation. By comparing a metropolitan environment with an industrialised rural area, it emphasises the range of possible ways of escaping unemployment depending upon the quality and type of resources afforded by the territorial contexts (Barbano 1987).

A comparison between the research devoted to the cassaintegrati and the problems of re-entering the labour market in Piedmont and Campania shows that the accumulation of educational and social experience can be a more important factor for an autonomous entry into the labour market than specialised credentials (Rebeggiani 1988). This experience may be acquired through trade unions, public relations, commercial contacts, the pooling of knowledge in the local community and acquired through the work of several members of the family.

Research devoted to job-seekers frequently overlaps with work carried out on young people, casual and illicit labour. Studies of unemployed youth have been influenced, at a theoretical level, by the research into industrial unrest and the effects of generations who have revived the debate on individual and collective identities, highlighting the emergence of new codes of behaviour among the cohorts derived from the youth movements of the late 1970s. These codes were then transformed by the promotion of the private sector and the individual, and the diversity of psycho-social factors following the collapse of belief in the community (Melucci 1984; Cavalli 1985).

A team of sociologists and psychologists has examined the problem of the transition from school to work, focusing its analysis on the variable duration of the occupational insertion of young people. Applied to a small group of job-seekers in northern Italy, the study highlights the subjects' different ability to take direct and active control of their transition to the world of work. It also emphasises that identical circumstances can acquire different values depending upon the individual's personal history and his or her living environment. The researchers maintained that the transitional phase from school to work illustrated the complexity of social processes and represents a measure of potential long-term difficulties in the labour market (Sarchielli *et al*. 1991).

The IARD research co-ordinated by Cavalli paints an overall picture of young people's condition which is not restricted to education and work. It draws a comparison between young people in the North and in the South, distinguishing between young men and young women. These analyses emphasise the importance of having recourse to social networks, notably solidarity in the family and between friends, which prove to be the principal instruments giving access to the labour market (in northern as well as southern Italy). They also show that many young people experience long periods of short-term, temporary employment, without obtaining a positive impact on their qualification. Not only does employment of this kind fail to promote the acquisition of skill, it also leads (more often than not) to occupational downgrading.

NEW ISSUES ON THE LABOUR MARKETS: STUDIES DEVOTED TO YOUNG PEOPLE AND WOMEN

Unemployment among the young, social malaise and deskilling

Analyses of youth unemployment stress the influence of socio-territorial factors acting upon the construction of the quality of human resources. 'Desocialisation' phenomena and the 'deskilling' of these resources lead to a weakening of the basic academic level, the disappearance of networks of social relations and shortcomings in the industrial production system, especially in the Mezzogiorno. As a result young people and women are discouraged and excluded from the world of work. A structural scarcity of job opportunities (or a serious blockage due to economic contraction) gives rise to the vicious circles of exclusion and impoverishment of human capital liable to lead, in certain cases, to chronic social exclusion.

In recent years, a body of research has been conducted in different parts of Italy to identify an Italian model of unemployment (Pugliese 1993). This research reveals the existence of three main problems: the difficulties encountered by young people in gaining access to employment; discrimination against women and their exclusion from the labour market; the fact that these problems (for young people as well as for women) are growing more acute in southern Italy (Calza Bini *et al*. 1993).

The most important aspect of Italian unemployment is that it chiefly affects young people looking for their first job, matching their needs and expectations, which the economy and labour market are unable to give them, particularly in the Mezzogiorno, where young women from a modest background are particularly forced into unemployment.

The difficulties encountered by young people – whether faced with mass unemployment, with no prospects, as in the Mezzogiorno, or enjoying a more favourable situation from the point of view of job opportunities, as in the case of Rome, for example – are linked to the lack of acquisition, or the loss, of competence and employable occupational skills. The longer they take to become economically active, or the longer they remain excluded from the job market, the greater their disadvantage compared with other young people of the same age who have entered the world of work. In a great many cases, this explains their subsequent difficulties in securing employment.

On the basis of a survey carried out on a representative group of young people registered at the local job centres in several districts (Catania, Naples, Rome and Genoa), Mingione points out the irrelevance of the distinction made in the statistics between short- and long-term unemployment where the majority of young job-seekers live for many years (frequently beyond the age of 30) in their families and receive no benefits (Mingione 1992). A comparison between the different areas shows that the length of young people's unemployment can mean different things depending upon their level of unease and the difficulties confronting them. People with low incomes (personal and family) are forced out of unemployment to accept extremely sub-standard working conditions, thereby entering the vicious circle of odd jobs alternating with spells of unemployment, and are not always registered among the long-term unemployed. In contrast, job-seekers enjoying greater resources (chiefly in the cities in central/northern Italy) continue to look for a job corresponding to their expectations. In both cases, the family gives the individuals concerned its support in looking for a job. The higher the family's social status (or the stronger the desire on the part of young people to rise up the social ladder), the more the family uses its resources to make this search possible. These analyses highlight how the availability of resources is a variable linked to unemployment pathways reflecting the identity of the subjects. These individuals, living in different regions, depend on the latent capacity for occupational development offered them by these contexts and the local labour market. The odd jobs, casual, illicit or temporary employment constituting the first 'work' experience of young job-seekers do not often provide them with new skills.

In the structurally most underprivileged regions where young people generally dispose of meagre resources (for example Campania), the atmosphere of general *malaise* highlighted by research may be summarised as follows:

When the work exists, it remains precarious, devoid of legitimacy and any form of security. More often than not, work is inaccessible if the individual is not a member of the social and political élite of people with 'contacts' or if he or she has not acquired a minimum degree of *professionalità*, which only a good job and an effective training system can provide. If a permanent job becomes available, it is only after years of insecurity. But for many women, work remains a dream buried under the chores and living conditions of the housewife. Frequently, they wait, for an entire generation, to inherit work in the shadow of the family or, alternatively, work is obtained indirectly, by helping someone.

(Rebeggiani and Veneziano 1993)

In Naples, a significant proportion of young people from the most under-privileged social categories start work at a very early age as apprentices but are dismissed after a few years when their employers lose the advantages linked, in particular, to the low cost of their recruitment. This loss of employment frequently goes hand-in-hand with the gradual loss of their skills – however small – and increases the risk of exclusion from the world of work and the danger of drifting into organised crime.

In Campania, these regressive forces – which play a major part in keeping young job-seekers at a low level of professionalità – are exacerbated by the influence of institutional factors such as early school-leaving, the inefficiency of a great many technical and vocational schools or the malfunctioning of the vocational training system.

Consequently, in the 'shadow of non-employment', we find two types of suffering. There is the suffering of those who have acquired the basic skills required to develop an occupational pathway but who fail to do so in a coherent and continuous manner. There is also the suffering of those who have never had access to training services and courses. In both cases, the deskilling of labour supply has been shown to reduce the level of skills on the demand side of the labour market, to young people's further disadvantage. In fact, a comparison between the occupational competences offered and required on the labour market highlights a sort of vicious circle between mass unemployment and the qualitative characteristics of a large part of the production system. The quantitative shortage of job opportunities is accompanied by a qualitative weakness leading to a loss of skills acquired in technical institutions, school and university, as well as occupational skills. Whereas in other markets, these skills would be developed and consolidated in work, in the context of mass unemployment, they are squandered in the transition from one sector to another, from one job to the next.

The quantitative and qualitative surveys carried out in Rome on the populations of young people enjoying 'average resources', but not coming from a particularly high social milieu (Calza Bini and Cavarra 1994), show that the theoretical possibilities of having access to a market for well-qualified labour afforded by an urban context and culture boost the social aspirations of a growing segment of the population and push large numbers of young people towards intermediate or advanced levels of education. These expectations are not often satisfied in terms of employment. A certain saturation of job opportunities in the most sought-after occupations creates 'major areas of joblessness' and adds to the queues of job-seekers with specific credentials. The young people who enjoy a high personal and family capital can afford to wait, accepting the 'turn-over' of casual employment or deciding to enhance their qualifications and training. Young people disposing of average resources try to follow the same path, but they have fewer opportunities and run the risk of long-term unemployment and the attendant loss of skills. Otherwise they must retarget their expectations on more general and lower prospects, but then their assets are not always the best or the most appropriate. A period of waiting such as this can subsequently damage the quality of human resources, and young people can become frustrated because their skills are neither used nor developed. This can lead to a decline in social relationships, depressive tensions and the onset of apathy, aggravating their situation as job-seekers and pushing them towards the brink of exclusion.

These phenomena, derived from global forces leading to micro-exclusion, become visible a long time after the damage has been done and has become irreparable. Faced with these forces, the individuals concerned do not adopt the same rational actions, the same goals and the same instruments. It has already been pointed out that variable social conditions and/or territorial disparities generate differences in the way individuals think. Individuals experiencing the same situation may adopt different forms of behaviour depending upon the structure of their personalities, their experience or the construction of their identities. Research of a qualitative nature reveals that young people develop three types of response to their awareness of the long-term nature of unemployment. The first group pursue their objectives (unremittingly and irrespective of the cost) even if their chance of success is virtually zero. The second group redefine their expectations after a longer or shorter period. Here there is a real danger not only of a subsequent loss of skill but also of 'occupational downgrading' and a shift towards still more insecure and marginal strata of the labour market, along with downward social mobility. The third group of young, underprivileged people either expect nothing or nourish ambitions greater than anything the labour market is capable of offering them. As failure follows failure and the period of waiting grows longer, these young people lose confidence in the market and, despite their needs, abandon the active search for employment. These categories of the unemployed tend towards a form of resignation and, ultimately, rely exclusively on their family networks.

GENDER DIFFERENCES: RESEARCH CONDUCTED BY WOMEN ON WOMEN

Along with research devoted to young people, work focusing on women is among the most innovative due to its success in distancing itself from the theories and paradigms of Economics and Sociology. The research referred to here is only that concerning the education/work relationship and the labour markets. Generally speaking, it focuses on themes such as the double shift (housework/paid work), discrimination, family strategies, the processes of socialisation and construction of identity of cohorts and generations of women, the themes related to the mass movements at the end of the 1970s.

Based on events in everyday life, the accumulation of experience and the interplay of collective memory, these analyses set out to occupy an intermediate level between descriptive empirical research and certain aspects of criticism and theoretical reformulation. They show how apprenticeship, behaviour, choices and strategies are the result of complex individual and social interactions, frequently originating within the individual's decision-making processes. Individual rationality cannot easily be interpreted on the basis of a standard model of rationality which applies to all people in the area of education as well as in terms of labour market entry. Viewed from this angle, it may be possible to improve our understanding and interpretation of the unexpected aspects or negative effects of the policies governing education and training for work.

Taking as their starting-point the inequality, discrimination and the double shift whereby women carry out tasks and functions without receiving economic, social or emotional recognition, feminists have adopted several thematic, theoretical and methodological approaches which cannot be discussed in detail here (Altieri *et al.* 1993). The question of the relationship(s) existing between work and education is approached from different angles but the analyses agree on the following conclusion: there exists a strong correlation between women's rate of participation in the labour market and their academic levels. Territorial differences confirm the importance of the education factor in determining women's participation in the labour market. In places where the possibility of women finding work is limited (the female unemployment rate in southern Italy stood at 32 per cent in 1990), women are, on average, more highly educated than men. They also have a relatively higher level of education than the women living in the North and Centre (9 per cent possess a *laurea* compared to 6.5 per cent).

The education factor favours a continued presence, or strengthens positions, on the labour market. Thus the proportion of women among wage-earners increases with the level of their academic attainment. This phenomenon is the consequence of two convergent factors. The first concerns a higher demand for work on the part of women who, precisely because they have studied, find it difficult to accept their traditional role. The second factor concerns the fact of studying for many years and of benefiting from an 'egalitarian' time during their studies, which allows them to escape from traditional expectations and roles. This is due both to the fact of being respected for these non-traditional qualities and skills and the expectations that arise from this investment. The search for new types of mediation between different identities and roles then seems possible and entry into the world of work becomes the first testing ground of their own value and expectations.

Schooling and the desire for education lie at the centre of the analyses emphasising the differences in behaviour, ethics and identity between different generations of women (Merelli *et al.* 1985). The observation of the determination of young women to acquire a good level of education has made it possible to verify a number of hypotheses concerning the role of education in identity-building processes and the importance attributed to work by the new generations of women and its significance in their value systems (CISEM 1987). Although the analysis of the data regarding educational choices merely adds to the complexity of the interpretation of the relationship between young women and the education system, this relationship exhibits certain contradictions and leaves two questions unanswered: the definition of the causes of discrimination in training and the assessment of their impact.

We encounter these questions and these doubts in the analysis of occupational segregation and the difficulties encountered by women in their careers. Recent work has focused on the analysis of women's work and careers in predetermined organisational contexts. The approach reveals the growing difficulties created by the use of the category 'gender difference' as a key for interpreting individual behaviour (AAVV 1993).

This vast field of sociological research highlights the fact that discrimination against women in the labour market is the result of masculine domination in practices, choices and behaviour. Although it is true that there exists a difference in qualification between men and women, this difference is the result of forms of socialisation and sexual division of roles and tasks in society and at home.

Despite the extreme differentiation in the construction of feminine identities, I consider that 'female socialisation' has, until now, developed at least one learning capacity specific to women, linked to domestic and occupational roles. Transposed in the world of work, this capacity would determine a specific qualification and occupational skill that could be used in particular roles and professions in the world of work and, in this respect, should be recognised, esteemed, appraised, appreciated and remunerated at its true value.

As yet, there are no convincing results on these aspects. A recent study set out to examine the extent to which 'gender' identity represented not only a resource for women but also a key for interpreting the organisational changes in companies in the wake of technological innovations and enhanced competitiveness. Although this study identified a number of specific forms of work behaviour in men and women, it did not identify clearly defined gender differences in the various types of leadership and forms of organisational behaviour. It noted the persistence of a few stereotypes and highlighted the growing convergence of values shared by men and women.

This research has been used as a basis for an interesting study of the new relationships between employment and domestic life and of the socialisation process at work in contemporary society. It is women's presence on the labour market that calls into question the traditional division of labour between men and women by also imposing on men the need to take account of the problems of organising their private lives (Luciano 1993).

If these issues seem to express fundamental trends in our society, it would be inaccurate to speak of a general model. It is enough to examine the different investment made by men and by women in family strategies, in the attribution of roles within the family, with regard to education or the length of time and resources necessary to secure employment. The effects of a different education or different socialisation through work are also evident in the comparison between the upper classes, or in the results produced by everyday social life in the hyperactive North and in the jobless South. In Italy, research also emphasises the different use (or non-use) of the institutions, of relational possibilities, of public and private services for accommodation, assistance and health care. In this respect, the most recent studies focusing on several generations of women show the different types of investment, depending on the different stages in the life cycle, that individuals, families, institutions and society have made in the family, work, professional roles and social relationships (Merelli 1989; Sgritta (ed.) 1988).

At present, research on women in the Mezzogiorno is highlighting the 'societal' specificities of the forms of socialisation in active life and the diversity of family strategies at a time when women's rate of participation in the labour market is becoming more significant both in the South and in the North. These analyses explain – through a series of cultural, social and class barriers – the really low levels of work available for women in the South. It reveals the gravity of the structural weaknesses of the demand for labour and the scale of the problem to be overcome in ending these discriminating dualisms. Nevertheless, according to these analyses, a stronger presence of women in the labour market (which is still partly discouraged today) would further exacerbate unemployment levels.

NOTES

1 The employees receiving the *cassa integrazione* while retaining formal, legal links with their company, are not obliged to work and are paid an allowance, chiefly funded by the state.

BIBLIOGRAPHY

AAVV (1993) *Doppi legami*, Rome: Ediesse.

Altieri, G. (1993) *Presenti ed escluse, Le donne nel mercato del lavoro frammentato*, Rome: Ediesse.

Altieri, G., Farinelli. F. and Meghnagi, S. (1993) *La cultura delle pari opportunità*, Roma: Ediesse.

Bagnasco, A. (1977) *Le Tre Italie. La problematica territoriale dello sviluppo economico italiano*, Bologna: Il Mulino.

——(ed.) (1986) *L'altra metà dell'economia*, Naples: Liguori.

——(1988) *La costruzione sociale del mercato*, Bologna: Il Mulino.

Barbano, F. (ed.) (1987) *L'ombra del lavoro*, Milan: Angeli.

Becattini, G. (1987) *Mercato e forze locali: il distretto industriale*, Bologna: Il Mulino.

Bellandi, M. (1996) 'Innovation and change in the Marshallian industrial district', *European Planning Studies* 4(3).

Bonazzi, G. (ed.) (1989) *L'espulsione tutelata*, Turin: Ires Piemonte.

Boudon, R. (1987) 'Rationalité subjective et dispositions', *Rassegna italiana di Sociologia* 2.

Brusco, S. (1975) 'Organizzazione del lavoro e decentramento produttivo nel settore metalmeccanico', *Inchiesta* 17.

Calza Bini, P. (1976) *Economia periferica e classi sociali*, Naples: Liguori.

Calza Bini, P. and Castellucci, L. (1990) 'Vincoli e risorsi nella costruzione sociale delle forme di produzione flessibile del caso Italia', *Economia e Lavoro* 4.

Calza Bini, P. and Cavarra, R. (1994) 'Giovani disoccupati tra reti sociali e marginalità', *Inchiesta* 100.

Calza Bini, P., Mingione, E. and Pugliese, E. (eds) (1993) 'Scenari regionali della disoccupazione in Italia', *Inchiesta* 99.

Calza Bini, P., Oteri, C., Bosco, C. and Pieri, D. (1996) *Sistema locale e distretto industriale: il caso di Civita Castellana*, Biblioteca Comunale 'Enrico Minio', Civita Castellana.

Cavalli, A. (ed.) (1985) *Il tempo dei giovani*, Bologna: Il Mulino.

——(ed.) (1990) *I giovani del Mezzogiorno*, Bologna: Il Mulino.

CISEM (Centre for Innovation and Experimentation in Education) (1987) *Donne a scuola, scolarizzazione e processi di crescita di identità femminile negli anni '70 e '80*, Milan: Angeli.

Favaretto, I. (1988) 'Minore impresa partecipe delle trasformazioni produttive', *Progetto e Economia* 1.

Luciano, A. (1993) *Tornei, Donne e uomini in carriera*, Milan: ETASLIBRI.

Melucci, A. (1984) *Altri codici*, Bologna: Il Mulino.

Merelli, M. (1989) *Quasi adulta*, Milan: Amgeli.

Merelli, M., Morini, M., Nava, P. and Ruggerini, M. G. (1985) *Giochi di equilibrio*, Milan: Angeli.

Mingione, E. (1990) 'Il sistema italiano delle divisioni regionali ed i processi di informalizzazione', *Inchiesta* 83–84.

——(1992) 'Aspetti sociali della disoccupazione: dalla disoccupazione industriale classica alla moltiplicatà della disoccupazione odierna', in P. Calza Bini *La disoccupazione: interpretazioni e punti di vista*, Naples: Liguori.

Paci, M. (1975) 'Crisi, ristrutturazione industriale e piccola impresa', *Inchiesta* 20.

Pugliese, E. (1993) *Sociologia della disoccupazione*, Bologna: Il Mulino.

Pugliese, E. and Altieri, G. (1990) 'Tre Italie, due disoccupazioni', *Inchiesta* 83–84.

Rebeggiani, E. (1988) *Disoccupazione industriale e Cassa integrazione: une ricerca sulla condizione dei cassaintegrati a Napoli*, Naples: Liguori.

Rebeggiani, E. and Veneziano, S. (1993) 'La disoccupazione in Campania, in Scenari regionali della disoccupazione in Italia', *Inchiesta* 99.

Regini, M. and Sabel, C. (1989) *Strategie di riaggiustamento industriale*, Bologna: Il Mulino.

Sarchielli, G., Depolo, M., Fraccaroli, F. and Colasanto, M. (1991) *Senza lavoro*, Bologna: Il Mulino.

Sgritta, G. B. (ed.) (1988) *Percorsi femminili: Lavoro, Formazione e famiglia nella regione Lazio*, Milan: Angeli.

INDEX